# How the Farmers Changed China

**Transitions: Asia and Asian America**
Series Editor, Mark Selden

# *How the Farmers Changed China,*

# Power of the People

Kate Xiao Zhou

*with a Foreword by Edward Friedman*

WestviewPress
*A Division of HarperCollinsPublishers*

*Transitions: Asia and Asian America*

Copyright © 1996 by Westview Press, Inc., A Division of HarperCollins Publishers, Inc.

Published in 1996 in the United States of America by Westview Press, Inc., 5500 Central Avenue, Boulder, Colorado 80301-2877, and in the United Kingdom by Westview Press, 12 Hid's Copse Road, Cumnor Hill, Oxford OX2 9JJ

Library of Congress Cataloging-in-Publication Data
Zhou, Kate Xiao, 1956–
    How the farmers changed China : power of the people / Kate Xiao Zhou.
        p.   cm. — (Transitions—Asia and Asian America)
    Includes bibliographical references and index.
    ISBN 0-8133-2681-8 (HC). — ISBN 0-8133-2682-6 (pbk.)
    1. Farmers—China—Economic conditions. 2. Rural industries—China. 3. Rural women—China. 4. China—Economic conditions—1976– I. Title. II Series.
HD 1537.C5Z46 1996
338.1'0951—dc20                                                                                        95-50485
                                                                                                                    CIP

The paper used in this publication meets the requirements of the American National Standard for Permanence of Paper for Printed Library Materials Z39.48-1984.

10    9    8    7    6    5    4    3    2    1

# Contents

# Illustrations

# Foreword

### Edward Friedman

Kate Xiao Zhou is a fresh voice who tells an exciting story about world-shaking events in *How the Farmers Changed China*. Trained in political science at Princeton University, where she earned her doctorate, and drawing on many years of hard work and deep friendships in China's countryside, Professor Zhou is one of a new generation of uniquely able American social scientists from China that includes Minxin Pei, Zhiyuan Cui, Huo Shitao, Suisheng Zhao, X.L. Deng, and many equally qualified others. These brilliant scholars offer a very special combination of life experiences and professional training that is contributing to a rapid and dramatic improvement in our understanding of how China really works.

Even Professor Zhou's striking use of unconventional language alerts us to misleading stereotypes that obscure the tremendous forces that have been expanding wealth in post-Mao China and facilitating a spectacular rise of China, perhaps comparable to the nineteenth-century rise of Germany. Kate Zhou vividly depicts how rural people in post-Mao China have been the core agents of this momentous transformation. She dubs the energetic people who have been the motivating force and the creative source of China's extraordinary liberation of productive dynamism "farmers," a term that conjures up images of market-oriented, hard-headed economic actors.

In contrast, the conventional term "peasant" seems popularly identified with an old-fashioned group entrapped in ancient ways. "Peasants" seem the objects of history-making action by others. Kate Zhou's powerful story, however, deals with leading dramatic actors on the stage of history, the human agency that is making China once again central to the global drama, hence "farmers." This book challenges conventional categories and conventional wisdom.

Kate Zhou tells us that Western theory does not yet readily accommodate the power and potential of this leaderless force in China, the farmers. Nor, she shows, is conventional theory, Eastern or Western, ready for the extraordinary dynamic power of women farmers, a core feature of this extraordinary enrichment of life in China. There is so much in *How the Farmers Changed China* that is new, challenging, and so very important

Professor Zhou clearly sketches *How the Farmers Changed China*. It is indeed true, and at times even acknowledged in writing in China, that

China's post-Mao leaders never imagined that their small, late 1978 reform of raising state purchasing prices and allowing surpluses beyond a state-imposed quota to be sold on the market would produce the monumental outburst of creative effort and competitive productivity that has given the people of China the greatest wealth expansion anywhere in the world since 1979. Taking advantage of a small political opening, farm households seized command of their destiny and began to free themselves from repressed labor on collectives and to turn a small experiment with contracting basic crops to their own much larger advantage. Farmers agreed to deliver a set amount of basic crops to the state. The government agreed that farmers then would be free to deploy their time, energy, talent, and capital as they chose. Power-holders did not foresee the resultant economic dynamism.

In fact, according to China's Ministry of Agriculture, "Initially, the decision makers did not acknowledge the family contract responsibility system, and it was even considered at first a move that opposed the system of socialism."[1] The nation's farmers, however, ran forward based on a few isolated experimental spots. As the conservative Wang Shan observed in his pseudo-nymous 1994 polemic, *China Through a Third Eye*, once rural families could calculate their own accounts, these "people themselves" destroyed the economically suffocating yoke of state plans.[2] Professor Hsi-sheng Ch'i sums up the process of change: "Peasants had taken things into their own hands. . . . In contrast to their leaders, the younger Chinese peasants were more resourceful, more receptive to change, and much more aggressive in exploiting new economic opportunities."[3] Thus, both supporters of and skeptics about reform accept as fact Kate Zhou's premise that the farmers themselves exploded the economically irrational system of socialist agriculture.

It is, of course, well known that, even in dictatorships, the seemingly powerless turn out in fact to have a certain amount of power. The scholarly contributions of James C. Scott establish that. It is even well understood that a state that concentrates and centralizes such extraordinary power as do Leninist systems inevitably touches people across boundaries in similarly painful ways and thus cannot help but engender "an aggregation of large numbers of spontaneous individual behaviors."[4] Kate Zhou clarifies something more: This collective behavior can be continuous and successful. It can change the structure of power. It is not limited merely to defensive resistance.

Yet, many Chinese fail to see how the farmers changed China. Instead, they still perceive peasants as passive, illiterate, and superstitious. Peasants are "remembered" by most urban folk as the people who staffed the Maoist system and blindly obeyed Mao's commands, bringing a tragedy of hate, stagnation, and destruction to China. Consequently, to most Chinese who live in cities, it is inconceivable that empowered rural people could have dynamized China's post-Mao growth. Peasants are essentially not movers and shakers. Like all who break their chains, the peasants have accomplished deeds that seem magical or impossible to those who see with the preconceptions of the old order, in this case, statist socialism.

What the so-called reform leaders did do that was important for the rural actors was to belatedly approve the wealth-expanding success of the farmers. The "most important contribution of China's reform leadership was that they refrained from making quick judgments and suppressing 'illegal' practices; instead, they let time be the judge."[5] Given how regularly politicians mess things up, this after-the-fact support is no small thing.

At political centers, party leaders also have had to beat back numerous attacks by entrenched conservatives and reactionaries, that is, assaults against reform by troglodytes who would yoke farmers back into the Sisyphean toil that locked them into the poverty of the Mao era, when hundreds of millions were malnourished and few had any cash.

Since 1953, by state confiscation of grain (called state purchase), by state prohibition of physical mobility after 1960, and by payment to farmers at below-market prices, China's rural dwellers had been ruined by repressive institutions and exploitation that were legitimated as socialism. Those crushed and dependent country people of the Mao era are unimaginable to conservatives as the empowered farmers they have become in the post-Mao era. Chinese who still see with Mao-era eyes cannot conceive how such old-fashioned people as peasants could turn into farmers and rapidly modernize China. Yet they did.

Kate Zhou makes this amazing tale of human liberation strikingly vivid. All too regularly, however, foreign journalists in China talk mainly to city folk, who conceive rural China in outmoded categories. Thus, news reports talk of peasants and virtually never about farmers. In the conventional wisdom, peasants are the beneficiaries of the action of great political leaders. As the pundits see it, "In the beginning there was Deng, who personally directed the first three waves of reform. . . . He created a market economy in food . . . by freeing prices . . . and . . . by . . . favor[ing] . . . essentially, family farms."[6]

Kate Zhou's very different story is about what happened when the chains were broken by China's farmers themselves. She leaves to others the job of analyzing the continuing struggle at the highest levels of elite power over how far to permit the reforms to go and grow, or whether reform should even be reversed. Such infighting has been continuous at the highest level of politics in Beijing. Conservatives who embrace China's rural dwellers as mere loyal peasants oppose the empowerment of farmers.

In fact, the state center is rife with elite individuals who fear the energies of China's farmers, with power brokers who prefer to think of an irrational and premodern peasantry that should be locked away in the countryside again, as in the Mao era. Although rural workers who have migrated to cities have stimulated urban economies, selling quality produce, toiling in construction, and providing cheap inputs for industry, nonetheless, the general perception of the migrant from the countryside in the city is that of peasants threatening urbanites, the backward threatening the advanced, the ignorant and undisciplined spreading crime, disorder, and filth. According to 1995 Chinese government statistics, over half a million of the migrants from the farms have been arrested in the cities on various charges.

So popular is this prejudiced—almost racist—presupposition about "peasants" that even reformist rulers appeal to condescending urbanites for support by promising to slow or stop the flow of seemingly alien people from the countryside. Stifling the physical factor, mobility of economic reform, can win great urban support when presented in the guise of a war on the backward peasant. Lenin's war against so-called Asianness, that is, against peasant consciousness, is presented in China as a true appreciation of the warmth of a rural community that is ruined when supposedly simple peasants become really sharp farmers focused on making and investing money. That extraordinarily liberating change is damned as unvirtuous and alien. Yet, as Kate Zhou establishes, farmers are making the future of a prospering and modern China.

Conservative rulers and frightened urbanites are not enamored of such a future. City folk, in China's age of rural dynamism, find themselves dealing with country people who apparently don't even speak right, virtual foreigners who have migrated into cities and live in ghettos populated by their own kind and who are allied to compatriots who have illegally bought residence permits in villages surrounding the metropolises. Urban dwellers speak of a second encirclement of the city by the countryside. Mao won power by the first encirclement during a prolonged civil war. Now, many city folk look at the rural influx and feel that all the first revolution won for them, through a monopoly of state-guaranteed benefits that marginalized villagers, may be lost in a second encirclement by peasants seeking their own prosperity. Hence, conservative power-holders opposed to continuing the productive and liberating thrust of rural reform, so ably captured by Kate Zhou, win popular urban support on a platform of sending peasants back where they came from. Indeed, there is a basis for the fears of privileged urban conservatives, some truth that these mobile farmers in the city, denied of any government benefits, harassed by the police, and looked down upon by urban folk, are angry and could yet be a force for further change.

The signal importance of China's spontaneous and unorganized farmers' movement for empowerment can be measured by the growing gap since the years 1984–1985 between the hope-filled aspirations of country people and the anxiety-laden actions of China's Leninist dictatorship, which has not permitted any further institutional progress for rural reform, such that farmers in China are hemmed in by painful institutional constrictions that preclude growing farm incomes, much as happened in Hungary during the reformist Kadar dictatorship.[7] If the farmers' movement has the power Kate Zhou finds, it could yet push China beyond the limits imposed by China's Kadar, Deng Xiaoping. As in post-Kadar Hungary, China's farmers find themselves frozen for over a decade by centralized state policies imposed by ruling groups who fear the further empowerment of farmers. The farmers could spur further change, true reformist breakthroughs.

Conservative rulers, opposed to further basic change, build on a nostalgia for supposedly simpler days when Mao was alive and life did not seem defined by money, connections, and corruption and the party spouted propaganda for a collectivistic egalitarian village called Dazhai. Then things seemed under control. Now the farmers are on the move and out of control.

> In the old days, when we were learning
> from Dazhai, we weren't even allowed
> to leave the village. Those who moved
> about illegally would find their families
> dragged to study sessions or . . . fined. But
> . . . that did not stop the people from
> moving. . . . Today, one may not see a young
> person in the village all day. Anyone
> who can leave has left.[8]

The success of the farmers, if extended, seems even to threaten the very base of the Leninist dictatorship. Farmers already surreptitiously buy, sell, and lease land. But taking property distribution out of the hands of party officials spells the end to the state's socialism, which condemns private property being bought and sold as the enemy of humanity and instead hands command of property to unaccountable officials. Such successful self-interested practices by farmers as buying, selling, and leasing land delegitimate the socialistic rulers' reason for existing. Also, farmers go where the money is. If not allowed to lease or sell land back in a natal village while working productively elsewhere, farmers are forced to leave the land untilled. This leads to a cutback on producing the money-losing basic crops that the state seizes at below-market prices. The wasted land seems to scream out to ruling and urban groups that something is fundamentally wrong. What is wrong is that an unaccountable command economy still reins in the productive energies of farmers.

The military looks at the abandoned land and fears it will lose the food needed to feed its soldiers in wartime. The rulers' nightmare is both a specter of food insufficiency, hunger, and riot that could threaten the regime's power and a specter of the farmers winning out against state-imposed low farmgate prices. If food prices rose, then urban subsidies would rise to keep pace, with living costs zooming up in cities. The rulers would then be faced by unhappy urban workers paying higher prices and fearing that the government would soon be compelled to reduce its mounting budget deficit by stopping the subsidization of money-losing state enterprises, throwing unproductive urban workers (whose state-owned enterprises lose money and are subsidized by productive farmers) into the streets, jobless.

To avoid facing up to the need to transform or shut down parasitic socialist industry, conservatives urge the party instead to compel farmers to work again as peasants locked away in the hinterland, compelled again to grow basic crops such as grain and cotton at below-market prices. Some places have already begun to reimpose grain rationing by distributing coupons to reduce the weight of money prices. In much of China, frightened and conservative rulers urge rural officials to keep peasants repressed and dependent on collective inputs that tillers need to make farming a success. The great wealth and power won by China's farmers remain threatened by ruling conservatives and chauvinists.

China's farmers thus see the government as the obstacle to the nation's continuing prosperity and the farmers' further empowerment, that which must be removed so dreams can come true. The conservative Wang Shan argues that (what he considers to be) the low-quality people in rural China cannot live with the differentiation caused by market development. The Mao era of shared poverty brought a stability that, for Wang, is much to be preferred. Consequently, for Wang, the only "guarantee of social security is a low level of equality."[9] The farmers' success consequently is presented as the enemy of a much-desired stability that most Chinese in fact are frightened to death they may already be losing. Wang concludes that outraged and ambitious rural dwellers are a "high danger" entity that is threatening the old order.[10] That China's farmers could really change China, Kate Zhou shows us, is, in fact, liberating. Of course, to defenders of repression, the popular empowerment depicted by Zhou is instead scary.

In short, what the socialist state wars against, as Kate Zhou powerfully establishes, is the better world the farmers have already made and would pursue yet further. These conservative forces oppose the empowerment that Zhou empathetically and dramatically recounts. These ruling groups prefer dependent peasants. In spring 1995, in the name of ending "social dislocation" caused by "China's surplus rural work force," a paper circulated among China's ruling groups arguing that Deng-era contracting of production to peasant households had long since outlived its usefulness. Instead, in the name of "economies of scale," that is, the old Stalinist gigantomania, the paper advocated "large-scale farming," in other words, recollectivization, to rechain and again crush empowered farmers.[11] Phony model collectives have been kept subsidized by conservatives during the reform era to "prove" what their antireform policies could achieve.

Most outside observers, misperceiving China's dynamic farmers as passive peasants, cannot imagine their centrality to the success of reform or to the political debate and struggle over China's future. Most analysts slight the profound reality that Kate Zhou highlights and instead give credit for the prosperity won by reform in China to the leader, Deng Xiaoping, or to the urban intellectuals who have learned to copy Hungary or Japan.[12]

Kate Zhou shows that nothing could be further from the truth. It is the farmers themselves who have changed China and in so doing have empowered themselves. In some villages, real local elections have even taken place that have ousted the old guard of the ruling Communist party.[13] The empowerment of farmers is a terrifying proposition to elements within China's dictatorship who prefer to keep peasants dependent and who appeal to anxious villagers through nostalgia for an imaginary golden age associated with the promise of Mao's original revolution and through chauvinistic outrage at aliens, including China's empowered farmers, presented as no longer really Chinese.

In short, Chinese society and Chinese ruling groups are split. A complex and politically explosive political struggle is under way. This struggle, in part pitting peasants against farmers, will decide whether the twenty-first-century rise of China will intensify repression, superpatriotic peasant passions, and territorial ambitions or will instead contribute to greater empowerment of China's farmers and to its other citizens and even be further open to mutually beneficial exchange and enrichment within the Asian-Pacific region. What is at stake in the fate of rural Chinese is whether the future brings war in Asia or a prospering Asian-Pacific economic community.[14]

The former dangerous prospect naturally makes headlines outside of China. Indeed, it should. What is seen is China as a threat. It is a prospect that emanates from chauvinists who fear the liberation of the farmers. But there is another powerful dynamic at work, one hidden by the invisibility of China's farmers.

This happier project of an open China tied to a dynamic and broadly enriching Asian-Pacific economic community is based on empowered farmers who can compete in the world market but whose value is usually hidden because observers are blinded by preconceptions about a backward and medieval peasantry. Yet farmers are, in fact, the driving force of China's rise. China's happier, mutually beneficial potential is centered in its farmers. Their destiny may decide the largest issues of war or peace in the Asian-Pacific region. It is important, therefore, at least to end the invisibility and also to see the great promise in what China's farmers have already achieved. This hope, this extraordinary drama of enrichment and empowerment, is eloquently and powerfully captured in Kate Xiao Zhou's profoundly important study, *How the Farmers Changed China*.

## Notes

1. Luo Yousheng and Zhang Hongyu, "Land Reform Innovations Examined," *Jingji yanjiu* (Economic Research), January 20, 1995, translated in FBIS-CHI–95–056 (March 23, 1995), p. 73.

2. *Di sanzhi yanjing kan zhongguo* (Taiyuan: Shanxi People's Publishing House, 1994), pp. 178, 177.

3. Hsi-sheng Ch'i, *Politics of Disillusionment* (Armonk, N.Y.: M. E. Sharpe, 1991), pp. 226, 253.

4. Xueguang Zhou, "Unorganized Interests and Collective Action in Communist China," *American Sociological Review* 58 (February 1993): 54.

5. Ping Chen, "China's Challenge to Economic Orthodoxy," *China Economic Review* 4, no. 2 (1993): 139.

6. John Naisbitt, *Global Paradox* (New York: Avon, 1994), p. 244.

7. Yu-shan Wu, *Comparative Economic Transformations: Mainland China, Hungary, the Soviet Union, and Taiwan* (Stanford: Stanford University Press, 1994).

8. "An Investigative Report on China's Surplus Rural Labor Force," *Zhongguo qingnian bao* (China Youth Daily), part 6, February 25, 1994, p. 3, translated in JPRS-CAR–94–029 (May 11, 1994), p. 22.

9. Wang Shan, *Di sanzhi yanjing kan zhongguo*, p. 193.

10. Ibid., p. 188.

11. Daniel Kwan, "Provincial Deputies Warn of Grain Supply 'Crisis,'" *South China Morning Post* (Hong Kong), March 13, 1995, p. 7.

12. Likewise, people found it hard to credit Polish workers for democratization in Poland, instead focusing on the work of intellectuals in KOR (see Roman Laba, *The Roots of Solidarity* [Princeton: Princeton University Press, 1991]. For an analysis of reform in China that details how the leaders actually stumbled around, see Barry Naughton, "What Is Distinctive About China's Economic Transition?" *Journal of Comparative Economics* 18 (1994): 470–490.

13. China Rural Villagers Self-Government Research Group, *Study on the Election of Villagers Committees in Rural China* (N.p., December 1, 1993), 175 pages.

14. Edward Friedman, "The Challenge of a Rising China: Another Germany?" in Robert Lieber, ed., *Eagle Adrift* (New York: HarperCollins, 1996).

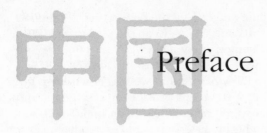# Preface

Much of this book rests on my "fieldwork." Since mine is not the trained professional fieldwork of an anthropologist, you have a right to know the nature of my "fieldwork."

How could someone like me, a privileged urban brat, write a book about farmers? The answer to this question is far from simple. Let me begin by describing my background and motivations for writing this book.

I was born in 1956 in Wuhan, one of the largest industrial cities in China. My father was a college professor of English, my mother was a high school teacher. Growing up, I had almost no contact with rural people, the great majority of China's population. The few I saw were beggars from rural Henan. In my eyes, beggars represented what rural people were all about—"dirty," "lazy," and "bad." Urban kids had many rhymes to describe the stupidity of rural people. I still remember one of them:

Henan hick carried a pile of shit,
When I tried to help him,
He said I beat him.
When I gave him a bowl of fried rice,
He said it was full of shit.

But in the summer of 1966 the Cultural Revolution started, and my privileged position suddenly disintegrated. First, my father was labeled a "bourgeois intellectual" and was locked up in an improvised prison at his school. Big posters proclaiming "Down with Zhou Mingshen" and describing my father's supposed sexual activities covered the whole campus where our apartment was located. Our dignity was stripped away. Red Guards sealed the door of our room with big posters, leaving one small hole to crawl in and out. My eleven-year-old sister, Zhou Ping, and I fled to my mother's home (my parents had divorced). Two days after we arrived, Red Guards from my mother's school gave her a *yinyangtou*, a half-man and half-woman haircut. They attacked her sexual identity because of her "good looks" and her two divorces. They forced her to walk fifteen miles barefoot on a day when the heat was above 100° F. A political struggle meeting against my mother was held in front of a public restroom in her neighborhood. All my mother's household belongings, our clothes, and our books were burned in the backyard. The high school Red

Guards also smashed the furniture and dug up the floor to find "bourgeois treasures." Whenever they found some jewelry or an old set of china, they shouted revolutionary slogans as they threw the jewelry into the fire and smashed the china against the wall. My mother was sent to prison.

My sister and I tried to flee the violence, but we had nowhere to go. Everyone we knew suddenly stopped talking to us. Even our friends and relatives avoided contact because my parents had been branded "bourgeois intellectuals." On many nights my sister and I held each other against the cold wind on the bench of a railway station. Occasionally, we saw police run after rural beggars and lock them up in the *shourongsuo*, the temporary jail station for rural people, before sending them back to their villages. In order to distinguish ourselves from those rural beggars, my sister and I would board the crowded buses to recite Mao's sayings from the Little Red Book to the passengers. We hoped that our accents, our education, and our political enthusiasm would distinguish us from those rural outsiders. We desperately wanted to be part of the urban crowd and to join the revolution in the name of Chairman Mao. Occasionally, we participated in struggle meetings against "the enemy of the people," both frightened and excited by the shouting and angry crowd.

When the revolutionary fever cooled in late 1969, my father was released from the improvised prison and sent to the countryside. My sister and I were also exiled to the countryside to be "reeducated" by the poor farmers. My mother remained in prison. Life in the countryside was desperately hard, so the loss of urban residential status was a serious punishment in itself. My sister and I settled in Tongxin Village, Jingshan County, in rural Hubei, more than 100 miles from Wuhan. We were assigned to stay with a poor farm family in Team Number Nine.

For us, the village was a completely strange world. There was no electricity, no running water, no toilet. Everything we took for granted in the city did not exist in the countryside. Still, we felt more relaxed because rural people were not as obsessed with politics as urban people.

As teenagers from the city, my sister and I immediately became celebrities of a sort among young people despite our "bad political" backgrounds. We wore factory-made clothes and shoes. Young girls were amazed that we used sanitary tissue paper for our period instead of ashes and rags. We had difficulty explaining such basic terms as "banana," "cakes," "running water," "coal," and "electricity." On many summer nights, several young village girls would lie on top of the rice straw stack listening to my stories of city life and talking aloud of their dreams. One hoped that someday she would walk on the Yangzi Bridge; another wanted to take a ride on a train; still another wanted a bike. At that time, however, even these simple dreams were only fantasies for those rural youths. Locked in a closed system, these young villagers had almost no chance of upward mobility.

Despite the hard and unfamiliar living conditions, I adapted to the rural environment. I tried hard to have a perfect local dialect and learned to carry heavy objects on my shoulders. I even learned some needlework from my village friends during political study sessions. Working and living together with rural people enabled me to establish close ties with farmers.

I left the village in 1972, when the government asked my father to come back to the city to teach English. Nixon's visit made people in Beijing realize that they needed more people who could speak English. My tie to the village did not end, though. My sister, who turned sixteen that year, was not allowed to leave with us. She stayed in that village for another six years. During that time I often visited her and my friends. One reason for my frequent visits was my guilt. I did not have to go to the countryside as long as she was there. I felt that my sister was forced to stay in the village to suffer for me. In the mid–1970s in Wuhan, the government would allow one child to stay in the city to care for his or her parents. I often brought her rare "goodies" such as soap, sugar, soy sauce, and crackers.

Yet the return to the city was not easy. I had lost my education in the countryside. When I was put into senior high school because of my age, I could not understand the classwork and lost interest. After two years in the countryside, I had lost the urban language and the urban style. It was difficult for me to make new friends, and I became purposeless and hopeless.

In 1975, after two aimless years, I was able to get a job at a factory in Wuhan making parts for copying machines. I worked between three and four hours a day in the factory, spending the rest of my time chatting with co-workers. We workers learned how to conserve our energy because we had to line up for groceries and then prepare food after work.

For most Chinese, landing a job in an urban state factory was the height of aspiration. Politically, workers were supposed to be the masters of the state, *laodage* (big brothers). Economically, workers had life-tenured jobs with free medical care and a pension. Having lived in the countryside, where these political and economic privileges did not exist, I treasured my job and at the same time felt tremendously guilty when I thought of my sister and friends trapped in the village.

When Mao died and his loyal followers, including his wife, were arrested in 1976, the whole nation experienced a period of agitation and anxiety. No one was sure what was permissible. Farmers in Tongxin Village experienced a period of social paralysis.

Then, in late 1977, farm families began to "bribe" their way out of collective chores by making deals with local cadres. One family in Team Number Nine was able to take control of a pigsty by promising high payment to the collective. Another made a deal with the brigade party secretary so that they were allowed to manage a small hillside of trees. This kind of private dealmaking gradually spread to farm production. At first, the production team was divided among several families. Since villagers were related, members of those small groups were usually relatives. In a very short time, small groups yielded to family production. The head of a family would promise to fulfill the production quota and gave the cadres a bit over. The family gained control over production decisionmaking. After fulfilling the quota, the farmer was able to keep or to sell the rest of the harvest. Known as *baochan daohu* (turning over production to the household), this system gave farmers great incentives to increase productivity.

During this period, the Beijing government was locked in factional struggle over the succession to Mao, and the confusion provided an opportunity for farmers' dealmaking to spread. When the rapid increase in farm productivity attracted the attention of central leadership in the early 1980s, the reform faction within the government tried to take credit for the farmers' achievements by institutionalizing *baochan daohu*. In regions such as Anhui and Sichuan, where provincial leaders and local cadres did not resist *baochan daohu*, the process went smoothly. Elsewhere, the process was slower and more complicated. However, the central government's recognition of *baochan daohu* provided legitimacy that local cadres could no longer resist, although the center did nothing to implement it as a policy. *No work team was sent to any village in Hubei to carry out* baochan daohu. No urban people were involved in the great transformation. Even the urban exiles had by then returned to the city.

As soon as *baochan daohu* became institutionalized, rapid changes took place in rural China that neither leaders nor farmers could have anticipated. Under this system, once a farm family satisfied the state quota and paid off the local cadres, it had the power to do whatever it wished to earn more money. Markets boomed across the nation, and the impact was felt by both rural and urban dwellers. Long lines for food in the city disappeared as farmers began to sell all kinds of agricultural goods. Throughout the 1960s and 1970s, city dwellers had had to line up for two or three hours for a piece of bad pork. Wuhan residents had been allowed to buy fish only twice a year. Having queued every day for several hours after a day's work in the factory, I was happy to begin seeing farmers selling fresh food at the gate of our apartment building. Farmers quickly replaced the state-run vegetable shops as the main source of produce for all Wuhan residents.

In 1980, when villagers from Tongxin came to Wuhan selling eggs, rice, pork, and other agricultural products, some stayed at my home for several weeks because the state hotels refused to take them in. My home became a magnet for my rural relatives and friends. I was impressed by their entrepreneurial skill. Many evenings I listened to stories of their new life.

When I in turn visited the village in 1982, it had changed beyond recognition. Almost everyone was building a new house. Every family was engaged in market exchanges. Dinner conversations focused on making money. Linked with moneymaking was the rise in consumption. There was at least one bike in each family. Talk of buying a TV and a small tractor preoccupied villagers.

During this period of rapid change, my life also was altered. In 1977, China held the first college entrance examination since 1966. The universities began returning to life. I entered Wuhan University to study English and was able to travel around China during school vacations. From 1979 to the early

1980s, I visited more than twenty villages in Hunan and Hubei. I also visited Guangdong in 1981. Everywhere I went, farmers were busily selling goods at markets, building houses, and raising chickens and pigs. Everywhere I went I saw farmers keen on making money as fast as possible.

My connection with farmers' go-getter activities and my life as a college student at one of China's most prestigious universities divided me between two completely different worlds. At school, my fellow students and I tried to follow the intellectual trends of the time. We were tantalized by the ideas of democracy. In 1980, I actively participated in the national intellectual debate on the meaning of life. We students were also interested in the notion of free speech. We liked to read writers who were out of favor with the regime. Liu Binyan and Bai Hua, two writers who were criticized by the government, were particularly popular among students. We also talked about the merits of the market system and the problems of a planned economy. Almost all of us were waiting for the government to assign us good jobs after graduation from college, but no one at school talked about the farmers who were actually creating and supplying Chinese markets. Most students from the countryside tried hard to hide their rural identity. There was a saying to describe those students: "As freshmen, they're 'earthy'; as sophomores, they become 'stylish'; by the third year, they refuse to recognize their parents."

The embarrassment of the students from the countryside indicates the common attitude toward farmers. Chinese intellectuals, regardless of their ideological orientation, had reached a curious consensus concerning the backwardness of farmers. Supporters of the regime argued that the Communist system was necessary because of the ignorance and illiteracy of the "peasants." Dissenters blamed the "conservative peasants" for the continuation of Communist rule.[1] Unaware of this strange agreement between the two worlds, I shared the intellectuals' contempt for villagers. Having grown up in a nonmarket culture, I also felt ambivalent about the commercial rush of those farmers and worried about the future of our nation.

In 1983, I was able to go to Beijing for a college teacher training program. The same phenomenon of the farmers' market fever was also infecting Beijing. In the Zhongguancun *jishi*, or farmers' market, farmers from Shandong, Hebei, and Henan were busy selling foods of all kinds, while nearby the state grocery stores were almost empty or stacked with products of bad quality. On many street corners, farmers were selling goods in defiance of the ban on private selling outside *jishi*.

In mid-1983, national leaders in Beijing launched the Anti-Spiritual Pollution campaign in order to attack "bourgeois ideas" that threatened the Communist party. This movement had no impact on farmers' attitudes, though. When I talked to rural merchants in Zhongguancun *jishi* and in Tazhongsi, a neighborhood in the middle of Beijing, few were aware that there was a "new cultural revolution" going on nationwide. When I told them about the campaign, some were worried that the new "Red Guards" would come to take away their money. I realized then how utterly irrelevant Beijing leaders, students, and intellectuals were to the interests and lives of farmers.

Sporadically, the Beijing government tried to crack down on farmers' market activities. On several occasions in 1983, I saw police rounding up farmers when they tried to sell goods along the road. One day in October, I saw local policemen hassling two young rural women who were hawking sunflower seeds at the Mu Xu Di subway station. The police wanted to fine them 100 yuan for unlicensed and illegal selling. When they refused to pay the fine, the police hit them with clubs and took away their money and the sunflower seeds. When the police left, I went up to the two women and offered to take them home. After some hesitation, they allowed me to take them to their Beijing residence, a farmhouse in Haidian District. The owner rented three rooms to rural migrants who came to Beijing for the market or to work, and every room was packed with people making things and planning new ventures.

I was also surprised by the rise of new landlords among Beijing farmers. Farmers dominated Beijing *caishichang* (free vegetable markets), but the suburban farmers were busy building houses to rent. Realizing that most rural migrants were violating *hukou* (household registration system or internal passport) restrictions, I began to have a new understanding of farmers' commercial and migration activities.

In the summer of 1983, I set out to see more of rural China, spending three months in Hebei. Energized by the family-based economy, Hebei farmers spent much of their time selling and making deals. In the capital, Shijiazhuang, I visited *jishi* daily and talked to farmers. Farmers from far-flung counties came to Shijiazhuang, some by tractor or horse cart, most by bicycle. *Two big baskets attached to a heavy-duty bicycle became the symbol of the rural entrepreneur.*

When I returned to Wuhan to teach in September 1984, I found small shops springing up like mushrooms along the city's main roads. Most were run by rural migrants, who, lacking urban *hukou*, found the urban setting hostile. In many cases, they had to depend on themselves and their friends to stay alive in the city and had to use the name of an urban resident to set up a small business. Yet, very quickly these small businesses began to dominate Wuhan's service sector.

Surprised by the dramatic change, I began to observe the farmers' activities keenly, occasionally even participating. I traveled with two Hunan rural entrepreneurs in Hubei and was impressed with their inventiveness. One important element was their ability to smooth the way with cadres of all kinds. Whenever they passed a truck check station, they offered "gifts" to the cadres there. They were also good at *laguanxi*, "cultivating relationships" with officials. These rural go-getters were able to create businesses for themselves in more than ten provinces between 1981 and 1993.

The wave of rural entrepreneurship was accompanied by a tide of rural migrants. Even in the mid-1980s, I felt the presence of rural migrants in my life. Many set up small restaurants and shops along the road I biked to school to teach. Suburban farmers rented rooms and houses to new rural migrants. These migrants were illegal in the eyes of the state because they did not have urban *hukou*. Most of them did not register as temporary residents. No matter which village I visited between 1983 and 1986, villagers, especially the young, eagerly sought employment outside the village. This had been impossible under Mao's collective regime.

While these great changes took place among farmers, state-sector employment stood still. *Up to 1986, when I left China, I did not know a single urban person who gave up a state job in favor of private employment.* By this time, almost everyone in rural China was working for his or her own family. Rural people were farming, selling, working in industries, and migrating. *I also did not know any urban people who gave up their* hukou *in order to live where they wished.* Urban people initiated few if any changes, instead reacting to the changes introduced by rural migrants. Gradually, however, more and more urbanites began to moonlight together with rural entrepreneurs.

City dwellers did feel the rural influence, of course, especially in the booming service sectors. They no longer had to line up for food, and they could eat anytime they wanted in small private restaurants, but urban people also resented the success that rural people had achieved. For more than twenty years, urban residents had occupied a superior position. Although they continued to enjoy privileges, they were now challenged by people from the countryside, who seemed ignorant and uneducated. In mid–1986, a new phenomenon arose in urban China, *tiqi kuaizi chirou, fangxia kuaizi maniang*. Roughly translated, it describes how people lifted their chopsticks to eat meat, but when they put down their chopsticks they began to curse. In other words, urban people benefited from the change brought by farmers (they had meat to eat), but they felt left out and betrayed by the process at the same time.

The rural atmosphere was quite different. Although incidents of attacking the newly rich did occur because of *hongyanbing* (red-eye disease, or envy), almost everyone I met had a vision of prosperity. Before I left China in 1986, I went to Tongxin to say goodbye. The villagers' hospitality was moving. I had to eat at every door. Many said, "You suffered with us before. In the past, we could not offer you even a simple meal. Now you are going away and will not come back for a long time. It is our pleasure to entertain you with good food. Do not look down upon us." On several occasions, I even had to sleep with a new bride because it was considered the most hospitable thing to allow an honored guest to sleep in the new bed. Profitmaking and the search for better opportunities dominated conversations at all dinner parties I attended.

With these impressions in my mind, I came to the United States for graduate studies. At Texas A&M University, where I studied sociology, I was surprised to find that almost everyone I met across the political spectrum took it for granted that Deng Xiaoping was the grand designer of

Chinese economic reform. Having been so involved with the farmers who had initiated the changes, I found this common perception irritating. In China, government officials tended to take credit for whatever looked good, and the Chinese press presented Deng as the designer of rural reforms. The press was controlled by the party, so I was accustomed to such sycophancy, but I had higher expectations of the U.S. media and academic community. When I said this to my then-adviser, James Copp, a rural sociologist, he asked me to write about it. Under his guidance, I wrote my master's thesis about changes in the village where I had lived. In 1989, I began work on my Ph.D. in comparative politics at Princeton University. When I gave a talk on Chinese farmers' proverbs in 1991, my adviser, Lynn White, urged me to make the best use of these sources for my dissertation.

In writing this book, I have made every effort to assure that farmers, who have long been spoken for by political and academic authorities, would speak here in their own voices. In the course of interviewing throughout the countryside in the years 1981–1986, I realized the importance of what James Scott has since called "hidden transcripts."[2] I began to collect proverbs, local songs, and popular sayings. I hope to bring farmers' voices into the analysis of contemporary Chinese politics by tapping those new sources. For thousands of years, Chinese people have used proverbs, popular sayings, and local songs to express their feelings and attitudes toward everything, especially politics. Those forms of popular expression differ from political posters because they rarely appear in print, but they are more popular and more widespread than posters and newspapers. Unlike most published literature, they have no known authors, but each proverb, each popular saying, influences many people. In fact, they are shared expressions of popular resentment and longing. "Especially in a largely illiterate community, shared values and handed-down wisdom are apt to be encapsulated in proverbs."[3] They are folk politics!

In order to take photographs for the book, I went back to China in December 1994. I had hoped to find the first farmer to own a twelve-wheel truck or the first farmer to become a landlord, but no one knows who they are. I was startled to find how prevalent materialism has become. Goods and services had lost all symbolic meaning except for their monetary implications. Many people seemed more interested in making money than in making China. The government, after all, was responsible for maintaining order, for maintaining the Will of Heaven. The people felt responsible for getting on with their own lives and watching over their own families. They rarely reflected on their role in creating the tide that had washed away so much of the old system.

## Notes

1. For example, Su Xiaokang and Wang Luxiang, the writers of "River Elegy" (Heshang), produced a controversial six-part TV documentary that was aired nationally in the summer of 1988 and subsequently banned. The

series contrasts the "backward" rural culture and the "outward-looking" coastal economy. For a translation and commentary, see Richard W. Bodman and Pin Pin Wan, *Deathsong of a River* (Northfield, Minn.: Department of Russian and East Asian Languages, St. Olaf College, 1991).

2. James C. Scott, *Domination and the Arts of Resistance: Hidden Transcripts* (New Haven: Yale University Press, 1990).

3. R. David Arkush, "If Man Works Hard the Land Will Not Be lazy," *Modern China* 10, no. 4 (1984): 462.

## Note on Measures
1 mu   = 1/15 hectares  = 1/6 acre
1 jin   = 0.5 kilogram   = 1.1 pounds
1 yuan  = approximately U.S. $0.50–$0.80 (the value has decreased since the late 1980s)

# Acknowledgments

The support of a number of individuals has been crucial to the process of my writing of this book. I am grateful to Lynn White, who never failed to encourage me with long and detailed comments. I would like to thank Marion J. Levy, Jr., who helped me in ways that defy identification, and Professor F. W. Mote, who has no peer in scholarship and hard thinking. Edward Friedman read each chapter and encouraged me all the way. Jeffrey Herbst, James Scott, Gilbert Rozman, Solomon Karmel, Michael Oksenberg, and Pei Minxin read all the draft chapters and provided me with helpful comments to improve the book.

A number of people read part of the book and provided helpful comments. They are Charles Tilly, Ansley Coale, Deborah Davis, Dorothy Solinger, Cathy Thelen, Kay Warren, Yongnian Zheng, Ben Steinberg, Bob Orr, Steve Davis, and Nancy Bermeo. Heidi Didier and Martin Heijdra in Gest Library at Princeton have been very helpful. Other friends and colleagues have given me both intellectual and moral support. They are Mildred Kalmus, Tom Moore, Chris Stancell, Robert and Jean Gilpin, George Downs, Zhuang Anqing, Jim Doig, Fred Greenstein, Seth Masters, Judy McPherson, Chen Yizi, Wang Feng, Wu Guoguang, Cheng Xiaonong, Jane Sell, and David Tubbs.

Hawaii has been a good place for me to revise my manuscript, as many friends and colleagues in the Political Science Department and the Center for Chinese Studies, especially Cindy Ning and Daniel Cole, have given me lots of support.

I have been fortunate to have Mark Selden, Susan McEachern, and Marian Schwartz as my editors. They have been essential in the manuscript preparation. Through Mark, I was able to communicate with quite a number of Chinese scholars, who helped clarify my confusion and misunderstanding. More than that, he has found time to go over this manuscript at least four times to try to save me from sin. Who can teach better? I owe him enormous *renqing* (good human feeling).

Finally, the love of my father, Zhou Mingshen, and my sister, Zhou Ping, has been an important sustaining force during my stay in the United States. David Burns deserves the most special thanks. David read each chapter many times and suggested improvement in both English language and ideas. I am dedicating the book to David. My son, Neil, also deserves many thanks. Neil constantly gave me lovely smiles and laughter.

# Introduction: Who Changed China?

In a very short time, in China's central,
southern and northern provinces, several
hundred million peasants will rise like a
tornado or tempest, a force so extraordinarily swift and violent that no power,
however great, will be able to suppress it.
They will break all trammels that now
bind them and rush forward along the
road to liberation. They will send all impe-
rialists, warlords, corrupt officials, local
bullies and bad gentry to their graves.

> Mao Zedong,
> "Report of an
> Investigation into
> Peasant Movement in
> Hunan"

China is undergoing rapid social change and high-speed economic
development. Since 1979, China is thought to have maintained a
two-digit economic growth rate, perhaps the world's highest growth
rate ever. According to a recent International Monetary Fund account,
China is now the third largest economy in the world after Japan and the
United States. The amazing thing about China's growth is that rural growth
is its basis. This book argues that Chinese political leaders are going with
the flow rather than directing the most dramatic elements of development.
This development is a product of a special kind of movement.[1] It is a spontaneous, unorganized, leaderless, nonideological, apolitical movement
(SULNAM),[2] and it is rapidly sweeping away everything in its path; it is a
new energy for China. The farmers of China are changing China this time
around—not the leaders, not the bureaucrats, not the cadres, not the intellectuals but the farmers themselves.

## The Background of Change

For over two thousand years, the Chinese maintained the largest-scale state in human history—both territorially and demographically. In recent times, only the Soviet Union, Canada, and the United States have exceeded China territorially—and the Soviet Union has now proved unstable. Before the Communist revolution (1949), Chinese farmers and villages avoided any centralized structure. Typically, Chinese farmers ran independent farms in an open class system, although granted the system often got clogged. Ideally speaking, however, it was an open class system for over two thousand years. In the villages, the family heads, who knew farming, managed the farms. A civil service–selected bureaucracy governed Chinese society, but officials rarely intervened directly beyond the *xian* (county) level. Considering the scale involved, the Chinese bureaucracy, for all its faults, ruled more effectively, efficiently, and continuously than any other in world history. Not the least of its practical achievements were irrigation systems covering territories larger than the state of Texas, grain storage, and famine relief.[3] Still and all, roughly 85 percent of the population, the farmers of China, kept themselves and the urban Chinese alive by farming that was planned and directed by family heads, not by government officials or overlords. The leadership of the People's Republic of China (PRC) changed those social structures radically, including some that had remained stable for over two thousand years.

## Basic Changes of the Communist Regime

After the revolution, profound changes occurred in the position of the rural family and the nature of society, the most profound of these, perhaps, associated with collectivization. The changes affected the source of farming decisions directly and decisively. The Communists set out to remove the Chinese family from the nexus of local organization and decisionmaking. The party organization represented by cadres took over the control and direction of farms. The commune and later the production teams replaced the family as the basic social unit of farming.

Specifically, the People's Republic's policies of socialist transformation, collectivization, procurement, *hukou*, and the rationing system (subsidized grain distribution for urban people and producer grain allocation for rural people) created a new farmer class.[4] By depriving all farmers of landownership and mobility, the state attempted to turn the farmers into rural proletarians. The new rural proletarians differed from their urban counterparts; they lacked the subsidies and social welfare that urban workers received. The government had no social contract with the farmers as they did with urban workers.

In the course of these changes, the lives of the farmers fell under the direct control of the cadres, the government-appointed officials, who became, in effect, their overlords. The state bound Chinese farmers to the cadres and to the land, denying them migration and social mobility based on family or individual decisions. Before the revolution, farmers traveled to participate in nonfarm work during the annual dry season. The collectives deprived farmers of these nonfarm opportunities. They walked a "peasant" road. Although in the previous two thousand years, most people who were born farmers died farmers, the official state examinations held out the hope that an educated son, even of a farmer, might acquire a bureaucratic post.[5] Previously, farmers could join the merchant class. The People's Republic closed social and geographical mobility for the new "peasant" class. The primary channels of mobility for rural people in the PRC were the party and the army, which enabled some young men to rise and in some instances to leave the village. Advancement sometimes came from loyalty to a party boss, which led to cynicism, opportunism, and sycophancy in all its forms. In short, the revolution closed classes and created a "feudal" relationship. The farmers were bound to cadres and tied to the land.

In medieval Europe, the feudal lords at least knew a great deal about farming and shouldered an obligation to feed the serfs.[6] Not so under Communist China. The party promoted cadres on the basis of their political loyalty and often failed to provide basic subsistence. In a time of difficulty (1959–1961), the state further deprived farmers to feed urban people, resulting in the famine deaths of 15 million–40 million farmers.[7]

These past–present, urban–rural contrasts motivated the new "peasants" to seek to regain their family autonomy through daily resistance, mostly by "foot dragging," against the cadres' control. Throughout the collective days, farmers tried to expand their private plots. Sometimes the government even compromised by giving over a small portion of private land (2–5 percent). Farmers were even allowed to sell some produce from private plots in the market. The "great" compromise between the government and the farmers did not change the key structure of the collective system. The private plots were tiny. Moreover, political campaigns repeatedly cut the balance of the compromise. The farmers, despite improvements in machines, seeds, and fertilizers, were left with little or no incentive to increase or even maintain collective productivity.

Soon after the Communists took power, after a few sunny moments, the lot of farmers worsened. Not only did the state set family autonomy aside, but it put people who were good at politics, but not necessarily at farming, in charge of farming. Chinese farmers had never before organized themselves primarily on a village basis. They had been organized, first and foremost, on a family basis. Each family had cared for its own farm. Cadres organized farming on a commune, brigade, or team basis, regardless of the implications for productivity. They gave farmers no individual incentives to work hard to increase the level of productivity. Cadre rule took centralization beyond any level necessary for productivity. As a result, per capita rural income stagnated and in some cases declined. Given the vast mobilization of labor (especially women) and year-round application of labor to capital construction, for instance, the return to labor measured by labor days also dropped. Farmers worked longer and harder for little or no gain. This is related to the government's view of China's collective farmers as having unlimited supplies of labor that could be tapped as essentially a free good by the collective or the political leadership.[8]

In the 1980s, farmers cut themselves loose of cadre control using the knife of *baochan daohu*.[9] By so doing, collective "peasants" reclaimed their status as farmers, setting off a chain of events startling in their implication for agrarian productivity. In the end, the unorganized farmers' drive for a return to family autonomy and direction changed the social structure of the People's Republic of China more than did any of the changes in the urban setting. The increase in productivity in the early 1980s, when a majority of Chinese farmers adopted *baochan daohu*, greatly intensified the revolutionary impact of unorganized farmers. Family organization provided farmers the incentives to use newly available technology, seeds, and fertilizers to increase productivity and income both per hectare and per worker. (Farmers had access to technical improvements before *baochan daohu*, but they did not have incentives.) Under *baochan daohu*, increased productivity released much labor power from farm work, making more labor available for rural industrialization and for migration to urban areas. The reduced need for farm labor and the farmers' "feudal" peasant status combined to motivate a migration of surplus labor away from the land. Farmers' increasing emphasis on local markets undermined monopoly control of the markets by government officials. The farmers took advantage of the corruptibility of the cadres rather than revolutionary action. Without anyone organizing a revolution, assuming leadership, or inventing an ideology, the farmers gained autonomy in farm planning, revived rural nonagricultural production, expanded old markets, and initiated new markets and migration to the city. Without intending to or realizing it, the farmers were bringing about a revolutionary change.

In the course of these changes, each and every unorganized effort contributed to the transformation of the Chinese Communist regime and prepared it, unintentionally, no doubt, for vastly increased productivity and remarkable increases in economic development. These spontaneous and apolitical efforts—rather than state ideology and in spite of Communist organization—formed the primary basis for China's current success in economic development. That success was directly due to a spontaneous, unorganized, leaderless, nonideological, apolitical movement (SULNAM).

Contrary to conventional thinking, unorganized increases in rural productivity, rather than any urban economic development, accelerated China's economic development (still overwhelmingly rural). Farmers attempted unorganized decollectivization, or surreptitious grass-roots land reform, in many parts of rural China throughout the 1960s and 1970s. Their efforts finally succeeded in the late 1970s and came above ground in 1982, when Deng Xiaoping eventually accepted this alternative to "peasant" revolution or Mao's mobilizational collectivism. He named it "the household production responsibility system" in order to avoid using the term "decollectivization."[10] With this renaming, the government reluctantly recognized the farmers' family autonomy in managing their economic lives. *Baochan daohu* gutted the rural people's communes, a system integrating party organization and farm management. The new Chinese "peasants" regained the status of farmers. They also redefined the "status of farmers" through the explosion of rural industry and commerce.

Farmers pounced on the party-state's concession in the Third Plenary of the Eleventh Party Congress (1978) loosening control over rural markets and increasing agricultural prices. They proceeded to dominate almost all new markets in the 1980s, both in urban and in rural areas. The farmers' commercial activities effectively killed the grain rationing system, the government's primary instrument for controlling the spatial and social mobility of the rural population.

Rural migration (both permanent and temporary) to cities helped farmers evade the government's control of the job market; it challenged, weakened, and bypassed the *hukou* system. The government had used the *hukou* system, combined with the grain rationing system, to tie "peasants" to the collective land. The government forced farmers to sell at a loss, on the one hand; on the other hand, the government imposed grain rationing in the city, while at the same time restricting migration from the countryside. "Compulsory purchase and urban rationing were two sides of the coin. The state replaced the market to increase control over the agricultural product and the labor power and movement of rural population."[11]

After *baochan daohu*, opportunities for alternative employment enabled farmers to bypass illicitly the *hukou* system. Farmers did not need rationing coupons to buy food. They could get it at the corners of the city where rural merchants dominated. So long as the family submitted their quota to the state and to the local cadres, cadres could not control the mobility of farmers. Rural migrants call themselves *ziliuren* (free people, i.e., free of collective controls),[12] creating jobs for themselves and taking jobs that city folk would not take.

Although a few wealthy farmers bought urban *hukou*, millions of poor migrants seeped through holes in the planned system. As a result, rural migrants flooded Chinese cities. By 1992, migrants numbered 100 million, although permanent migrants are few.[13] And the number is rapidly growing.

Likewise, the successful results of farmers' pursuit of autonomy encouraged some urban workers, intellectuals, and even government cadres to leave their own *danwei* (urban or state work unit, which provides welfare and exercises political control). Rural industries provided opportunities for urban people to participate in "second shift" (i.e., moonlighting) activities.

Family autonomy also widened farmers' job choices. They could choose entrepreneurial roles, factory work, or whatever the expanded market offered. The diversified life opportunities spurred rural enterprises to grow twice as fast as state-owned firms.[14] Before *baochan daohu* (in 1978), rural industry generated only 7 percent of the gross national product, but it created 40 percent of the total output value of all national industry by the end of 1992.[15] In some coastal areas, many rural industries were export-oriented, and some were linked to foreign investment. By 1993, rural industry constituted 50 percent of all industrial production.[16]

Although the government now encourages (or at least legally accepts) many autonomous farmers' efforts, others remain outside the legal system. Graft, bribery, corruption of every imaginable sort, smuggling, *guanxi* (use of personal connections), and surreptitious economic activity (opening a factory or a business without state permission) allow farmers to undermine, avoid, and evade government control. This evasion runs counter to the notion that the state relinquished controls in the post-Mao period. Farmers' SULNAM reduced the degree of government control. A special illustration of rural people's power in reducing the government's control is rural resistance to the state's one-child policy. Since 1979, the government has insisted that *jiben guoce* (basic state policy) mandates one child per couple. Despite the government's ability to reduce even the rural birthrate, it was never able to carry out its one-child policy in the countryside to the extent that the one-child policy succeeded in the cities. Decollectivization and the relaxation of controls on population movement made it vastly more difficult for the government to enforce its population program in the countryside. As of 1985, the government was forced to tacitly accept a second child for rural people when the first child was a girl.

Finally, rural women are active participants in the *baochan daohu* movement, the development of markets, rural industrial employment, and migration. These developments in turn have provided opportunities for rural women, increasing their economic power and social status.

## The Forgotten Farmer in the Analysis of Chinese Politics

Few can doubt that great changes have shaken China. Many analysts believe that deliberate economic reforms caused virtually all the changes, but scholars do disagree as to the force behind the economic reforms. Until recently, the farmers' role in the transformation of Communist China has been largely neglected. Literature on the origins of Chinese economic reforms centered mainly on three driving forces: the elite (especially Deng Xiaoping); the impact of the Cultural Revolution (1966–1976); and institutional sources (a statist view).[17] All three focus on the state.

Most in the West regard Deng Xiaoping as the mastermind behind rural reforms, for which *Time* twice made him "Man of the Year" (1979 and 1986).[18] The Chinese honor Deng as *zongshejishi* (the great architect) as a result of the economic reforms. Yet Deng himself opposed *baochan daohu* until 1982, by which time it had already brought a rapid increase in productivity.[19]

A preoccupation with the elite, especially Deng Xiaoping, dominates the thinking of most observers, both Chinese and non-Chinese. *China Quarterly* introduced its special issue on Deng Xiaoping with the statement:

> Yet there is no denying that Deng was responsible for a monumental transformation of one-fifth of humanity, awakening China from its socialist slumber with the prospect of an unprecedented future. . . . Consequently, in 1992 Deng reignited radical economic reform. The results were impressive indeed: 12.8 per cent GNP growth in 1992. Foreign direct investment poured into China at unprecedented levels.[20]

But 1992 is relatively late, and 12.8 percent growth is small when compared to the growth rates (more than 20 percent) built by rural industries beginning in the late 1970s. In fact, most growth in China since 1978 has come from agricultural and rural industrial growth.

Many compared Deng to free-marketers like Margaret Thatcher and Ronald Reagan. Such remarks make one wonder whether Deng had a magic wand in his hand. Deng himself made little effort to appeal as a charismatic leader, as Lucian Pye pointed out: "The extraordinary and dramatic changes in China would seem to have called for a larger-than-life charismatic leader-magician who could project his persona so as to captivate the imagination of a whole population. Yet, consider the astonishing fact that Deng rarely appeared in public and almost never used the mass media personally."[21]

Further, Deng never renounced the four cardinal principles of socialism: (1) adherence to socialism; (2) adherence to the People's Dictatorship; (3) adherence to Marxism, Leninism, and Mao's thought; (4) adherence to the leadership of the Communist party. Not until 1992 did Deng suggest that socialism means increasing people's material well-being and that slow growth is not socialism, but by 1992, who else in China believed in socialism at all? As Zu Ping, a farmer of Tongxin Village, Hubei Province, said well in 1978: "Only the cadres pay attention to political lines; the farmers are only interested in what works."[22]

Even if Deng did favor market reform, could he have achieved the Chinese miracle by political means alone? If so, what were his means? Mikhail Gorbachev and Boris Yeltsin have said and done much more to push for market reform in Russia. Yet how much have they achieved?

How much control have they wielded? The answer appears to be very little, indeed.

*Dilemmas of Reform in China,* by Joseph Fewsmith, is probably the best book to focus on "elite intrigue politics" in China.[23] While recognizing the role of central leadership, Fewsmith also argues that rural reforms followed a "bottom-up" process. For Fewsmith, the bottom started with provincial and prefecture leaders like Wan Li and Wang Yuzhao in Anhui and Beijing intellectuals of the Rural Development and Research Center. For me, the bottom started very low, with the ordinary farmers. Without farmers' initiative in *baochan daohu* and without the *baochan daohu* demonstration effect, Wan Li and Beijing intellectuals would not have discovered *baochan daohu.* The most powerful demonstration of "bottom-up" rural reform is the flow of millions upon millions of rural migrants, which is missing in Fewsmith's book. Although we can find ample evidence of antimigrant policies at every level of government, we could not find a single politician or intellectual leading this massive flow of rural migrants.

For Fewsmith, a bottom-up process was possible in the countryside because the bureaucratic organization was weak there. It is quite possible that a SULNAM would have been impossible in the city because officials were constantly on the lookout.

It is a fundamental theme of this book that the farmers were able to accomplish what they did because the elite leadership was mostly looking the other way. Professor Fewsmith, however, does give us the most thoroughgoing description and analysis of the elite that I have seen. He tells us who they were, with whom they went to what schools, which officials and commissions they served, their likes and dislikes, where they lived, their hopes, their fears—he knows them and gives them to us in unbelievable detail.

The second conventional explanation for the economic reforms gives credit to the aftermath of the Cultural Revolution. The government itself admitted that it needed to repair the damage done by the Cultural Revolution. The Cultural Revolution explanation also centers upon the elite, claiming that the Cultural Revolution convinced Chinese leaders to abandon Mao's legacy.[24] This interpretation, however, fails to tell us why reforms did not occur first in the city, where the violence of the Cultural Revolution centered.[25] I try in this book to demonstrate that the leadership has lagged well behind farmers' initiatives. When the government lifted restrictions, it did so only in recognition of the fact that the sea of unorganized farmers had already made them irrelevant.

The third interpretation of economic reforms employs an institutional argument. Focusing on the state's intention to mend its fences, Vivienne Shue wrote this about the origins of rural reforms: "Of course, we do know why what has happened happened so suddenly. Those who lead and support the power coalition in Beijing today include many of Mao Zedong's oldest and bitterest political enemies, and they are quite naturally undoing much of what they had long opposed in the Maoist political and economic program."[26]

Again, this explanation fails to reveal why reform occurred first in the countryside. Neither Mao's friends nor his enemies were known for their appearances in the countryside. Some argue that Deng and his colleagues initiated rural reform first because they thought it would be easier to undertake rural reforms than to start with urban reforms, as if they had planned the whole thing. But Deng himself admitted that reform is like *mozhe shitou guohe* (crossing the river by feeling the stones). He was groping his way in the dark. The very success of *baochan daohu* convinced Chinese leaders to undertake urban reforms that have proved less successful.[27] The state reacted to change rather than initiating it.

The above approach also assumes that the center initiates reform and that the government can manipulate the rest of society at will. All of these interpretations of rural reform, to a large extent, center upon the elite, largely ignoring farmers.

This fixation on the elite as the source of reform may flow from the influence of the totalitarian model, which stresses the power of the state and views society as a collection of atomized individuals unable to take action: "The penetration of the state into all realms of life did not extend a public sphere so much as negate it, for without attachment to the party or one of its subsidiary organizations no particular individual could make claims with any general validity."[28]

This penetration by the state means that only the top initiates reform, as expressed by well-known Chinese scholars:

> In contrast to a society where property and citizenship rights are well-established and government policies have to take fully into account the private sector's motives and behavior, it should be borne in mind that in state socialism where the government is a sole de facto ultimate owner of everything, the government always takes the lead and others follow.[29]

The strength of the farmers, however, lay in the fact that they did not undertake organized resistance. They sought family gains, and they washed as a sea around the myriad cadre fish.

When scholars study the state–society relation, they treat the government as if it were an autonomous entity, apart from society. So often, the study of the Chinese people has become the study of the government's policies. It has seldom occurred to analysts that the interaction between the representatives of the state and ordinary people may cut both ways. Scholars take for granted the idea that China developed rapidly in the past

because the Leninists guided development. The idea that China is following other Asian authoritarian states in pushing economic reform suggests
that government officials have built more control over peoples' lives. But
*baochan daohu*, markets, rural industry, and migration all reduced official
control over peoples' lives, particularly rural people's lives. This great
increase of autonomy surpassed anything experienced before in the
People's Republic. Now, as a popular saying well states: "Beijing people
dare to curse anyone they like; Guangdong people dare to eat anything
they wish; Shanghai people dare to wear anything they fancy; farmers dare
to sell anything they can get their hands on."[30]

Alternatives to the totalitarian model also neglect the Chinese farmers.
Although critical of the totalitarian model, some scholars of structural insti-
tutionalism attribute China's lack of political initiative to the institutional
impediment of the Communist state. The Chinese party-state, like any other
Communist state, does not tolerate nonstate actors seen as competing with
itself and will crack down on any potential competitors who raise their
heads. The party-state is alert for signs of political organizations, leadership, and ideology, witness Tiananmen. By exchanging material goods
(welfare, housing, medical care, and pensions) for party loyalty, the party-
state compels individuals to compete against each other to show who is
most loyal.[31] Consequently, the organizational structure of the socialist state
exhibits an "extraordinary ability to prevent organized political activities
even from reaching the stage of collective action."[32] This structural analysis
implies that nonstate action with political implications is stillborn.

There were gaps in this institutional armor, though. Urban people did
not enjoy their dependence, as a result of negative impacts (lack of personal
freedom and political monitoring at the workplace). Chinese farmers
received little from the party boss in terms of social welfare. The restructuring
of the Communist state only benefited farmers because they never received
much, if any, economic security from the existing Communist system. This
difference between urban workers and farmers in terms of social welfare
means that rural people have more incentives for seeking fundamental
changes than any other social set in China, but the way farmers changed was
through a spontaneous, unorganized, leaderless, nonideological, apolitical
movement. Had farmers shown any signs of organization, challenged ideological leaders, waved banners, or posted ideological declaration on walls,
the state would have struck them down early on as surely as they trampled
the students and intellectuals in Tiananmen. The farmers either cared little or
were too sophisticated to waste effort on such patently dangerous gestures.

## Views of Farmers

The state-centric analysis dominates not only the China field but most
analyses of Communist countries. To some extent, the state-centric analysis
in Communist countries is inevitable because scholars so seldom have the

chance to do extended fieldwork in rural areas, or in urban ones for that matter. That may be why the collapse of communism in the former Soviet Union and Eastern Europe came as such a surprise. Certainly none of the party-state entities planned their own demise. State-centric analyses never suggest elite-guided state suicide.

Although the Potters, Helen Siu, Graham Johnson, Edward Friedman and his associates, Viviene Shue and Mark Blecher, Myron Cohen, Ellen Judd, Christine Wong, and Jean Oi were recently provided opportunities for fieldwork in China,[33] with the exception of Judd and Friedman and associates, their studies have focused overwhelmingly on various levels of party-state power, especially the local level. They either stress the power of the state, exposing how the government exploits the farmers, or emphasize the importance of local government for the improvement of rural China. They either show what the government did to farmers or argue what the local government did for the people. They say little about farmers as a driving force. This book illustrates what the farmers did for themselves.

Intellectuals both in China and in the West have been so preoccupied with the idea of a despotic state and a passive uneducated peasantry that they credit any social change, marketization, or liberalization almost uniformly to "reforming elites." This view demeaning farmers comes to us via Chinese intellectuals, the people who inform Western thinking about China.[34] Analysts intensified their fixation on intellectual and political elites and the corresponding denigration of the Chinese "peasantry" in the aftermath of Tiananmen.[35] Immediately after the Tiananmen tragedy, a social survey on democratic culture was conducted. It indicated that educated people seek more eagerly for democracy, whereas the less educated show indifference. Since the majority of Chinese people, the farmers, have little formal education (at least one-third are illiterate), the survey concludes that a democratic China faces dim prospects:

> The contrast between the two patterns (educated and uneducated) suggests that if a political crisis between the regime and the intellectuals occurs again, the majority of the population may once again not offer much backing for the demands for democratic change. But if this is true, the implications for a democratic outcome are uncertain.[36]

It may also be that the vast majority of farmers knew little or cared less what happened to the students and intellectuals at Tiananmen. The universities and intellectuals understood the farmers even less than the government did. The intellectuals despised the farmers.

Other influential Chinese intellectuals specifically cite rural culture and economic interests as a source of support for the Communist regime:

Scattered farming, a self-sufficient economy and a narrow gap between the rich and the poor had always been the solid foundation of China's autocratic political system, and contracting output to the household, in fact, re-created this situation within a very short period of time, helping Deng Xiaoping and the other reformers to consolidate their political power greatly.[37]

The farmers did not self-consciously seek democracy. They sought more immediate, perhaps more far-reaching goals, such as family control of land use. But their modest seeking restored an open class system and laid a greater emphasis on decisionmaking by individuals. None of their effort will be wasted if democracy comes to China, although the farmers' movement treated here does not, consciously or unconsciously, embrace democracy. Such an open society could become a basis for democracy. Movements that change Communist states are not necessarily democratic movements, anticommunist though they may be.

With rare exceptions, scholars have not studied the farmers' unorganized revolutionary role in the transformation of socialist states and in modernization.[38] However, as formal resistance under Communist China was rare, it is important to pay attention to the informal resistance, for, as Jean Oi pointed out, "In China, as in the Soviet Union, and the developing nations of the Third World, there is a need for the informal system of politics that circumvents the contradictions inadvertently created by the formal political and economic system."[39]

## The Revolutionary Power of Unorganized Farmers

The focus in this book is on the Chinese farmers' spontaneous, unorganized, leaderless, nonideological, apolitical movement (SULNAM) in *baochan daohu*, markets, rural industries, migration, rural resistance against the one-child policy, and the changing position of rural women. The movement as treated here has far-reaching effects, including social effects in general and political and economic effects in particular. The farmers' movement is a political movement in that it has had the extensive political effects discussed throughout this book, but the farmers achieved those results apolitically. They did not band together to overthrow the government or even the party. They tried, as individuals, to get out from under the government. They tried and were spectacularly successful in getting the government off their backs. The farmers' movement is an economic movement in that it has broad effects on the allocation of goods, labor, and services.

My interpretation of farmers' political behavior differs from most recent studies on farmers' roles in economic reforms by highlighting the impact of *baochan daohu* on the structural change of China. I identify *baochan daohu* as the jolt that broke the log jam in the countryside. Recent studies of farmers' leadership in economic reforms stress the context of "structural political opportunities" provided by the Communist regime.[40] Chen Yizi stresses farmers' economic deterioration under Chinese collectivization as the motivation behind farmers' political behavior. Focusing on the devastating effect of famine on Chinese farmers, Dali Yang argues that the memory of the Great Leap Famine (1959–1962) turned "peasants" against collectivization in the countryside and sowed the seeds of reform. The famine destroyed the aura of the party but not the organization. Economic deterioration motivated farmers less than their coerced submission to management by agrarian incompetents, though. Famine was important in the changing relationship between the state and farmers, but the primary cause of farmers' discontent lies in the Chinese socialist creation of a "feudal" structure and its incompetent management. Farmers preferred not to submit to the cadres' rule, and they resented their collective ties to state-owned land. They wanted to restore their lost family autonomy.

Others stress the change in elite policies that led to Chinese farmers' political behavior. In *Peasant Power in China*, Daniel Kelliher documents farmers' initiative for rural reforms but concludes that farmers' political behavior responds only when the elite stresses a policy of balanced growth:

> Because peasants derive almost all their leverage over the state from their position in agriculture, their small power is greatest when the state is bent on balanced economic growth. This is why peasant power in the People's Republic bloomed only under Deng Xiaoping. . . . Deng's coalition feared that peasant dissatisfaction, expressed in traditional modes like passivity and noncooperation, could doom the whole enterprise. Consequently, Deng's government displayed unprecedented restraint toward peasant defiance, an urge to accommodate peasant desires, and, above all, an openness to peasant initiatives.[41]

Despite recognizing the elite's interest in reform, the policy of balanced growth did not necessarily further the farmers' initiative. First, the elite does not speak with a unified voice. The policy of balanced growth was in fact proposed by Chen Yun, but Chen Yun ardently opposed *baochan daohu*:

> Agriculture is an important part of the national economy. Agriculture must also keep to the principles of planned economy as primary and market economy as subordinate. The reason for stressing this point is that after implementing various responsibility

systems it looks as if agriculture might be taken out of the plan. . . .
We cannot allow farmers to choose the path which only serves
their narrow interests. . . . Otherwise, the so-called freedom of 800
million farmers will result in the collapse of the state plan.[42]

Second, privatization does not strengthen the government, as Kelliher
suggests, but erodes it. Kelliher uses the absence of rural people in
Tiananmen to indicate farmers' support for the regime. He disregards the
fact that Chinese farmers' power lies in the unorganized sphere, as this
book demonstrates. The farmers resemble Mao's guerrillas more than modern "Westernized" protesters: They strike where they expect the fewest
casualties and retreat from confrontation. Unlike Mao's movement, though,
the contemporary farmers' movement is not organized. There is no Mao in
their movement.

Chinese farmers differed from Eastern European protesters. Protesters
seek to gain publicity; the Chinese farmers' movement succeeds surreptitiously. The protesters organized, usually as overtly as they could; the farmers simply acted for themselves, as individuals. I stress those unorganized
aspects of farmers' political action and the constraints they place on the
elite's choice of policies. It may be hard, especially at first, to detect unorganized movements; and when detected, they are hard to swat, like mos-
quitoes! The best indicator is the movement of rural migrants. As millions
upon millions of Chinese farmers moved, the economy was transformed.
The government would have suffered great economic loss and generated
profound social unrest if it had tried to stop this movement.

In addition, none of the studies pays attention to the impact of "feudalization" on the political behavior of rural people. Most writers use the term
"peasants" to describe rural people as if they have never changed in China.
The term "peasant" ignores the immense changes associated with collectivization. If "peasant" means a subsistence farmer who does not sell goods
or services on a local, national, or international market, then this term,
although still commonly used in English-language articles and books on
China, is no longer appropriate to describe even the Chinese farmers living
in the most remote regions.[43]

I argue that Chinese farmers in Communist China are not reactionary,
passive, anticapitalist, or antimodern. In their effort to regain their lost family autonomy, farmers formed a dynamic force for development and thus
modernization and the transformation of the Communist state. The creation
of a new "feudal peasant" class and the control of farming by cadres who
knew little of farming made Chinese farmers revolutionary. Farmers chafed
under this "feudal" arrangement and did not want foolish cadres bossing
them around. By forcing "feudalization" upon Chinese farmers, the
Communist leadership inadvertently forged their revolutionary potential.
One must not forget that the Chinese Communist "feudalization" of

Chinese farmers affected more than 80 percent of the total Chinese population. Correspondingly, it motivated 80 percent of the Chinese to seek alternative conditions. Even though the rural population may have now dropped below 80 percent, it still contains the overwhelming majority of all Chinese, and many nonfarmers come from a rural background.

In the context of Communist states, the farmers' lack of organized confrontation brought them strength rather than weakness.[44] Given the fact that no Communist state has ever tolerated any organized confrontation, any action that challenges the state must remain unorganized if it is to be effective, as Zhou Xueguang pointed out: "In the Chinese context, on the one hand, if interests are organized, they are basically state organizational apparatus and hence not autonomous; if interests are independent of the state, they are often unorganized."[45]

Most of the farmers' acts against the Chinese Communist state discussed here have been unorganized.[46] There is no Mao nor Deng in *baochan daohu*, in rural industrial development, or in rural migration. Social scientists often pay attention only to organized collective masses, ignoring individual human beings. Piven and Cloward have illustrated in a comparative context that unorganized popular movements can be powerful and that an explicit organizational structure can make a movement less powerful.[47] By focusing on the unorganized farmers' movement, I pay attention to the micro level of farmers' actions as well as to the aggregate effect of individual farmers' behaviors on the system as a whole.[48]

The Chinese farmers' role in the structural revolution of Communist China turns a new page in the understanding of political movements. Onlookers generally assume that political movements, and farmers' movements in particular, are organized political events, that is, a demonstration, a strike, or a waving of rakes and scythes in a mass gathering. Onlookers either do not regard unorganized or unmobilized political behavior as a revolutionary movement or else they assume someone arranged it when they did not! It has been taken for granted that political movements need conscious strategic planning and leadership from nonfarmer political entrepreneurs.[49] Worse, they assume no radical change without violence.[50] But the Chinese farmers' movement of 1978 to the present as analyzed here is a spontaneous, unorganized, leaderless, nonideological, apolitical movement (SULNAM) that has succeeded longer and more broadly than any comparable unorganized movement. China offers an extraordinary case in which farmers leached away the economic dominance of an authoritarian government and replaced it with a phenomenal real growth rate, powered almost entirely by farmers' initiative and ingenuity. The China so moved is the world's most populous nation.

Political science neglects the unorganized apolitical movement. That is why so few social science theories fit the Chinese case adequately. Most of the social movements studied have been organized, led, and ideological, but not so for the farmers in post-Mao China, especially since 1979![51] Recently, however, a growing literature gives notice and prominence to the creative unorganized or organized movements of farmers. A few scholars, such as James Scott, talk about changes from below and give recognition to the power of unorganized resistance, but for Scott, peasants occupy the margins of the political arena and thus wield limited power, which is symbolized by his book's title, *Weapons of the Weak*.[52] Scott's peasants do not make great changes in contemporary politics. The difference between Scott's peasants and Chinese farmers is that the latter are making major changes. When you add Chinese farmers one by one up to 1 billion, you no longer have the power of the weak. The best example of the power of farmers lies in markets and industrial production (rural production increased from 7 percent in 1978, to 50 percent in 1993). Farmers in China have developed new weapons of the strong, and they have done it in SUL-NAM fashion.

Chinese farmers offer a different way to look at revolutionary potential. Through their unorganized pursuit of family autonomy, farmers undertook a silent structural revolution without outside help or even the help of other farmers. The Chinese farmers' "movement" restored family decisionmaking and economic independence. We may see it as "political" because of the far-reaching and striking implications of this movement for the structure of governance in the PRC. Although its source was largely apolitical, its striking effects are such that it appears to us as an anomaly—a spontaneous, unorganized, leaderless, nonideological, apolitical movement by farmers—a movement that had broad political and economic effects. The farmers followed no leaders and formulated no explicit credo or doctrine. The farmers who did these things wanted most to be let alone, left to their own devices. They did not seek out any Tiananmen.

This is not a study of comparative economic development or of the comparative fates of Communist states. It is a study of the pivotal role of China's farmers in the economic development from the late 1970s through the early 1990s. It is a study of farmer-based initiatives shaping the fate of economic development in China in the face of a Communist regime that had sought to restructure the countryside through imposed collectives and a politics of mobilization.

I have used the term "farmers" as a kind of generic, emphasizing the similarities among rural people's experiences. Although I have used different examples of different farmers' participation in these processes, I have made no systematic attempt at analysis of the detailed differences among Chinese farmers on regional or other bases. I am concerned with generalizations about farmers who are involved in farming and nonfarm activities (industry and commerce) that struck me as crying out for recognition and analysis. If the hypotheses presented holds up at all, nothing is surer than that systematic pursuit of differences among the farmers in these processes will yield a rich harvest. Studies of regional differences in China have been extremely fruitful in the past and will continue to be useful in the future.

This book is divided into nine chapters. Chapter 2 tells of the "feudalization" of Chinese farmers under the Chinese Communist state. Chapter 3 details the process of *baochan daohu*, which broke the log jam in China. Chapter 4 discusses farmers' role in commercial activities, especially the expansion and creation of markets. Chapter 5 depicts the development of rural industry and private enterprises. Chapter 6 discusses the farmer's freedom movement in labor allocation and in residence (i.e., migration). Chapter 7 looks at rural resistance to the one-child policy. Chapter 8 focuses on the changes in the position of rural women. Finally, Chapter 9 summarizes the continuing transformation of the Chinese Communist regime. For this time—perhaps for the first time in two thousand years— unorganized farmers are changing the basic social structures of China and in doing so are changing themselves, the urban Chinese, and even their authoritarian government.

## Notes

1. I define a movement as any change in place or position. I define a social movement as any change in place or position not adequately explicable at present in terms of human heredity and the nonhuman environment. I define a political movement as any social movement's implications for change in the allocation of power and responsibility. I define an economic movement as any social movement's implications for changes in the allocation of goods, labor, and services.

2. The term "spontaneous" is intended to convey farmers' initiative in the spread of *baochan daohu*, markets, rural industries, and migration. The initiative and spread of the movement is best described by the farm saying about chicken pests quoted in Chapter 3 of this book. The term "unorganized" is sometimes more of a problem. Few advocated *baochan daohu* on an organized basis. The market element was not organized, although individual markets were as they had been from time immemorial. Rural-urban migration was not organized, although individual elements of it may have been organized on a family basis rather than within any organized superstructure. Similarly, each individual rural factory was organized. But there was no organization for the promotion of rural industry. Individual farmers and their families resisted the one-child family policy, but the state birth control policy involved intensive organizations. Finally, despite continuing changes in the position of rural women, these changes are neither directed nor stimulated by any women's organization. Indeed, they are glaring examples of growing individualism in China. Cutting across all of the elements in these spontaneous, unorganized, leaderless, nonideological, apolitical movements were age-old organizations and, as in

all other societies, families, local ties, networks of kinship, and so on. What can be described as SULNAM was not organized formally, however. The nonideological and apolitical nature of the movement is clear enough, although it is expected that the success and the spread of the movement will lead sooner or later to a superimposition of political and ideological elements.

3.    Pierre-Etienne Will and R. Bin Wong, *Nourish the People* (Ann Arbor: University of Michigan Press, 1991); and Kung-Chuan Hsiao, *Rural China: Imperial Control in the Nineteenth Century* (Seattle: University of Washinton Press, 1960).

4.    As far as farmers were concerned, the most important aspect of *hukou* was its control over grain rationing. Therefore, I shall use *hukou* to refer to control of both mobility and food. The residence registration system also monitored the identity, social status, party status, and residence of all mainland Chinese. For a good description of the Chinese *hukou* system, see Cheng Tiejun and Mark Selden, "The Origins and Social Consequences of China's Hukou System," *China Quarterly* 139 (September 1994):644–668.

5.    Marion J. Levy, Jr., *The Family Revolution in Modern China* (New York: Atheneum, 1948).

6.    Karl Polanyi, *The Great Transformation* (Boston: Beacon Press, 1957).

7.    The data range from 40 million, according to new data from China, to the lower estimate of 15 million given by the Chinese government. As far as I am concerned, even the lower estimate (say, 15 million–25 million) makes this the largest famine death count in world history. A few important Western sources on the famine death toll are Thomas Bernstein, "Stalinism, Famine, and Chinese Peasants: Grain Procurement During the Great Leap Forward," *Theory and Society* 13, no. 3 (1984): 339–377; Carl Riskin, *China's Political Economy: The Quest for Development Since 1949* (New York: Oxford University Press, 1987); and Basil Ashton, Kenneth Hill, Alan Piazza, and Robin Zeitz, "Famines in China 1958–61," *Population and Development Review* 10, no. 4 (1984): 613–645.

8.    Mark Selden, *Political Economy of Chinese Development* (Armonk, N.Y.: M. E. Sharpe, 1993).

9.    Farmers also used other terms like *dabaogan* (comprehensive contracts), *baogan daohu* (household contracts with fixed levies), and *fentian daohu* (divide the land among the households), which were more radical claims. But the term *baochan daohu* was what initially enticed cadres, and that is also the term used by the government. Thus, I shall use the term throughout the book, although it may also include more radical practices of comprehensive contracts in some rural areas.

10.    The Chinese phrase Deng used was *jiating zeren zhi.*

11.    Selden, *Political Economy of Chinese Development,* p. 130.

12.    Edward Friedman, "Deng Versus the Peasantry: Recollectivization in the Countryside," *Problems of Communism* 39 (September 1990): 33.

*Ziliuren* is a play on words. It comes from *ziliudi* (private plots). Here it means personal autonomy.

13. Jiang Liu, et al., eds., *Shehui lanpishu 1992–1993 nian zhongguo: shehui xingshi fenxi yu yuce* (China in 1992–1993: Analysis and Forecast of Social Situations 1992–1993 China) (Beijing: Zhongguo Shehui Kexue Chubanshe, 1993).

14. Nicholas R. Lardy, "China: Sustaining Development," in Gilbert Rozman, ed., *Dismantling Communism* (Princeton: Princeton University Press, 1992), p. 68.

15. *People's Daily* (Overseas), September 15, 1993.

16. Rural enterprises are not state-sector enterprises. Many are owned and operated in part or full by local governments—townships, villages, counties—sometimes with private or even foreign capital. However, there is an extraordinary "third sector" that is not the pure private family enterprise. These enterprises must sink or swim in the market, yet they have elements of the organizational economy. Some are even legacies from the old collective era (Jiangsu Province in particular). The development of rural industries is overtaking that of the urban-based state sector.

17. Deborah Davis and Ezra F. Vogel, eds., *Chinese Society on the Eve of Tiananmen: The Impact of Reform* (Cambridge: Harvard University Press, 1990); Harry Harding, *China's Second Revolution: Reform After Mao* (Washington, D.C.: Brookings Institute, 1987); and Susan L. Shirk, *The Political Logic of Economic Reform in China* (Berkeley: University of California Press, 1993)

18. Daniel Kelliher, *Peasant Power in China: The Era of Rural Reform 1979–88* (New Haven: Yale University Press, 1992), p. 33.

19. Chen Yizi, *Zhongguo: shinian gaige yu bajiu minyun* (China: Ten-year Reform and 1989 Democracy Movement) (Taiwan: Lianjing Chuban Shiye Gongsi, 1991).

20. David Shambaugh, "Introduction: Assessing Deng Xiaoping's Legacy," *China Quarterly* 135 (September 1993): 409.

21. Lucian W. Pye, "An Introductory Profile: Deng Xiaoping and China's Political Culture," *China Quarterly* 135 (September 1993): 414.

22. Personal interviews with Zu Ping, a farmer in Tongxin Village, Jingshan County, Hubei, December 1978.

23. Joseph Fewsmith, *Dilemmas of Reform in China: Political Conflict and Economic Debate* (Armonk, N.Y.: M. E. Sharpe, 1994).

24. Ezra F. Vogel, *One Step Ahead in China: Guangdong Under Reform* (Cambridge: Harvard University Press, 1989).

25. For a good discussion on urban violence during the Cultural Revolution, see Lynn T. White, *Policies of Chaos* (Princeton: Princeton University Press, 1990).

26. Vivienne Shue, *The Reach of the State: Sketches of the Chinese Body Politic* (Stanford: Stanford University Press, 1988), p. 126.

27.   Sheng Hua, et al., *China: From Revolution to Reform* (London: Macmillan Press, 1993).

28.   David Stark and Victor Nee, "Toward an Institutional Analysis of State Socialism," in Victor Nee and David Stark, eds., *Remaking the Economic Institutions of Socialism: China and Eastern Europe* (Stanford: Stanford University Press, 1989), p. 22.

29.   Sheng, et al., *China: From Revolution to Reform*, p. 25.

30.   *Beijingren shenme dou ganma; Guangdongren shenme dou ganchi; Shanghairen shenme dou ganchuan; nongmin shenme dou ganmai.*

31.   Jean Oi, *State and Peasant in Contemporary China: The Political Economy of Village Government* (Berkeley: University of California Press, 1989); Andrew Walder, *Communist Neo-traditionalism: Work and Authority in Chinese Society* (Berkeley: University of California Press, 1986).

32.   Walder, *Communist Neo-traditionalism*, p. 19.

33.   Shue, *The Reach of the State*; Sulamith Heins Potter and Jack M. Potter, *China's Peasants: The Anthropology of a Revolution* (New York: Cambridge University Press, 1990); Jean Oi, "Fiscal Reform and the Economic Foundations of Local State Corporatism in China," *World Politics* 45, no. 1 (1992):99–126; Helen F. Siu, *Agents and Victims in South China: Accomplices and Victims in Rural Revolution* (New Haven: Yale University Press, 1989); Christine Wong, "Material Allocation and Decentralization: Impact of the Local Sector on Industrial Reform," in Elizabeth Perry and Christine Wong, eds., *The Political Economy of Reform in Post-Mao China* (Cambridge: Harvard University Press, 1985); Edward Friedman, Paul Pickowicz, and Mark Selden, *Chinese Village, Socialist State* (New Haven: Yale University Press, 1991); and Ellen R. Judd, *Gender and Power in Rural North China* (Stanford: Stanford University Press, 1994).

34.   Many prominent intellectuals such as Lu Xun and Jin Guantao attribute Chinese backwardness to farmers' culture. Most influential is the documentary film, *Heshang* (1988). Many of the films about rural China by Zhang Yimou and others also show farmers in an unsympathetic light.

35.   Lowell Dittmer, "Tiananmen Reconsidered: Review Article," *Pacific Affairs* 64, no. 4 (1991): 529–535.

36.   Andrew Nathan and Shi Tianjian, "Cultural Requisites for Democracy in China: Findings from a Survey," *Daedalus* 122, no. 2 (1993): 116.

37.   Sheng, et al., *China: From Revolution to Reform*, p. 61.

38.   The exceptions are Kelliher, *Peasant Power in China*; David Zweig, "Struggle over Land in China: Peasant Resistance After Collectivization, 1966–1986," in Forrest D. Colburn, ed., *Everyday Forms of Peasants' Resistance* (Armonk, N.Y.: M.E. Sharpe, 1989), pp. 151–174; and Judd, *Gender and Power in Rural North China*.

39.   Oi, *State and Peasant*, p. 229.

40.   The phrase "structural political opportunities" comes from Peter K. Eisinger, "The Condition of Protest Behavior in American Cities," *American Political Science Review* 67 (1973). Some of the best studies of

this kind for rural China are Kelliher, *Peasant Power in China*; Chen, *China: Ten-Year Reform*; Andrew Watson, "The Family, Land Use and Accumulation in Agriculture," *Australian Journal of Chinese Affairs* 17 (1987); Dali Yang, "Making Reform: Great Leap Famine and Rural Change in China" (Ph.D. dissertation. Princeton University, 1993); and David Zweig, *Agrarian Radicalism in China: 1968–1981* (Cambridge: Harvard University Press, 1989).

41.   Kelliher, *Peasant Power in China*, pp. 246–247.

42.   Chen Yun, *Selected Works of Chen Yun: 1956–1985* (Beijing: Renmin Chubanshe, 1986).

43.   I am grateful to Professor Marion J. Levy, Jr., who first pointed out the distinction between "farmers" before the People's Republic and "peasants" afterward. Professor Levy has constantly reminded me of this important distinction. Solomon Karmel at the Department of Politics of Princeton University also helped me to clarify this point. For a good discussion on the misuse of the word "peasant," see Myron L. Cohen, "Cultural and Political Inventions of Modern China: The Case of the Chinese 'Peasant,'" *Daedalus* (1993):151–170. On Chinese farmers' influence in international trade, see David Zweig, "Internationalizing China's Countryside: The Political Economy of Exports from Rural Industry," *China Quarterly* 128 (December 1991):710–741.

44.   Perhaps Solidarity in Poland is the exception, as a faltering regime desperately sought to save itself.

45.   Zhou Xueguang, "Unorganized Interests and Collective Action in Communist China," *American Sociological Review* 58, no. 1 (1993): 57.

46.   There were organized farmers' actions in the countryside, particularly of a religious and lineage nature, after *baochan daohu*, but those organized activities resembled the prerevolutionary rural China and thus did not have the transforming nature of the unorganized movement that is the focus of this book. For a good discussion of organized rural protests, see Elizabeth J. Perry, "Rural Collective Violence: The Fruits of Recent Reforms," in Perry and Wong, *The Political Economy of Reform*, pp. 175–192.

47.   Frances Fox Piven and Richard A. Cloward, *Poor People's Movements: Why They Succeed, How They Fail* (New York: Vintage Books, 1977).

48.   Kelliher, *Peasant Power in China*.

49.   See Samuel Popkin, *Rational Peasant* (Berkeley: University of California Press, 1979), especially the last chapter.

50.   Barrington Moore, Jr., *Social Origins of Dictatorship and Democracy* (Boston: Beacon Press, 1966.)

51.   In a personal letter (November 25, 1993), Professor Charles Tilly alerted me to the literature on collective and individual behavior. Among the most useful works I found were John A. Brass and Mitchell Seligson, "Peasants as Activists: A Reevaluation of Political Participation in the

Countryside," *Comparative Political Studies* 12 (1989):29–59; Tom Brass, "Moral Economists, Subalterns, New Social Movements, and the (Re-) Emergence of a (Post-) Modernized (Middle) Peasant," *Journal of Peasant Studies* 18 (1991):173–205; Stephen G. Bunker, *Peasants Against the State: The Politics of Market Control in Burgisu; Uganda 1900–1983* (Urbana: University of Illinois Press, 1987); Mancur Olson, Jr., *The Logic of Collective Action* (Cambridge: Harvard University Press, 1965); Fox Frances Piven and Richard A. Cloward, "Collective Protest: A Critique of Resource Mobilization Theory," *International Journal of Politics, Culture and Society* 4 (1991):435–458; and Sidney Tarrow, "Cycles of Collective Action: Between Moments of Madness and the Repertoire of Contention," *Social Science History* 17 (1993):281–308. The movements discussed in the literature differ from the Chinese farmers' movement presented here because they are, in one way or another, organized.

52. James Scott, *Weapons of the Weak: Everyday Forms of Peasant Resistance* (New Haven: Yale University Press, 1985).

# 2 The "Feudalization" of Chinese Farmers: Bound to the Land

Farmers are not the heads of the households; the heads of the households are not farmers

> Popular saying of
> collective commune
> members in the
> 1970s

In the early days of the People's Republic of China, many people were grateful to the new Chinese government because it had ended civil wars and brought about peace after a century of war and national humiliation. The fact that many rural sons fought and died for the cause strengthened the bonds. In addition, building on earlier movements in the base areas, land reform won a significant rural and intellectual following to the banner of the party both in distributing the land of the rich and relatively rich and in preserving the system of the family farm. But the short honeymoon lasted only three years. Between 1953 and 1954, the Chinese Communist state, in the name of socialist revolution and industrialization, confiscated farmers' land and imposed upon them a serflike status. Farmers' struggles to survive the resented action of the state inspired their search for alternatives to socialism.

It may seem strange that leaders and a party that could so effectively mobilize farmers against the Guomindang regime and the Japanese invaders would turn their backs on farmers once they had achieved power. After all, these leaders were sardonically referred to as simple agrarian reformers who substituted the farmer as a base of power, the agrarian proletariat for the urban proletariat, who, in theory, were the classic Marxist base for Communist accession to power. Once in power, the Communist leadership turned the screws on the farmers more effectively than the Guomindang ever had.

Part of the problem may have inhered in Marxist ideology, but there was a structural basis as well. For all of China's previous history, most of its productivity was farmer-based. Although China had a higher level of foreign trade than most other countries in those times, the greatest part of China's productivity was agrarian. A certain outflow composed of rents, taxes, profits and usury, was extracted from the tillers of the soil and was taken for granted. The amount of this outflow varied, with some regions as high as over 50 percent and others as low as 30 percent. This outflow supported a bureaucratic elite and made urban life possible. When graft and corruption, warlords, and grasping officials pushed exactions beyond the point of endurance, farmers rebelled and used force to improve their lot. Such a situation existed when the Communists made their move to power. Mao and his associates practiced the movement of *jianzu jianxi* (reduce taxes and rents). That went well, indeed, as long as the Communists had to seek support only for themselves and the farmers, and they could even make productive agrarian nonmilitary uses of their military when the soldiers were not fighting (the so-called Nanniwan spirit). Any urban hardships were a further aid to the Communist accession to power.[1] By 1949, neither the farmers nor most urbanites were sorry to see the Republic of China fall.

But when the Communists "won," the support of the cities as well as the rural areas devolved on them. They, too, had to extract a surplus from the farm to support life in the cities. Far more than the Guomindang, however, the Communist party and its front advisers were committed to a program of accelerated industrialization. The party's ambitions centered on heavy industry. When ideological preferences led the party leadership to destroy rural incentives, the rural-urban imbalance worsened and continued to worsen until, in the late 1970s, the farmers saw a ray of hope and unleashed their initiative.

Table 2.1 provides a comparison between farmers of Republican and Imperial China and cadre-bound farmers (dependent upon the cadres) of the PRC. Before collectivization, Chinese farmers lived a life marked by considerable differences from the conventional European ("Western") feudal arrangement, which included closed social classes, a well-defined hierarchy of power holders, identification, at least ideally, of each individual as responsible to some particular individual higher in the hierarchy and related to others outside that direct line by virtue of his overlord's relation to them, a distribution of goods and services, especially landownership and control, based primarily on the ranks distinguished in the hierarchy of power and responsibility, succession to both such ranks and property, ordinarily determined on the basis of inheritance via kinship.[2]

With the exception of the last pattern, rural society under Communist China resembled the feudal pattern more than the traditional patterns of Imperial China or the Republic of China (1911–1949). Sons of leaders tended to join the leaders' network. Class became inherited, although rank was not formally inherited. How could the Communist leaders, supposedly the ultimate antifeudalists, "feudalize" Chinese farmers? The "feudalization"

**Table 2.1**
Ideal Patterns of Rural Life Before and Under Collectivization

| | Pre-Collective Rural China | Rural China Under Collectivization (1956–1978) |
|---|---|---|
| Basic unit of production | family | members of the production team, brigade, and commune |
| Basic unit of consumption | family | family |
| Relation to land | private proprietor, tenant, hired labor | tied to the land as membership of collective |
| Production decisionmaking | family | village and state cadres |
| Village self-sufficiency | substantial food self-sufficiency but local market networks vital | tight restrictions, even on local markets* |
| Main purpose of production | family consumption and local exchange | sale to the state, tax, and immediate use |
| Ownership of resources | family | collective or state |
| Market activity | some | limited |
| Inheritance of land | yes | no |
| Social mobility | open | closed |
| Economic class differentiation | a great deal | very little except the cadres |
| Autonomy of local "community" | great | little |
| Marriages | arranged by parents or kin | arranged by parents or kin |
| Patriarchal authority | high | high |
| Contact with the outside | through family, relations, and markets | through cadres |

*Rural people relied on state inputs such as fertilizer, electric power, and insecticide.

of Chinese farmers was an unintended and unrecognized result of socialist industrial development, a latent function, an unwanted side-effect of the socialist ideals themselves.

## Socialist Transformation: Becoming Communist "Peasants"

The Chinese Communist state transformed farmers fundamentally. Through the party administration represented by the cadre system, and through collectivization and control over mobility, the Chinese state transformed traditional Chinese farmers into land-bound peasants. They no longer owned land, they could not move from the land, and classes were closed (see below). They were subject to direct and comprehensive controls by the Communist state.

Collectivization was the most important means of transformation of Chinese farmers. Communist leaders implemented collectivization in China by using two effective methods that consolidated their control in the countryside: class labeling and land reform.

The state used class labeling to divide the rural population, which had formerly organized itself along lineage, family, and village lines. The Communists assigned each family to a class based on the family's economic circumstances at the time of land reform (1947–1952). Mao defined six classes: the landlord class; the rich peasants; the upper-middle peasants; the middle peasants; the lower-middle peasants; and the poor peasants. The landlords and rich farmers were considered wicked classes; the lower-middle and poor farmers were considered virtuous classes. Through the struggle against former local elites, the state recruited new local leaders who were loyal to the party.

In the beginning, the state used the image of a helpless and impoverished peasantry to mobilize the majority against the rural elites. During land reform (1950–1953), the class struggle offered a tangible reward— land—to many poor farmers. By promising "land to the tiller," the state mobilized the poor against the rich, destroying the power base of the traditional elites.

Land reform did not give land entitlement to the poor. It confiscated land from all classes. The state allocated land for the farmers' use, *but denied them both ownership and control*. Although before communism many farmers lived a life of landless rentier subsistence, at least 60 percent of the rural population consisted of small, relatively independent landowners.[3] Many both owned and cultivated rented land; some rented and others rented out, including even some who were rather poor. This varied regionally, with high tenancy rate in the South and Central areas and low tenancy rate (but more hired labor) in the North. Land reform transferred the land from independent proprietors, most of whom were poor, to the collective (i.e., local state organization).

Even before land reform started, the Communist leadership was already committed to a collective future modeled on the Soviet collective experience. From the political point view, Mao used land reform as a steppingstone to collectivization. Immediately after land reform, the government launched a campaign against the antirevolutionaries (most landlords, other rich people, and people who had a connection with the former Nationalist government). Many people were killed or imprisoned. The repression used in the campaign set a precedent, establishing the state as the source of coercion and silencing the population.

## The Procurement System

With the abolition of private landownership, beginning with restrictions on the right to buy, sell, or rent land, farmers experienced control and oppression before they had the chance to enjoy the fruits of land reform. In 1953, the state further reduced farmers' autonomy by introducing *tonggou tongxiao* (the compulsory procurement system). On November 23, 1953, the state issued a directive to ban all private grain sale: "After *tonggou tongxiao*, no private grain merchants are allowed to deal with grain."[4] Never before had the state controlled the sale of grain on a nationwide basis. Before the PRC, the government had collected taxes, sometimes years in advance, but the government had never in effect laid claim to the entire crop. With establishment of the procurement system, there were few private grain markets, although black markets in grain emerged. Government leaders sought to eliminate them, but those black markets kept reappearing. In twenty-six years, the state's control over grain prices alone extracted 25 billion yuan from farmers.[5]

The shrinking of markets was not limited to grain. In its effort to eliminate small and private businesses, the state reduced employment in rural industry (mostly family handicrafts), sidelines (raising vegetables, fowl, and pigs), and services, stimulating a rapid decline in rural market towns.[6]

In addition, twenty-five years of collective organization brought increased labor days and virtually no increases in per capita rural income. First, there was a vast expansion of the labor force, especially rural women in production lines. Although most women in rice-growing areas worked in the fields before 1949, fewer women in the North worked in the fields at that time. Second, labor days also greatly increased. Farmers had to work all winter, although winter was regarded as the leisure season.

The state's ownership of all resources and control over the market subjected farmers to the mercy of the state planning system. Through the *jiandaocha* (a scissors price—high prices for industrial goods and low prices for agricultural goods), the state extorted, as it were, surplus value from farmers for industrial development. Through the procurement system and the "scissors price," the state extracted 800 billion yuan from farmers between 1953 and 1978.[7] We may readily assume that no previous Chinese regimes had been as successful in extracting surplus value from the farmers or in removing so much of it from local areas.

The state forced farmers to pay their tax in grain, not in cash. Farmers with insufficient grain bought grain at a premium (nonsubsidized) price to meet government demands. This hidden tax contributed to rural poverty.[8] Land reform and class labeling consolidated political controls in rural China, and the procurement system gave the state complete control over grain marketing. All three policies paved the way for collectivization.

## Collectivization

*Collectivization gave the state control over production processes and the daily lives of farmers.* For the first time in Chinese history, the state wrested farm management decisionmaking power from family heads.

Farmers interacted with the state through local cadres and thus were effectively bound to their intermediaries. Between 1955 and 1956, the state transferred farmers' land,[9] cattle, and tools to the collectives. A local rural leader of Fujian Province expressed his anger in the 1980s when talking about the coercive confiscation of farm land:

> They [farmers] were ordered to join the advanced cooperatives and contribute their land to the collective. All return from the cooperative was to be divided according to the members' labor, without regard for how much land they owned after land reform. Peasants were turned into mere farmhands. In a single stroke the government took away land owned privately by peasants.[10]

The collective system depended on the elimination of all private ownership of the means of production, especially land. With the imposed collectivization, members of collective farms were masters in the state-dominated collectives in name only. Those who had better land were particularly unhappy, whereas some with less or poorer land may have hoped that collectivization, like land reform, might bring redistribution benefits. But the development of the collectives and especially the Great Leap Forward made farmers deeply hostile to the collectives.

With the abolition of household farming, the state transformed independent farmer proprietors into rural proletarians struggling to earn work points under the command of powerful local cadres. Those who had better land and/or higher incomes were particularly unhappy. Those with lower incomes, often less or poorer land, were not necessarily unhappy at the time, but they soon felt the constraint imposed upon them. He Liyin, a farmer in Tongxin, compared the collective farming in the 1970s to many pairs of small feet trapped in a big shoe, dragging along the *yangguang-dao* (shining road) of socialism: "We could not walk one step without hurting our flesh."[11]

*After 1955, the collective agricultural system, combined with the procurement policy, enabled the state to provide cheap agricultural products to the urban population.* When the problems with collectives became clear, especially after the Great Leap debacle, many farmers became deeply hostile to the collective. As in all other Communist states, rural people provided "primitive socialist accumulation."[12] Chinese collectivization enforced this principle of distribution: the state comes first, the collective second, and the individual last, contradicting the traditional Chinese ethic, which placed loyalty to the family above all.

All production decisions flowed from the top. People from outside the family and often outside the village now told farmers what to produce, how much to grow, and how to grow it. Since the state focused on extracting a surplus to feed both industry and urban people, grain production was stressed. Farmers became single crop producers (mainly grain producers), deprived of other sources of income ranging from sidelines to off-farm season employment to marketing. Farmers in Sanyankuang Village, Yuanjiang County, Hunan Province, had grown ramie for more than two thousand years. They also grew oranges and exported them to Hongkong. But the state required farmers to abandon the crops they were known for in order to produce grain. Within a few years, state policy requested cutting 1,000 mu of ramie and 2,000 mu of orange trees. In 1979, impoverished farmers complained to reporters about state grain policies: "[The government] never looks at concrete reality and only stresses grain production. In the end, it was not able to get more grain. Instead, it destroyed diversified crops. It's like chasing a chicken into a hole and losing it deep inside."[13]

Hunan farmers were not the only ones enraged by the state's "grain first" policy. Farmers in Hubei resented the interference of the state, as some complained: "The state is like a crazy man, always picking those things that will hurt us most."[14] Other complained: "Whatever would hurt us most the Communists would choose to do."

The reconstruction of rural society left little room for farmers to innovate or even any incentive to work hard. As soon as the collective was imposed in 1956, farmers complained bitterly: "The agricultural cooperatives have to obey the state's plan. Farmers cannot grow what they want! Outside the cooperatives, farmers could grow whatever makes the most money and is most convenient. How free that is!"[15]

Forced collectivization met with rural resistance. In many places, farmers slaughtered their animals or tried to sell their valuable water buffaloes. When the collectives did not deliver the promised common prosperity, many farmers demanded to withdraw, and some attempted to take back their horses and farm animals. Many complained that collective agriculture took away their freedom to control their own lives:

> Individual farming was free. We could decide when to go to work. The collective farming is hard and fixes the basic work days. In addition, labor discipline is also required. Thus collectivization is not free. . . . When we did not have the collectives, we had control over our harvest. We could decide how much to eat and how much to save. In the collectives, this kind of freedom died.[16]

The government suppressed farmers' calls for autonomy in various political campaigns. But periodic revolts against collectivization and continuous quiet efforts to expand household enterprise efforts never stopped. Between 1956 and 1978, there were four large-scale decollectivization movements. The first three movements, which I shall discuss in detail later, were suppressed.

When farmers lost control over their harvest, the incentives to work diminished and productivity dropped. As a rural saying goes: "The public work is slowly done, following the crowd. Everyone gets ten work points. Why should I work harder?"[17]

From 1952 to 1978, labor productivity fell below the 1952 level (the only exception being 1956), while the cost of production increased rapidly (264 percent).[18] The state regarded low productivity as an indication of farmers' lack of political enthusiasm and their attachment to the old ways of farming. Political movements ensued.

In the years ahead, political movements successfully sought to keep farmers on the socialist track. These included the 1958 Great Leap Forward, the 1963 Socialist Education Movement, and the 1966–1969 Cultural Revolution. These relentless political campaigns further undermined farmers' incentives.

## Local Emperors

Collectivization resembled serfdom not only in that farmers no longer owned the land but also in that cadres decided what work farmers should do and when. Local elites combined economic and political power and effectively controlled the rural people.

Unlike the pre-Communist traditional elites, whose power bases varied from landed and commercial wealth to military power, the power of the new rural elites, the cadres, came from the state, and they gained advancement in return for political loyalty.[19] The cadres' monopoly control over local resources gave them a big stake in supporting the socialist system. A rural proverb states, "Socialism is a plate of *jiang* [a Chinese soy bean pastelike dip]. Only those with power can dip in."

With rare exceptions, local cadres implemented state policies without regard to—at times to the direct detriment of—the economic interests of local people. They enforced the state "grain first" policy, extracted the large quantities of grain demanded by the state, and neglected other forms of agricultural production. They prohibited farmers from engaging in economic activities outside the collective farm. Whenever farmers tried to do something to benefit their families, the cadres attacked them as "capitalist roaders." The power structure regarded material improvement from household or market activity as a "capitalist tail" to be cut off:

> The more the state preached ascetic equality, the more it exposed itself as hypocritical to the many excluded, who were forced to live austerely, while the privileged manifestly profited from the entrenched system. Whereas the excluded sought to survive outside the walled-off socialist system, any favored unit was compelled by the structure of the system to try to grab everything, no matter how redundant. The favored, logically, favored more socialism.[20]

Cadre-bound farmers, farmers who were bound to cadres in a feudal relationship, resented their overlords and called them *jiandao ganbu* (cadres with scissors). Some farmers subsequently described their bondage and their lack of free action on the collective farms: "[We] could not stretch our hands without touching our fathers and could not move one step without kicking our mothers."[21] This rural saying was hardly an exaggeration of cadre-bound farmers' life. In addition to losing control over production and consumption, farmers lost almost all of the freedom they had had. They even had to ask for leave when they wanted to visit their relatives. The most poignant example is that farmers had to ask cadres for permission to go begging.[22]

Restrictions on movement interfered with the Confucian practice of *li* (showing proper respect to one's relations). This restriction struck women particularly hard. Traditionally, women used those visits to maintain contact with their native villages; it was a means for married women to escape abuse and seek protection. Under the rule of the party elites, however, married women could not visit their parental village without permission from the cadres, which in many cases was denied. In Tongxin village, except for the Spring Festival, a woman's request to visit her parents was often denied unless the woman had some connection with the cadres. Cadres, not individuals or farmers, controlled the labor power of collective members. In fact, cadres controlled all social contact with the outside.

With collectivization, the state curtailed the solidarity based on lineage and local networks through control of the markets, mobility, and ritual: "Peasant production and marketing outside the state-planned sector was reduced to a trickle, and all the various sorts of horizontal linkages between peasant communities that rested on the trellis of the rural free marketing network were further weakened."[23]

The market had been an important locus of rural culture. People went there to see and perform plays and local operas, lion dances, drum corps, stilt dancing, comic dialogues, shadow puppets, stories, and much more. All that died after 1957, when market festivals ended and it became difficult to leave the village or to sustain markets.

The cadres curtailed other important village customs, such as *ganji* (going to the local market). Cadre-bound commune members had to get permission to go to the local market. Without local cadres' permission, farmers could not leave the collective land to take a job elsewhere. If anyone disobeyed the cadres, punishment followed, ranging from struggle and criticism meetings, *youjie* (parading someone through the streets), and beating, to cancelation of the offender's family's food rations.

Cadres also tied members to the land through long working hours and big state projects. In winter, when there was no farm work on the land, the state carried out a corvée policy, making cadre-bound commune members work on public roads, railways, and reservoirs without pay. They had to provide and carry their own food; the state did not give them coupons to buy food. They received no pay, bonuses, or even food from the state, only work points from their villages. In addition, farmers were responsible for projects in the village, such as soil improvement and irrigation.

The imperial state had forced farmers to undertake public projects, like the Great Wall and the Grand Canal, but every household could decide who to send. The scale of the public projects, moreover, was far larger in the PRC, and the new public projects involved more members of the family (women with children were not exempt) and fundamentally disturbed the daily life of the family. Throughout Chinese history, projects away from the village were for men only. For example, for more than ten years (1966–1977), farmers in Tongxin had to work on the Huitian reservoir every winter for two months. Only one adult member of each family was allowed to stay in the village; the rest had to go to the reservoir, about thirty miles from the village. Villagers had to live in a makeshift tent and sleep on straw mattresses in the coldest weather. From the mid-1950s forward, such winter projects were carried out widely throughout rural China. In most rice-growing areas in Hubei and Hunan, for example, this is how most farmers spent their winters in the 1970s.

Cadres often imposed state policies, but some joined forces with farmers to deceive the state. This was especially true at the team level. Team leaders whose roots were in the community and who had no prospect of climbing the bureaucratic ladder often sided with farmers, helping them hide part of their land and part of their harvest. This power provided a limited source of relief as long as the collective structure remained intact. Although caring team leaders, to a limited degree, might reduce harm done to team members through *manchan* (the hidden production quota) and *mandi* (the hidden land),[24] the power of the collective remained intact.

Power flowed through the secretary of the brigade and the party boss at the commune level. With militia and police at their disposal, these cadres had absolute power over farmers, who called them *tuhuangdi*, local emperors.

Frequently, outside interference took the form of a work team sent by the state to supervise the implementation of state policy. Sometimes the work team made surprise visits to villages to check on farmers; at other times, during political campaigns, the "visits" lasted as long as two or three years.

For example, in the late 1960s and early 1970s, the state tried to implement "double planting" in all rice-growing areas. Although there were places where a double or even triple crop was profitable, the party's procrusteanism often forced farmers to double or triple the crop where doing so was inappropriate, and farmers resented this policy. In Tongxin Village, farmers used the climate as a reason to refuse to carry out the central policy, so a work team was sent there to enforce its implementation. Teams that refused to carry out the policy were given no fertilizer and had to provide the state with more grain as punishment. Every team had to set aside a certain amount of land for double planting. Farmers used passive resistance to defend against this intrusion by the state. The farmers often selected the worst land for double planting and sent children to work on it. After seeing the failure of double planting the following year, farmers and the work team reached a tacit agreement. Farmers had to waste some land and labor for double planting so that the work team had something to report to the state, but large-scale double planting was never carried out. The tacit agreement between cadres and farmers made it difficult to carry out double planting according to the expectation of the state, but farmers paid a price for it in the inefficient use of labor and land.

Whatever the economic failures of the collectivization system, the collectives did succeed in controlling villagers. Their power flowed from the state, not from the people. From the cadre-bound farmers' point of view, rural cadres cared only about maintaining their own wealth and power and not at all about the interests of the majority of villagers, as one popular saying in Anhui shows: "Your promotion does not depend on my begging; my begging does not affect your promotion."

## Urban and Rural Segregation: A Castelike Society

China was not alone in using collectivization and control over markets to extract surplus from the farmer, that is, to provide resources for industrial development. Other states, especially socialist states, carried out a "scissors price" through their control over the market.[25] But China was highly effective in controlling both the physical and social mobility of farmers, tying them to the collective land.

In the early days of collectivization, many farmers sought to migrate to respond to the job opportunities opened by industrial development in the city. In the mid-1950s, massive numbers of farmers left their villages to find work in the cities.[26] Facing this influx of farmers, the state adopted a strict policy banning rural–urban migration. This policy was the basis for a caste-like system, a social hierarchy that had farmers at the bottom with no chance of social mobility and city people, especially cadres, at the top.

In 1956, Zhou Enlai, then premier, signed a state "Order to Stop Blind Rural Migration." This order instructed factories, mines, railways, construction firms, and transportation firms to stop employing rural migrants. From 1956 to 1957, the central government issued four documents to stop the flow of rural–urban migration. In all of these documents, the state ordered police specifically to prevent rural–urban migration and to capture peddlers. A state coalition composed of public security (police), railways, transportation departments, service companies, the food supply bureau, and the supervisory committee prevented rural migration.[27]

In 1958, Mao signed a document, "Regulation for Household Registration of the People's Republic of China," legalizing the *hukou* system.[28] The chief purpose of *hukou* was to prevent rural–urban migration, especially to the largest cities. Every household's booklet registered the family origin, class affiliation, personal identity, birth date, and occupation of all its members. Farmers with rural *hukou* could not move into the city, nor could they obtain nonagricultural jobs or housing, or even buy food. With the exception of limited army recruitment and temporary contract work (mostly male), *children of farmers remained farmers*. All other occupations were denied to them, all other doors closed. The Chinese village became a closed society.

*Hukou* provided the basis for a rationing system that discriminated against farmers in an obvious way. The availability of coupons became a mark of urban class status. With an urban *hukou*, one received *liangpiao* (food rationing coupons) for food, staples, and nonstaples, all at a subsidized price. Without these coupons, rural migrants who found jobs in the city were unable to buy food. China denied the purchase of grain to rural migrants. Without *hukou*, farmers could not find housing in the city. Farmers had to get a letter of introduction from their commune cadres even to stay in a hotel in the city.

By 1978, there were between forty and fifty kinds of coupons distributed to urban residents for everything from grain, cloth, and matches to cooking oil and soap. With economic benefits attached only to urban *hukou*, rural *hukou* were worth next to nothing. Every household in the city had a booklet, but a rural household could never get its hands on one. Since rural *hukou* had nothing to do with coupon redistribution, the commune kept possession of rural household *hukou* before 1978.

Through the rationing system (especially grain rationing), *hukou* divided the Chinese people into two main groups: urban and rural. Under communism, the source of food provided the most important class differentiation in China. *Urban people possessed guaranteed subsistence and employment; rural families confronted nature alone.* The food coupon, the most important source of subsistence for city residents, signaled the differences between rural and urban dwellers. Urban people enjoyed state welfare rights and benefits and received grain from the state; rural people had no state-provided welfare rights and benefits and received grain rationed through the production team. Rural people called those having food coupons the eaters of *guojia liang* (government grain). Gradually this differentiation based on food sources was institutionalized and universalized through *hukou, danwei* (the urban work unit), and coupons.

Normally before, most farmers had been able to produce food for themselves in times of peace, although many rural families experienced the immense weight of poverty in the first half of the twentieth century due to wars. Because the state determined production, marketing, and consumption, though, the rationing system enabled the state to take food from cadre-bound commune members for the subsistence of the urban population. For example, when the Great Leap brought famine between 1959 and 1961, starving more than 30 million people, almost all of the deaths were in the countryside. Since *hukou* could determine the difference between life and death, urban people's struggle to hold on to *hukou* became an effective means of social control. Convicted criminals suffered confiscation of their urban *hukou*. Life in the countryside threatened urban people.

The state rationing system created a system of bureaucratic control over access to goods and services, with farmers as the underclass. At the top of the hierarchy sat the party cadre class, who shopped at special restricted access stores and received special coupons. Some shops served only the party elite and excluded the general public.[29] Ordinary urban people waited in long lines for many goods. They sometimes used personal connections or bribery to get access to additional, restricted goods and services. They at least knew where to line up. By contrast, the farming people, the lowest class in socialist China, found no opportunity for extra goods, either legitimately or via corruption. Many barely had enough to keep them alive.

China's farmers, in short, paid a heavy price for the early stages of industrialization achieved in the initial decades of the People's Republic of China. There were achievements as well as hardships for the countryside, of course. Rural people suffered low levels of rural income and consumption with little gain as the state extracted the rural surplus, and they were the victims of famine death, while cities were protected. Farmers were bound to the land and locked within their villages. Nevertheless, China's life expectancy rose dramatically, from about forty to over sixty in the first decades of the PRC. Also, after the early 1960s, famine was controlled, hard-core poverty areas remaining at the barest subsistence level.[30]

The state excluded cadre-bound commune members from benefits and services. Take train service, for example. Only high-ranking officials could travel first class; second class served middle-ranking government workers; the "hard seats" were left for ordinary people. Anyone who wanted to buy first-class or second-class tickets had to present a letter of introduction from their workplace indicating their rank. After 1960, even a "hard seat" ticket required a letter from the commune of a rural person. A sense of injustice prevailed, as revealed by one saying popular throughout most of China in the 1970s: "High-ranking officials have goods sent to their door; middle cadres open the back door; city people knock from door to door; rural people have no door."[31]

Rural residents differed markedly from other social classes. The food they ate, the houses they lived in, the transportation available to them, even the clothes they wore differentiated them from the other social classes. Cadre-bound rural people received the worst of everything. *Cu* (coarse), *yu* (ignorant), *zang* (dirty), and *qiong* (impoverished) became synonyms for farmers in the eyes of city people. As villages in the North complained, "Of all occupations, the worst is to be a grain grower."

The inherited status in the countryside, the procurement system, "scissors prices," the state's antirural policies, and strict control over rural–urban migration and markets transformed Chinese independent farmers into cadre-bound peasants:

> China's collective system locked rural people into an identity as peasants that became the first and the last fact of their social existence. They lived a life of enforced separateness. Rural people were effectively tied to the land, with the army (mainly for men) and marriage (mainly for women) as the only likely avenues out. They were barred by law from residing in the cities by a system of household registration (*hukou*) that severely restricted internal migration (and continued to do so through the 1980s). In effect, state socialism in China created a structure in which ascript status was personal destiny, albeit in the guise of a "modern" social system. People were born into peasant status and most were bound to die with it.[32]

Structurally, socialist agriculture tied cadre-bound farmers to the land but prevented them from owning it, bound them to cadres but deprived them of the power to make production decisions. Cadres, many of whom lacked agricultural experience, made production decisions for experienced farmers.

Although circumstances limited social mobility for the poor majority before communism, upward mobility was an ideal pattern for virtually all classes. The ambition of rural families focused on this possibility. Many popular stories tell of poor mothers who helped their sons acquire an education, pass the state examinations, and become officials.[33] With the exception of the post of emperor, all ranks of government were open to men with merit: "Through careful planning and shrewd management of the available resources, a 'peasant' family might successfully push one of its more talented sons to become a merchant, a handyman, or even an official. Peasants had never been excluded from acceptable avenues of upward social mobility."[34] This contrasted sharply with the cadre-bound farmer's frozen low status. With the exception of the army and cadre routes, the state closed off the avenues for farmers' ambitious fantasies. Village mobility was controlled by the party-state, whereas for a long time markets and education had been the mobility routes on which individuals and their families depended.

Ironically, one of the goals of the revolutionary government was to destroy "feudal elements" in farmers' culture and practices: ancestor worship; the focus on the family; organization by lineage; geomancy; and patriarchy. As early as 1943, Mao stated this goal clearly:

> In terms of the farmer masses, private individual economy has existed for several thousand years with each family as a production unit. This private economy is the economic basis of feudal regimes, which impoverished farmers. The only way to overcome this problem is gradual collectivization. The only path to collectivization is through cooperatives as pointed out by Lenin.[35]

Under communism, the state itself created a "feudal" system that tied farmers to the land and closed off social mobility, transforming farmers into virtual serfs. Edward Friedman nicely summarizes the farmers' "enserfment":

> Not only are the peasants forced to work land they do not own; others decide what work they will do. They cannot legally choose to leave the land and seek work elsewhere, and their children cannot go to school elsewhere. They cannot travel, eat, or reside elsewhere: scarce state ration coupons for grain are specific to a place, and permission slips for travel have to be shown to the security services. Theirs is a demeaning and alienating social existence.[36]

## Endogamy and the Perpetuation of the Patrilocal System

The control of physical mobility has important implications for gender roles. A special provision of the *hukou* system—a somewhat surprising one at first glance for a patriarchal society—dictated that children inherited their mother's residence status. Children could not change their residence status. This antitraditional policy did not reduce the patrilocal and patriarchal system, however, nor did its authors intend to do so. The power kept women and children in the village, unable to join husbands who might find urban jobs or become army officers.

Traditionally, some rural women moved out of the villages by marrying urban people, but the People's Republic of China reduced this practice. The state refused to grant married women and their children legal urban status, making long-term stays in the city impossible and even short visits difficult. State control over mobility produced the unintended consequence of "two endogamous groups crosscutting all of Chinese society."[37]

Martin Whyte's investigation of Chengdu, Sichuan, confirms the existence of two endogamous groups. Whyte's research suggests that 50–60 percent of Chengdu women who married in the early 1950s came from the countryside. After 1958, rural people were excluded from urban marriage and urban work, and less than 10 percent of women who married after 1958 had a rural background.[38]

As a result of *hukou*, a strange pattern of social structure existed in the People's Republic of China—the coexistence of patrilocality (women still married into men's families) and matrilocality (officially, children followed their mothers' residence). The result of this kind of coexistence and weakening of standard markets in the countryside reduced extravillage cultural and marital ties. In both South and North, the circle of marital ties became smaller, and intravillage marriages increased.[39]

## Exclusion from Socialist Welfare

The state excluded cadre-bound peasants not only from the industrial labor work force but also from the socialist welfare system. The pattern of unequal allocations began with massive urban subsidies. Beginning in 1953, the state spent millions on urban subsidies, and the budget for subsidies grew quickly. In 1965, subsidies to urban people were 261 million yuan; in 1978, the state spent 938.6 million yuan.[40] The state also gave city dwellers subsidies for cooking fuel. Urban residents enjoyed subsidized electricity for many years, whereas electricity was unavailable to most rural people before the 1970s. The state invested in urban schools and guaranteed most urban children nine years of free schooling, leaving farmers to rely upon themselves for substantial parts of their education funds. Partly as a result, almost one-third of rural people (most of them rural women) were still illiterate in 1986.[41]

Apart from direct subsidies from the state, most urban workers received additional benefits from their *danwei*. These work units formed the key structure for the Chinese regime in the city. By providing job security (*tiefanwan*, "an iron rice bowl"), medical care, pensions, child care, paid sick leave, maternity leave, housing, and other welfare-related services, the party boss of each *danwei* gained absolute power over the workers. The boss became their feudal overlord. The party representative punished workers' political disobedience with a negative record in their *dang'an* (files; refers to the secret personal dossier). A substantial portion of the real income for the average urban worker in 1978 came from workplace welfare, which was under the control of the party boss. As a result, workers depended upon the party boss as their patron.

The "feudalization" of the factory differed from the "feudalization" in the countryside because the agricultural workplace (the work team or the commune) did not provide welfare to its workers. Negative incentives (punishment or coercion) were the means used to rule the countryside, whereas positive incentives (welfare and job security) played this role in the city workplace. *Danwei* became an expression differentiating urban and rural people. Membership in a *danwei* implied certain social rights. This key difference determined that farmers were more eager than urban workers to get out from under the new "feudal" system. Farmers suffered the disadvantages of the new "feudal" structure without gaining from it.

In fact, the "feudalization" in the city was based on the coercive control of the countryside. Welfare was expensive. A guaranteed low price for agricultural products made it possible for the state to provide welfare to urban workers. Much of what farmers sold to the state became a contribution to urban workers, and most of what urban workers and enterprises bought from the state was welfare. The cost of this welfare provision gave the state an incentive to reduce the number of welfare recipients. With a huge rural population (more than 80 percent of the country), only strict control of rural–urban migration made the "feudalization" of *danwei* possible.

As a result of urban subsidies and the *danwei* welfare system, every job in the city cost the government money, which went for housing, utilities, education, and subsidized grain, none of which the government paid for in the rural areas, although it did provide disaster relief and subsidies to chronically impoverished counties, while barring migration. *China's socialist welfare system sacrificed the majority for the benefit of a minority*, not in a capitalist fashion but none the less.

For a long time, the image of "barefoot doctors" in the Chinese countryside fascinated the "West." China was regarded as a model for other Third World nations for providing health care to millions of poor farmers. In fact, the "barefoot doctors" were a hoax. Most of those doctors received little training at all, and many could not even perform the simplest emergency care. With the important exception of preventive vaccines in some rural villages and some first aid services, farmers received little help from the state in terms of health care. The "barefoot doctors" camouflaged the lack of medical attention in the countryside. Moreover, the traditional system of physicians (private Chinese traditional medical practitioners) was disrupted.

As a result of the state's two-track system, one-third of rural people lived in poverty (less than 100 yuan per year), and another 31.7 percent received 100–150 yuan, whereas the poorest urban resident received at least 200 yuan and all urban residents received subsidies.[42] With little assistance from the state, farmers had to depend on themselves for almost everything: "Rain or drought, insects or hail, the illness of a father, the birth of only female children—these and other determinants like them remained as central to the livelihood of Chinese peasant families under Mao as before."[43] As a result, farmers depended on the family to provide welfare. From the delivery of a baby and taking care of the sick to protection of the old and burial of loved ones, the family was as important under Mao as before. The Communist state provided little welfare to farmers but took away their autonomy, thus placing itself in structural opposition to farmers.

The Communist leaders wanted to industrialize China. For them, industrialization meant a high percentage of industry in the national economy. They made progress toward that goal—by 1978, the rural share of the national growth rate was only 28 percent, although the rural people accounted for 80 percent of the population.[44]

Because the new industrial state provided little welfare to the farmers, the gap between rural and urban life widened. The poorest 20 percent of families lived in the countryside, possessing only 7 percent of the national wealth; the richest 20 percent lived in the cities, possessing 41 percent of the national wealth.[45] Through collectivization, the procurement system, and the *hukou* system, the state transformed independent farmers into a rural "proletariat," a class with no ownership. However, Chinese rural "proletarians" differed from proletarians in capitalist states in that they did not have the right to sell their labor on the market. Control over rural mobility smothered the labor value of the rural "proletariat" and helped to lower the prices of agricultural products. The collective farm captured the Chinese rural "proletarians." *The Chinese industrial state was built on a social contract that depended on the sacrifice of the majority—the collective farmers.* Because the system excluded them, the farmers resented both *hukou* and socialist welfare.

## Self-Awareness

The actions of the state awoke farmers to their common interests, but the farmers did not attempt to organize against the system. Rather, they watched shrewdly for any opportunity to evade, circumvent, get out from under it.

Elsewhere, industrial development accompanied urbanization, but Chinese industrial development curtailed the urban share of the total population. As a result, urbanization in China, which had always been comparatively high in Imperial China, was low compared to the level in other developing nations. The state sent urban people to the countryside during urban employment crises, shifting this burden onto the cadre-bound farmers. During the famine (1959–1961), the state sent 20 million urban people to the countryside. In 1968, more than 20 million middle school graduates and 10 million urban residents arrived in the countryside. Purged urban residents (many of them intellectuals) did penal labor in rural areas. The farmers fed these inexperienced laborers with their meager rations.

These newcomers strengthened the cadre-bound farmers' awareness of the polarity between the city and the countryside. Their inferior status enraged farmers, perhaps partly because the Communist ideology of equality for all conflicted with its strict control of social mobility. Ironically, Communist indoctrination provided cadre-bound farmers with the moral high ground to fight the socialist state's claim of equality for all. Farmers' growing awareness formed a social basis for fundamental changes.

The state's urban bias excluded the farmers, whom the state controlled but did not represent. Farmers labeled urban people *guojia de ren* (the people of the state), whereas urban people called rural people *xiangxia ren* (rural people). The state categorization of rural classes after the land reform became economically irrelevant. No matter what classes cadre-bound farmers came from, economically they formed one class.

The Communist ideology of equality for all contradicted farmers' daily experience of exploitation and restriction. He Liyi, a farmer in Tongxin Village, Hubei Province, associated socialism with "an empty stomach" and "a caged bird."[46] Many old farmers in Shuide County, Guangdong Province, told the state investigation team in 1979 that "for thirty years, the Communists did not allow us to have enough to eat. We had no freedom to speak out." Farmers in Henan said: "We dreamed about socialism. But who thought that it would bring us misery?" In Anhui Province, farmers told the same state investigation team, "We helped the Communist Party defeat the GMD [the Nationalist party]. If next time, the GMD comes, the Communists better hope we will not use our *biandan* (carrying poles) to beat the Communists."[47]

Farmers' resentment against the rule of the Communist state under Mao gave rise to their self-consciousness and solidarity. Shue pointed out: "The state policies consolidate the solidarity and the interests of Chinese peasants against 'statist' domination."[48] The state's antifarmer policies—confiscating land, control over markets and mobility, and exclusion of cadre-bound farmers from welfare—brought suffering to the rural people. Cadre-bound farmers, as the victims of socialism, found it in their common economic interest to resist the exploiting state. It is not an exaggeration to say that the socialist revolution in agriculture—the wholesale transformation of Chinese farmers into commune laborers—sowed the seeds of its own destruction. In *Peasant Power in China*, Daniel Kelliher states clearly the structural opposition between farmers and the state:

In China, the structure of state socialism itself gave peasants cohesion. This was never the state's intention, of course. The collective structure had the primary effect of giving the People's Republic the ability to reach directly and immediately into the lowest level of society anywhere in the vast countryside—*an intrusive power possessed by no other state in Chinese history*. Yet the quiet, almost unnoticed, consequence of this structure was to lock peasants into a sameness of circumstances that could produce *unconsciously* uniform peasant action on an enormous scale.[49]

What is important is not the farmers' cohesion but the millions acting largely as individuals. Since farmers could not organize as a tangible opposition group under the Communist regime, farmers' actions were unorganized and unled. In seeking economic independence and family autonomy, the new farmers flowed around the cadre fish, who wanted to keep farmers trapped in the new feudal system. Those unorganized farmers finally moved China to new horizons.

## Notes

1. See Marion J. Levy, Jr., "The Problem of Our Policy in China," *Virginia Quarterly Review* 25, no. 3 (Summer 1949): 360–362.

2. Marion J. Levy, Jr., *Modernization and the Structure of Society* (Princeton: Princeton University Press, 1966), p. 282.

3. Chen Jianyuan, *Zhongguo shehui: yuanxing yu yanhua* (Chinese Society: Original Pattern and Transformation) (Shengyang: Liaoning Renmin Chubanshe, 1988), p. 142.

4. Li Yingsheng, "Woguo chengxiang eryuan shehui gejiu de dongta kaocha," *Zhongguo shehui kexue* (China's Social Science) 2 (1993):114.

5. Wang Genjin and Zhang Xuansan, *Woguo nongye xiandaihua yu jilei wenti yanjiu* (A Study on Agricultural Modernization and Capital Accumulation in China) (Tanyuan: Shanxi Jingji Chubanshe, 1993), p. 93.

6. For a good discussion of Chinese rural markets before the People's Republic of China, see John Winthrop Haeger, *Crisis and Prosperity in Sung China* (Tucson: University of Arizona Press, 1975); Dwight H. Perkins, *Agricultural Development in China: 1368–1968* (Chicago: Aldine, 1969); Dwight H. Perkins, *China's Modern Economy in Historical Perspective* (Stanford: Stanford University Press, 1975); Yoshinobu Shiba, *Commerce and Society in Sung China*, translated by Mark Elvin (Ann Arbor: Michigan Abstracts of Chinese and Japanese Works on Chinese History, 1970); G. William Skinner, ed., *The City in Late Imperial China* (Stanford: Stanford University Press, 1977).

7. Wang and Zhang, *Woguo nongye xiandaihua yu jilei wenti yanjiu*, p. 93.

8. Nicholas R. Lardy, "State Intervention and Peasant Opportunities," in William Parish, ed., *Chinese Rural Development: The Great Transformation* (Armonk, N.Y.: M.E. Sharpe, 1985), pp. 33–56.

9. Collectivization left *ziliudi* (tiny private plots) for farmers to grow vegetables for their own consumption. The *ziliudi* totaled only 3–7 percent of

all the land. See Zhou Jianming, *Geren zai jingji zhong de quanli* (Individual Rights in the Economy) (Beijing: People's Press, 1989), p. 151. For a good discussion on the coercion of collectivization, see Mark Selden, "Cooperation and Conflict," in Mark Selden and Victor Lippit, eds., *The Transition to Socialism in China* (Armonk, N.Y.: M.E. Sharpe, 1982), pp. 32–97.

10.   Huang Shu-min, *The Spiral Road: Change in a Chinese Village Through the Eyes of a Communist Party Leader* (Boulder: Westview Press, 1989), p. 54.

11.   Interview with farmers in Tongxin Village, Jingshan County, Hubei Province, in 1976. The phrase *yangguangdao* (shining road) came from a book, *Jinguang dadao*, by Han Lan.

12.   Frederic L. Pryor, *The Red and the Green: The Rise and the Fall of Collectivized Agriculture in Marxist Regimes* (Princeton: Princeton University Press, 1992), p.47; and Ivan Szelenyi, *Socialist Entrepreneurs: Enbourgeoisement in Rural Hungary* (Madison: University of Wisconsin Press, 1988), p. 64.

13.   *People's Daily*, November 6, 1979. All translations are my own unless otherwise specified.

14.   Personal interview with farmers in Jinshan in 1976.

15.   *Guangxi Daily*, November 12, 1957.

16.   Ibid.

17.   Chen Yizi, *Zhongguo: shinian gaige yu bajiu minyun* (China: Ten-year Reform and 1989 Democracy Movement) (Taiwan: Lianjing Chuban Shiye Gongsi, 1991), p. 24. In Chinese: *Gongjia dehuo manmanmo, renjia zhazuo wozhazuo; yitian doushi shifenduo, ganduole huabuzhe.*

18.   Wu Xiaoying, "Zhongguo nongcun renkou jingji jiegou jiqi zhuanbian yanjiu" (Chinese Rural Population Economic Structure and Its Transformation), in Zhu Jiaming, Ji Yanshi, and Chang Xiuze, eds., *Dandai zhongguo: fazhan, gaige, kaifang* (Contemporary China: Development, Reform, and Opening Up) (Hongkong: Wenhua Jiaoyu Chubanshe, Culture and Education, 1987), pp. 41–49; Yu Wang, ed., *Da zhuanbian shiqi* (Great Transformation) (Shijiazhuang: Hebei Renmin Chubanshe, 1987), p. 19.

19.   For good discussions on different patterns of rural authority before the People's Republic, see Helen F. Siu, *Agents and Victims in South China: Accomplices and Victims in Rural Revolution* (New Haven: Yale University Press, 1989); and W. E. Willmott, ed., *Economic Organization in Chinese Society* (Stanford: Stanford University Press, 1972).

20.   Edward Friedman, Paul Pickowicz, and Mark Selden, *Chinese Village, Socialist State* (New Haven: Yale University Press, 1991), p. 275.

21.   The party-state often compares itself to one's father and mother. References to fathers and mothers allude to the local officials.

22.   Both Mark Selden and Chen Yizi have also known cases where farmers (often after the Great Leap) asked permission to go out begging.

Personal communications with Mark Selden, February 1995, and with Chen Yizi, March 1993.

23.   Vivienne Shue, *The Reach of the State: Sketches of the Chinese Body Politic* (Stanford: Stanford University Press, 1988), p. 135.

24.   Jean Oi, *State and Peasant in Contemporary China: The Political Economy of Village Government* (Berkeley: University of California Press, 1989).

25.   For a good discussion of the statist bias for industrial development in developing countries, see Robert H. Bates, *Markets and States in Tropical Africa: The Political Basis of Agricultural Policies* (Berkeley: University of California Press, 1981). For discussions on Communist states' anti-rural policies, see Karl-Eugen Wadekin, ed., *Communist Agriculture: Farming in the Soviet Union and Eastern Europe* (London: Routledge, 1989).

26.   Mark Selden, *The People's Republic of China: A Documentary History of Revolutionary Change* (New York: Monthly Review Press, 1979).

27.   Guo Shutian and Liu Chulin, eds., *Shehen de Zhongguo* (Unbalanced China), (Shijiachuang: Hebei Renmin Chubanshe, 1991), p. 16.

28.   Sulamith Heins Potter and Jack M. Potter, *China's Peasants: The Anthropology of a Revolution* (New York: Cambridge University Press, 1990), p. 301. The term "castelike society" is from them.

29.   For a detailed discussion of a privileged hierarchy in a Communist state, see Milovan Djilas, *The New Class: An Analysis of the Communist System* (New York: Harvest/HBJ, 1957). Party officials and military officers live in special compounds guarded by armed soldiers. In each compound, there is a service department providing cheap and varied goods for the families within the compound. In addition, there are small shops in many expensive hotels in major cities—Beijing, Tianjing, Wuhan, and Shanghai. Ordinarily, they require foreign currency, but a special waiver may be given to party officials and military officers, especially during an important meeting. In *The Private Life of Chairman Mao* (New York: Random House, 1994), Dr. Li Zhisui describes how he and other members of Mao's entourage went on a shopping spree in the early 1960s in Shanghai's Jingjiang Hotel, when the whole nation was suffering from famine. Ordinary people were not allowed to enter those fancy hotels.

30.   Mark Selden, *Political Economy of Chinese Development* (Armonk, N.Y.: M.E. Sharpe, 1993).

31.   In Chinese: *Gaoji ganbu song shangmen; Zhongji ganbu kai houmen; chengshi jumin ren tuoren; xiangxia nongmin meiyou men.*

32.   Daniel Kelliher, *Peasant Power in China: The Era of Rural Reform 1979–88* (New Haven: Yale University Press, 1992), p. 103.

33.   The most popular story is Mengzi's mother, a poor widow, who worked day and night weaving clothes so that her son Mengzi could get an education. Mengzi later became the most important Confucian scholar in Chinese history.

34. Huang, *The Spiral Road*, p. 3.

35. Nongyebu Jingji Zhengce Yanjiu Zhongxin (Economic Policy Research Center of Agricultural Ministry), *Zhongguo nongcun: zhengce yanjiu beiwanglu* (Rural China: Policy Research Memorandum) (Beijing: Nongye Chubanshe, 1988), p. 299.

36. Edward Friedman, "Maoism and the Liberation of the Poor," *World Politics* 39, no. 3 (1987):414.

37. Potter and Potter, *China's Peasants*, pp. 303–304.

38. Martin King Whyte, "Chengdu diaocha: nongcun jiating xingshi shiying chengshi shenghuo wenti," (Chengdu Survey: Rural Family Pattern in Urban Life) *Shehui xue yanjiu* 3 (1990): 66–73.

39. Mark Selden, "Family Strategies and Structures in Rural North China," in Deborah Davis and Stevan Harrell, eds., *Chinese Families in the Post-Mao Era* (Berkeley: University of California Press, 1993), pp. 139–164; William L. Parish and Martin King Whyte, *Village and Family in Contemporary China* (Chicago: University of Chicago Press, 1978), p. 171; Potter and Potter, *China's Peasants*, p. 217. There is another interpretation of the increase in intravillage marriages: Young people tried to defy the intravillage taboo on intralineage marriage. This point is made by Anita Chen, Richard Madsen, and Jonathan Unger, *Chen Village: The Recent History of a Peasant Community in Mao's China* (Berkeley: University of California Press, 1984).

40. Wang Shiyuan, et al., *Zhongguo ganke daquan* (Chinese Reform Encyclopedia) (Dalian: Dalian Chubanshe, 1992), p.5.

41. For the data on Chinese illiteracy, see Joint Economic Committee, *China's Economy Looks Toward 2000*, vol. 1 (Washington, D.C.: Congress of the United States, 1986), p. 319; and Guo and Liu, *Unbalanced China*.

42. Nongyebu (Agriculture Department), *Woguo nongmin shenghuo de juda bianhua* (The Tremendous Change in the Peasant's Life in Our Country) (Beijing: Zhongguo Tongji Chubanshe, 1984), p. 402.

43. Shue, *The Reach of the State*, p. 49.

44. Zhongguo shehui kexueyuan nongcun fazhan yanjiusuo, *1992 nian zhongguo nongcun jingji fazhan niandu baogao* (A 1992 Report on Chinese Rural Economic Development) (Beijing: Zhongguo Kexue Chubanshe, 1993), p. 167.

45. Liu Xiaojing. "Woguo cheng xiang jiating shouyu chaju di jizhong tixian" (The Concentrated Embodiment of the Disparity in Family Income Between City and Country in China), *Shehui xue yanjiu* (Sociological Studies) 2 (1990): 91–98.

46. Personal interview with He during my visits in 1977.

47. Chen, *Zhongguo*, pp. 18–22.

48. Shue, *The Reach of the State*, p. 53.

49. Kelliher, *Peasant Power in China*, p. 101. Emphasis added.

# 3 Baochan Daohu: Breaking the Log Jam

*Nizou nide yangguangdao; wozou wode dumuqiao*

(You walk on your shining road, I walk on my single-log bridge.)

A popular farmer
saying in the 1970s

*Baochan daohu*, the practice of turning production over to the household, is the key source of the most important transformation in rural China since 1978. Farmers' enthusiasm and the rapid increase in their productivity after *baochan daohu* caught on illustrates their proclivity for family farming and a range of household enterprises. The origins of *baochan daohu* in various forms can be traced back to long before 1978. This chapter examines four phases of it and explains why farmers were finally able to achieve their goals in the late 1970s and early 1980s.

In examining four phases of *baochan daohu*, I show that it involved an unplanned struggle between farmers and the state and an important learning process for farmers. The fourth phase of *baochan daohu* succeeded when farmers learned from their past failures and adopted different strategies. They made deals with cadres instead of making demands. They did not organize among themselves or with others. They made effective use of provincial and local reform policies whenever they could to achieve their goals of autonomy in production and marketing.

## The First Phase (1956–1957)

As discussed in Chapter 2, family landownership rights were the bases of production for pre–People's Republic of China farmers (i.e., the farmers of Imperial China and the Republic of China) as independent proprietors. Farmers began attempts to recover these "tools of autonomy" immediately after collectivization took them away. As soon as the collectives began to dominate the organization of the farmers' way of life in 1956, farmers voiced dissatisfaction with their lack of autonomy. They pressed for greater autonomy, including the freedom to engage in sideline production and marketing. Farmers in Guangdong demanded *erduo yiziyou* (two "mores" and one "autonomy," i.e., *more* private family plots, *more* allocation of grain, and the *freedom* to go to work).[1]

The phrase *baochan daohu* first appeared in *Zhejiang Daily* on January 27, 1957. At that time, *baochan daohu* contained four elements: *baochan daodui,* output quotas contracted to the production team; *zeren daohu,* each household responsible for part of the production quota; *dinge daoqiu,* the output of land was fixed and anyone responsible for the land could decide how many work points a worker could receive; and *tongyi jingying,* the production and distributive decisions were made by the team leaders. This responsibility system won the support of some local leaders in Zhejiang. Li Yunhe, deputy party secretary of Yongjia County in Zhejiang, was a well-known advocate of the first *baochan daohu* movement. Yongjia's experience soon spread to other parts of rural Zhejiang. By the summer of 1957, more than 15 percent of the rural areas in Zhejiang had adopted *baochan daohu.*[2]

Official *baochan daohu* provided cover for the more radical actions of farmers, some of whom openly called for a return to family farming. In Sichuan, some farmers were reported saying, "They [farmers under the collective] contract for 400 hundred jin per mu. I will produce 500 or even 600 jin per mu. I am willing to be fined even if I have to sell my water buffalo and tools. But I have one condition—that the cooperative give back my land, my water buffalo, my boat and farm tools."[3]

This became the well-known *la niu tui she* movement (formally withdrawing from the cooperative, taking back one's family ox or buffalo) in the countryside between 1956 and 1957. In Guzheng Township, Zhongshan County, Guangdong, some farmers openly grew crops on their family's original land. Some even defied rural cadres and demanded to withdraw from the collective. Most farmers in Guzheng began to work on the land allocated to them during the land reform (1952–1953).[4] Riots broke out when cadres refused to let farmers take back their tools and animals. Some farmers even demanded compensation when they withdrew from their cooperatives. On May 14, 1957, four farmer leaders led fifty-six other farmers from Da Shi Qiao Cooperative in Shandong and surrounded the *xiang* (township) government, shouting, "Better to die killing than die starving!" They demanded that the director of the township government settle their accounts and give them grain. Some of the riots involved beating cadres. In Jing County, Shandong Province, rural riots over redistribution of land and farm tools took place in 47 percent of the villages. In one collective, forty farmers beat cadres and took back farm tools and wheat.[5]

In other places, farmers redistributed land and practiced family farming on their own. In Sichuan, farmers referred to the return of family farming as "the second land reform" and claimed, "A good harvest is possible only if the land is distributed to the household and each person is left free to be responsible for production."[6]

In Wenzhou County, Zhejiang Province, farmers in 1,000 collectives adopted family farming in 1956, involving 178,000 rural households.[7] In the same year, farmers in Fushan County, Guangdong Province, also adopted family farming. By the end of 1956, around 20 percent of the members in the cooperatives formally had withdrawn from collective farming.[8] Closely reading the official press at that time, I discovered that the withdrawal was particularly widespread in Guangdong, Henan, Zhejiang, Jiangsu, Hebei, Anhui, Jiangxi, Shandong, Shaanxi, and Liaoning provinces. Farmers' demands for the return of the family farm with individual land rights came to the attention of the state, as did rural riots.

Before the farmers who withdrew from the collective could enjoy the fruits of their family farming, Mao attacked the *la niu tui she* movement. *Baochan daohu* was attacked as the capitalistic idea of some nouveau riche farmers. This effort was combined with the 1957 antirightist movement, in which thousands of intellectuals were persecuted for making criticisms (often minor) against the state. In fact, some intellectuals were stigmatized as rightists after they voiced sympathy for farmers.

The political response to the farmers' *la niu tui she* movement was nationwide, effectively smashing the dreams of other farmers who wanted to restore family autonomy. This anti–*baochan daohu* campaign and the antirightist movement silenced the farmers, led to an expansion of the collective system in 1958, and gave rise to the People's Commune, the new form of the collective system. This set the stage for the Great Leap and the subsequent famine.

## The Second Phase (1961–1962)

The Great Leap famine fundamentally changed the relationship between the state and the farmers. Millions of farmers held collective farming and cadre incompetence responsible for the famine. As one farmer jingle in Hubei Province put it:

> Cadres are subjective pigs;
> Wanting to change the way of farming.
> For the sake of good appearances,
> They would impose cotton growing on bad land.

The famine forced most leaders at all levels to accept at least temporary retreat from their great plan of higher-level collectivization. Some leaders, like Chen Yun, Zhu De, and Deng Zihui, head of rural work, called for a reexamination of policies toward rural people. In 1960, the central government issued documents again allowing farmers limited private plots (5 percent of the total land) and raising the price for grain and other agricultural products.[9] More importantly, by devastating rural China, the famine created space for local and regional leaders to push for agricultural reforms. This included some leaders who had zealously supported the Great Leap movement.

A variety of policy changes occurred in many rural areas as rural cadres embraced reform initiatives. Their goal was to repair the damage of the famine. In 1960, when famine swept Hubei and Guangxi, their provincial governments called for *sanbao yijiang* (three contracts plus reward), in which the production team contracted with the production brigade to produce a certain quantity of grain at a certain cost using a certain labor force. Teams that surpassed the quota were permitted to retain the surplus as reward. A 1960 Hubei government directive specified that the production team should receive 70 percent of above-quota grain.[10]

In Guangxi, task rates were introduced in order to increase farmers' work incentives. In 1960, 42 percent of the production teams in Longsheng County adopted this task rate system.[11] With the officially sanctioned reform, farmers in many places began to push for more radical change. In Tongxin Village, Hubei, farmers subdivided the production teams and started to contract production to *zuoyezu* (small work groups). In many cases, the members of small groups were kin.

Some localities went further in terms of contracts. In 1959, in Xinxiang Prefecture, Henan, one of the worst devastated by the famine, Party Secretary Gen Qichang created his own version of *baochan daohu*, which required that each worker be assigned responsibility for a piece of land with a set output target. The worker would be rewarded for above-contract output (often 70–90 percent of the above-quota amount). In order to encourage farmers, Gen even pledged that this policy would not be changed in the near future. By the end of 1959, 60 percent of Xinxiang villages had adopted this policy. Wang Huizhi, the second party secretary of Luoyang Prefecture, Henan, advocated the system of *baochan daolao* (contract production to labor or task rates). By 1959, more than eight hundred production brigades had adopted task rates, in which the brigade set specified work points for each task.[12] In some areas of Jiangsu, some local governments also promoted the task rates system.

The best-known case of *baochan daohu* was in Anhui Province. Even though the farmers initiated the practice of *baochan daohu*, provincial and local leaders were responsible for its spread. In 1960, a seventy-five-year-old farmer in Su County pleaded with the commune head because his only son suffered from tuberculosis. With a single shovel and one four-prong hook, they harvested 3,300 jin of grain, giving 1,800 jin of grain and 60 yuan obtained from hog raising to the commune, an astonishing feat at a time when famine was sweeping the nation. This sharp contrast between the success of the old farmer and the failure of the commune system was reported to the governor of Anhui, Zeng Xisheng.[13] Zeng, a radical follower of Mao's Great Leap Forward, having witnessed the disaster that he and his comrades had inflicted upon farmers, began to take this report seriously. It is possible that Zeng used the old man's story exactly as collectives used the Dazhai story to formulate his policies at this time.

Facing a severe famine in Anhui, Zeng was motivated to take the advice of the old farmer. In the spring of 1961, Zeng and his associates in the Anhui provincial government proposed a system of *zerentian* (responsibility land system), in which commune members received work points according to the output of the land they were assigned. Crucial to *zerentian* was unified distribution within the collective. The cadres were in charge of distribution. Although *zerentian* was limited in terms of autonomy, it did give farmers more incentive to work on the land by tying farmers' work points to their productivity.

Zeng was not alone in promoting the new system. One provincial leader in Anhui, Qian Nengrang, wrote a letter to the central government quoting farmers on the superiority of *zerentian*: "To be honest, under the Communist policy of cooperation, the best policy is the policy of *zerentian*. If this policy is allowed to continue, we don't mind paying a higher duty [more government procurement of grain]."[14]

With the support of the provincial leaders, *zerentian* spread rapidly in Anhui. By August 1961, 75 percent of production teams had adopted the new system.[15] By October, the total reached 84 percent. Farmers in Hebei also became interested in the idea of the responsibility system in the early 1960s. In one public forum, farmers in Nanjia Village, Hebei Province, discussed the importance of *zerentian*. One said, "As far as I am concerned, the important thing is to place responsibility on the shoulders of the laborer."[16] In Henan, 85 percent of rural areas adopted *zerentian* in 1961; in Guangdong, half of the production teams adopted it. By the end of 1961, 25 percent of rural areas in Guizhou were practicing *zerentian*. By May 1962, more than 30 percent of all rural households had adopted it.[17] *Zerentian* was so crucial to rural China's recovery from the famine of the early 1960s that farmers called it *jiumingtian* (lifesaving grain field).

The *zerentian* system and other similar reform systems in the early 1960s differed fundamentally from the *baochan daohu* practices of the late 1970s. In the early 1960s, the distribution of the portion of the output specified in contracts in most cases was handled at the brigade level. In most cases, the crucial farming decisions were handled at either brigade or team levels. *Only field management was left to individual households.*

Provincial leaders reported on their experiment to the higher authorities. At first, the center was very supportive of local initiatives because the famine forced the center to grasp at any effective straw to promote agricultural production. In fact, many local policies became national policies by the end of 1960, when famine swept the country. A 1960 emergency directive from the central government called on production teams to have *san-bao yijiang* (three contracts, one reward system) and gave farmers permission to have a limited amount of private land (5 percent) to produce sideline products.[18] Some central government leaders, among them Deng Xiaoping, Deng Zihui, and Chen Yun, became supporters of the *zerentian* system. In June 1962, at a meeting of the Central Secretariat, Deng Xiaoping made his well-known pragmatic speech: "All kinds of methods should be used in poor rural areas where farmers live a hard life. Some comrades in Anhui say, 'No matter whether the cat is black or yellow, the cat is good as long as it can catch mice.' This saying contains some truth. *Zerentian* is a new thing worth a try."[19]

In late July 1962, Mao launched an attack against *zerentian* at a party conference in Beidaihe. Also at this conference, Mao advanced his famous slogan, "Never forget class struggle." Mao, however, was not sobered by the Great Leap famine. He remained convinced that collectivist socialism would bring wealth and power to the nation and prosperity to the countryside. He launched the Socialist Education Movement (1963–1965) to force farmers back to collective farming. Zeng Xisheng and other provincial and local leaders who promoted *zerentian* and other rural reforms were stripped of power, and farmers were forced back to collective farming. Since leaders from both the center and local governments were responsible for the spread of *zerentian* and other reforms, the rapid change of policies generated cynicism among farmers.

## The Third Phase (1967)

Mao sent work teams, including cadres, intellectuals, and college students, to press the campaign in the countryside. The urban outsiders were able to use farmers' bitterness toward local cadres to create struggle meetings. The Socialist Education Movement had barely come to an end when Mao launched the Cultural Revolution in 1966. The chaotic condition in the early stages of the Cultural Revolution (1966–1976) provided farmers with an opportunity to voice their dissent. (During the later stages, this was reversed.) In the very beginning, farmers and workers did not participate in the Cultural Revolution, but after the January 1967 Shanghai workers' revolt, people from all walks of life began to organize, challenging bureaucracy and party cadres. The farmers' movement followed the arrival of Red Guards from the cities.

In some areas, farmers took advantage of the chaotic situation during the Cultural Revolution to press for the expansion of the household and market. Farmer Wang in Anren County, Hunan, for example, led a group of his villagers to engage in commerce.[20] They traveled to cities like Guangzhou and Changsha and made money. At a time when other villagers did not have enough to eat, Mr. Wang built a new house. He was caught by the local militia when he was going to Guangzhou, however. The local cadres held a struggle meeting against his capitalist ideas and paraded him through the village. Humiliated, Mr. Wang hanged himself.

In Gaozhou County, Guangdong Province, farmers assigned production tasks to work groups and earned work points on the basis of output rather than labor time.[21] Farmers in some villages refused to hand over their grain taxes. Some tried to divide the collective land. Some farm leaders organized farmers and called for self-government. In Xishui, Hubei Province, Wang Renzhou, who was kicked out of college because of his counterrevolutionary ideas, became a well-known farmers' leader in 1967. Inspired by the Paris Commune revolution described by Marx in *The Civil War in France*, Wang demanded "rural self-autonomy" from the state and asked farmers not to submit grain to the state. Wang even allied with rebel leaders (college students) in Wuhan in an attempt to increase the influence of his farmers' organization. In the fall of 1968, Zeng Siyu, commander-in-chief of the Wuhan military garrison, sent troops to smash Wang's farmers' organization and arrested Wang and other rebel student leaders.[22]

Elsewhere, farmers took advantage of the chaotic situation in 1967 to "invade" collective and state property such as forests and fish ponds. For example, hundreds of villagers living close to the Qinling Mountains stole trees from the state forests and sold them on the black market.[23] The mass tree-stealing activities came to an end in the spring of 1968, when a small number of "tree stealers" were punished to scare villagers. We may never know the extent of organized rural violence during that period because of the chaotic situation and the lack of any formal data collection. According to a central government directive, however, farmers in Jiangxi, Sichuan, Zhejing, Hubei, Hunan, Henan, Anhui, Ningxia, and Shanxi provinces were involved in the armed power struggle. Some even advocated the slogan "the countryside encircles the city," an ironic borrowing from Mao's revolutionary struggle of the era of guerrilla warfare. A directive to rural people from the central government in late 1967 called for rural people to struggle against four tendencies: speculating and profiteering; graft and theft; *contracting land to the household*; going it alone.[24] The party set out to destroy the rural movement toward family farming and free markets. Incidents like those in Hubei may have taken place in other areas as well. In fact, in 1967 and 1968, the central government called for many college students and professors to go to the countryside, where farmers had taken measures into their own hands. In 1983, an interview with four former college students who were sent to crack down on rural resistance in Ersi Prefecture, Hubei, suggested that in 1967 farmers throughout Ersi used the chaotic situation to openly call for *baochan daohu*. One recalled the bold behavior and words of local leaders: "All of us were shocked by the words of the local leaders. One said that the movement against Liu Shaoqi was crazy. Without *baochan daohu* advocated by the center and local government in the early 1960s, all farmers would have died."[25]

The organized attempt to force collective farming during the Cultural Revolution was fairly successful. Work teams and military forces from the city were able to impose the unpopular state policies. Having witnessed the official shutdown of organized movements and experienced the failure of the leader-promoted movement, farmers learned bitter lessons.

## The Fourth Phase (1977 to the present): The "New" *Baochan Daohu*

Throughout the Cultural Revolution and beyond (1966–1978), farmers' resistance against the collective farming took a silent but daily form. This resistance prevented government leaders from moving China to even higher stages of collectivization by attempts to raise the level of accounting from team to brigade.[26] The government intensified its effort in the years 1974–1975 by curtailing rural markets and private plots, and farmers' activities went further underground, on the defensive. Farmers' incentives to work on the collective were further undermined. At the height of the Cultural Revolution, in the years 1966–1967, agricultural production stagnated. In order to boost production in the early 1970s, the government introduced a wide variety of modern technology: farm machinery, fertilizers, plastic sheets (for nurturing rice seedlings), improved seeds and pesticides. In 1970, Zhou Enlai and other conservative modernizers were the moving force behind the North China Agricultural Conference, where agricultural technology was stressed. This and a great expansion of irrigation contributed to expanded grain production, but because costs were heavy and state purchasing prices of agricultural commodities remained fixed, farmers did not raise their income. In the 1970s, grain production increased in spite of low morale, but the increase was very slow, less than 2 percent per year, barely keeping up with population growth. According to Carl Riskin, the per capita expenditure for the rural population actually declined.[27] These technologies would prove crucial for increased productivity after the fourth phase of *baochan daohu.*

### *Baochan Daohu : The Corruption That Cut the Farmers Loose*

The death of Mao in 1976 certainly provided an opportunity for farmers to pursue family autonomy. In 1978 (in some places as early as 1977), when farmers began to pursue family autonomy anew, they had learned a lesson from their bitter history. This time, with few exceptions, they did not try to organize. They made no demands. They succeeded by making individual deals with individual cadres. They offered cadres more than the cadres expected. That broke the log jam. In almost all cases, farmers guaranteed a certain percentage to both the state and the local cadres—as captured in a well-known saying, "Give enough to the state and to the collective and the rest to ourselves"—to win approval for family farming.[28] The proportion given to the collective was under the direct control of rural cadres. This unofficial "bargaining strategy" was very attractive to many cadres, although some refused to make deals with farmers.

In the very beginning, farmers promised to give a bit more to the cadres themselves (surcharges). That additional offering to the cadres cut farmers loose. After *baochan daohu* became institutionalized, this form of surcharge also became expected. As Jean Oi points out, rural cadres "engage in activities ranging from illegally withholding a portion of peasant receipts from sales to the state, to imposing ad hoc surcharges, to extorting money from peasants at the purchasing station."[29]Although all rural cadres benefited economically from the deal, the brigade cadres with whom farmers made the most deals benefited most. A social survey of cadres in four counties of Anhui suggests that *baochan daohu* was directly responsible for pay increases of rural cadres: 20 percent for commune cadres, and 164 percent for brigade cadres.[30] In Shandong, most cadres were able to get for themselves 20–40 jin of grain per mu once farmers practiced *baochan daohu*.[31] This was, in effect, bribery to entice cadres.

This deal-making strategy worked best in poor areas, where cadres found it hard to turn down farmers' offers given the poverty-driven economy. Thus, *baochan daohu* spread from poorer to more developed rural areas. In one poor village in Heilongjiang Province, poor farmers had to depend on state loans to buy food. One farmer couple in 1981 asked the cadres' permission to practice *baochan daohu*: "No one wants us because we are so poor. We have an idea to get rid of poverty—which is to divide the land and allocate it to the household. We will pay 4.5 yuan per mu to the team, if the team leaves us alone."[32]

Although the provincial government in Heilongjiang opposed *baochan daohu*, poor farmers like this couple were able to practice family farming by offering bribes to cadres. Such bargaining was quite common. According to one survey in Dongmin County, Shandong, most farmer households that pursued *baochan daohu* promised not only to fulfill the grain quota set up by the commune cadres but also to give them more than they had asked for, the bribes ranging from 5 percent to 10 percent of the quota.[33] According to one report from rural Guizhou, more than 50 percent of the goods belonging to the collective (including cash) were allocated to the private use of village cadres during the *baochan daohu* movement.[34] The ingenious farmers used material goods to bribe their cadre overlords to look the other way while the farmers practiced *baochan daohu* and broke the log jam.

Poor farmers were the initiators of *baochan daohu*, but other farmers achieved autonomy by contracting for the pigsty, the woods, the waste land, the fish pond, and the vegetable land. In most cases, individual farmers made deals with cadres. For example, in 1978, the Ziqiang production team in Heilongjiang spent 1,000 yuan to run a pigsty. When Liu Shilin promised to give some money to the cadres from the pigsty in 1979, Liu was able to give the team cadres 590 yuan and keep 1,050 yuan for himself. As early as 1980, at least fifty thousand farm households like Liu's scattered throughout Heilongjiang contracted for the collective's sideline production.[35]

Some farmers tried to make deals with local cadres (mainly at the team and brigade level) in order to be left alone in farming and sideline production; others bought their way out of collective farming altogether. For example, farmer Ma Youcai, Zhonghen Village, Niulin County, paid cadres 1,750 yuan for the use of 157 mu of waste land and made a profit every year.[36] This is especially true for farmers in densely populated areas of Zhejiang and Jiangsu. One farmer would go to the brigade party secretary and ask permission to leave the collective land: "I am willing to pay what the strongest laborer will make in the brigade by the end of the year. Please let me go out to do something else. If I make more money, I shall pay more."[37] This sort of bargaining enabled farmers to leave collective farming. Jurgen Domes even discovered the unorganized farmers' abandonment of collective fields in the late 1970s:

> Peasants in the communes—in particular in Zhejiang, Jiangsu, Jiangxi, Gansu, and Liaoning—had begun to engage in the "restoration of capitalism." They "speculated," "started small production," and "corrupted the cadres and party members." They "left agriculture to engage in commerce," and in this way, "the individuals made money while the collective fields were neglected and became barren land."[38]

It is apparent that the combination of local cadres' corruptibility and unorganized farmers' individual deals allowed numerous farmers to breach the collective dike. If the cadres had not been corruptible and if the farmers had organized, the farmers could not have succeeded. To some extent, the poorer the area, the easier it was for farmers to make deals with cadres, for the cadres were more susceptible to the farmers' offering. When famine and drought struck Anhui and Sichuan, cadres in those provinces found it difficult to reject farmers' offers. Anhui and Sichuan farmers were not alone. In fact, farmers in Gansu, Guizhou, Henan, and Hubei also started to make deals on their own.

Of course, not all farmer's action was unorganized. Some farmers secretly organized to pursue *baochan daohu.* Organized *baochan daohu* sometimes took place in small groups, but the small-scale group behavior was subject to local politics. If local cadres were not sympathetic to farmers' initiatives, the small group *baochan daohu* became vulnerable. A well-known case is Xiaogang Village, Anhui Province. Three former beggars from Xiaogang Village, Fengyang County, were the earliest to initiate the practice of *baochan daohu* in the late 1970s. Twenty years of collective farming had devastated the village. Migration and starvation had reduced it from thirty-four to eighteen households in 1978. Everyone in the village had had the experience of begging throughout the days of the collectives. On November 24, 1978, farmers from those eighteen households held a secret meeting and passed a resolution to guarantee *baochan daohu*:

## The Pledge

1. The contracting of production to individual households is to be kept strictly secret and not divulged to any outsider.
2. When the grain is harvested, the amount to be rendered to the state will be rendered to the state, and the amount to be rendered to the collective will be rendered to the collective. Should there be a large amount of grain, more should be contributed to the state, no one shirking.
3. Should they come to grief because of contracting production to individual households, we are willing to raise the children of village cadres until they are eighteen years old.[39]

The heads of household of the eighteen families signed the contract with their thumbprint. But the news of Xiaogang's *baochan daohu* leaked out. Soon, other places demanded the same treatment. The party secretary in the commune, Zhang Minglou, issued an order: "Anything the Communist Party provides for planting rice, making loans, and getting chemical fertilizer, Xiaogang cannot enjoy!"[40]

The organized nature of the Xiaogang movement had caught the eye of the authorities. The village was denied fertilizers and other important farm inputs. Production suffered. The cadres used this to try to convince farmers to try to stop the "new" *baochan daohu*. While the cadres' eyes were fixed on those organized *baochan daohu* at small group levels, *baochan daohu* action spread. Local cadres could not stop it, if, indeed, they had wanted to. As one Anhui farmer saying goes, "*Baochan daohu* is like a chicken pest. When one family's chicken catches the disease, the whole village catches it. When one village has it, the whole county will be infected."[41]

One example will illustrate how women helped to spread *baochan daohu* by marriage! When more farmers in poor Anhui Province were able to practice *baochan daohu* in 1979, farmers in neighboring Jiangsu Province became restless, but leaders in Jiangsu launched a political campaign to prevent the spread of the decollectivization movement. Loudspeakers and slogans set up in villages adjacent to Anhui blasted, "Resolutely oppose the tendency to go it alone!" In Liu Chen Village, Anhui Province, adjacent to Jiangsu, six weddings took place within one year, 1979 (one year after the decollectivization movement). Five of the new brides came from Jiangsu Province, an occurrence unthinkable in the height of collective days given Anhui's comparative poverty.[42] The flight of women to "decollectivized" farms was the last straw for farmers in Jiangsu. Soon the practice of *baochan daohu* spread to Jiangsu in spite of the resistance of provincial and local Communist leaders.

Rural women used their marriages to voice their preferences. Zu Fengjiao, a rural migrant from Tongxin Village, Hubei Province, liked to quote a proverb: "Water flows downward; but people strive upward."[43] For many rural women and their parents, striving upward meant running to a village where people had more power to make their own decisions and to earn money.

Through struggle, corruption, hard work, and migration, farmers actually succeeded in overcoming the central government's rejection of *baochan daohu.* In 1982, an important central document formally recognized *baochan daohu* as one of the responsibility systems of the socialist collective economy.[44] But throughout the whole process, farmers' action preceded the state's reformist agenda.

### The Benefits of Baochan Daohu

The "new" *baochan daohu* was quite different from the previous three movements. First of all, farmers did not ask for landownership as they did in 1957. They did not fight with cadres. There were no riots. Second, farmers did not organize. They made individual deals with cadres so that the distribution of the rest of the harvest belonged to them, whereas in 1961 the cadres had been responsible for the annual redistribution. After submitting the grain he had promised to the cadres, the farmer became the master of the rest of the harvest. The quota grain included taxes to the central government and taxes to the local government (village and commune). Third, farmers did not demand self-government as they did in the Cultural Revolution. In fact, they made no demands of any sort. They posed no overt threat to the regime. They were able to achieve a great deal of autonomy without ever raising the question of landownership. Theirs was a peaceful, unobtrusive, rural revolution. It was also a spontaneous, unorganized, leaderless, nonideological, apolitical movement (a SULNAM).

Even though under *baochan daohu* farmers had to sell some grain to the state as a form of rent and to give some to local cadres, farmers knew how much that contribution would be. In this respect, the *baochan daohu* initiated by farmers in the late 1970s was radically different from its usage in the first three stages. To differentiate it from former ones, farmers in Anhui and Henan used the term *dabaogan* (comprehensive household contracting, returning everything—distribution, production, labor—to the household). They no longer had to go to cadres on questions of production, labor allocation, and redistribution.

In a 1985 interview, Zhou Mingzu, from Zhou Village, Hunan, used a popular saying to express the importance of the distinction between the state, the collective, and the farmers: "As the old saying goes, if we are shortchanged, let the world know. Now we know exactly how much we give to the state. It feels good to have that knowledge." Other farmers in Tongxin referred to the division this way: "It is very easy to tell green onions from tofu." This means that the boundaries between the state, the collective, and the household are distinct. Farmers in other places used other expressions like *kandejian* (visible) and *modezhao* (tangible) to describe the new distinction among the household, the collective, and the central government. Under the collective system, farmers had no idea how much the state took from them or how much they could keep for themselves. This confusion among the state, the collective, and the individual over the allocation of crops enabled the state and the local government to take what they liked in the name of the people. This lack of control over "their own" crops was the heart of the problem for farmers. They saw their relationship with the collective as adversarial. In Tongxin Village, Hubei, in the early 1970s, villagers complained about the ambiguity of collective ownership: "Only ghosts know how much in that collective is ours and how much is theirs (the cadres')."[45] Clearly, the farmers were "us" and the cadres were "them." In a 1976 interview, Zu Choushu of Tongxin Village compared the lack of that knowledge to a mute eating *huanglian* (a bitter Chinese herbal medicine), unable to express the bitterness. Whenever an opportunity arose, cadre-bound farmers evaded the collective for their own benefit, but the cadres were able to take advantage of the situation to get more. In more than twenty villages I visited between 1978 and 1984, farmers used the saying "catching fish in muddy waters" to describe cadres who benefited from the confusing jurisdictions among the state, the collective, and the individual.

After *baochan daohu*, the family head once again became *dangjiaren*, the master of his own house. Apart from the state quota on oil, cotton, and grain, the producers were able to decide what crops they wanted to cultivate for the market. Decisions often were made according to the family's labor situation, the environment (climate and soil condition), and timing. The farmers were once again acting as household heads in control of farming.

Farmers became the masters of their own labor. All work was allocated within the family. Farmers happily said, "Busy time and leisure time alternate, how comfortable it is," referring to the return to the natural rhythms of farm life. Since there was finally an incentive to work, efficiency improved dramatically and a work ethic came back into farming. Formerly cadre-bound farmers put it clearly: "Now is different from the past. We work for ourselves." In a 1982 interview farmers in Tongxin told me that they would go to the fields without waiting to hear the whistle from the team leaders: "You cannot be lazy when you work for your family and yourself."

*Grandma Pan is well known for her smoked chickens. She will sell some but keep some for the Spring Festival. Photo by Kate Xiao Zhou*

After *baochan daohu*, farmers had direct control over their harvest. In the past, they had to take from the team whatever the team distributed regardless of quality. Now every household had control of its finances. As one farm saying goes, *Baochan daole hu, renren shi ganbu* (after *baochan daohu*, everyone becomes a cadre). Now, "everyone uses his brain, every household becomes a team leader and an accountant." If collectivization had deprived tens of millions of farmers of their initiative to plan and carry out the myriad tasks of farming and markets, *baochan daohu* restored these powers.

A clear division of labor at home was restored along sex and generational lines. This undoubtedly recognized the patriarchy within the family. In Chapter 9, I will expatiate on all the implications of the transformation from public patriarchy to family patriarchy. Now, "the family is like a home again." All elements of *baochan daohu* were nicely summarized by a farmer in his conversation with Jan Myrdal in the early 1980s: "Things are better nowadays. I make my own decisions. I can fertilize at exactly the right moment. No one tells me what to do. No materials go to waste; no time is wasted; no one interferes. I know what I do in order to reap a good harvest."[46]

Amazingly, *this grass-roots decollectivization was conducted without leadership, organization, or plan.* One can always identify the leaders of the student movement and of most other movements, but one cannot name the leaders of this or any aspect of the "new" *baochan daohu* movement in the late 1970s. There was only *laobaixing* ("old one hundred surnames" or ordinary people). No help was needed. No work team was sent by the state to initiate or supervise it. Indeed, the state long sought to repress it. The rapid pace of decollectivization reflected farmers' desire for autonomy. Many farmers called it *zhenzheng de jiefang* (authentic liberation). When the opening to *baochan daohu* was perceived, the response was spontaneous.

## Provincial and Local Governments

Although farmers were the initiators of institutional change in rural areas, their success was linked to the political environment in China and the roles of provincial leaders like Zhao Ziyang and Wan Li; some local rural cadres were also important for the spread of *baochan daohu*. In 1977, one year after the death of Mao, the political environment in China changed. The Chinese people and some leaders were tired of Mao's style of political campaign. Cadres as well as the other Chinese people began to show interest in their individual material betterment. Some provincial leaders took measures to reduce the harm inflicted by Mao's radical agricultural policies. These reform initiatives at the provincial levels and in some localities, limited as they were, did create an umbrella, as it were, for the rapid spread of *baochan daohu.*

### Sichuan Reform

*Baochan daohu* developed most rapidly in those places where officially sanctioned reforms took place in the late 1970s. Sichuan and Anhui were the best examples.

Sichuan used to be well known as the "grain warehouse" of China. Twenty years of collective farming devastated Sichuan, which became known as the "home of beggars." The flow of hungry rural migrants posed a threat to the existing collective entity in Sichuan. In an attempt to revive the stagnant commune system, Party Secretary Zhao Ziyang and the Sichuan provincial government issued Twelve Rules on Rural Areas in late 1977, and called for a system of farming that linked productivity to work points. Zhao supported three important local initiatives. First was the policy of "specialized contracts" *(zhuanye chengbao)*, in which the production team contracted with individual households to produce specific sideline items. The households sold their contracted items at lower prices to the team, and the team resold those items at a higher price. The profit was to be redistributed to all team members. The second local reform initiative was *baochan dao-*

*lao* (task rates). The task rates system adopted in several provinces (earliest in Sichuan in 1977) was the same as *zerentian* in the early 1960s. The collective production team was responsible for unified redistribution, production planning, and accounting; the work group *(xiaozu)* was responsible for cost, production output, and labor. Apart from a small portion of grain delivered to the team, the work group would keep the rest of the above-quota grain for distribution among its members.

The third reform, *baochan daozu* (contract production to work groups), developed later but became more important. *Baochan daozu* was developed first by Sichuan farmers in Guanhan County. In 1975, farmers in some localities in Guanghan divided the existing production into small groups (six to ten households per group). Each group was responsible for supplying a required quota to the state and the collective; in turn, group members were allowed to keep the rest of the harvest. Given the fact that relatives often lived close together, farmers were able to form groups along kinship lines.

*Baochan daozu* increased farmers' work incentives. In 1978, Zhao Ziyang began to support the Guanghan practice, which spread to other parts of Sichuan and to neighboring provinces such as Guizhou and Yunnan.

The Sichuan example spread to other provinces. Leaders in Fujian, Jiangxi, Tibet, Guangdong, Xinjiang, Henan, and Jiangsu called for task rates in 1978.[47] Like Zhao, the provincial leaders in those provinces intended to use mild reform to save the collective systems from the unofficial spread of *baochan daohu*. Zhao later admitted that his 1980 remark had delayed the spread of *baochan daohu.*[48]

The work groups provided a formal pretext for *baochan daohu* to spread. When production was officially allowed to be divided into small groups, it became easier for farmers, most often family heads, to make deals with local cadres.

### Anhui Reform

In addition to task rates reform, the Anhui provincial government took a more radical step in 1978. When a severe drought fell upon the province adopting the *jiedi* (lending land) policy, they allowed farmers to farm uncultivated land and keep all the harvest. Under the pretext of this official policy, the unofficial practice of *baochan daohu* spread quickly. First, *jiedi* made it easier for farmers to make deals with local cadres. For rural cadres, *jiedi* also helped to conceal the practice of *baochan daohu*. It was difficult for outsiders to figure out which plot was *jiedi* land and which was collective land. Farmers in Anhui "spontaneously enlarged the scope of the loaned land, some of them not only dividing up all the land, but also dividing up all livestock and farm implements."[49]

For example, when farmers practiced *baochan daohu* in Anhui's Shannan Commune in the late 1970s, all claimed that they *jie* (borrowed) the land from rural cadres. For fear of political fallout, cadres, especially brigade and team leaders, insisted that they *jie* (loaned) land to farmers. As a result, *baochan daohu* spread widely in 1979, one year after the *jiedi* policy.

Although *jiedi* played an important role for the rapid spread of *baochan daohu* in Anhui, Wan Li and other provincial leaders had not intended *baochan daohu*. In fact, farmers' spontaneous *baochan daohu* movement in Anhui was in direct confrontation with the provincial government reform document, the Six Articles, which specified "not permitting the contracting of production to individual households and not permitting the figuring of compensation according to output." On March 17, 1978, Wan Li wrote an article in the *People's Daily* and pointed out specifically that "*baochan daohu* is not allowed." Wan Li may have used the reform policy to replace the farmers' *baochan daohu* movement, or he may have been in a position where only lesser reforms could be advocated. In any event, Wan did not organize or lead the *baochan daohu* movement.

When the farmers' illegal practices proved to be highly productive, however, Wan acquiesced to it and adopted a wait-and-see attitude that is best expressed by his three "should nots": "It [*baochan daohu*] should not be publicized; it should not be promoted; and it should not appear in newspapers."[50] Wan's three "should nots" were important for two reasons. First, by doing nothing to stop it, Wan in fact acquiesced to the farmers' *baochan daohu* movement. Second, Wan's acquiescence gave farmers enough time to demonstrate the superiority of *baochan daohu* without being discovered by the central government.

But it is farmers who initiated and spread the "new" successful *baochan daohu* movement. Even Zhou Yueli, deputy director of the Anhui Agricultural Commission, admitted, "In a few communes, production brigades, and teams, output quotas were fixed on a household basis *on the initiative of the commune members themselves.*"[51]

In short, the reform policies and provincial leaders in Sichuan and Anhui created a congenial environment for farmers to spread *baochan daohu*. They made it possible to hide the real practice of *baochan daohu*. In both cases, the illegal spread of *baochan daohu* won the acquiescence of local and provincial leaders when high productivity was achieved. *The farmers wanted to get out from under, and the officials were looking the other way.*

Due to the agricultural crisis across the nation, leaders in other places also adopted some mild reforms to stop the farmers' *baochan daohu* movement. For example, in Shandong, the team accepted the practice of *zhuanye chengbao* (contract to produce sideline production) and contracted with farm households for certain sideline products while maintaining control of marketing. In Henan, provincial leaders tried to use *lianchan daolao* (contract production to labor) to shift away farmers' *baochan daohu* movement. But they could not sidetrack *baochan daohu*. As one Henan farmer saying went, "Neither sidelines nor labor could fence in household contracting."[52]

In Jingshan County, Hubei, farmers made deals with local cadres and called their farming families "work groups." For example, in late 1979, Zu's work group in Tongxin Village, Jingshan, consisted of members of his extended family: Zu and his wife, Zu's two sons and their wives, and Zu's two daughters. Jingshan farmers were not alone. In fact, "Wu family groups" and "father-son" groups appeared all over China.[53] There is no doubt that the work groups were not able to constrain the farmers' *baochan daohu* movement. Farmers were able to make deals with local cadres to go ahead with *baochan daohu* under varied guises. The deals struck created problems for administrative management at lower levels. As the Hubei party newspaper pointed out: "The household contract system has come about only because the chaotic situation in production management has failed to put a stop to it."[54]

## The Government Response

At the Third Plenum of the Eleventh Party Congress in late December 1978, the leaders tried to improve farmers' incentives by raising the prices of agricultural products. In order to raise farmers' enthusiasm for production, the central government passed a resolution that gave more decisionmaking authority to the team and proposed to raise agricultural prices by 20 percent. In addition, the resolution also encouraged small family sideline production. The central government was neither willing nor prepared, however, to go so far as to dissolve the collective system as farmers had in effect already done in many places. All measures passed at the meetings were ways to mend the fences of the old collective systems. The often-cited 1978 resolution, which Deng Xiaoping was deeply involved in drafting, specified that *baochan daohu* was illegal.

Farmers in many places simply ignored the state prohibition, however. In Henan, Gansu, Guizhou, and Anhui, *baochan daohu* spread quickly wherever deals could be made—apparently everywhere. Conservatives within the party tried to use farmers' decollectivization movements to undo any changes proposed by the reform group. On March 15, 1979, three months after the Third Plenary Session of the Eleventh Party Congress, a letter from Zhang Hao was published in the *People's Daily* denouncing the farmers' decollectivization movement as threatening the socialist system. In addition, a long editorial, "The System of Triple-Ownership with the Production Team as the Basic Unit Should Be Consolidated," supported Zhang's letter and attacked the decollectivization movement.[55] The letter clearly pointed out the unorganized spread of *baochan daohu* in Henan. Zhang was an official from Gansu Province and worked under Wang Renzhong, the former governor of Gansu, who was chairman of the Agricultural Commission in the State Council in 1978. It is apparent that Zhang's letter was an effort by some top leaders to attempt to stop the *baochan daohu* movement.

Zhang's letter put reform leaders on the defensive. After much maneuvering, the reformers published a letter from an Anhui leader praising "contract to the groups," a less radical form of decollectivization, on the grounds that it would strengthen the collective system because the new forms made the collective richer by increasing production. This approach ignored the issue of *baochan daohu* altogether. To show their adherence to the collective track, the editorial and Lu's letter explicitly rejected *baochan daohu.*[56]

The persistence of the reform faction in support of collective structure showed that socialist ideology was so ingrained in the mind of Deng and his reform associates that they were ready to crush any radical departure from the collective structure. However, they soon accepted precisely that. When Guo Congyi, a high-ranking official from Anhui, went to Beijing and tried to appeal on behalf of farmers for *baochan daohu,* few government officials would see him. When Guo tried to show that the achievement of Anhui farmers resulted from *baochan daohu,* he was pushed away and told that the central government did not allow the practice of such a system; they were not interested in what Guo had to say.[57] Only a few people had any patience for Mr. Guo. One of the few people willing to listen to Guo was Chen Yizi, a research fellow and government adviser who had just returned from the countryside after many years of exile. Chen went to Anhui to investigate the practice of *baochan daohu.* After a three-month investigation, Chen wrote a report that spread among top leaders. The main finding of Chen's report was that whenever farmers practiced *baochan daohu,* their production increased much more rapidly than under any other form of local reform initiative.

We do not know the "inventor" of the fourth phase of *baochan daohu.* His identity has not surfaced. We cannot tell, therefore, what inspired, moved, or encouraged him to "go for it." Some will want to believe that it was the relaxation of control, even encouragement by the government, for small private household gardens for family consumption in hard times. We may never know for sure, but we do know that various loosening proposals made before or during the fourth phase of *baochan daohu* paled in creating increases in productivity in comparison with those that followed the fourth phase of *baochan daohu,* which "spread like the chicken pest." The evidence presented clearly indicates that whatever concessions the government reforms made in small personal plots or various schemes of commune management did not achieve major increases in productivity—and those concessions did not include support or approval of *baochan daohu* until well after *baochan daohu* had resulted in major increases in productivity nowhere else achieved by alternative stimuli. Early on it was disapproved. The sense that something needed fixing may have laid a foundation of acceptance that came into play after *baochan daohu* had proved effective, but *baochan daohu* was not a "chosen instrument" before it proved its worth.

Apart from rapid increases in productivity, Chen Yizi's report contained another important message: *Baochan daohu* improved living conditions for all, including the poor. With the increasing living standard for all and the increase in production in villages practicing *baochan daohu* reaching more than 30 percent, this report opened the eyes of reform leaders, including Deng Xiaoping and Hu Yaobang. It also gave them a basis for rationalization. In fact, Hu Yaobang told Chen Yizi in 1981, "Your report played a decisive role in the new policy formation."[58] After reading this report, on May 31, 1981, Deng talked about the *baochan daohu* miracle with a few senior leaders:

> Most production teams in Feixi county of Anhui province practice *baochan daohu* and the grain output of these teams has increased significantly. Most production teams in Fengyang county, a county known to all because of the "Fengyang Flower-drum," have introduced a practice called "assumption of total responsibility." The county's grain output was twice as high as in the previous year, and now these production teams have already taken on a new look. Some comrades are concerned about the possibility that this may weaken the collective economy, but in my opinion, there is no need for them to worry.[59]

Fengyang farmers were not alone in achieving the growth miracle. In Dezhou District, Shandong Province, farmers who practiced *baochan daohu* achieved a 44 percent rate of growth in 1981 alone.[60]

Because *baochan daohu* was so ideologically incorrect within the party, many cadres from top to bottom tried to distance themselves from it as much as possible. In the late 1970s, Deng's power base was too weak for him to take on a touchy issue like *baochan daohu*, as illustrated by the 1978 party resolution of the Third Plenary conference. Perhaps the most important contributions of the 1978 reform policy were the price hike for agricultural products and the access to rural markets. These two reform policies in fact strengthened the power of *baochan daohu* because farmers who practiced *baochan daohu* could benefit more from the two reform policies and thus show the superiority of the system. The demonstration effect of *baochan daohu* began to divide leaders, and more debates on *baochan daohu* appeared in the party's newspaper, the *People's Daily*.

The *People's Daily* always represented the voice of the party, so the debate between the conservatives and the reformers confused both the public and the local governments. This confusion was important for the farmers, who needed to gain time if they were to demonstrate the superiority of their action. Meanwhile, as the debate dragged on in Beijing, more and more cadre-bound farmers took advantage of this confusion to decollectivize the land. Many adopted *baochan daohu* despite the state's prohibition. This situation is like a well-known line from China's most beloved poet, Li Bai: "While monkeys on both banks scream their lungs out, my small boat has already passed through thousands of mountains."[61] There is no doubt that the post-Mao factional struggle for power within the party hierarchy became the leaders' main focus. While the battles were being fought in Beijing over ideological correctness and factional struggles, the spread of *baochan daohu* became a social reality in many parts of China. Later, Deng's group was able to use the success of *baochan daohu* to defeat the Maoist group within the party.

After the summer harvest, the demonstration effect of *baochan daohu* enabled the reformers to gain the upper hand. Most of the places that adopted *baochan daohu* had bumper crops. Reform leaders in the central government could thus become more forceful in the rebuttal of the conservatives.

By the spring of 1980, 25 percent of production teams in Anhui had switched to *baochan daohu.* This movement tended to develop first in poor areas and to help the poor areas most. It later spread rapidly to other better-off areas as well. In Jinbaoyu, the wealthiest district of Anhui, 98 percent of the teams switched to *baochan daohu* between the fall of 1979 and the spring of 1980.[62] Interestingly, farmers also used this pragmatic approach to rationalize their decollectivization movement. While the debates about the socialist road and the capitalist road continued, poor farmers in Anhui would say: "A full stomach (not a needy one) is the main direction." The increase in production determined the superiority of the system because the past failures of agricultural production made it more difficult for cadres to resist a change that could bring about such dramatically increased production.

After twenty years of collective farming, the average grain consumption for rural people had in fact dropped several points below the 1955–1957 level.[63] Beginning in the 1970s, the state was forced to import foreign grain to meet more than one-third of urban grain consumption. If the new system provided more grain for the state, the state would not have to use its limited foreign currency to import grain. Of course, not all leaders took this practical approach to meet the agricultural crisis. For example, Chen Yun, who introduced the notion of a planned economy with some market mechanisms, consistently rejected *baochan daohu.* For Chen, collective agriculture was the key to the planned economy, and family-based agriculture would destroy the basis for a socialist planned economy. While advocating balanced growth, Chen became a fierce fighter against *baochan daohu* .

On November 14, 1979, the *People's Daily* published an important article, "Why Do Farmers Love *Zerenzhi* [the responsibility system]?" The article used convincing data from Anhui to show the power of *zerenzhi.* One telling example was the Qianwang production team of Anhui. Before collectivization (1955), Qianwang, with a population of 127, was able to produce

more than 180,000 jin of grain. Under collectivization and after repeated
political movements, the village was impoverished. Production dropped to
30,000 jin. Cadre-bound farmers had to depend on the government for seed
and animal feed. Many villagers fled the village. Yet, within one year of
*zerenzhi,* production vaulted. Farmers in Qianwang not only had enough to
feed themselves but also were able to give the state 6,700 jin of grain.[64]

Other success stories came to light, revealing the rapid increase in productivity. In Gansu, Guizhou, Shandong, and Hebei, wherever farmers
adopted *baochan daohu,* they stopped having to eat *fanxiaoliang* (the
grain supplied by other rural places), usually within one year.[65] The
demonstration effect of *baochan daohu* in those poor areas put the conservatives on the defensive and altered the thinking of the "reformers."

Even with the demonstration effect, few leaders at the top were willing
to give up collective farming. In fact, even in June 1980, there was opposition to *baochan daohu* even among reform leaders. On June 19, 1980,
Zhao wrote a letter to Wan Li and Hu Yaobang expressing his negative attitude toward *baochan daohu.* The letter in fact set the tone for the basic
attitude toward collective agriculture. Using the success story of a collective
team in Mizi County, Shaanxi Province, the old revolutionary base area that
was the party's wartime capital, Zhao Ziyang advocated task rates and
openly called for *baochan daohu* to halt:

> It seems that under the unified leadership of the team, contract
> production to labor with the collective arranged production speci-
> fication, is superior to *baochan daohu.* This [*baochan daolao,* or
> task rates] is a form of responsibility. The direction should be
> directed toward this system. This should apply not only to those
> places with a good collective economy but also to those farmers
> who practiced *baochan daohu* in backward areas.[66]

In the fall of 1980, a meeting of governors was held in Beijing.
Everyone at the meeting except Zhao Ziyang (then governor of Sichuan)
and Wan Li (then governor of Anhui) opposed the idea that *baochan
daohu* be allowed in poor and mountainous areas. After political maneuvering, the minority was able to gain permission for poor and mountainous
regions to practice *baochan daohu,* but the document from the conference
insisted that the more developed areas remain under the collective system
because it would not be desirable for those areas to adopt the "backward"
*baochan daohu.* In fact, the final resolution of the conference restricted
*baochan daohu* to 15 percent of rural China.[67]

The top leaders took it for granted that *baochan daohu* was a reaction
to backward productive forces in those poor areas. Concession to *baochan
daohu* in the poor areas was a way to readjust production relations to fit the

backward productive forces. In more developed rural collectives, *baochan daohu* would not be attempted because the forms of rural production management were supposed to follow the development of production forces. They failed to realize that farmers' desire for autonomy was (and is) a common desire and that farmers in both poor and rich areas were practicing *baochan daohu* without approval from the central government. In fact, the new system worked best in suburban areas, where there was nightsoil from the city and a huge market for vegetables and anything else, where roads were good and markets accessible. Any concession from the central government would encourage farmers everywhere to destroy the collective system and the imposed cadre-bound status. The state restriction of *baochan daohu* did not deter farmers in more developed areas from adopting the practice.

The concession from the center made it possible for various kinds of agricultural systems to coexist at the same time as *baochan daohu* was gaining momentum. The demonstration effect in both poor and developed areas where farmers defied state restriction on an unorganized basis rapidly raised productivity. In fact, no matter how developed the production team, the farmers who practiced *baochan daohu* in 1980 did much better than those within the same region who did not.[68]

When the central government received convincing statistics on these increases in productivity, some reform leaders (or followers) used the data to gain the upper hand in the power struggle and began to show support for *baochan daohu*. As Yao Yilin later recalled:

But during the process of [*baochan daohu*], this trend took place not only in the economically backward areas but also in the rich areas. The majority of the people all demand to carry out the family responsibility system. Under such circumstances the family responsibility system evolved. We have never fixed on this system as the only pattern. We did not cut everything with one knife.[69]

After *baochan daohu* spread, however, the reform faction began to shift its political strategy and started to bring the *baochan daohu* issue out into the open. On November 5, 1980, Wu Xiang, a reform adviser, wrote an important article, "The Shining Road and the Single Log Bridge" in the *People's Daily.* In his article, Wu directly challenged the conventional metaphor—"the shining road" (socialism)—to "the single log bridge" (individual family farming). Mao and the conservative factions had used the metaphor to attack *baochan daohu*. Using convincing data, Wu defined socialism as the increase of production and the improvement of people's lives: "Whatever best encourages producers to care about collective production, whatever facilitates the increase of production and commodities and the improvement of people's life, are responsibility systems to be supported. It is wrong to force people to have only one form, the symptom of *yidaoqie* [one knife that cuts everything, i.e., a Procrustean bed]."[70] This article signaled another turning point for reform leaders. Just three months before, in September 1980, all but two provincial governors (of Sichuan and Anhui) had opposed *baochan daohu* .[71]

The demonstration effect after the 1980 harvest and again after the 1981 harvest began to change the political scene. Some became supporters of *baochan daohu*. At a party conference in October 1982, Deng and other leaders in the central government lent their support to the farmers' movement and thus facilitated the decollectivization movement, especially in those provinces where leaders both at the provincial and the local level resisted *baochan daohu*. By the end of 1980, 40 percent of the production teams in Anhui, 50 percent of those in Guizhou, and 60 percent of those in Gansu were already shifting into *baochan daohu*.[72]

Deng and his reform leaders facilitated the spread of *baochan daohu* in 1983, when they saw the increased productivity *baochan daohu* brought. Deng was able to use the success of *baochan daohu* for his own political gain, taking credit and undermining the Maoist faction in 1983. In January 1983, the central government finally gave legal recognition to *baochan daohu* and called it the "household responsibility system." This Document No. 1, and another central government document in January 1984, encouraged the development of *baochan daohu* in most of rural China. This legal recognition and encouragement were important for the *baochan daohu* movement wherever local cadres resisted change. In places that followed the spontaneous movement, many farmers did not even notice the new policy. For example, a 1986 survey in rural Shanxi discovered that more than 46 percent of farmers had never heard of the central document that allowed *baochan daohu*, although family farming was spreading in Shanxi in the early 1980s.[73]

Chen Yizi, an important policy adviser to Zhao Ziyang, summarizes nicely the role of Chinese leaders in *baochan daohu*:

> At that time, the majority of leaders opposed it. Only a couple of leaders thought to give it a try by not suppressing it. At that time, those leaders played a role. But they neither advocated nor wanted to adopt the practice. To be fair, they adopted a rational attitude toward farmers' demands, thus opening the dike for the success of the rural reform.[74]

## Conclusion: The Snowballing of *Baochan Daohu*

From this discussion of the four phases of *baochan daohu*, we see that seeking family autonomy was a continuous struggle for farmers from 1956 to 1977, as farmers tried to recover the autonomy lost under collective agriculture. In 1977, twenty-one years after collectivization, many farmers still remembered the art of individual family farming. Their history served as a reference point for life.

The first three phases of attempts to resume family farming failed. Each involved some sort of organization and leadership that brought their efforts to the attention of the cadres before they could get a good start. Moreover, the first phases of *baochan daohu* and some reform initiatives by local leaders did not provide farmers the determination of use right and distribution decision. The fourth phase of *baochan daohu* was successful mainly because farmers had learned from their past failures. They made deals with individual cadres while seizing every opportunity to pursue their goals. They did not seek recognition or make high demands. They literally bribed their way out from under. Once they showed their ability to increase productivity, even political leaders who opposed them or who had simply been looking the other way began to support them. The farmers succeeded.

To be sure, the reform attempt by provincial leaders in Anhui and Sichuan provided conditions favorable to farmers. Deng's later support also was crucial in the legalization of *baochan daohu*. Deng could certainly have stopped the movement by military force had he chosen to do so. But who would have tried to stop a movement in the face of such drastic increases in productivity? Perhaps not even Mao himself—certainly no proven pragmatist like Deng—could have ignored such economic growth! Leaders like Deng Xiaoping, Chen Yun, Wan Li, and Zhao Ziyang advocated some measures merely as a temporary adjustment to resolve an economic crisis (e.g., the famine in the early 1960s and agricultural stagnation in the 1970s). Moreover, those leaders had no intention of turning *baochan daohu* into the model for all Chinese reforms. Only after great success did political leaders begin to incorporate *baochan daohu* into the reform program. They had no idea what door they were opening. As Daniel Kelliher points out, "But by acquiescing, the state ceded the initiative for charting the course of rural reforms. Reform thus carried China in a direction the leaders never planned, creating more radical policy changes than they anticipated at the Third Plenum."[75] But the latent consequences of state action always outweigh anticipated and intended consequences. *Baochan daohu* laid the basis for tremendous change well beyond what the farmers or the government leaders had expected.

The farmers' pursuit of autonomy was the source of Chinese reform initiatives. *Baochan daohu* increased farmers' resources, liberated them from the rigid control of the state bureaucracy, and enabled them to make the best of the market. *Baochan daohu* liberated more than 100 million Chinese farmers from *wenbao buzu* (not enough to eat or to wear) in its first six years and unleashed farmers' initiative. According to a survey by the *Economist*, "Grain output grew by one third in six years, cotton almost tripled, oil-bearing crops more than doubled, fruit production went up by half. Real incomes in the countryside grew even more spectacularly—threefold in eight years."[76]

All the Chinese achievements under Deng Xiaoping would have been impossible without the decollectivization movement in rural China. After decollectivization in the countryside, the ideal pattern of Communist agriculture (ownership and organization by the state) was in direct confrontation with the actual pattern, in which the family took responsibility for all important decisions. It was through decollectivization that rural people, more than any other sector, changed Communist China. After *baochan daohu* became generally effective, China entered a new stage of development—the new China was swamped by the productivity of millions upon millions of farmers who managed to achieve the kind of growth that the party leadership had sought but had not achieved.

The unanticipated success of *baochan daohu* led directly to the vast proliferation of markets, rural industries, and migration, which I will discuss in later chapters. Farmers obtained independent decisionmaking regarding diversity of crops, new industries, market activities, and the power of allocation of rural laborers and capital. None of these farmers made any attempt to seize control from the government, but they did leach away the government's control over farming, markets, industries, migration, and even family reproduction. Without firing a shot, without raising any placards, without posting any ideological statements on any wall, the farmers' movement moved as silently and unexpectedly as an electric automobile. This silent movement not only restored the position of the family in the Chinese social structure, to some extent, it also reopened the class system and loosened farmers' bonds to cadre lords and to the land. It did all this and more without any of the signs ordinarily associated with a "political" movement, although few "political" movements have had such far-reaching political effects as this apolitical movement did.

## Notes

1. *Nanfang ribao* (Southern Daily), October 19, 1957. All the newspaper citations between 1956 to the 1960s hereafter are taken from Zhongguo fazhan wenti yanjiu zu (Research Group on Chinese Development), *Baochan daohu ziliao xuan* (Selected Material on Contracting to the Household) (Beijing: Internal Government Document, 1981).

2. *People's Daily*, October 9, 1957.

3. *Xinhua Daily*, April 6, 1957.

4. *Nanfang ribao* (Southern Daily) October 11, 1957.

5. Shandong Sheng Nongye Hezuohua Shi Bianji Weiyuanhui, *Shandong sheng nongye hezuohua shiliao ji* (Collective Agriculture in Shandong Province) (Jinan: Shandong Renmin Chubanshe, 1989), p. 107.

6. *Sichuan Daily*, November 4, 1957.

7. *People's Daily*, October 9, 1957.

8. Cong Jin, *Ouzhe fazhan de suiyue* (Years of Torturous Development) (Zhengzhou: Henan Renmin Chubanshe, 1989), pp. 68–70. Ma Qibin, et al., *Zhongguo gongchandang zhizheng sishi nian 1949–1989* (Chinese Communist Party's Forty Years in Power, 1949–1989) (Beijing: Zhonggong Dangshi Chubanshe, 1991), pp. 120, 128, 133.

9. Chen Yun, *Selected Works of Chen Yun: 1956–1985* (Beijing: Renmin Chubanshe, 1986), pp. 132–133.

10. Guojia Nongye Weiyuanhui Bangongting (General Office of the State Agriculture Commission), *Nongye jitihua zhongyao wenjian huibian* (Compendium of Important Documents on Agricultural Collectivization), vols. 1 and 2 (Beijing: Zhongyang Dangxiao Chubanshe, 1981), pp. 53–361.

11. Cong, *Years of Torturous Development*, p. 487.

12. Guojia Nongye Weiyuanhui Bangongting, *Compendium of Important Documents*, pp. 254–257; and Cong, *Years of Torturous Development*, p. 234.

13. Wang Lixin, "The Years After Mao Zedong," *Kunlun* 6 (1988):4–53, translated in JPRS-CAR 89–079 (July 1989):1–16.

14. Qian Nengrang, "A Letter to the Central Government," in Zhongguo Nongcun Fazhan Yanjiu Zu, *Baochan daohu ziliao xuan* (Selected Material on Contracting to the Household) (Beijing: Internal Government Document, 1981), p. 330.

15. Wang, "The Years After Mao Zedong," p. 19.

16. *Hebei Daily*, February 19, 1963.

17. Guojia Nongye Weiyuanhui Bangongting, *Compendium of Important Documents*, p. 562.

18. Ibid., pp. 377–383.

19. Cong, *Years of Torturous Development*, p. 493.

20. Yuan Zhixin, *Guozhong zhi guo* (A Country Within a Country) (Guangzhou: Jinan Daxue Chubanshe, 1992), pp. 22–23.

21. Dali Yang, "Making Reform: Great Leap Famine and Rural Change in China" (Ph.D. dissertation, Princeton University, 1993), p. 137.

22. The crackdown on farmers' autonomous organizations was nationwide. At least in Sichuan, Hunan, and Guangxi, farmer rebel leaders were arrested.

23. Dachang Cong, "The Tree Stealers in Central Shaanxi During the Cultural Revolution," Paper presented to the Annual Meetings of the Association for Asian Studies, Washington, D.C., April 6–9, 1995.

24. Guojia Nongye Weiyuanhui Bangongting, *Compendium of Important Documents*, pp. 869–870.

25. Personal interviews in Wuhan in 1983.

26. David Zweig, *Agrarian Radicalism in China 1968–1981* (Cambridge: Harvard University Press, 1989).

27.   Carl Riskin, *China's Political Economy: The Quest for Development Since 1949* (New York: Oxford University Press, 1987).

28.   In Chinese: *Jiaogou guojiade; liuguo jitide; shengxia doushi zijide.*

29.   Jean Oi, "Market Reforms and Corruption in Rural China," *Studies in Comparative Communism* 22 (1989):227.

30.   Wang Xiaoqiang, et al., "Nongcun shangpin shengchan fazhan de xindongxiang" (The New Trends of Rural Commodity Production Development), in *Nongcun, jingji, shehui* (Rural China, Economy and Society) (Beijing: Nongcun Dushu Chubanshe) 3 (1985):84.

31.   Heilongjiang Sheng Nongye Hezuo Shi Bianweihui, ed., *Heilongjiang nongye hezuoshi,* (Beijing: Zhonggong Tangshi Ziliao Chubanshe, 1990), p. 291.

32.   Ibid., p. 481.

33.   Ibid., p. 290.

34.   Jiang Ruxiang, "Shichang, zhengfu yu shehui bianqian" (Markets, Government and Social Transformation) (Ph.D. dissertation, Beijing University, 1993).

35.   Ibid., p.502.

36.   Luo Yousheng and Zhang Hongyu. "Jiatin chengbao ziren zhi hou de nongdi zhidu chuangxin" (Institutional Innovations on Agricultural Land After Household Responsibility System), *Jingji yanjiu* (Economic Research Journal) 1, no. 1 (1995):69–80.

37.   This was said by one Zhejiang rural carpenter in Wuhan in 1978. I also interviewed several painters, cotton puffing men, and shoe repairmen. Their story was the same. They had to pay a substantial amount of money in order to leave the collective land. In this way, their families would be guaranteed food rationing.

38.   Jurgen Domes, *The Government and Politics of the PRC: A Time of Transition* (Boulder: Westview Press, 1985), p. 128.

39.   Wang, "The Years After Mao Zedong," p. 57.

40.   Ibid.

41.   In Chinese: *Baochan daohu xiang jiwen, yihu wenle, jiu quancun wen; yicun wenle, jiu quanxian wen.*

42.   Wang, "The Years After Mao Zedong," p. 35.

43.   In Chinese: *Shuiwang dichuliu, renwang gaochuzou.* Between 1969 and 1971, I lived with Zu's family. Since then I have revisited the village many times and helped Zu Fengjiao find a job in the city in 1985.

44.   Wang Shiyuan, et al., *Zhongguo ganke daquan* (Chinese Reform Encyclopedia) (Dalian: Dalian Chubanshe, 1992).

45.   My own personal observation in the early 1970s.

46.   Jan Myrdal, *Return to a Chinese Village* (New York: Pantheon Books, 1984), p. 46.

47.   Yang, *Making Reform,* p. 176.

48. Dangdai Zhongguo Congshu Bianjibu (Contemporary Chinese Series Editorial Board), *Dangdai zhongguo de sichuang* (Contemporary China's Sichuan), vol. 1 (Beijing: Zhongguo Shehui Kexue Chubanshe, 1990), p. 199.

49. Wang, "The Years After Mao Zedong," p. 28.

50. Ibid.

51. Zhou Yueli, "The System of Responsibility in Agricultural Production in Anhui Province," in Xue Muqiao, ed., *Almanac of China's Economy, 1981* (Hongkong: Modern Cultural, 1982), p. 368.

52. In Chinese: *Zhuanye chengbao bao buzhu; lianchan daolao wen buzhu; da baogan dang buzhu.*

53. *Far Eastern Economic Review* (April 6, 1979):15; and also in Daniel Kelliher, *Peasant Power in China: The Era of Rural Reform 1979–88* (New Haven: Yale University Press, 1992), p. 67.

54. *Hubei ribao,* May 14, 1980, p. 1, translated in Kelliher, *Peasant Power in China,* p.68.

55. Ibid., March 15, 1979.

56. *People's Daily,* March 30, 1979.

57. Chen Yizi, *Zhongguo: shinian gaige yu bajiu minyun* (China: Ten-year Reform and 1989 Democracy Movement) (Taiwan: Lianjing Chuban Shiye Gongsi, 1991), pp. 27–28.

58. Personal interviews with Chen Yizi, March, April, and May 1993.

59. Deng Xiaoping, "On Problems Concerning Our Rural Policy," in *Selected Articles of Deng Xiaoping* (Beijing: Renmin Chubanshe, 1983), p. 276.

60. Shandong Sheng, *Collective Agriculture in Shandong Province,* p. 295.

61. In Chinese: *Liangan yuansheng di bu zhu, qingzhou yiguo wan chong shan.*

62. Chen, "Why Did the Economically Developed Shuyan Commune Adopt *Baochan Daohu?*" in Zhongguo Nongcun Fazhan Yanjiu Zu, *Baochan daohu ziliao xuan,* p. 106.

63. Riskin, *China's Political Economy,* p. 261.

64. *People's Daily,* November 14, 1979.

65. Du Runsheng, *Zhongguo nongcun jingji gaige* (The Reform of China's Rural Economy) (Beijing: Zhongguo Shehui Kexue Chubanshe, 1985).

66. Zhao Guoliang, ed., *Zhongguo nongcun jingji tizhi gaige dashiji 1978–1988,* (Significant Events of Economic System Reform in Rural China) (Beijing: Qiushi Chubanshe, 1988), p. 82.

67. Personal interviews with Chen Yizi, October 1994.

68. Chen Yizi, "Nongcun di shuguang zhongguo di xiwang (The Rural Dawn Is the Future of China)," in Zhongguo Nongcun Fazhan Yanjiu Zhongxin, *Nongcun, jingji, shehui* (Rural China, Economy and Society), vol. 1 (Beijing: Nongcun Dushu Chubanshe, 1985), pp. 33–53.

69.  Yao Yilin, "Speech on Grain Bureau Ministers of China (Oct. 18, 1985)," in *Selections of Documents on Commerce Reform* (Beijing: Chinese Commerce Press, 1989), p. 43.

70.  *People's Daily*, November 1980.

71.  Personal interviews with Chen Yizi, March 1993.

72.  Gu Zhong, "Speeches on *Baochan Daohu* in Beijing Economics Association," in Zhongguo Nongcun Fazhan Wenti Yanjiu Zu, *Selected Material on Contracting to the Household.*

73.  Chen Shi and Mi Youlu, eds., *Zhongguo nongcun jiating di bianqian* (The Transformation of Rural Families in China), (Beijing: Nongcun Duwu Chubanshe, 1989), p. 273.

74.  Chen, *China: Ten-Year Reform,* p. 43.

75.  Kelliher, *Peasant Power in China,* p. 41.

76.  "When China Wakes: A Survey of China," *The Economist* (November 28–December 4 1992):4.

# Markets: Currents in the Farmer Sea

Wherever water flows, channels form.

Chinese proverb

The structural change of *baochan daohu* not only altered rural productive relations, it also affected market relations between the state and the rest of society. While the state did much by direct allocation, farmers flowed easily into markets, the freer the better. Eventually the market sea of farmers swamped the state monopolies.

*Baochan daohu*, the most generative structural change in China, has led some people to assume that in restoring family farming farmers sought to restore primordial attachments. It is regarded as a simple restoration of the old China, where millions of farmers lived a life primarily oriented toward subsistence. This conclusion ignores the importance of markets in farmers' lives, that is, the markets' intermediary role in rural life prior to the People's Republic and especially since the 1980s. To a degree even greater than most farmers of Imperial China, the Republic (1911–1949), and the early decades of the People's Republic (1949–1978), the new farmers aim at markets, which play a crucial role in their lives. Farmers have again pioneered in market creation, as they did for a thousand years. This rapid development of markets ended the state monopoly and altered many of the social structures of the People's Republic of China. The new markets radically undermined food rationing, the most important control in the *hukou* system, and this made a rural–urban migration of over 100 million people possible, a topic I focus on in Chapter 6.

## The Power of *Baochan Daohu*

The development of markets accelerated after *baochan daohu*, which permitted farmers to gain a sense of planning and controlling their destiny. After *baochan daohu*, farmers were able to make use of the better technology, especially fertilizers and varieties of seeds, thus leading to a rapid increase in productivity per hectare and per worker. The increase in productivity not only released "surplus" goods for which the farmers, not the state, had to seek outlets, not in direct allocation but in markets, but also released "surplus" people for rural industries and urban migration. Collectives concealed a surplus of labor—100 million to 300 million people, by various estimates. Farmers were motivated to produce more suitable, more diverse, and more profitable crops, from medicinal herbs to fruits, vegetables, and other specialty items. Not only was the variety of seeds increasing; existing varieties were becoming more widely known. Farmers were increasingly motivated to use seeds from outside their locality, to experiment with hybrid seeds. The *People's Daily* reported that even farmers in underdeveloped Guizhou Province became fascinated with hybrid seeds after *baochan daohu*:

> Guizhou farmers became preoccupied with hybrid seeds. They climbed mountains to visit their friends and relatives in order to get the best seeds. With mass stress on hybrid seeds, their use increased rapidly across the whole province. Every new kind of hybrid seed would bring a new set of technology. Many farmers are obsessed with studying the new technology. The "hybrid fever" led to a "science fever." Village after village, household after household, all commune members (farmers) look up to scientific farm households.[1]

With family farming the center of production management and a motivating condition, the efficient use of labor and new technology enabled farmers to increase productivity in grain, agricultural sidelines, and nonagricultural work. Sales of chemical fertilizers, improved seeds, and farm equipment rose rapidly.

When the basic production quota was fixed and farmers were allowed to keep or to sell the rest of the harvest, farmers' incentives soared, leading to the greatest sustained increase in productivity both per worker and per hectare in Chinese history. The striking aspects of the rapid increase in productivity in China are its long duration (1978–1992) and the diversity of agricultural products affected. The diversification of agricultural production ended the single-crop pattern under the collective, on the one hand, and also broke the traditional production pattern that was heavily oriented toward family consumption, although certain regions in Central and South China stand as exceptions to this pattern. This breakthrough is crucial for understanding the current development and modernization of China.

## Manipulation of the State's Procurement System

*Baochan daohu* restored initiative to the farm family not only in production but also in its basic responsibility for management, including paying taxes and especially marketing. For quite a few years after *baochan daohu*, farmers began to deal with the state directly with little interference from the local party apparatus. The *baochan daohu* relationship gave farmers strength and reduced the cadres' power in virtually everything else. The weakening of the cadres' power over the farmers can best be seen in the marketing of grain. After *baochan daohu*, the farmers sold products directly to the state procurement station. In order to encourage the farmers to produce more and to reduce its grain shortage, the state made a three-year contract (in 1982) with farm households, fixing the basic quota of grain to be paid to the government and to the village. After submitting their quota, farmers had control over the rest of the harvest. Thereafter, what goods and services farmers gave and received, on what occasions, and in what amounts, was a matter not of obligation but of economic calculation.

Some farmers were able to manipulate the old procurement system in the early 1980s. Others quickly imitated them. As a result, the manipulation of the government procurement system spread very rapidly. To put it simply, the state found it difficult to purchase those goods whose market value was higher than state prices, and the state procurement station was flooded with farm products (especially grain and cotton) whose market value fell below the state above-quota price. The farmers were adept at marketing. So was the state: It often refused to buy or issued an IOU rather than cash.

Government officials were not prepared for such widespread manipulation of prices and markets. The procurement system was adapted to agricultural shortages fostered by the command economy and thus could not handle the abundance of farm products fostered by market incentives. The problem of scarcity was replaced by one of surplus. In order to encourage farmers to produce more grain, the state raised prices in 1978 by 20 percent for all agricultural products and an additional 50 percent for above-quota grain. The price increase from the state created conditions favorable for farmers to outsmart the state. At the same time, however, the state also raised prices on all agricultural production input goods, such as fertilizer and pesticides, thus offsetting the gain from the agricultural price. In 1991, the total rural agricultural input purchase was 988.8 billion yuan, while the total rural export to the city was 852.31 billion yuan. Thus, rural net imports totaled 136.49 billion yuan.[2]

Once the basic quota was fulfilled, the farmers could sell at the above-quota price. When the rapid increase of production brought down prices, the above-quota prices sometimes exceeded the market prices, encouraging farmers to sell most of their grain at the above-quota prices at the state purchase stations. There were two ways for farmers to make profits through their sale to the state.

First, they increased production so much that large quantities of grain could be sold at the above-quota price, for the quota was set according to the productivity expected by the cadres under the collective system. For example, many farmers in Shandong devoted all their energy to cotton production and increased their production tenfold so that they were able to sell almost all their cotton at the above-quota price.[3] The rapid increase in edible oil production forced the state to lower the purchase price of oil and even use *fengding* (capping, or setting a ceiling, i.e., to limit the amount that farmers could sell).

Second, farmers could manipulate the system. Some farmers would declare that they had a bad harvest and could not meet the quota but actually let other farmers sell their products at the above-quota price and split the bonuses among them.[4] Farmers also colluded with cadres in the state purchasing station to achieve higher-priced sales. As a result, more grain was sold to the state at the above-quota price, by 1983 reaching 72 percent from just 32 percent in 1978.[5]

Market prices soon dropped below above-quota prices, so Chinese farmers gained by selling most of their grain to the state. This reversal of the farmers' fate had important political implications. It challenged the government's emphasis on urban industrial development and its view of the agricultural sector primarily as a source of resources or cheap food subsidized for urban dwellers. This "challenge," however, was not organized; it had no leaders and no ideology. It was the result of the structural implications of the major changes of *baochan daohu*. Collective farming had "feudalized" farmers and had made production and labor an obligation to the state, not a matter of price and market. Under the government's monopsony control, collective peasants had to sell at low prices and buy at high prices. *Baochan daohu* enabled farmers to make a profit manipulating government controls. The rapid increase in production and the manipulation of the procurement system enabled farmers, at least for the moment, to make the state a cash cow.

Another argument says that the high agricultural productivity came from raising purchasing prices, paying above-quota prices, and permitting private marketing on the part of the state. It is true that between 1978 and 1983 the state bought much more grain, 31–72 percent, at above-quota prices, producing real gains for farmers in more prosperous areas, but the state also raised the prices for agricultural inputs (fertilizers and gas), thus balancing the price gain. *Baochan daohu* was essential because it allowed farm families rather than the collectives to enjoy the gain. Under the collective structure, farmers had little incentive to manipulate the above-quota sale.

## The End of the State Procurement System

Farmers' actions, both in increased production and in marketing, caught the state unprepared. In contrast to the "reformed," newly motivated farmers, state commercial organizations did not reform in the early 1980s. They were still under central command. The state was as inept at marketing as it was at planning farming. This created marketing problems that allowed farmers to become the leaders in commerce.

First, state commerce organizations were simply not staffed to deal with 200 million farmer households. The lack of staff in the state purchasing stations in the countryside produced an explosive situation, because farmers had to stand in line for days and nights to sell their products to the state.

Second, the government lacked the technical capacity to receive all the produce from farmers because of a shortage of storage facilities. There were not enough warehouses to hold all the agricultural products. In 1982, farmers hit a record increase of 70 billion jin of grain, and in 1983, another 50 billion increase over 1982.[6] In 1983, many provincial government leaders sent emergency messages warning of the shortage of warehouses and asking the central government to help them export the grain. But state transportation could not deal with the new rural abundance, either. After the bumper crop in 1984, 10.3 billion jin of grain in Jilin and 14.4 billion jin of grain in Henan were awaiting storage.[7] It became technically impossible for the state to absorb the agricultural produce by 1984. Edward Friedman has vivid memories of a 1984 train trip from Dezhou to Tianjin during which he saw endless piles of cotton for miles and miles.[8]

Third, farmers' incentives to sell their products at above-quota prices created problems for the unreformed state commercial departments, whose staff did not have price flexibility in reselling the goods purchased by the state. Thus, the more the state sold, the less the state made. This loss was damaging to the state commercial sector, which was already in the red because of the lack of staff work incentives. Consequently, many state commercial organizations simply gave up buying goods from farmers.

When the government bought agricultural goods from farmers, it did not take good care of those goods, and this led to waste. Because their pay was not tied to their productivity, workers in state purchase stations cared little what happened to the goods they purchased. Fruits, vegetables, fish, and grain rotted in the county warehouses, *but after the farmers had been paid for them*. The waste was so appalling that farmers in Qing County, Hebei Province, coined a jingle to describe the inadequacy and waste of the state purchase station:

Retain the good, and sell the rotten;
Sell the rotten, and rot the good;
Get rid of the old, and store the new.[9]

Fourth, the staff in the state commercial sectors were not able to meet the consumption needs of farmers. After *baochan daohu*, increases in productivity enabled farmers to have more cash to buy desired goods (fertilizers, bicycles, gas, building materials, and farm tools). Farmers' "needs" were no longer limited to food. They now extended to consumer goods. But the state commercial outlets were not meeting their needs.

Fifth, the continuation of urban grain subsidies and the purchase of so much agricultural output led to a state fiscal crisis, a budgetary nightmare. On the one hand, farmers took advantage of the procurement system and sold most of their grain at high prices. On the other hand, the state continued to spend money subsidizing the urban population and urban enterprises. The state's costs remained high because of agricultural abundance and farmers' manipulation of the procurement system, but the sale price in the cities remained low. The state lost money by this arrangement. *The more grain the state took from farmers, the more money the state lost.* Unintentionally, the state marketing system redistributed more to the farmers than it subsidized urban workers in the early 1980s, momentarily closing the long widening gap between the countryside and the city. It was under this budgetary pressure that the state, even the most conservative faction, advocated further loosening control over farm products.[10] The government had created an anomalous system in which the more commodities they bought the higher the prices they paid. Open markets could have changed all that because the rapid increase in grain and other agricultural goods had already driven down the free market prices for all agricultural goods. The government's desire to decrease its debts finally led to more tolerance for markets. As a result, the state made the changes in the rural economy possible. The opening of markets in turn put pressures on collectives to go to *baochan daohu.*

## The State Budget Crisis

The loosening of market control over farm products led to rapid increases in farm goods, which flooded urban markets. Many farmers produced agricultural sideline products and brought them to the city. Urban people welcomed the abundance of food, especially chickens, eggs, fish, pork, and vegetables, but they also needed money to buy those goods. Due to the fact that the wages of workers in state factories had long been frozen and because of inflation pressures, subsidies for urban people increased rapidly. From 1980 to 1987, annual state spending on urban pork subsidies were more than 100 million yuan for Beijing residents, 100 million yuan for Shanghai, and another 100 million yuan for Fujian.[11] Every new baby born with a Beijing *hukou* automatically received 7.5 yuan per month for food subsidies during the 1980s. Throughout the 1980s, the state spent more than 20 billion yuan on urban food subsidies.[12]

In addition, the *danwei* distributed additional subsidies to workers. In Wuhan, workers received money to buy eggs, pork, and fish every month.[13] Subsidies were gradually extended to clothes and furniture and subsidies reserved exclusively for urban residents added to the state budget crisis. It soon became impossible for the state to purchase all the surplus goods of the farmers and to subsidize urban people without causing runaway inflation and serious damage to its fiscal interest.

*The government's inability to handle rural abundance sparked initiatives from farmers, including the independent marketing of their own goods.* Farmers tried to make up for the state's inefficiency by marketing goods on their own. Farmers had always contested the boundaries of household, collective, and market, even under the collectives. After *baochan daohu*, farmers opened up markets with a vengeance. In 1983, the state purchase station was not able to purchase 1 million chickens from farmers in Haian County, Jiangsu Province. Farmers carried chickens on their bicycles to Nanjing markets rather than sell to the government or in local markets. This benefited both urban residents and farmers.[14] Mutual benefits encouraged reform-minded leaders to lift or ignore controls over markets. They argued that the alternative would be a return to the old collective days, which would lead to a depression in farm production. Thus, in 1983, the government expanded produce access to markets and even allowed farmers to participate in long-distance trade. The same government that had prohibited long-distance trade three years before now had to lift its sanctions. Farmers were even allowed to buy trucks and to open restaurants in the cities. Nonetheless, this reform policy did not solve the budget crisis. It could not eliminate the farmers' spontaneous, unorganized, leaderless, nonideological, apolitical, and continuous manipulation of the procurement system.

## The Elimination of the Procurement System

In 1985, the government sought to reduce its financial burdens by ending the procurement system.[15] The state's purpose was to relieve the budget crisis and to insure the purchase of essential goods (grain, cooking oil, and cotton), but the end of official procurement created a quandary for farmers. On the one hand, the further loosening of control over markets gave farmers ever more motivation to engage in commodity production. On the other hand, the end of the procurement system ended the farmers' ability to manipulate procurement. A new system of exchange, *paigou*, replaced the old procurement system.

Under *paigou* (government cadres sent to purchase the grain quota), the state contracted with the individual farm family to set up a sales quota. In this way, the state began to reassert its control over production and marketing by using local cadres to enforce the state's demands. The control over money for sales was not enough to make farmers sell to the state at the low price, however. In many cases, cadres gave farmers IOUs rather than cash. Incentives to sell to the state plummeted. In order to entice farmers to sell grain at the low price, the state adopted a policy of *sanguagou* (three links), in which the state provided 30 percent of agricultural inputs (chemical fertilizer and diesel oil) at a subsidized price and awarded cash advances,[16] but this 30 percent enticement was not attractive in and of itself. In addition, since cadres controlled the subsidized coupons, *sanguagou* frequently did not materialize because the cadres gave them to their relatives or resold them in the markets.

*Paigou* showed how vulnerable farmers were under continuing state domination. It made it easy for the government to make a 15 percent cut in its purchase of grain (80 million tons) in 1985, greatly reducing its budget crisis.[17] In addition, the state lowered the grain purchase price by 10 percent. This policy change led to a decrease in grain, thereby realizing the state goal to lower prices. When the market price rose above the state price after the decrease in grain, farmers did not want to sell to the state anymore. They aimed at the markets.

## The Farmers Take over the Markets

*Paigou*, with its coercion, shows why farmers remained in opposition to the state even after decollectivization. The continuation of the antifarmer policy and the increase in subsidies to urban residents suggest that patterns of political interests have not changed much under Deng's government. The continuation of antirural politics under Deng was well summarized by Edward Friedman:

> The view that the peasantry is satisfied and supportive of the Communist party ignores the continued power of the command economy, whose bloated urban ministries and anti-rural scissors prices have been, since 1985, undermining the agricultural price gains of the original post-Mao reforms; it ignores the corrupt party-state nomenclature that is plundering the rural beneficiaries of the extraordinarily productive early post-Mao reforms; and it ignores the most recent attempts by party conservatives to woo urban workers at the expense of the peasants.[18]

This sharp observation points out the conservative nature of Deng's regime and its exploitation of farmers.

Other scholars, including Daniel Kelliher and Vivienne Shue, have also stressed the post-Mao state domination after *baochan daohu*. But they have only examined the setbacks of farmers and ignored ingenious farmers' tactics in reducing their losses and transforming the system. Although the policy of *paigou* demonstrates the power of the state, farmers did their best to sabotage this new policy, and they were successful.

The most effective way to escape *paigou* was the development of rural industry and a service sector, as well as commercial activities.

Farmers used the power of markets, leading to a rise of commercialization in the countryside. If unplanned *baochan daohu* fundamentally weakened the political structure of the Communist state in rural China, unplanned commercialization weakened its marketing power. Like baochan daohu, the process of commercialization centered on the struggle between farmers and the state, altering the patterns of politics in Deng's era.

## Resistance and the Growth of the Commodity Economy

The elimination of the procurement system was incomplete. On the one hand, through a kind of grain "poll tax" on the contracted land, the state restored some command in production and over marketing grain. Local cadres began to gain some control over the production quota. On the other hand, the state lifted controls over surplus items, especially agricultural sideline items. In fact, the state could not market the items that it controlled. For grain contracts alone, every county had to spend thousands of yuan and send many cadres to work for one or two months.[19] Even so, the state had difficulty making farmers meet its demand. Farmers' defiance can be best expressed by a jingle: "If I don't buy subsidized fertilizer, I do not sell cheap grain. Please Party, forgive me."[20] Local cadres had to spend a lot of time trying to convince farm households to meet the grain quota. As a popular saying among rural cadres says, "Visiting numerous households; speaking numerous words; inevitably offending numerous families."[21]

Although open confrontation did occur, the most important means for farmers to protect their interests and weaken the damaging effect of state policies was by commercializing agriculture. Farmers tried to avoid producing products that were subject to state procurement, focusing their efforts instead on commercial products. Although many farmers still produced grain for their own consumption, the land used to harvest commercial crops (sold on the market) increased 49 percent after 1985, and the land used for grain dropped 9 percent, intensifying the powerful trend observed since the market opened in 1978, with acceleration in the 1984 bumper year.

Table 4.1 shows that the growth rate for grain and oil (somewhat controlled by the state) was much slower than the growth rate for other commercial products.[22] This shift in planting was a net economic gain for farm families, the locality, and the country as a whole. Since most cash crops were bought and sold at the free markets, which were free by default if not by ideal, their increase helped to expand the development of markets.

Although the end of *tonggou* procurement gave impetus to farmers' commercial activities, farmers had begun to produce goods for the market as soon as *baochan daohu* took hold. In 1980, 36,000 rural markets were set up,[23] but after the end of the procurement system, market growth in the countryside accelerated. Farmers could participate in the commodity economy in two ways: selling products themselves; and processing their products and selling them in markets directly as consumer goods.

## Garden Economy and the Rise of Rural Merchants

At the very beginning of the reform, farmer families everywhere began to produce goods for the market. Eighty percent of farm families developed a *tingyuan jingji* (garden economy), which could actually include any of the following: two gardens (vegetables and fruits); two pens (for fowl and livestock); one fish pond; and one small factory. Farm families made effective use of the land around their houses and gardens to produce for the markets. In one survey in 1986, 85 percent of farm households gave cash income as the principal reason for raising pigs.[24] Although the commodity economy was small in scale, it contributed a substantial part of farm family cash income. Since so many farm families produced those goods, the aggregate impact of the garden economy on the market was great. In Shengyang, for example, by the mid-1980s, 42 percent of milk, 45 percent of eggs, 50 percent of pork, and 90 percent of fowl came from garden economies.[25]

In addition, a substantial portion of grain was also sold at the market despite the state supply system. The proportion purchased by the state decreased rapidly throughout the 1980s. In fact, by 1991, two-thirds of all grain was sold at markets, despite the *paigou* system.[26]

While farmers flooded markets with their produce, increasing numbers went to the markets without any commodities and engaged in purchase and sale, both in the local areas and in the cities. They became middlemen. Prices varied from region to region, so they could make a living by long-distance trade, which enabled supply to meet demand. They bought low at one place and sold high at the next, making a profit. Before 1983, the state tried to prohibit profitmaking by trade and forbade farmers to buy large vehicles to transport agricultural goods for profiteering purposes. The farmers used bribes to pass the driving test. Some farmers with illegal licenses drove farm vehicles, decreasing efficiency gains and greatly increasing the highway death toll, especially since some farmers do not consider beer alcohol.[27] The very prohibition, however, pointed to a practice already out of hand.

Although some rural merchants undertook long-distance trade, most were locally oriented in the beginning. Most farm families were engaged in local trade, both as producers and as merchants. Very quickly, though, as productivity increased and state marketing organizations proved unable to take in farmers' goods, rural merchants increased. At first, their numbers were small and their scale limited, but small-scale merchants, especially

**Table 4.1**

Growth Rate of Goods in the Market (percentages)

| Product | 1981–1984 | 1984–1985 |
|---|---|---|
| Grain and oil | 7.3 | 8.8 |
| Eggs and poultry | 21.5 | 52.6 |
| Fish produce | 26.9 | 37.8 |
| Vegetables | 15.5 | 47.4 |
| Fruits | 25.5 | 37.1 |

Source: *Fazhan Yanjiusuo (Development Research Institute), Gaige mianlin zhidu chuangxin (Reform and System Innovation) (Shanghai: Sanlian Chubanshe, 1988), p.51.*

rural peddlers, restored the longstanding interdependence between the countryside and the city that had been disrupted for twenty-five years. For farmers living close to the city, selling goods to urban people was part of daily life. They brought their produce to the city to sell. Rural peddlers and merchants from farther away traveled with their farm goods and family handicrafts everywhere, finding their way onto the city streets. Rural merchants and peddlers packed the buses bound for the city. Often those buses were so full of carrying poles, sacks of grain, potatoes, fruit, vegetables, fowl, and locally produced tools and handicrafts that the farmers in the buses were known as "acrobatic troupes" coming to town.

These merchants and peddlers also brought consumer goods to local villagers. Farm families spent more and more on consumer goods. Nonmarketable production decreased from 54 percent in 1978 to 27 percent in 1985.[28]

Very soon, the rural merchants began to participate in longer-distance trade. In order to increase their cash income, many farmers gave up agricultural production to specialize in trading, to become merchants. Farmers pioneered in trading in the People's Republic. In Xinmin County, Liaoning Province, more than ten thousand farmers in the mid-1980s specialized in trading, known as *wanren mabang* (thousands of mobile merchants), and a whole village specialized in egg trading, known as *daodan jidi* (a pun, that sounds like both "egg trading base" and "causing trouble").[29] The importance of trade in the farmers' life could be seen from the machines they owned. Trucks, small trucks, and tractors were the most popular machines (all used for transport). According to a 1986 government survey, the percentage of farm families that owned trucks increased by 100 percent after 1984, and the average farm household spent 239 yuan on transportation facilities, a 62 percent increase over 1984.[30] *Farmers were the first class in China to own private cars, trucks, and tractors.* The possession of modern transportation enabled farmers to become national merchants. By 1982, rural merchants were responsible for 80 percent of agricultural sideline marketing.[31] Yet, officially, long-distance trade was still illegal. The state did not legalize long-distance trade until 1983.

In Fuzhou District, Jiangxi Province, 105,000 farmers became merchants in the mid-1980s.[32] There were 11,000 rural merchants in Zhucheng County, Shandong Province, in 1987, 610 of them trading fowl and livestock.[33] In 1986, they helped the local farmers trade 17 percent of the pigs, 41 percent of the ducks and the geese, and 40 percent of the eggs outside the county.

Furthermore, rural merchants went from a single agricultural product and a single trade into a wide variety of goods. At the beginning, in 1980, rural merchants were seasonal. They went to markets when certain agricultural commodities were in their harvest season. Some of those rural merchants later became professional, even full-time traders. Gradually rural merchants began to trade nonagricultural products as well. With the rise of rural industry in the 1980s, rural merchants were also trading industrial goods and consumer goods. By the end of the 1980s, annual sales of largely industrial goods from rural Zhejiang alone amounted to 5 billion yuan at *jishi*, the farmers' markets.[34]

Rural merchants became formidable competitors for urban state sales organizations for five reasons:

First, they are competitive because of their economic independence. As former farmers, they benefited from *baochan daohu* and ran their businesses as independent entities. They pay attention to their profits and the market. They respond to market signals.

Second, they are more competitive in terms of agricultural products. As farmers, they have a good working knowledge of their products, which the urban state staff does not have. For perishable agricultural products, this knowledge is crucial for the success of businesses, especially if the goods are overproduced and must be stored or processed.

Third, farmers work hard to take care of their goods because every rotten product costs them money. They are responsible for their losses. Their counterparts, the state workers, do not have to worry about whether their goods will be sold. Independent rural merchants try hard to sell their goods.

Fourth, rural merchants can purchase their high-quality goods when they are plentiful. With supply surpassing demand, the more competitive survive. It is no surprise that the state sales enterprises went under. Rural merchants are able to lower their prices when the market is in recession because their costs are also lower. Very quickly, they took over a substantial part of the state commercial sectors.

Finally, farmers want to get the cadres off their backs and to work for family profit. Those motivations have made them competitive and tough in the market. For them, economic freedom offered a great opportunity.

Almost all state sales organizations were soon running in the red. For example, twenty-six out of twenty-nine state commercial organizations in

Yinde County, Guangdong Province, lost 480,000 yuan in 1985. Rural merchants threatened the production of food processing factories in the city. One rural merchant in Changsha City, Hunan Province, sold as much as a dozen workers in a state shop in 1985, costing the government more in subsidies for those workers.[35]

Moreover, the rise of rural merchants restored social mobility. Trading became the fastest way to climb the social ladder. In virtually all Chinese villages, merchant families (mostly peddlers and petty traders) were the best off. For social mobility, the merchant route is the preferred one. This rural social mobility affects urban social mobility as well (see Chapter 6).

## The Rise of the Rural Service Sector

The rise of rural merchants promoted rural specialization. Frequent urban contacts enabled some rural people to open restaurants, shops, and beauty shops in the city, a topic to be dealt with in Chapter 5. *Services became a second source, after rural industry, of nonagricultural employment.*

### Transportation and Construction Services

Many rural people were involved in sending agricultural production into the city and bringing urban industrial and other consumer goods back to the countryside. For example, in Xinmin County, Liaoning Province, there were 10,789 farmer households that specialized in trade in 1984; they possessed 7,700 trucks and tractors to transport goods. In that county alone, 1,800 farm households established business contacts with more than 100 urban restaurants, shops, and urban *getihu* (individual private business) in three big cities—Shenyang, Fushun, and Bengxi.[36]

More and more farm families began to own their own means of transportation. By 1986, they possessed 4,164,000 small tractors (92 percent of the total tractors) and 318,000 trucks (64 percent of the total trucks in China).[37] This is consistent with my observation in Tongxin Village, Hubei, where one-fifth of the households in the village had a small tractor by 1986.

Rural construction trade boomed after *baochan daohu*, when farmers used their newly made money to build new houses. By 1986, the total value of rural construction reached 59,193,000,000 yuan, almost 8 percent of the total social output in the countryside.[38] Farmers' per capita housing space increased from 8 square meters in 1978 to 15 square meters in 1986.[39] The rural construction boom led to the rise of rural construction teams in the urban areas. In 1978, rural transportation output was valued at 35 billion yuan and rural construction at 135 billion yuan, but in 1993, transportation was worth 1.5 trillion yuan, increased by a factor of 40, and construction was multiplied by 20, to 2.7 trillion yuan.[40]

### Rapid Development of Jishi

In the course of a decade, the sale of vegetables, meat, eggs, and fish passed from overwhelming dominance by state commercial organizations to a strong majority of sales in private markets. For example, there was an increasing share of *jishi*, the periodic rural markets (see Table 4.2), whose essence is distribution.

*Jishi* originally meant the market town in the countryside, but it has played such an important part in the daily life of urban people that there is a saying among urban Chinese: "One can get by without going to the stores (usually government owned) for ten days, but one cannot survive one day without going to a *jishi*." In contemporary China, the main body of commercial activities at *jishi* was conditioned by farmers and rural craftsmen. Through the efforts of rural merchants, the life of urban people became increasingly linked to the services of rural-based merchants. With the disappearance of long queues and coupons for food, urban people's dependence on urban cadres and *danwei* for food coupons weakened. The urban folk, too, have enjoyed the freedom, efficiency, and ease of rural-based markets. An escape from personal dependency to the impersonality of the market feels liberating.

In 1983, the number of *jishi* reached 48,003, constituting 14 percent of retail sales. In 1989, 70 percent of goods in the cities were sold at *jishi*, mainly by rural merchants. By 1991, there were 6,390,200 rural nonstate marketing organizations, involving 13,980,800 rural merchants, who controlled one-third of retail sales of agricultural products. With the exception of grain, cotton, oil, tobacco, and silk cocoons, by 1990 almost all agricultural products came from *jishi*, whereas in 1979, only 15 percent of all products came from *jishi*.[41]

The development of *jishi* proved economically beneficial to the state from the budgetary point of view. First, the state collected taxes from *jishi* markets. From 1980 to 1989, merchants at *jishi* paid 20 billion yuan in taxes.[42] Second, everything sold at the state shops was subsidized by the state, whereas there were no subsidies for products sold in *jishi*. Thus, the larger the *jishi* share, the less the state spent. *Jishi* were not limited to agricultural goods and later evolved into comprehensive markets across China, but rural merchants and farmers have remained the key players in the *jishi* system both in the countryside and in the cities. Because urban people rely on *jishi* for their daily food, farmers and exfarmers, in fact, are in charge of the urban grocery business. Farmers and merchants (most of them exfarmers) were the dominant sellers both in the countryside and in the cities.

### Village Trade

All buying and selling among farmers did not occur in markets. In fact, many trading activities took place inside the village between villagers and rural merchants. Special rural traders collected goods in villages. Every household had something to sell and wanted to buy things. Until very recently, state regulations made it clear that trading was legal only after state quotas were fulfilled, but local avoidance was easy and successful. In addition, the state prohibited the trading of some agricultural products. Farmers close to the cities would take produce to the cities, but local merchants (exfarmers) would go to gather goods from farm households and sell them in the city. Across the nation, even in small villages, there were sales networks. In one village, two hundred households were involved in trade. They established dozens of sales networks across the nation, selling 2 million kilograms of oranges per year. By 1992, in Kai County, Sichuan Province, alone, more than one hundred thousand farmers were involved in trade. They possessed a thousand trading boats.[43]

## Roadside Markets, Specialty Markets, and Wholesale Markets

The rapid development of wholesale markets is an important aspect of the rural service sector. Farmers used every opportunity to make a profit. Farmers living close to a highway developed roadside markets. They planted cash crops along the highway and piled up their products along the road for sale. In this way, they expanded local *jishi*. Some even put up a small shop that could also be used as a watch post for their products at night. Since those products (fish, vegetables, watermelons, and other agricultural products) did not involve transportation costs, they were both cheap and fresh. Road markets became popular. When a certain product was in season, rural merchants and urban government organizations would go to road markets to buy fresh agricultural products.

The wholesale vegetable market in Jiang County, Shanxi Province, was formed in the following way. At first, vegetable farmers living close to the county seat gathered along the road to the county trying to sell their vegetables to truckers and passers-by. But the road market grew so huge that thirty-four organizations with different ownership structures and two hun-

**Table 4.2**

Sales Share of *Jishi* vs. the State Commercial Organizations in Cities (percentages)

| Year | Vegetable | Beef/Mutton | Eggs | Fowl | Fish |
|------|-----------|-------------|------|------|------|
| 1979 | 7 | 12 | 31 | 39 | 10 |
| 1989 | 139 | 188 | 103 | 232 | 184 |

*Source: Liu Xuemin, Zhongguo shangye bao (Chinese Commerce News), October 11, 1990.*

*The Ta Zhongsi agricultural sideline retail market,
"Beijing City's Big Vegetable Basket," attracts
farmers from all over the country, providing hundreds of kinds of vegetables for Beijing residents.
Photo by Tang Zhaoming*

dred vegetable farmers lined up forming a five mile–long road market. This
became a market that specialized in vegetables and did business with more
than ten neighboring counties and dozens of big and medium-sized cities.[44]
     Of course, product-based specialty markets were not limited to roads.
Many specialty markets grew because of the famous products of certain
places. For example, Gaozhong and Mu villages in Jiangsu Province were
well known for rabbit fur. Good quality and high productivity drew many
merchants and factories to the area. Gradually, Gaozhong became a rabbit

fur specialty market selling truckloads of fur to several provinces and involving hundred of merchants.[45]

Development of wholesale markets was not limited to the countryside. Rural merchants also went to cities and formed roadside markets on the busy city streets. Since state regulations made it difficult or too costly for rural merchants to rent a shop at commercial centers, rural merchants took to the streets to sell to commuters and travelers and to form markets close to train and bus stations. These spontaneous markets grew so fast that some of them developed into wholesale or specialty markets. One of the most successful wholesale markets is the Beijing Dazhongshi market. Dazhongshi was a busy *jishi* dominated by rural merchants (most from Hebei, close to Beijing) selling their agricultural products. The market grew so quickly that many farmers began to specialize in wholesale trade. Beijing-area farmers seized the opportunity to formalize the wholesale trade center. In the early 1990s, rural merchants from twenty-six provinces and six hundred counties across China sent their goods there. The Dazhongshi wholesale market occupied such an important place in the Beijing agricultural markets that 80–95 percent of vegetable sales in Beijing were soon coming through the Dazhongshi wholesale market.[46]

Although the state also developed some wholesale markets for agricultural goods in the city, those wholesale markets are different from the ones developed by rural merchants. First, all prices in the spontaneous wholesale markets are subject to fluctuation, whereas those in the state-run wholesale markets are generally fixed. Second, anyone is allowed to participate in trade in the spontaneous wholesale markets, whereas only licensed members are allowed to trade in the state-controlled markets. Most members are organizations and enterprises of the government. In other words, rural merchants dominated wholesale markets that were markets of equals, one of the primary requirements of a free market! Any buyer or seller, regardless of residence, origin, occupation, or wealth, is allowed to participate in exchange. Third, the spontaneous wholesale markets deal with agricultural and nonagricultural businesses, whereas the state wholesale markets are largely limited to grain and meat. In fact, many markets trading goods throughout China evolved from the agricultural *jishi* run by rural merchants. By 1990, there were 1,267 wholesale markets for agricultural goods and 239 small commodity markets, all developed on a nonplanned base.[47] The spontaneous wholesale markets could increase diversity at will; the state markets were fixed in this sense as well.

In addition to their multiple uses as marketplaces, roads both in the cities and in the countryside have become selling grounds for almost anything.

### Roadside Inns, Shops, and Restaurants

In addition to the sale of goods, farmers also pioneered in private restaurants and innkeeping. In almost all cities, exfarmers run restaurants every-

*This eighty-year-old grandmother from rural Guangdong sells aprons on the street. Photo by Kate Xiao Zhou*

where. Along major highways, thousands of restaurants and motels flourish because traders need somewhere to eat and sleep. For example, there were 107 restaurants and motels in one section of Highway 320 (the Zhejiang–Fujian highway), averaging 1 restaurant every 317 meters. In 1987, there were more than 550,000 private roadside restaurants in Guangdong, employing 109,000 rural people; by 1988, the number had jumped to 779,000 roadside restaurants and 171,000 rural people.[48] The farm-based development of restaurants and services is an important part of Chinese privatization. By 1993, out of 1.6 million shops and restaurants, 1.2 million were in either farmers' or cooperative rural people's hands; out of 1.7 million hotels and travel agencies, 1.3 million were owned by private families and joint households.[49] The rise in roadside service did not cost the state one penny. There was no leader to tell the farmers to open the restaurants. The development was spontaneous and leaderless. With so many farmers selling goods and engaging in services, the regulations over migration that had been reinforced by urban food coupons and other forms of rationing were losing their power. This development meant that the use of food coupons and other form of rationing to control either urban or rural people became virtually useless—another leaching away of

*Wuchang farmers in Hubei provide fish for the market. Photo by Li Yifang*

authoritarian control. The government may again try to use food coupons to please urban residents, but the use of the rationing coupon to control rural–urban migration is past history in China.

## Corruption and Marketing

Corruption has played an important role for rural people trying to gain market share in both agricultural and industrial products. A particularly profitable area for collusion between rural industries and state officials is that of marketing goods for rural industries. At the beginning, state marketing organizations would not take products from rural industries. Rural industries had to sell everything on their own. Some rural industries began to give state marketing cadres *huikou* (kickback money) and bribed their way to a public market for their products.

Marketing people from rural industry often bribed an important marketing cadre by giving him or her a percentage of the sale of their products. The commissioned cadre often tried his or her best to sell the products to the state shops and *danwei*. The Liushi (Zhejiang Province) low-voltage electrical appliance markets are a good example. The high commission encouraged buyers from all over China to buy electrical appliances at Liushi. Orders poured in from all over the nation. One market town in Liushi received 25,000 telegrams every month. By 1985, there were 90 transport consignment stations in 3 markets, in charge of shipping 2,500 tons of goods per month.[50] The Liushi low-voltage electrical appliances market developed into a national market and further stimulated the growth of electrical appliance production in the area.

When the director of a state railway company in Harbin City, Heilongjiang, became known locally as a "greedy cat," many rural sales people began to knock at his door. One Shandong man found the director's home and told his wife: "I am from a light fixture factory in Zhaoyuan County, Shandong. I would like the director to help us by buying our factory products. I am from far away and did not bring anything with me. Please accept the 1,000 yuan and buy some cigarettes and wine for the director."[51]

*Farmers from all over China came to Shenzhen to make money. This female restaurant owner from the rural North opened a restaurant catering to those who prefer the Northern style. Photo by Kate Xiao Zhou.*

It is important to note that rural merchants and sales people approached the official first. So when the director was arrested, he insisted on his inno-cence: "I think bribery is an exchange between power and money. But my case is different since they came to me and sent me money and gifts. I never asked them for anything."[52]

*Huikou* encourages important state officials to purchase products from rural industries. Although *huikou* is an old standard business term, under the People's Republic this supposedly indicated a covert practice. It is through rural industrial firms that sales clerks in the state firms learned the linkage between pay and profitmaking.

## Local Government

There is no doubt that where the economy boomed in the countryside and local government grew rich, local officials had more resources. Issues were complex, however, because the power of the local governments was also encroached upon by the increased power of the markets and rural merchants. When farmers' production became linked to market demands, the farmers sought to maximize profits; they developed a drive difficult for the cadres to contain. Because they were not organized, they could only be contained separately. Local cadres whose authority was challenged tried every means to reverse the market trend. After 1985, a decrease in grain drove the market price up 10 percent, but the state refused to raise its price. Some farmers abandoned grain farming, but grain farmers tried to avoid the state plan system and tried to sell at the market price. In order to guarantee the purchase plan, the state set up regulations for every level of administration to enforce the purchase of cheap grain from farmers. Whenever one level of government failed to deliver the fixed quota, that government body would have to buy high-priced grain to meet urban demand. In order to provide lower-level cadres with incentives to enforce the plan, the state allowed local cadres to control the sales money and allowed some control over agricultural inputs. By so doing, the state attempted to restore the relations of depen-dency between cadres and farmers. Under family farming, the relation-ship between farmers and cadres was not important. By giving cadres some control over the finances of farmers, the Deng regime restored some of the former unhappy elements, but farmers had now tasted mar-kets. They tried to escape the new command economy or to reduce the power of the plan by selling in the market. Local governments' response was to close local markets, making it "illegal" to sell grain at the markets. In Hubei, farmers had a saying to describe the government behavior: "When grain is scarce, the state wants all; when grain is plentiful, the state wants multiple channels in the markets. It's not ghosts in the world but human beings who make trouble."[53]

To counteract the new impositions, farmers tried to sell their produce outside local markets. Many local governments had to use road blockades and repression to try to stop the flow of farm goods. This pattern of local antimarket behavior tightened when the reforms decentralized power. During the reform period, local governments (both provincial and county governments) also adopted an industrial development policy that sought to keep farmers as cheap providers of raw material and food. In order to make sure that farmers sold to local governments at lower official prices, many local governments set up blockades to prevent farmers from seeking profits elsewhere. In order to increase local revenue from local industries, local governments at all levels tried to capture more local farm goods at below-market prices. In provincial, county, and township government, each added its own version of procurement targets.[54]

For example, in 1981, Jiangxi orange farmers had a good harvest, but the Jiangxi provincial government prohibited farmers from selling oranges to Guangdong and demanded that all oranges be delivered according to the plan to Nanchang's canned fruit factories and other local factories. When the harvest came, however, those local factories refused to take oranges from Jiangxi because of the high transportation cost; oranges then rotted in many farmers' homes. In Xingan County alone, 1 million jin of oranges spoiled. Interference hurt the economic interests of the farmers, and anything that hurt the economic interest of the farmers was difficult to enforce. Farmers tried their best to flow around the local government restrictions and sell their goods at a higher price. They had learned market participation. Smuggling was not new to the Chinese and was readily relearned. Even in 1981, the farmers in Jiangxi were rushing their goods to Guangdong, frustrating the plan leaders.[55]

Farmers' market exchanges created markets and destroyed the wall that separated areas. When the local government tried to force farmers to sell their products to local enterprises, farmers waited for the best bidders. The politics of regional protectionism failed as a result of farmers' noncooperation. In 1986, when rice production fell and prices rose, the Hunan government decided to place a rice trade embargo against neighboring Guangdong. In one neighboring county, Lin Xiang, Hunan, the government sent the militia to patrol the provincial border and set up more than twenty road posts along the border in an attempt to prevent Hunan rice from being sold in Guangdong markets. They captured 200 grain merchants from Guangdong and confiscated 550,000 jin of grain, but this local government effort was not able to stop the flow of rice to Guangdong. Hunan farmers organized their version of the "Ho Chi Minh Trail" (as it was referred to in rural Hunan); thousands of farmers carried loads of rice to Guangdong. A substantial portion of Hunan rice went to Guangdong markets through this Ho Chi Minh Trail despite the local government's blockade.[56]

# Rise of Guilds

Farmers also sought mutual aid by setting up neighborhood or kinship organizations, such as *hui* (associations in which several households, more often perhaps from the same locality or relatives, pool money together to help someone in need, and every other household in turn gets money from each *hui* member). Such *hui* have existed in China for thousands of years. Apart from *huitou* (the head of the *hui* is someone who starts the *hui* or for whom the *hui* is established), the rest of the *hui* members determined their chance of receiving money in turn (often through a lottery). The *hui*, a very old form of organization, was a way of starting up private farm businesses. The *hui* could function as a network for capital formation.

The more developed the market, the more widespread the use of rural *hui*. In Wenzhou, Zhejiang Province, for example, *hui* have contributed to the success of the rural market economy. In 1985, when the state budget crunch affected enterprises, economic activities in many enterprises were constrained, but the local credit networks remained active and guaranteed the necessary capital for investment, assuming thereby a crucial banking function. In 1985, rural family industry in Wenzhou grew 42 percent despite state budget controls.

By 1986, private credit organizations had emerged in Wenzhou, including two private banks. These were the first private banks in the People's Republic of China. But the government was alarmed at the rise of private financial power and in 1986 issued a banking law to ban private financial organization.[57] Although formal banks were banned by decree, informal capital markets flourished in rural Fujian, Guangdong, Zhejiang, Anhui, Shandong, and Hunan. As a result, rural areas became the source of private finance. For example, a Zhejiang stock company started with 30,000 yuan from the informal rural credit market and initiated financial undertakings that contributed to considerable changes in China's financial system.

Another important organization was the *xiehui* (mutual assistance association). *Xiehui* were first organized among farmer households that specialized in commodity products. Rural *xiehui* combined many features of traditional commercial guilds. The chief purpose of these organizations was to provide farmers with information about production and marketing. Their primary moral motto was *zijiu zizhu* (self-reliance and self-help). The *xiehui* were apolitical. Economic benefit was the main concern of every member. As a result, *xiehui* were allowed to exist in China as nonstate organizations, making farmers the first group to organize nonstate organizations at all levels in the People's Republic of China. Another focus of *xiehui* was the goods themselves. This is reflected in the fact that a whole series of *xiehui* were named for the farm production they organized, such as cotton, rice, or fish. There was suddenly a sense of pride in being a cotton grower or an orange grower. One was admitted as a full *xiehui* member by producing special agricultural goods. For example, chicken producers organized a chicken *xiehui* and cotton growers set up a cotton *xiehui*. They exchanged information on the market, new technology, and state policy. For example, the chicken *xiehui* provided necessary immunization for its members' chickens. Some *xiehui* even began to have their own publications.

Since *xiehui* provided economic benefits to their members, they grew rapidly. In 1986, there were seventy three chicken and vegetable *xiehui* in Fengren County, Hebei.[58] In Hanyang County, Hubei, alone, there were eighty-eight *xiehui* even in 1986.[59] Their activities aroused considerable contemporary enthusiasm. No Chinese county was without numerous associations. These organizations greatly altered dependency relations in the countryside and reduced cadres' control over information and markets. Although they had political effects, they were themselves nonideological and apolitical: Some of the functions they performed had been carried out by lineage organizations and guilds of various sorts in pre-Communist China. There has so far been no recognized attempt at overall organization and leadership of those broadly scattered organizations. Thus, they are often autonomous in nature.

In addition, these *xiehui* often extended over many provinces, providing mechanisms for members to evade local intervention. One of their most important consequences is that *xiehui* became marketing organizations for farmers.

## Conclusion

The rising supply of rich and varied agricultural goods after *baochan daohu* led to a rapid increase in free markets in China. The growth of farmers' markets ended the state's market control and increased interdependence on a grand scale. If *baochan daohu* altered the relationship between the local cadres and the farmers within the collective structure, the development of markets altered the relationship between the state and farmers outside the villages. This development touched off and at the same time deflected conflicts among the state, urban consumers, farmers, local governments, and the whole national economic system. Above all, rural merchants simplified the process of administrative bureaucracies and delivered goods directly to consumers. As they flourished, they furnished the distributive sinews for rapid economic growth—sinews the formal bureaucracies of the People's Republic did not provide.

When previously unavailable opportunities opened, farmers eagerly seized them to make money. They took the state by surprise through rapid increases in productivity and manipulation of the state plan, forcing an end to the *tonggou tongxiao* procurement system. Farmers were far ahead

of urban people in market activities. Urban people left markets to special-
ists, who were easily replaced by rural merchants. As a result of market
expansion and the hard work of rural merchants, a substantial portion of
farmers' total economic activities was transferred to the market. Even in
1985, when very few urban people participated in market activities, the
rate of rural-produced commodities reached 64 percent of all rural production; cash income per capita accounted for 66 percent of total individual
income, more than 60 percent of the total volume of retail sales was realized in the countryside, and 60 percent of the market currency of the
whole country was in the farmers' pockets.[60] By 1988, there were over
sixty thousand markets in the countryside, double the number in 1980.[61]
Rural merchants, not urban merchants, came to lead commercial activities
both in the cities and in the countryside.

The growth of markets greatly increased interdependence and altered
the structure of the countryside. In 1989, the value of nonagricultural production surpassed that of agricultural production, reaching 55 percent.[62]

The rise of rural merchants has far-reaching implications for social
mobility in China. In Imperial China, the ideal and often actual pattern for
social mobility was to get an education and take the official examinations
in order to become a government official. However, another actual pattern
was becoming a merchant.[63] Successful merchants, if they could, would try
to educate their sons to become officials.

A new pattern for social mobility has formed now, and trading has
become a preferred vehicle of social mobility. For millions of farmers,
becoming merchants is *the way* to gain economic independence. As one
rural saying goes, "If one wants to become wealthy and powerful, one
gives up farming and becomes a merchant."[64] The more a farm family sells
and buys, the more its economic life is attached to the market and freed
from state control. Commercial activity is liberating—not democratic, but
liberating—a major way out of governmental control.

This changing pattern for social mobility has far-reaching social consequences for Chinese economic development. A general shift toward commerce is taking root in the thinking of people both in the city and in the
countryside. In the 1950s, when the Communist state copied elements of
Stalinism, engineers were highly respected. One popular saying went, "If
one is good at math, physics, and chemistry, one will have good fortune
wherever one goes." In the 1960s and 1970s, when social mobility became
fixed by *hukou* and status categorization, there was a saying: It is more
important to have a good father [i.e., from a "good" social class] than to be
good in math, physics, and chemistry." By the end of 1980s, the slogan
was, "It is more important to be engaged in commerce than to be good in
math, physics, and chemistry."

Almost all studies of development attribute the growth of markets to
urbanization.[65] The Chinese experience suggests that rural-based market

development can be an alternative pattern. It was primarily the farmers who founded markets and sparked China's market-oriented renaissance. From 1979 to 1988, the average growth in consumption was 7.6 percent, and farmers accounted for an 8.1 percent and urban residents for a 5.9 percent increase.[66] This contrasted sharply to 1.8 percent growth from 1958 to 1978. Government subsidies created some of the urban increase, but private family initiative was the source of the farmers' increase. The political consequence of this socioeconomic transformation is an open question. Can farmers' networks constitute something comparable to earlier republics such as the Italian city-states or the Hanseatic League? So far, everything the farmers have accomplished has been without any organized political movement, without any identifiable leadership, and without any ideology into which a still powerful state apparatus could sink its teeth.

The central government, which literally had at least potential control of virtually everything in China, really did not think much about the farmers. They thought about heavy industry and the urban sector, so what took place among the farmers slipped right out from under them, caught them unawares, until the results were so widespread and powerful in terms of a double-digit real growth rate that officials were more likely to claim credit than to interfere.

## Notes

1. *People's Daily,* July 6, 1982.

2. Zhongguo Shehui Kexueyuan Nongcun Fazhan Yanjiusuo, *1992 nian Zhongguo nongcun jingji fazhan niandu baogao* (A 1992 Report on Chinese Rural Economic Development) (Beijing: Zhongguo Kexue Chubanshe, 1993), pp. 153–154.

3. Cai Ji and Fang Jia, "Gaige jiage butie de shexiang" (Tentative Plans for Reforming Price Subsidies), *Jihua jingji yanjiu* 21 (1983):15, quoted in Daniel Kelliher, *Peasant Power in China: The Era of Rural Reform 1979–1988* (New Haven: Yale University Press, 1992), p. 128.

4. *Nongmin ribao* (Farmers' Daily), September 26, 1988.

5. Kelliher, *Peasant Power in China,* p. 133.

6. Gao Xiaomeng. "Lishixing de zhuangzhe" (The Historical Turning Point), in Zhongguo Nongcun Fazhan Wenti Yanjiu, ed., *Nongcun, jingji, shehui* (Rural China, Economy and Society), vol. 4 (Beijing: Nongcun Dushu Chubanshe, 1986), pp. 8–23.

7. *People's Daily,* January 16, 1985.

8. Personal communication with Edward Friedman, December 1993.

9. In Chinese: *Cunhaode maihuaide, mailande huai haode-tuijiu cunxin.*

10. Chen Yizi, *Zhongguo: shinian gaige yu bajiu minyun* (China: Ten-Year Reform and 1989 Democracy Movement) (Taipei: Lianjing

Chuban Shiye Gongsi, 1991); and Sheng Hua, et al., *China: From Revolution to Reform* (London: Macmillan, 1993).

11. *People's Daily*, February 1, 1988.

12. Shang Xiaoyuan, *Zhongguo guoming de ziwo yizhixing renge* (Self-inflicted Depressed Personality in China) (Kunmin: Yunnan Renmin Chubanshe, 1989), pp. 4–34.

13. Personal interviews with factory managers in the Wuhan Copier Factory in 1985.

14. *People's Daily*, January 5, 1984.

15. Sheng, et al., *China: From Revolution to Reform*.

16. For a good discussion of *sanguagou*, see Terry Sicular, "China's Agricultural Policy During the Reform Period," in Joint Economic Committee, Congress of the United States, eds., *China's Economic Dilemmas in the 1990's: The Problems of Reforms, Modernization, and Interdependence* (Washington, D.C.: Government Printing Office, 1991), pp. 340–364, esp. 354–355.

17. Sheng, et al., *China: From Revolution to Reform*.

18. Edward Friedman, "Deng Versus the Peasantry: Recollectivization in the Countryside," *Problems of Communism* 39 (September 1990):30.

19. Gao Xiaomeng and Xiang Ning, *Zhongguo nongye jiage zhengce fenxi* (Policy Analysis of Chinese Agricultural Price) (Hangzhou: Zhejiang Renmin Chubanshe, 1992), p. 57.

20. In Chinese: *Pingjia huafei wobumai, pingjia liangshi wobumai; qing dang yuanliang*.

21. In Chinese: *Zoubian qianjia wanhu; shuojin qianyen wanyu; dezui qianjiawanhu*.

22. Aubert also argues that farmers raised production most slowly on commodities for which state extraction was highest. See Claude Aubert, "The Agricultural Crisis in China at the End of the 1980s," in Jørgen Delman, et al., eds., *Remaking Peasant China: Problems of Rural Development and Institutions at the Start of the 1990s* (Aarhus, Denmark: Aarhus University Press, 1990), pp. 16–37.

23. *People's Daily*, March 10, 1980.

24. Lu Mai and Dai Xiaojing, "Xianjieduan nonghu jingji xingwei qianxi" (A Preliminary Analysis of Economic Behavior of Contemporary Farm Households), *Economic Research* 7 (1987):68–74.

25. Zhang Zhiwen, *Zhongguo nongcun jiating jingying* (Family Management in Rural China) (Beijing: Jingji Guanli Chubanshe, 1989), p. 103.

26. Lu Wen, "Nongcun ruhe fazhan shehui zhuyi shichang jingji?" (How Should We Develop Socialist Market Economy in the Countryside?), *Nongye jingji wenti* (Problems of Agricultural Economics) 12 (1992):7–11.

27. Edward Friedman, personal communications, 1994.

28. Statistical Bureau of China, *Statistical Year Book of China 1986* (Hongkong: Longman Group, 1986).

29. Wen Tiejun, "Nongchanpin liutong zhong xinjingyingzhe xingwei fengxi" (The Behavior of Newly Engaged Managers in Agricultural Marketing), *Nongye jingji wenti* (Problems of Agricultural Economics) 7 (1991):44–52.

30. Zhang, *Family Management in Rural China*, p. 160.

31. *People's Daily*, May 16, 1983.

32. He Qianfeng, "Nongmin jinru shichang wenti di tansuo"(Farmers Enter the Market: An Economic Analysis), *Nongye jingji wenti* (Problems of Agricultural Economics) 5 (1987):26–32.

33. *People's Daily*, February 19, 1987.

34. Liu Xuemin (Director of the State Commercial Bureau), "Speech on National *Jishi* Conference," *Zhongguo gongshang pao* (Chinese Commerce News), October 11, 15, 18, 1990. *Jishi* originally meant rural markets, but rapid development of rural markets swept the city in the 1980s. Now *jishi* means any markets dominated by rural people.

35. Diao Xinshen, "Shichang xing cheng zhong di gaige renwu" (Task of the Reform in Market Forming), *Jingji yanjiu* (Economic Research) 8 (1986):43–48.

36. Zhou Yu and Zhang Tie, "Cong xinmin xian kan cheng xiang jiehe zhenxin jingji di xin chaoshi" (A New Trend: The Combination of City and Village and the Vitalization of Economy in Xinmin County), *Jingji yanjiu* (Economic Research) 3 (1985):72–77.

37. Dong Fureng, *Industrialization and China's Rural Modernization* (London: Macmillan Press, 1992), p. 37.

38. Statistical Bureau of China, *Statistical Year Book of China, 1987* (Hongkong: Longman Group, 1987).

39. Dong, *Industrialization*, p. 38.

40. Guojia tongji ju nongcun shehui jingji tongji shi. *Zhongguo nongcun tongji nian jian, 1994* (Chinese Rural Statistics, 1994) (Beijing: Zhongguo Tongji Chubanshe, 1994):33.

41. Liu, "Speech on National *Jishi* Conference."

42. Ibid.

43. Liu Benrong, "Guli nongmin jinlu liutong, luli qidong nongcun shichang" (Encourage Farmers to Enter into Circulation and Develop Rural Markets), *Nongcun jingji* (Rural Economy) 3 (1993):15–17.

44. Wang Guohe, "Nongchanpin zhuanye pifa shichang chutan" (Specialized Wholesale Market of Agricultural Produce), *Nongye jingji wenti* (Problems of Agricultural Economics) 5 (1987):18–22.

45. Cheng Naiwu and Cheng Xi, "Tigao nongmin jinru liutong zhuzhihua changdu chutan" (Raising the Organizational Level of Farmers to Improve Their Performance in Marketing Agriculture Products), *Nongye jingji wenti* (Problems of Agricultural Economies) 4 (1992):10–13.

46. Nongchanpin Pifa Shichang Ketizu (Wholesale Market Research Group), "Woguo nongchanpin pifa shichang gean tiancha yu fengxi"

(Agricultural Wholesale Markets in China: Analysis on Selected Case Studies), *Nongye jingji wenti* (Problems of Agricultural Economics) 4 (1992):2–9.

47. Liu, "Speech on National *Jishi* Conference."

48. Lu Bingyi, "Laizi Guangdong lubian fadian di baogao" (Report from Guangdong Roadside Restaurants), *Falüyushenghuo* (Law and Life) 3 (1990):7–13.

49. Zhongguo Xiangzhen Qiye Nianjian Bianji Weiyuanhui (Editorial Board of Chinese Rural Industrial Enterprises Yearbook), *Zhongguo xiangzheng qiye nianjian—1994* (1994 Book of Chinese Rural Industrial Enterprises). (Beijing: Nongye Chubanshe, 1994), p. 39

50. Dong, *Industrialization*, p. 69.

51. Cheng Baokun and Lin Bing, "Gongcheng 'shuoshu'" (A Construction Rat: The Fall of the Director of Ha'erbin Railway Company), *Minzhu yu fazhi* (Democracy and Law) 9 (1990):23.

52. Ibid.

53. In Chinese: *Liangshao quan douyao; liangduo duoqudao; shishang benwugui, quan shi renzainao*. Personal interviews with Wang Wenhua and Zu Ping of Tongxin Village, February 1986.

54. Andrew Watson, et al., "Who Won the 'Wool War'?," *China Quarterly* (118 1989):213–241.

55. Sun Fangmin, et al., "Nongcun shangpin liudong zhong de 'zinan' wenti" (Four Difficulties in Rural Commodity Circulation), in Zhongguo Nongcun Fazhan Wenti Yanjiu, ed., *Nongcun, jingji, shehui* (Rural Areas, Society and Economy) (Beijing: Zhishi Chubanshe, 1985), pp. 246–254.

56. Su Ya and Jia Lusheng, *Shuilai chengbao: Zhongguo jingji xianzhuang toushi* (Who Is Going to Contract: Analysis of the Chinese Economic Situation) (Guangzhou: Huacheng Chubanshe, 1990), p. 321.

57. Dong, *Industrialization*, p. 79.

58. *Hubei ribao* (Hubei Daily), March 29, 1986.

59. Fazhan Yanjiusuo, *Reform and System Innovation*, p. 143.

60. Ibid., p. 4.

61. Wu Xiang, "Shenhua gaige qianghua nongcun jingji xin tizhi" (Deepen the Reforms and Strengthen the New Rural Economic System), *Nongye jingji wenti* (Problems of Agricultural Economics) 1 (1988):11.

62. Guojia Tongji Ju Nongcun Shehui Jingji Tongji Shi (Rural Social Economic Statistics Group of the State Statistical Bureau), *Zhongguo nongcun tongji nian jian, 1992* (Chinese Rural Statistics, 1992) (Beijing: Zhongguo Tongji Chubanshe, 1992): 55.

63. Marion J. Levy, Jr., "Contrasting Factors in the Modernization of China and Japan," *Economic Development and Cultural Change* 2, no. 3 (1953):161–178.

64. In Chinese: *Yaoxiang fuqiang, qinong jingshang*.

65. For instance, see Bert F. Hoselitz, ed., *The Progress of Underdeveloped Areas* (Chicago: University of Chicago Press, 1952); Samuel P. Huntington, *Political Order in Changing Societies* (New Haven: Yale University Press, 1968); William Arthur Lewis, "Development with Unlimited Supplies of Labor," *Manchester School* 22 (1954):139–192; G. Ranis, et al., "A Theory of Economic Development," *American Economic Review* 51 (1961):533–565.

66. Dong, *Industrialization*, p. 46.

# Rural Industries: Waves of the Farmer Sea

The soft and the weak overcome the hard
and the strong.

Lao Tzu

O n June 12, 1987, Deng Xiaoping told a group of Yugoslav visitors of his surprise about the rapid development of rural industries:

> Generally speaking, our rural reforms have proceeded very fast, and farmers have been enthusiastic. *What took us by surprise completely was the development of township and village industries.* The diversity of production, commodity economy, and all sorts of small enterprises boomed in the countryside, as if a strange army appeared suddenly from nowhere. *This is not the achievement of our central government.* Every year township and village industries achieved 20 percent growth. . . . This was not something I had thought about. Nor had the other comrades. This surprised us.[1]

Incredible as the 20 percent annual growth is, the real figure for rural industrial development has been even higher in some years. In fact, some development of rural industry occurred in the 1970s before 1978, when the government chose to announce reforms. The government's initial reaction was to use rural industrialization as a means to prevent rural–urban migration, stressing that villagers would be encouraged to leave the village but not to leave the countryside. That is, they would not be permitted to migrate to cities. The development of rural industries was at first restricted to a few provinces, but after the household responsibility system (*baochan daohu*) in the late 1970s and early 1980s, rural industrialization spread throughout the nation despite its regional differences, reaching an average annual increase of 26 percent throughout the 1980s.[2] By 1993, 50 percent of China's industrial output came from rural industries. The state no longer maintained its industrial monopoly. According to the *Economist*, by 1992, the state's share of Chinese output had fallen below 25 percent if one includes agriculture and services.[3] Rural industries and joint ventures (4.4 percent of all industry in 1990) have been the most dynamic sources of export earnings. By 1991, the export share of rural industry jumped to 30 percent, and in Jiangsu, Zhejiang, Fujian, Dalian, and Qingdao it exceeded 50 percent.[4] In 1993, rural exports made up one-third of Chinese exports and were responsible for two-thirds of the growth.[5]

In this chapter, I examine how the small rural unorganized fish (rural industries) outsmarted and outperformed the big fish (the state industries administered by cadres). Then I focus on the phenomenon of *guahu*, the rural industries' equivalent of *baochan daohu*, to examine the complex relationship among the state, local governments, and rural entrepreneurs in terms of transformations of ownership and control. These two developments provide a clearer understanding of the transition from the Communist state to the Chinese industrial development of the Deng years and beyond. Other latecomers to modernization have generally focused on urbanization, and so did the government in Communist China. In China, however, in the last decade and half, the most spectacular actual development has been rural, not just in agriculture but in industry as well. What China may have to teach the world is how to develop by "rural industrialization," although that is certainly not what the Chinese government originally intended.

A variety of terms can describe Chinese rural industry. According to the government, rural industry refers to "those enterprises organized by the commune (now the *xiang*) or by the brigade (now the village), or by one or several individual commune members."[6] This definition obviously departs from actuality because by 1983 the family had become an important additional unit of production and entrepreneurship. In their excellent work on the subject, Lin Qingsong and William Byrd define rural industry as "all nonagricultural activities in rural areas and small towns other than those on state farms."[7] Although Lin and Byrd capture the essential economic aspects of the activities of rural entrepreneurs, their definition confines rural industries to a local setting. But the scope of rural-initiated economic activity very quickly overleapt those bounds and reached beyond the countryside. I define rural industries as industrial-related activities performed by rural people or people only recently moved out of rural settings (after 1978). By defining it thus, I highlight the differences between rural and urban industries. My description of rural industry includes household firms, township enterprises, village enterprises, and partnership firms (enterprises held jointly by several households).

The speed of Chinese rural industrial development has captured the world's attention. In both China and the "West," the success of rural industry is nicely summarized by Jan Svejnar and Josephine Woo:

TVPs (rural enterprises) have been able to thrive in a variety of environments. In contrast to state enterprise, TVPs are characterized by great flexibility, harder budget constraints, costs of capital that are more reflective of scarcity, and much heavier reliance on worker incentives. . . . Their ability to maintain growth under the restrictive macroeconomic policies of the mid-1980s attests to their viability and superior performance.[8]

Scholars disagree as to what drives farmers to develop industry and how they have achieved what they are achieving. Some argue that the state led the development of rural industry; others suggest that the state has created barriers to rural industry. For example, Barry Naughton argues that the state's policy of reducing the barriers to entry ended the state's monopoly over industry and weakened the power of state.[9] David Zweig, on the other hand, argues that the state has been constraining the growth of rural industry, despite the miracle of rural industrial development.[10] Along the same line, Louis Putterman notes that the state has tried to "suppress encroachments on its product monopolies" from nonstate sectors.[11]

Few publications have looked at the struggles of rural industries or measured the impact of those struggles on the erosion of the PRC's structure. This chapter focuses on the tension between rural industries and urban industries and describes how rural entrepreneurs are swamping state planned industries and bursting the dike of the state industrial monopoly.

The state initially encouraged some rural industries in the early 1970s, in an attempt to prevent rural–urban migration and to promote agricultural mechanization. This enabled some rural areas to develop industries that went beyond the state's control. Prior to 1978, the scale of rural industries was small and relatively concentrated in a few provinces, Jiangsu and Zhejiang, in particular. Despite its rapid growth, the rural share of industrial production was only 7 percent in 1978. An important feature of this rural industrial development was its dependence on urban state industries. Almost all those early rural industries in Jiangsu were subfactories of Shanghai and Nanjing state factories.

The rapid development of rural industries after *baochan daohu* differed from the early 1970s' rural development. Many independent small industries boomed. First, *baochan daohu* enabled farmers to control labor allocation. Farmers tended to look for sectors (often industry) that paid better. Second, the rapid increase in productivity after *baochan daohu* released rural surplus labor. Third, the booming markets put funds in the hands of farmers to start small-scale businesses. Facing the reality that state factories refused to hire rural residents, rural people had to fall back on their own devices for industrial employment and development.

With so many farmers trying to participate in rural industry, industrial development in China flourished. Farmers used every possibility to increase family income. When industrial goods became profitable, industrial production boomed in the countryside. Millions of farmers wracked their brains to find out what the market wanted. As soon as some farmers came up with a new idea to make products to sell, all the neighbors knew about it. Very quickly the whole county knew about it. The exponential growth process became endemic. When one family became successful, soon other families followed suit, as expressed by one rural saying in the 1980s: "One household influences one village; one village affects one district; every village has an [industrial] smokestack; every household emits smog."[12] The growth of rural industries was another "chicken pest" that spread in rural China. This is another side of the coin. Thus, a village could even become a national center for a product, just as rural Fujian took the lead in making shoes. Other times, when everyone tries the same thing, the market becomes saturated and many fail. This is especially true in less dynamic areas.

Thus, patterns of specialization developed despite the fact that most family factories were small. For example, in Zhuo County, Hebei, eighty thousand farm households engaged in synthetic clothing production during the 1980s. The annual production of clothes from those farm households reached twenty million units and sales reached several hundred million yuan.[13] As a result, family cottage industries mushroomed in the countryside. A rural saying has this to say about rural industrial development: "Dig under the foundation," i.e., undermine the planned economy.

## Corruption: A Base for Rural Industrial Development

Farmers achieved the development of rural industries only through tremendous effort. The greatest obstacle to rural industrial enterprise was the lack of access to raw materials. According to a 1988 survey, 97 percent of managers in rural enterprises felt the pressure of the lack of raw materials and capital.[14] China's socialist economy meant state control of all marketing and distribution of raw materials and goods. The State Planning Department did not allocate raw materials to rural industries. The state's commercial departments would not help them sell their goods.

This pattern of resource allocation followed the "feudal" arrangement of Chinese farmers under collective farming. The government banned farmers from engaging in any nonagricultural activities (commercial and industrial activities). Rural areas could only provide raw material for state urban industries. Farmers were forced to sell low to and buy high from the state.

The structural changes in the early 1980s altered this situation, making it difficult to run the state as usual. The rural industrial takeoff did not begin until *baochan daohu* enabled the family head to resume economic decisionmaking.[15] Family farming rationalized labor and the use of technology, leading to an increase in productivity both per hectare and per worker. Once the family paid its taxes in grain, the cadres could no longer prevent farmers from engaging in nonagricultural work. Restrictions on rural entry into urban factory jobs pushed farmers to set up their own factories. After the fourth phase of *baochan daohu* began, incentives spread everywhere. It is against this background that rural industrialization took off in the early 1980s.

The government's response to this unexpected development was to make sure that developing rural industries did not compete with urban state factories for raw materials and energy. The state sought to bind rural industry to the guiding principle of *sanjiudi* (the three locals: get material locally, process locally, and sell locally). *Sanjiudi* revealed the state's desire to confine rural enterprises to the local areas, as documented by the 1979 central government on rural industry:

> Commune and brigade enterprises should adhere to socialism and actively produce what society needs, but mainly serve agricultural production and serve the people while serving big industries and export. But at the same time, they should organize their production according to the local resources and energy. Do not engage without local resources. Do not process those products that are already oversupplied. *Do not compete with the advanced big industries for raw material and energy supply. Do not destroy state resources.*[16]

The government held its policies toward rural industry consistent throughout the 1970s and 1980s. The government wanted to keep rural industries away from urban industrial development and to prevent competition from the nonstate sector for resources and markets, but the state's efforts to maintain its monopoly proved ineffective. Rural industries from the very beginning were competing with state industries for both raw materials and market shares.

Rural industries were often able to get around the state restrictions because they were willing to pay higher market prices for raw materials. This was especially true of light industries, which eventually received a substantial portion of their raw materials from the countryside (70 percent in 1991).[17] In family farming, farmers controlled some nonstaple products (or all, in the case of sideline production) and sold to the highest bidders. Farmers sold the best quality wool, silk cocoons, and tobacco to those rural industries willing to pay more. Rural industries also had an advantage since they had more knowledge of the territory. They could depend on their own entrepreneurial initiative in locating raw materials. State-owned factories had to wait for the state to locate materials for them. Thus, state-owned factories frequently could not get sufficient raw materials quickly enough to exploit shifts in the market for light industrial production.

Very quickly, rural industries, the latecomers, took the lead in consumer goods production. For example, by 1990 more than 70 percent of clothing production and two-thirds of clothing exports came from rural enterprises.[18] This rapid growth spread to other industrial products as well. In 1991, rural industries provided 45 percent of China's silk, 32 percent of China's silk products, 28 percent of China's coal and cement, 38 percent of China's paper, and 78 percent of China's bricks.[19]

When more and more rural industries competed with one another for scarce light industrial raw materials, prices soared, making it difficult for the state to make farmers sell those products to the state at low prices. The government lost its position as the single buyer of raw materials. State wool factories and cigarette factories ran short of raw materials. The Shanghai Cigarette Factory, the oldest and one of the largest state cigarette factories, ran out of tobacco for a while in the mid-1980s.[20] The state issued a document on May 4, 1981, trying to stop rural enterprises from producing cigarettes, textiles, and salt,[21] but raw materials prices continued to rise. In September 1987, the State Council issued yet another document concerning tobacco:

Since the purchasing of tobacco began this year, many tobacco production areas independently raised the price and the grade of tobacco. . . . This has affected the normal procedure of state purchases. If this situation continues, it will make the state suffer a great economic loss and will also affect the production of cigarettes. This must be stopped.[22]

The state prohibition seemed to have little effect, however. The state factories were finding it more and more difficult to obtain raw materials. In August 1993, the No. 1 Cotton Mill, a major manufacturer in Wuhan, had to shut down for two weeks because of a supply shortage. Zhang Baoxin, director of the mill, attributed the shortage to the corruption of bureaucrats who profited from selling cotton to rural factories. Zhang believed that individual cadres had sold much of the subsidized cotton designated for his mill to rural factories, "where second-hand looms are being set up overnight to exploit the raw cotton with even cheaper labor, [and] at the same time avoid taxes."[23]

Rural enterprises often won victories in the competition for raw materials from light industries, but they faced a tougher battle to get energy and steel. The state's central plan officially allocated all energy and steel, and it did not reserve any for rural enterprises. Furthermore, the plan allowed only state enterprises to produce such goods. Rural industry by necessity turned to the "back door" to obtain these goods at high prices from those enterprises that received goods as part of the plan. Because state enterprises received materials cheaply from the state, they obtained huge profits from this illegal "middleman" trade. Since the state did not control the money made from these transactions, the managers in those enterprises

**Table 5.1**

A Comparison of Prices for Some Raw Materials, 1988

| Item | Unit | State Price | Market Price |
|------|------|-------------|--------------|
| Coal | 1 ton | 50 yuan | 110 yuan |
| Steel | 1 ton | 1,050 yuan | 1,680 yuan |
| Electricity | 10,000 kilowatt-hours | 850 yuan | 1,500 yuan |
| Timber | 1 square meter | 90 yuan | 500 yuan |
| Aluminum | 1 ton | 4,800 yuan | 12,000 yuan |

Source: Hu Heli, "1988 nian woguo zhujin jiazhi de gusuan" (Estimation of Rent-Seeking in 1988), Jingji shehui tizhi bijiao (Journal of Comparative Economic Social Systems) 5 (1989):10–15.

used the money as bonuses for workers. Bear in mind that the urban workplace acts as a small welfare state, shouldering responsibility for its workers.[24] Because urban wages are fixed, this form of "illegal" dealings provided an important source of funding for the welfare of the urban enterprises. Table 5.1 illustrates the price differences between the state planned price and the market price of some raw materials. It shows that state enterprises were protected by prices frequently well below half those prevailing in the market, and sometimes a third or less (as in the case of timber and aluminum).

As more and more rural enterprises competed for raw materials, the differences between fixed and market prices increased greatly, eroding the pattern of price stability in the PRC. To a great extent, these illegal dealings benefited both rural and urban industries: rural industries got badly needed material and energy, and urban state factories received extra cash to improve the welfare of their workers. Although they were discriminated against, rural enterprises were able to use these "illegal" transactions to survive. The only "loser" in the game was the state, which lost money through the "illegal" deals and which failed to stop the rural industries from penetrating, undermining, and leaching away the planned system. As several leading Chinese reformers have pointed out:

> Exchange between state enterprises with soft property constraints and rural enterprises has broken the monopoly on scarce resources by the state sector and therefore broken "rent," which has inevitably led to a state budgetary crisis. As the rural enterprises have tried their best to seek "rent" from the state sectors and to share "rent" with state employees, the moral standards of the whole society have also degenerated.[25]

Nevertheless, even the state profited in one quite fundamental respect: The government benefited from the higher rate of economic growth and job creation. The result was added government tax revenues and spinoff effects boosting other sectors of the economy. However, the economic benefit brought key structural changes. The interdependence between rural and urban factories not only altered the ownership structure of the state plans but also altered the working structure of the state enterprises as well.

## *Siqian Jingshen* (Four Thousand Spirits)

Rural entrepreneurs rewarded anyone in the rural enterprise who through personal connections arranged to get raw material or to expand the sales of rural products. In order to obtain badly needed raw materials from state factories, rural factories hired a large army of *caigouyuan* (purchasing agents who specialize in buying and selling goods). *Caigouyuan* in rural enterprises make independent decisions and can offer cadres gifts, meals, commissions, money, and other benefits in return for materials in short supply or for sales opportunities. Using personal connections and money, these rural *caigouyuan* established contacts with urban state factories. The practices of giving *xiaohongbao* (a small red bag containing money) or *huikou* (kickbacks) prevailed. Above all, this meant that the *caigouyuan* from rural enterprises could act swiftly and the *caigouyuan* in the urban industries could not. The motto of rural *caigouyuan* was "endure numerous hardships; cross one thousand mountains and ten thousand streams; speak one thousand dialects and ten thousand words; and use one thousand means and ten thousand schemes."[26]

Since rural people had limited contact with urban industry, they sometimes had to hire urban people to look for contacts for them. Thus, a group of people known as *guandao* (official profiteers) emerged, specializing in transferring scarce resources from state enterprises to rural industries. Through *guandao*, rural industries were able to get raw material at the state price and foreign currency at the official exchange rates. *Guanxi* is best described by a well-known song from the 1980s:

> Old acquaintances are all underground party members,
> Everyone has his own web of connections;
> Benefiting oneself and others,
> It's as good as two hundred ingots of gold.
> Having *guanxi*, one depends on *guanxi*,
> Without *guanxi*, one looks for *guanxi*;
> When all fails, buy *guangxi*.

"Illegal dealings" between rural and state enterprises accelerated when urban reforms allocated more decisionmaking to factory managers. One Chinese scholar noted:

> The shrinking of administrative controls and the strengthening of the profit motive for state enterprises under the reforms have led

to rampant growth of activities such as barter trade, unplanned sales of products listed in the state plan, and speculation on commodity quotas at the state prices. This environment provides an opportunity for TVPs (rural enterprise) to shift part of state enterprises' profits into their own hands by such means as giving sales commissions, paying sales agents, and making out blank invoices. Hence TVPs, whose backward technology is often coupled with high input costs, can sometimes out-compete state enterprises that have advanced technology and low input prices.[27]

"Illegal" transactions between state and rural enterprises were so widespread that state planning was on the verge of becoming irrelevant. Moreover, illegal transactions weakened the bureaucracy and party discipline. In April 1983, the State Council issued an order demanding that state industries stop illegal transactions, but to no effect. In order to guarantee the safe delivery of planned goods, the state in 1984 formally recognized the existence of the black market. They allowed state factories to sell their products at 20 percent above the state fixed price (*guojia zhidao jia*, the state guided price) once the enterprises fulfilled their production quotas.[28] This was an attempt to develop an urban equivalent of *baochan daohu*. In fact, the success of *baochan daohu* motivated Deng Xiaoping and Zhao Ziyang to initiate urban reform in 1984. As Deng said: "The success of the rural reform gave us confidence. Thus we decided to apply the rural experience to urban economic system reforms."[29] In 1985, the government lifted price controls on nonquota products, thus giving formal recognition to the two-tier price system.[30] The system divided products into two parts: one part submitted to the state at the state price, and the remainder sold at the market price. This recognition accelerated the selling of the planned share of raw material and energy supply. In 1985 alone, rural industries spent so much money buying raw materials and energy from state enterprises that state enterprises gained a net profit of 10.7 billion yuan from this exchange.[31] Since the after-quota sales take place at near-market prices, the two-tier price system, in effect, legitimated the buying of raw material by rural enterprises. The result of the two-tier system threatened the state planned system, as one Chinese scholar points out:

It is obvious that the two-tier system prevents the state from fulfilling those important commanded plans. Those enterprises that produce highly demanded raw material would try their best to squeeze the planned quota out, failing to meet the quota while at the same time increasing unplanned sales on their own. Those aggregated incidents have made it impossible for the state economy to fulfill its plan. Thus the function of the state for stability and controlling the economy was weakened.[32]

In other words, the two-tier system funneled raw materials to the more efficient rural industries. Rural industries were more efficient in labor, capital, and land. Since rural industries depended on market-priced (or near market-priced) goods, the increase in rural industry led to increased market allocation of goods and materials, as opposed to direct allocation. The state's control over allocation of goods and energy decreased rapidly. By 1993, the state plan only allocated 30 percent of industrial raw materials, compared to its 100 percent control in 1978.[33] Now even state factories compete with rural industries to buy most of their raw materials and goods on the market.

Rural industries also had to find markets for their products because the state commercial bureau did not help them sell their products. Rural *caigouyuan* are responsible for both purchases of raw material and sales of rural products. Their role is so crucial to the operation of rural enterprises that they constitute 10 percent or even 20 percent of the total work force.[34] According to one estimate, rural *caigouyuan* controlled more than 70–80 percent of rural industry's product sales and purchases of raw materials.[35] In Wenzhou, Zhejiang, where rural industries developed fastest, rural enterprises employed a hundred thousand *caigouyuan* in 1984; they traveled across the nation delivering as well as buying goods from thousands of shops and factories, both private and public. They created markets nationwide.

With high raw material costs and less-educated technical personnel, how could rural industries compete with state industries with low material costs and better-educated personnel? Rural industries survived the competition with large urban enterprises because their "hard budget" constraint forced them to make good products, respond to customer desires, and operate efficiently—or go bust. State factories with "soft budgets" saw no reason to compete with rural industries.[36]

Moreover, rural industries enjoyed lower labor costs and were more aware of their lower social status, consciously competing with the state industries. A 1988 survey based on 5,600 rural enterprises suggests that the people who ran rural industries were very conscious of the existing state-owned enterprises and intended to compete with them. When asked, "What is your relationship with the state factories that produce the same products?" 48 percent responded with "competition" and an additional 19 percent replied "cooperation and competition."[37]

Competition with urban state factories was apparent in the urban market. Rural industries were able to sell their goods in the urban market despite the formal and informal discrimination against them. Government department stores at first refused to sell products from rural factories. The official newspapers were full of stories about the inferior quality of rural products and the deception of rural merchants. The informal discrimination involved urban customers who always looked down upon rural people

*This factory in rural Anhui employs 100 workers
and exports more than 100 kinds of pottery and
tens of thousands of pieces of imitation Sung, Yuan,
Ming, and Qing pottery. Photo by Lu Xun-chen*

and were suspicious about rural products. Exfarmers developed marketing
strategies to overcome those barriers. For example, one rural enterprise in
Shishi, Fujian Province, produced sanitary napkins. In order to break into
the Shanghai market, the company sold its products to Shanghai women at
below cost and used commercial ads. When more and more women got to
know the products, Shishi products became popular because of their good
design and high quality. Very soon, orders flooded the rural company.[38]

Combined with marketing strategy and market mechanisms, rural
industrialization surged against urban industries and drove them to greater
efficiency or ruin. Table 5.2 clearly suggests that for every one hundred
yuan worth of fixed assets, rural enterprises produced more than the state
enterprises in both heavy and light industries. The output value per fixed
assets is of course only one criterion; state enterprises also paid much more
for labor and benefits.

Some state factory managers even hired rural managers to help them run
factories. For example, Mudanjiang Boiler Manufacture hired Bi Yuanli, the
head of a rural enterprise, as manager. He turned a moneylosing state factory
into a profit-making factory within six months. When asked his secret, Bi
said: "I was asked to adopt the management of rural industry and did things

**Table 5.2**

Economic Efficiency in State and Rural Enterprises, 1985

| Type of Industry | State Enterprises (Output Value per Y100 of Fixed Assets) | Rural Enterprises (Output Value per Y100 of Fixed Assets) |
|---|---|---|
| Heavy | 67 | 177 |
| Light | 209 | 256 |
| Average | 95 | 207 |

Source: Zhongguo gongye jingji tongji ziliao 1986 (Statistical Materials on China's Industrial Economy) (Beijing: Zhongguo Tongji Chubanshe, 1987), pp. 98, 211.

in the farmers' way. I have independent decisionmaking power. . . breaking the iron-rice bowl [life-tenured job], creating a new environment."[39]

Apart from the market mechanism, the small size of rural industry also made it more competitive. Farmers' small savings and limited access to outside capital usually kept their businesses small. At the early stage of market creation in a socialist state like China, smallness can be a blessing for at least five reasons. First, entrepreneurs take a political risk to establish a large-scale private firm, because neither the people nor state officials are used to the idea of nonstate entities. Smallness also protects rural industry from the state. When industry is small, confiscation of inventory is always a risk, but if a plant is large in terms of both inventory and capital, there is a greater risk. Large enterprises are more noticeable. It is easy for little fish to hide from big fish—especially in the great state reef. Moreover, it is difficult for the state to see small-scale private firms as organized movements with a potentially political leadership.

Second, a small business is flexible and thus able to respond to market signals. When a new product is in demand, a small business can change its production quickly. A rural saying goes, "Only small boats can easily change direction." As a result, rural entrepreneurs were sensitive to market signals, and their commercial impulses were strong. Small businesses enabled rural entrepreneurs to create new products to meet changing market demand. Flexible small rural firms fit well in a global market that required small quantities but diversity and flexibility.

Third, small-scale businesses encourage innovation to meet diversified market demands. Farmers' commercial impulses led to innovation despite their lack of education. When people found it difficult to sell local textile products, for example, they tried to produce acrylics. An old woman in Zhejiang rebuilt the old weaving machines to weave acrylics, and within a few years a whole district became the biggest acrylics textile center in China, resulting in multi-million-yuan profits.[40]

Fourth, consumer goods were in demand nationwide. Thus, the small family businesses had a market impact on the whole nation. The best-known commercial market is in Wenzhou. Many Wenzhou businesses aimed for a broader market. For example, when the state announced in the newspaper that it would issue personal identification cards and undertake rural credit reform, rural entrepreneurs in Jinxing, Zhejiang Province, immediately sent the government their blueprint samples of farmers' credit cards and personal identification cards and offered to produce them for 1.2 billion people![41] The consumer goods production within small firms created a big commercial market, which greatly improved the lives of farmers as well as those of urban people.

The most important reason for their success is that rural industries did not depend on the state for support. Their strength came from within. After 1978, in fact, the state continued to cut capital investment in rural areas while at the same time granting loans to bail out troubled urban state enterprises and to increase pay and subsidies for unproductive urban state workers. The result was a huge gap between the competitive rural industry and the dependent state industrial sector. As rural industries produced for markets and responded to market signals, they grew stronger.

Fifth and finally, the lack of dependence on the state meant that many rural factories went bankrupt. Private household firms that could not keep up washed out quickly, but even if the worst befalls a small enterprise and it fails, it leaves no large gap in the market scene. Many farm families suffered losses. Because the state did not help them, they had always to rely on themselves. As a result, they became tougher in the market compared with the state factories. For example, when the state cracked down on rural industries in 1989, many small firms managed to survive and some even aimed to produce for the global market. As David Zweig points out, "Despite the state intention to crack down, exports from TVE (town and village enterprises) reached $10 billion in 1989, and increased 25 percent in 1990."[42]

The flexibility of rural industries enabled them to compete even in the international market, and their export shares increased rapidly. For example, in 1991, rural industries earned 77 percent of total export earnings in clothing, over half the export earnings in handicrafts, about a third of the export earnings in light industry and chemical products, and a quarter of the export earnings in textiles and machinery. By then, rural industries had become the major force among export producers. In three major export industrial provinces, Zhejiang, Fujian, and Jiangsu, and two cities, Dalian and Qingdao, rural industries claimed more than 50 percent of the exports.[43]

Rural enterprises were able to survive in spite of high raw material costs and low sales prices partly because of their low labor and overhead costs. There is little welfare protection within the rural factory, but there is much welfare built into the rural family. (Of course, rural factories in the very rich areas, like the Pearl River delta, Jiangsu, and many suburbs, are increasing their welfare resources far more than what collective farming could provide.) The rural family is the age-old welfare unit of China, its basic unit for more than two thousand years. In addition, there were varieties of charitable institutions in the village such as lineage and religion.

Because the comparative advantages for rural industries are higher than in farming, rural workers prefer staying in the factories. This motivation to do good work is strong among rural workers. Often when a factory faces financial difficulties, rural workers are willing to take pay cuts to stay with the factory. This is especially true for factories that take relatives and friends as employees.

## Rural Industry Exploits the Weakness of the Centralized State

Not positioned to mount effective opposition to state factories, small rural firms have tended to occupy those places left vacant by state-owned industries. The success of rural industries depended on the three weaknesses of the planned economy. First, small rural firms were able to spread quickly because Chinese socialist industry left space for small businesses to grow. All state enterprises in China are big fish. In 1970, socialist countries had double the average employment per firm and double the percentage of workers employed in large firms as did the capitalist countries. According to one estimate, the size of Chinese state enterprises was something like 10:1 to private enterprises.

Second, the state gave the highest priority to the military and heavy industries. As a result, consumer goods and services lagged behind. Long lines and rationing coupons in the city revealed the demand for consumer goods and services. The shortage became more obvious after *baochan daohu*, when increased agricultural productivity and family sidelines gave farmers cash to buy consumer goods. The urban state factories were not able to produce sufficient consumer goods to satisfy urban residents, let alone the rural demand. Urban people depended on the rationing system for various goods (from matches, pots, soap, and toilet paper to basins) that the system denied to rural people. This shortage provided farmers a golden opportunity to develop rural light industries. Rural industries corrected that inefficiency and led to the mass production of light consumer goods. To a certain extent, the initial success of rural industries depended on shortages, as Byrd pointed out:

> For goods that are chronically in short supply at low government-set prices, TVPs may have an artificial market niche. TVPs usually produce those goods at higher cost and sell at higher market

prices, but the shortage situation protects them from the full brunt of competition from state enterprises. Under those circumstances TVPs can be viable and competitive even though they are producing goods of lower quality or with more backward technology.[44]

In other words, rural industries were able to make the best use of the weakness of the Chinese planned state, pioneering the structural change of industry.

Third, the planned state and its bureaucracy were so preoccupied with urban industrial sectors, especially eight thousand large and medium-size state-owned enterprises, that the small-scale rural industries escaped their attention. In other words, rural industry developed in interstices opened due to weaknesses in the state bureaucracy. Once again the central government was looking away. In contrast, the attention of the state brought problems for the urban state sector: "Since the performance of the urban industrial sector was directly related to the revenues of the state and affected the state's ability to attain its goals, the center could halt or at least slow the process of urban industrial reform in a way that was not possible in the countryside."[45]

While the state's attention centered on the urban sector, farmers developed industries with a vengeance. With little capital support from the state bureaucracy and few subsidies, rural industries emerged strong and powerful. Now the state could not eliminate small businesses without damaging itself. Rural small businesses made market reforms irreversible. The shortcomings of the planned system helped rural businesses boom, especially family businesses in the rural areas.

## *Guahu:* An Eddy in the Farmer Sea

Much attention has been paid to *baochan daohu*, putting rural China at the forefront of privatization. The published statistics on the share of the private sector in the gross value of industrial output remained low during the 1980s (5.4 percent). But this figure is only a small part of the whole privatization because it does not include industrial output from *guahu* enterprises in the countryside. According to the State Council's calculation, the number of registered private enterprises was only half of the calculated number. *Guahu* has played and continues to play a part in the structural transformation of the Chinese state.

Literally, *guahu* means to attach oneself to someone else's household, but in the context of rural industry *guahu* means using the name of a formal legal organization to engage in economic activities. Another common name for the *guahu* phenomenon is *jiajiti* (fake collective enterprise). Roughly speaking, there are three forms of *guahu*: *danhu* (single household or one individual) *guahu*; *lianghu* (more than two households) *guahu*, and *gufen* (joint-stock holders) *guahu*. While individuals in *danhu* and *lianghu* are responsible for the management of the *guahu* businesses, owners of *gufen guahu* do not necessarily get involved in management. All three types use formal organizations for *sandai sanjie* (three substitutes and three borrowings): to issue receipts, keep books, and pay taxes; to issue letters of introduction, write contracts, and open bank accounts. The formal legal organization (i.e., the organization that provides the cover) gets a certain percentage of the profits from the private rural entrepreneurs, varying from 8 percent to 15 percent in Zhejiang and 1 percent to 5 percent in Hubei.[46] Like *baochan daohu, guahu* was under the table, a way around official patterns.

Rural entrepreneurs in Wenzhou were the first to adopt the practice of *guahu*. Interestingly, *baochan daohu* was responsible for the appearance of *guahu* in Wenzhou. When in 1979 Wenzhou farmers went back to family farming, the rapid increase of production after *baochan daohu* stimulated villagers in Jingxin to try a similar reform for the previously money-losing office supply factory in the village. At first, they divided the factory into four shops and carried out a policy of *wutong shizi* (five coordinations and ten independences). Roughly, *wutong* refers to the same leadership, the same factory name, the same bank account, and the same tax rate (7 percent); *shizi* can be summarized as voluntary cooperation, independent work contract; self-improvement of technology; independent production, self-investment, independent instruments, independent production quota, independent responsibility for loss and profits. As this reform spread, profits soared. When *baochan daohu* infected China, families began to contract to run factories that still carried the name of their village.[47] The demonstration effect of *guahu* attracted villagers in other rural places, and *guahu* became popular and widespread in the countryside. *Guahu* also spread like the chicken pest!

There are eight reasons for the development of *guahu* in the countryside. First, despite the rhetoric of the state's support for private enterprises, the social and political environment throughout the reform period was hostile to private business. The Four Cardinal Principles (Socialist Road; Marxism, Leninism, and Maoist Thought; the People's Dictatorship; and the Leadership of the Communist Party) upheld socialism as the only proper social structure for the PRC. The government did not give legal recognition to *siying* (private enterprises) until 1987.[48] Thus, rural entrepreneurs feared becoming the targets of political campaigns. The state made a conscious effort to devalue the private entrepreneurs. In 1989, the central government issued document no. 9, specifying, "The relationship between the boss of a private business and its workers is exploitative. No head of any private business will be allowed to join the Communist party."[49] Party members working in private firms lost access to the party since no party organization was allowed in private firms. Political campaigns always attacked private business first. For example, after the 1989 Tiananmen incident, the government launched a national campaign to attack private businesses. All major Chinese newspapers criticized the private entrepreneurs as an exploiting class and as causing instability. Often rural entrepreneurs have four fears: fear of confiscation; fear of being forced to take in new employees and new leaders when efficiency improves and wages grow; fear of becoming targets of attack when making any mistakes; fear of not being allowed to continue to do business when the business grows. Thus, many rural entrepreneurs use *guahu* to hide, *beikao dashu haochengliang* (in the shade of a big tree). *Guahu* helps rural entrepreneurs overcome their fear by giving them a red cap to wear, putting the trappings of communism on the practice of capitalism. One rural proverb in Henan depicts a vivid image of the *guahu* phenomenon as a battered daughter-in-law looking to her parents for protection.

Second, from a social point of view, *guahu* also reduces tension among villagers. The newly rich have been under pressure to hide their wealth from their fellow villagers in order to avoid becoming the victims of *hongyanbing*. *Guahu* is able to achieve this.

Third, *guahu* enables rural entrepreneurs to get around government restrictions on private businesses. For example, a 1983 state regulation prohibited private businesses from hiring more than five workers. Although the state did not specify punishment for those who violated it, this regulation made many rural entrepreneurs reluctant to expand their private business. *Guahu* enabled private businesses to hire more workers. In Chongqing, Sichuan Province, some *guahu* enterprises hired two hundred workers.[50]

*Guahu* overcame other restrictions on banking and loans. In Shuqian County, Jiangsu Province, village collective enterprises did not have to get approval from the county bank if the loan was less than 5,000 yuan, but a private business needed approval from the county bank if the loan was more than 1,000 yuan.[51] Whereas a private enterprise has to go through red tape to issue a receipt, a *guahu* company can issue receipts easily. Banks either refused to give loans to private business people or charged them high interest rates. In some places, the interest rate for loans reached 18 percent for private loans.[52] With *guahu*, rural entrepreneurs were able to get bank privileges extended through the collective enterprises. Moreover, no state-owned enterprise would take receipts from private enterprises, especially rural ones, and exhibitions refused entry to nonstate enterprises. *Guahu* overcame the structural barriers and enabled rural entrepreneurs to acquire the social cover of collective enterprises.

For example, when the former party secretary of one village in Heilongjiang tried to form a private construction firm, he had to use the collective name in order to register the business because the provincial government did not allow private businesses.[53] In 1988, the private company made 4 million yuan. Clearly, *guahu* enables rural entrepreneurs to break through state restrictions on the size or scale of private businesses.

Fourth, *guahu* also gave rural enterprises and merchants access to bank transfer notes and checks that they are otherwise denied. Rural entrepreneurs had to carry cash for their business transactions. Some had to pay money to police in order to get protection if they carried a large sum of money. One rural entrepreneur, Zhou Minghui, from Baoqing, Hunan Province, tired of paying police money and so attached her businesses to a formal organization in her county seat, saying: "With *guahu*, I am able to get checks from the bank and do not have to carry cash with me all the time. Although I have to pay some money to the county government for using its name, I am able to get bank loans and carry bank notes just as collective firms do."[54]

Fifth, *guahu* brings direct economic benefits to rural entrepreneurs through tax privileges and economic privileges. For one thing, collective enterprises pay lower taxes than private ones. According to the state 1986 tax law for private businesses, a private firm must pay 60 percent of its earnings in taxes if the net earnings do not exceed 30,000 yuan and 84 percent if it earns more.[55]

Since this heavy tax does not include the enterprises tax or management fees, the state progressive tax law makes it impossible for any private business to make money legally. *Guahu* enables rural entrepreneurs to make the best use of government policies, especially regarding tax privileges for collective enterprises. Many rural private businesses could not have survived the tax burden without *guahu*. Two farmers in one village of Fujian Province gathered 140,000 yuan to set up a package factory and owned everything in the factory. Everyone in the village knew that the factory belonged to these two farmers, but the factory had to carry the name of a village collective. By using the name, the village private factory paid lower taxes to the state and was able to get low interest loans. After paying 5,000 yuan in management fees to the village head and another 1,000 yuan to the township government, the village factory went about its business unhampered. In Guangdong, collective enterprises pay no taxes for the first three years of operation. In another example, when one private tractor repair shop in one village of Heilongjiang Province heard that any collective enterprises that hired handicapped people would be granted a tax exemption, the manager immediately recruited several handicapped people and attached the factory to the Civil Affairs Bureau.[56] With good management and without paying taxes, this village-based private business grew into a big enterprise with capital assets of more than 1 million yuan. Apart from paying a 30,000 yuan management fee, the company actually had nothing to do with the Civil Affairs Bureau, even though it was officially attached to it.

Similar cases of *guahu* combine a collective firm with a private firm. The private firm pays management fees to the collective firm and is entitled to use its name to conduct business transactions, enjoying the same tax status. Through *guahu*, rural entrepreneurs have been able to avoid a substantial tax burden. (Independence in economic decisionmaking distinguishes *guahu* enterprises from other collective forms of ownership.) Thus, the very privileges that stifled state industries fructified rural small-scale enterprises.

Sixth, private businesses have to pay management fees to local governments. Through *guahu*, rural entrepreneurs are able to avoid tremendous fees aimed at private business. According to one survey, there are more than sixty-seven state bureaus collecting eighty-nine different fees from private businesses, of which forty-one have no legal basis.[57] One example from a rural factory in Jieshou, Anhui Province, will illustrate this benefit of *guahu* for rural entrepreneurs:

> In 1980 a farmer applied for permission to establish a factory in the county seat. A private person was then not allowed to use land in town, nor could he open an account for his firm with the bank. The law was sidestepped by designating the business a TVP at the commune level under the direct control of the county. This status made the firm eligible for more liberal bank loans than ordinary private enterprises and gave it exemption from taxes. In addition, it obtained easier access to low-cost inputs through the government channels that served rural industries, advantages in obtaining fiscal assistance from the government (such as a Y5000 interest-free loan for working capital, better credit standing because of being able to use the county's name, and the privilege of selecting a plant site anywhere in the county). . . . We were amazed to find that the firm had just bought 1 mu of land at the new site for Y10,000, although China's constitution forbids private ownership of land. The purchase would have been impossible had the firm not been designated a township enterprise. In return for all these privileges, the enterprise pays 1 percent of its gross sales as a management fee to the county business administration every year.[58]

This case indicates that rural entrepreneurs have been able to use the status differentiation among different enterprises to get the best possible deal through the practice of *guahu*. Rural entrepreneurs in Henan have an expression to describe this rent-seeking behavior, *zhaokaoshan* (looking for a reliable mountain): "Small enterprises depend on three *suo* (taxation office, police office, and commercial office); medium size depends on three bureaus (police bureau, tax bureau, and commercial bureau); the big one depends on the county magistrate."

Seventh, apart from economic benefits and political protection, *guahu* increased the social status of rural enterprises, particularly regarding the legal transfer of *hukou* from rural to urban. Once a rural enterprise enjoyed the legal status of a county or township collective enterprise, entrepreneurs and sometimes even workers gained urban *hukou* and other privileges of urban residents. Politically, the entrepreneurs could be promoted to formal cadres, enjoying life-tenured appointment. Even their family members would be able to obtain *hukou*. William Byrd also finds that moneymaking is not the only concern of rural entrepreneurs: "Nonpecuniary goals include providing employment and a secure future for family members and, to a lesser extent, other relatives; improving one's social and official status (for example, by becoming a second-class urban resident as many Jiezhou entrepreneurs did); and even contribute to local community welfare and employment."[59]

The pressure to secure urban *hukou* privileges among workers in *guahu* enterprises has perpetuated the *guahu* practice. For example, one successful company in Tahe, Anhui Province, was forced to become a "collective" company to help all its employees to obtain urban *hukou* status.[60]

As a result of those benefits from *guahu*, many rural business people tried their best to seek *kaoshan* (a "reliable mountain," i.e., a big shot), and *guahu* flourished. By the early 1990s, *guahu* had become a common way for farmers to expand their businesses. In Sixia County, Henan Province, *guahu* businesses comprised 36 percent of *getihu* and 30 percent of private enterprises.[61] In Wenzhou, Zhejiang Province, out of 12,000 private enterprises, only 40 registered as private businesses, with the rest falling in the category of *guahu* companies.[62] In Changle County, Fujian Province, 80 percent of rural industries are *guahu*, while in Shantou, Guangdong Province, *guahu* enterprises occupy 90 percent of all enterprises.[63]

Eighth, finally, *guahu* also occurred when a collective firm facing difficulties asked a private rural company to take over, promising to pay the debt. This was especially true in rural areas where rural industry was not developed. According to Lou Xiaopeng, in the 1980s, 50 percent of all private companies in less developed areas took over collective enterprises but used *guahu* to keep all the privileges of the collective enterprises.[64] The old collective enterprise continued to exist in name and to get all the benefits from the government, but the enterprise became private, enjoying independence. Since it saved a rural enterprise from bankruptcy, local government leaders often encouraged this form of *guahu*. This was another attempt to approximate the effects of *baochan daohu*. As long as the firm paid the fees, the local government left it alone. The protection furnished by *guahu* sheltered private enterprises.

Although most *guahu* businesses arose voluntarily, some cases involved coercion and confiscation of private property. In many cases, *guahu* businesses sacrificed their profitability for their borrowed legitimacy. Sometimes, when *guahu* businesses grew, the local government gave in to the temptation to get involved with running the business and just took over. The blurring of ownership caused problems. Some local leaders used the diffusion to take over the enterprises and become managers themselves. In general, though, *guahu* strengthened the power of rural entrepreneurs. Once the situation becomes favorable, many rural private businesses will come out of the *guahu* closet.

## The Impact of *Guahu*

*Guahu* significantly influenced the structure of the PRC by redefining the role of government cadres. *Guahu* links the personal material interest of cadres directly to rural industrial privatization. The local government receives substantial fees from *guahu*. Some local governments prefer to give a red cap to those private businesses so that they can collect more management fees. In fact, *guahu* enterprises have become *xiaojingui* (small gold treasure boxes) for local cadres. This new form of patron–client relationship is different from the old one in that the participants all try to weaken the state's economic power for their personal benefit and local interests. As long as *guahu* enterprises pay the management fees to the local government, they get tax-free status like other collective enterprises in the countryside. Local tax exemption makes it difficult for the state to collect more money from *guahu* enterprises, while at the same time strengthening the power of local government and local entrepreneurs. A popular rural saying in the mid-1980s captured a *guahu* exchange between rural cadres and rural entrepreneurs:

> Your name is specialization (rural entrepreneurs),
> my name is power;
> You want a stamp, I want money;
> you want to get rich, I will support you.
> Signing a contract is easy.
> Maotai wine helps me write.[65]

By so doing, the former political cadres become the state's gravediggers. Rural governments are motivated to reduce state taxes and increase the revenues of local enterprises. Since local government budgets come from local industries, more development means more money for local cadres. Thus, cadres became monetary dependents rather than controllers of rural industries. *Guahu* changed the local cadres from political commissars into economic parasites. Some of them even made patrons of rural entrepreneurs. Of course, local cadres still retain political control. What is important is that the new power base combines politics and money. When the state launches a campaign against private business, rural entrepreneurs are often protected by those formal organizations. For example, when the 1983 anti-spiritual pollution campaign destroyed many private businesses, rural entrepreneurs with *guahu* remained intact. This also explains the surge of *guahu* after the 1989 Tiananmen massacre, when the state attacked private businesses.

In addition, the very success of *guahu* businesses allowed local cadres to take part in private enterprises. When the state lifted the restrictions that forbade cadres to participate in private businesses, rural cadres used *guahu* to become de facto owners or partners of rural enterprises. Through *guahu*, rural entrepreneurs drafted cadres to help them cultivate the non-state sector. Some cadres became rural entrepreneurs themselves.

The impact of *guahu* also affects the city. In fact, the tables turn and the village and rural small towns sometimes become the sources of *guahu* for urban private entrepreneurs to expand their businesses or to initiate a private business. For example, when one high school teacher invented a water tank for urban high-rise buildings, he used the name of a rural collective enterprise to set up Maoning Water Tank Instruments.[66] *Guahu* enabled the former high school teacher to save 9 million yuan in taxes. By 1988, the enterprise produced output worth 85 million yuan, while the *xiang* government received 800,000 yuan. In short, *guahu* changed the context of the local government.

Moreover, numerous rural industries established relations with urban factories through *guahu*, greatly increasing the interdependence between the rural and urban people. Although the state factories benefited from the efficiency of rural industries, rural factories gained new technology from urban state factories.

*Guahu* made it easy for rural private businesses to contact urban state organizations. In Suzhou, Jiangsu Province, several hundred rural enterprises attached themselves to State Foreign Trade companies, accounting for one-third of all exports in that city in 1985.[67] *Guahu* enabled many private rural enterprises to march into urban markets under the flag of a legal entity. In fact, the emergence of rural corporations in the cities in the early 1990s came from *guahu*.

Guahu fused the public and private spheres, allowing private sectors as well as local governments to begin to dominate. The diffusion of the *guahu* phenomenon provided an important path of expansion for private businesses on the one hand and the erosion of the state's power on the other. In November 1986, the state business and commercial administration bureau issued a document trying to stop the spread of *guahu*. The document points out that 80–90 percent of cooperatives are in fact private partnerships and demands that the local government change their licenses to private business licenses. *Guahu* has been so important for the growth of rural industries, however, that the state could not undo it without giving up its economic benefits.[68] *Baochan daohu* restored family farming, but *guahu* facilitated and expanded the growth of private businesses, which absorbed the surplus labor released from agriculture.

## Conclusion

The sudden rise of the rural industrial sector has far-reaching significance in Chinese politics. Before the takeoff of rural industrialization, the state took virtually "all of the surplus generated by industry, including profits and indirect taxes, and local governments were able to retain only a portion of the profits of selected local enterprises."[69] The rapid growth of rural industry has changed this pattern. Rural industries eroded the state's main source of revenue: monopoly profits of state-owned industry. As a result, the central state budget shrank from over 40 percent of national income in 1978 to only 22 percent in 1989.[70]

From the ownership structure, the rural industries with private, *guahu*, and collective enterprises challenged the dominance of the state industrial sector and became the backbone of Chinese industrial production.

Rural industry developed unevenly in China, varying from region to region. The rural regions of the East and South developed faster than the rest of the country. This uneven development complicates the analysis of Chinese farmers' industrial development, but rural industrial development in the less developed regions has also been crucial (see Figure 5.1). Even in Gansu, one of the poorest provinces, between 1984 and 1990, the real growth rate of output value for rural industry was 31.2 percent. Nowhere in China is rural industry irrelevant to development, although its scale can vary greatly. What is more, rural industry gave the local governments more access to goods from rural enterprises, diminishing the revenue share of the central state. *Guahu* broke through the barriers between different enterprise structures, breeding private initiatives under the collective structure. *Guahu* diversified the Chinese ownership structure by undercutting the socialist state and collective ownership structure and by blurring the division between public and private spheres. In contrast to the previous blurring line between the collective and private that smothered private interests, the new blurring line serves to strengthen private individual interest at the cost of public power. *Guahu* is like jungle vines that have twined around a tree and strangled it. Eventually the tree rots out and only the vines remain. Like parasitic vines, the instigators of *guahu* overwhelm their hosts. When the government's attitude becomes less hostile, the *guahu* business gradually come out of the closet. By 1993, 54 percent of all rural industry was owned by individuals or private joint-stockholder companies.[71]

The rural influence threatened state planning so much that in his 1989 government report, Li Peng called for a reduction of rural industrial development and advocated the return of *sanjiudi*.[72] The growth of rural industries has constrained the state function as the result of the two-tier price system and *guahu*. The rapid development of rural industries and the changes that accompanied it made it impossible for the state to stop the growth of rural industry without hurting itself. Although state industry still

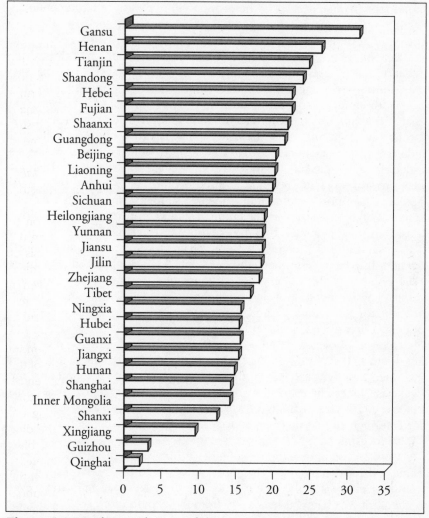

**Figure 5.1**  Real Growth Rate of the Output Value of Rural Industry, by Province, 1984–1990

*Source: Zhongguo Xiangzhen Qiye Nianjian Bianji Weiyuanhui (Editorial Commision of Chinese Rural Industrial Enterprises), Zhongguo xiang-zheng qiye nianjian 1992 (1992 Book of Chinese Rural Industrial Enterprises) (Beijing: Nongye Chubanshe, 1992).*

monopolizes some sectors of the economy, if the current trend continues, China's most productive industry will actually move to the countryside or come under rural enterprise control by the end of the 1990s.

Despite the great achievement of rural industries, much of the world's attention has focused on the elite (especially Deng Xiaoping) or on overseas Chinese investment. There is no doubt that elite permission for rural people to set up small-scale industries opened the gate for farmers. The goal of the elite was to stop rural–urban migration. Their real concern was for the state factories. Since the elite power base was built upon the state industries, they, including Deng, often tried to constrain rural industries, especially when the state factories' revenue share was shrinking. This sudden erosion of state revenue startled Deng. As late as 1989, Deng Xiaoping's support for rural industries was still wavering. When the dominance of state industry was threatened by the competition of rural industries, Deng said in a speech to the Politburo in 1989 that "it was all right to shut down the inefficient, or wasteful village and township enterprises."[73] Farmers have a saying about the constant changes of the state policies: "The policies of the Communist party are like the moon; they wax and wane."[74] Wavering support in an authoritarian society could not possibly account for the explosive and continued increases in development that originated in the rural areas and among rural people.

In terms of overseas Chinese investment, rural industries received very little before 1990. After 1990, the share of overseas Chinese investment increased rapidly, especially in the cities. Rural people also tried to attract overseas Chinese investment by using their village and family connections, but the total share of foreign investment in the rural areas is still low. In 1991, foreign capital investment accounted for only 4 percent of all rural capital investment.[75]

Unlike in other developing countries, Chinese industrial growth is now being led by the farmers. The most active force for modernization and industrialization is in the countryside. The Chinese state's industrial development tried to keep farmers away from industrialization. For a while, the state succeeded, binding the majority of the Chinese population to the collective land, but once the farmers reassumed family autonomy, the base of the former pattern was shaken. Rural industrialization not only changes rural China; it also transformed urban China.

The Chinese experience makes clear that the rural population is not inevitably antagonistic to modernization. How fast would Chinese industrialization have been if farmers had not in Mao's time been largely overlooked in favor of urban industrial development? No one will ever know. The marginalization of Chinese farmers in Chinese elite politics may have also benefited rural industrialization because the leaders did not pay much attention to rural people. The state apparatus continues to run under the

*A rural-based foreign joint venture in Shandong
makes silverware for the European and American
markets. Photo by Wu Zengqiang*

urban heavy industrial model but becomes increasingly irrelevant by doing
so. The present army of urban firms is disappearing into nowhere. During
the whole reform period (1978–1993), state rural investment in fact
declined from 10 percent of capital investment in 1978 to a little over 2 percent in 1992. State leaders did not know much about farmers' industrial
development until it grew too strong to reverse.

The rural population took advantage of the central leadership's ignorance or lack of interest in them to develop industries with a vengeance
and, above all, on a spontaneous, unorganized, leaderless, nonideological,
and apolitical basis. *Even now, when rural industries contribute more than
50 percent of China's overall industrial output,*[76]*there is no ministry of rural
industry in Beijing.* There are also no parades or placards touting rural
industry as such. Individual businesses have leaders and develop organizations, but there are no leaders or organizations supporting the rural industrial movement as such. Yet that spontaneous, unorganized, leaderless,
nonideological, and apolitical movement is increasingly responsible for
most of the industrial growth of China.

# Notes

1. Deng Xiaoping, "Gaige de buzi yaojiakuai" (To Speed up Reforms), in *Shierda yilai zhongyao wenjian xuanbian* (Selections of Important Documents Since the Twelfth Party Congress) (Beijing: Renmin Chubanshe, 1988), p. 1444. Deng's comments also appeared in *People's Daily*, June 13, 1987. Emphasis added.

2. Dong Fureng, *Industrialization and China's Rural Modernization* (London: Macmillan Press, 1992), p. 54.

3. "When China Wakes: A Survey of China," *Economist* (November 28, 1992).

4. Zhongguo Xiangzhen Qiye Nianjian Bianji Weiyuanhui (Editorial Commission of Chinese Rural Industrial Enterprise), *Zhongguo xiangzheng qiye nianjian 1992* (1992 Book of Chinese Rural Industrial Enterprises) (Beijing: Nongye Chubanshe, 1992), pp. 260–262.

5. Zhongguo Xiangzhen Qiye Nianjian Bianji Weiyuanhui (Editorial Commission of Chinese Rural Industrial Enterprise), *Zhongguo xiangzheng qiye nianjian 1994* (1994 Book of Chinese Rural Industrial Enterprises) (Beijing: Nongye Chubanshe, 1994), p. 436.

6. *Zhongguo xiangzhen qiyebao* (Chinese Rural Industry News), March 23, 1984.

7. Lin Qingsong and William Byrd, eds., *China's Rural Industry: Structure, Development, and Reform* (New York: Oxford University Press for the World Bank, 1990), p. 3.

8. Jan Svejnar and Josephine Woo, "Development Patterns in Four Counties," in ibid., pp. 47–62.

9. Barry Naughton, "Implications of the State Monopoly over Industry and Its Relation," *Modern China* 18, no. 1 (January 1992):15.

10. David Zweig, "Rural Industry: Constraining the Leading Growth Sector in China's Economy," in Joint Economic Committee, eds., *China's Economic Dilemmas in the 1990s: The Problems of Reform, Modernization and Interdependence* (Washington, D.C.: Government Printing Office, 1991), pp. 418–436.

11. Louis Putterman, "Institutional Boundaries, Structural Change, and Economic Reform in China," *Modern China* 18, no. 1 (January 1992):6.

12. In Chinese: *Yihu dai yicun; yicun dai yipian; cuncun dianhuo; huhu maoyan.*

13. Yang Youzhe, "Jiji fazhan jiating he nianhu qiye" (Actively Develop Family and Joint-Capital Enterprises), *Zhongguo nongcun jingji* (Chinese Rural Economy) 4 (1986):1–4.

14. Hou Xiaohong, "Xianjieduan nongcun shenyu laodongli xingwei tezheng" (Characteristics of Behavior of the Surplus Rural Labor Force at Present), *Jingji yanjiu* (Economic Research) 2 (1988):66–77.

15.  The development of rural industry started first in the Great Leap Forward but was abandoned after the complete failure of that program in 1959. The government did not allow rural people to participate in industrial activities until 1970, when the state advocated the mechanization of agriculture, allowing farming machine tools factories to open in the countryside. In some places, peasants took this opportunity to develop industries, but development did not take off until *baochan daohu*. For more on rural industrial development in the 1970s, see Dwight Perkins, *Rural Small-Scale Industry in the People's Republic of China* (Berkeley: University of California Press, 1977); and Carl Riskin, "Small Industry and the Chinese Model of Development," *China Quarterly* 73 (March 1977):145–173.

16.  *People's Daily*, editorial, September 10, 1979.

17.  Guojia Tongji Ju Nongcun Shehui Jingji Tongji Shi (Rural Social Economic Statistics Group of the State Statistical Bureau), *Zhongguo nongcun tongji nian jian, 1992* (Chinese Rural Statistics, 1992) (Beijing: Zhongguo Tongji Chubanshe, 1992), p. 35.

18.  Lu Xueyi and Li Peilin, *Zhongguo shehui fazhan baogao* (A Developmental Report on Chinese Society) (Shengyang: Liaoning Renmin Chubanshe, 1991), p. 140.

19.  Guojia, *Chinese Rural Statistics, 1992*, pp. 162–163.

20.  Wu Jilian, "Guomin jingji de kunjing he chulu" (The Difficulties and the Solution of the State Economy), *Bijiao jingji shehui tizhi* (Economic and Social System Comparison) 6 (1990):6.

21.  *People's Daily*, May 4, 1981.

22.  Guowuyuan Nongcun Fazhan Yanjiu Zhongxin Bangongshi (Rural Development Research Center of the State Council) "Guowuyuan bangongting guanyu zhizhi jiajia qianggou he tiji shougou yanye de tongzhi" (State Council Office Bans Price-rising, Purchase-Snapping and Grade-Raising of Tobacco), in *Nongcun zhengce wenjian xuan* (Selections of Agricultural Policies, 1985–1989) (Beijing: Zhonggong Zhongyan Dangxiao Chubanshe, 1989): 344.

23.  Patrick E. Tyler, "Between Marxism and the Market, Chinese Manager Finds Corruption," *New York Times*, May 25, 1994, D 3.

24.  There is a considerable difference in wage and welfare packages in the urban state sector, in contrast to the urban collective and private sectors, but the largest differences remain those between city and countryside.

25.  Sheng Hua, et al., *China: From Revolution to Reform* (London: Macmillan Press, 1993), p. 166.

26.  In Chinese: *Qianxin wanku; qianshan wanshui; qianyan wanyu; qianfang baiji*.

27.  Du Haiyan, "Causes of Rapid Rural Industrial Development," in Lin and Byrd, *China's Rural Industry*, p. 55.

28.   Sheng, et al., *China: From Revolution to Reform*.

29.   Deng, "To Speed up Reforms," p. 1444.

30.   Miao Zhuang, "Zhidu bianqian zhong di gaige zhan lüe xuanze wenti" (Choice of Reform Strategies During Institutional Changes in China), *Jingji yanjiu* (Economic Research) 10 (1992):72–79.

31.   Wang Shiyuan, et al., *Zhongguo ganke daquan* (Chinese Reform Encyclopedia) (Dalian: Dalian Chubanshe, 1992), p. 30.

32.   Jiang Mao and Jiang Sung, *Zouchu migong* (Walk out of the Maze) (Beijing: Xueyuan Chubanshe, 1989), p. 93.

33.   Jiang Liu, et al., eds., *Shehui lanpishu 1992–1993 nian Zhongguo: shehui xingshi fenxi yu yuce* (China in 1992–1993: Analysis and Forecast of Social Situations, 1992–1993, China) (Beijing: Zhongguo Shehui Kexue Chubanshe, 1993).

34.   Huang Laiji, "Guanyu xiangzhen qiye suoyouquan yu jingying fangshi" (A Survey of Management and Ownership of Rural Industries), *Zhengzhi yu falü* (Politics and Law) 4 (1987):50–53.

35.   Liu Guoguang, *80 niandai Zhongguo jingji gaige yu fazhan* (Chinese Economic Reform and Development in the 1980s) (Beijing: Jingji Guanli Chubanshe, 1991), p. 400.

36.   The concepts of "hard budget" and "soft budget" come from Janos Kornai, *The Socialist System: The Political Economy of Communism*, (Princeton: Princeton University Press, 1992). Kornai points out that "hard budget constraint" is a concept akin to the principle of "profit maximization" but not exactly synonymous with it (p. 143). The "soft budget constraint" involves vertical bargaining: "A firm (or a branch directorate on behalf of several firms, or a ministry on behalf of several branches) bargains for more subsidy to cover its excess expenditure. Negotiations are made either in advance, before the amount of subsidy has been laid down, or during and after the period covered by the subsidy, to improve on the sum promised in advance" (p. 140).

37.   *Nongmin ribao* (Farmers Daily), September 8, 1988.

38.   Zhongguo Xiangzheng Qiye Nianjian Bianji Weiyuanhui, *1992 Book of Chinese Rural Industrial Enterprises*, p. 230.

39.   *Zhongguo Xiangzhen Qiyebao* (Chinese Rural Industry News), August 8, 1988.

40.   Wang Xiaoqian, et al., "Nongcun shangpin shengchan fazhan de xindongxiang" (New Trends of Rural Commodity Production Development), *Nongcun, jingji, shehui* (Rural China, Economy and Society) 3 (1985):77.

41.   Fei Xiaotong, "Xiaoshangpin, dashichange" (Small Commodities but a Big Market), in *Fei Xiaotong xuanji* (Selected Works of Fei Xiaotong) (Tianjin: Renmin Chubanshe, 1988), pp. 364–383.

42.   David Zweig, "Internationalizing China's Countryside: The Political Economy of Exports from Rural Industry," *China Quarterly* 128 (December 1991):719.

43.   Zhongguo Xiangzheng Qiye Nianjian Bianji Weiyuanhui, *1992 Book of Chinese Rural Industrial Enterprises*, pp. 260–262.

44.   William A. Byrd and N. Zhu, "Markets Interactions and Industrial Structures," in Lin and Byrd, *China's Rural Industry*, p. 96.

45.   Joseph Fewsmith, *Dilemmas of Reform in China: Political Conflict and Economic Debate* (Armonk, N.Y.: M. E. Sharpe, 1994), p. 80.

46.   Wang, et al., "The New Trends." The data in Hubei are from my own investigation in Wuhan fringe areas and in Jinshan of Hubei Province, 1984 and 1985.

47.   *Nongmin ribao* (Farmers Daily), September 23, 1987.

48.   According to official definitions, a *siying* enterprise is different from *getihu* in that the foreman hires more than five workers, whereas *getihu* is often a family or individual business. In the early 1980s, the state lifted restrictions on *getihu*, but the formal recognition of *siying* remained in force until 1987.

49.   Nongyebu Jingji Zhengce Yanjiu Zhongxin (Economic Policy Research Center of Agricultural Ministry), *Zhongguo nongcun: zhengce yanjiu beiwanglu* (Rural China: Policy Research Memorandum), vol. 2 (Beijing: Nongye Chubanshe, 1991), p. 312.

50.   Zhang Jinjiang, "A Preliminary Analysis of Private Enterprises Under the Name of the Collective," *Social Sciences in Chongqing* 1 (1988):60–64.

51.   Nongyebu Jingji Zhengce Yanjiu Zhongxin, *Rural China: Policy Research Memorandum*, vol. 1 (Beijing: Nongye Chubanshe, 1988), p. 375.

52.   Guowuyuan Yanjiu Shi Geti Siying Jingji Tiaochazu (State Council Investigation Team), *Zhongguo de geti he siying jingji* (Chinese Private Enterprises) (Beijing: Gaige Chubanshe, 1990), p. 17.

53.   Ibid., p. 97.

54.   Personal interview with Zhou Minghui from Baojin, Hunan Province, in 1985.

55.   Guowuyuan, *Chinese Private Enterprises*, p. 289.

56.   Ibid., pp. 57, 98, 102.

57.   Liu, "Woguo feigong youzhi qiye jin qunti jiben xianzhuang" (An Analysis of Nonstate Entrepreneurs and Their Basic Conditions), *Shehui xue yanjiu* (Sociological Research) 6 (1992):17.

58.   Lou, "Ownership and Status Stratification," in Byrd and Lin, *China's Rural Industry*, p. 146.

59.   William A. Byrd, "Entrepreneurship, Capital and Ownership," in Lin and Byrd, ed., *China's Rural Industry*, p. 199.

60.   Lou, "Ownership and Status Stratification."

61.   *People's Daily*, July 3, 1993.

62.   Liu, "An Analysis of Nonstate Entrepreneurs," pp. 13–20.

63.   Guowuyuan, *Chinese Private Enterprises*, p. 7.

64.   Lou, "Ownership and Status Stratification."

65. In Chinese: *Ni xing zhuan, wo xing quan; ni yao zhang, wo yao qian; ni zhifu, wo zhiyuan; Dingge hetong lidangran; Maotaijiu dang mushui, qiangzi gaizhang haozizai.*

66. Guowuyuan, *Chinese Private Enterprises*, p. 99.

67. *People's Daily,* May 16, 1985.

68. Nongyebu, *Rural China* (1988): 378.

69. Christine P. W. Wong, "Fiscal Reform and Local Industrialization: The Problematic Sequencing of Reform in Post-Mao China," *Modern China* 18, no. 2 (April 1992):197.

70. Ibid.

71. Zhongguo Xiangzhen, *Zhongguo xiangzheng qiye nianjian 1994*, p. 4.

72. Li Peng states: "The township and village industries should concentrate on developing the processing of agricultural and sideline products, the production of certain raw materials, and production of export commodities that earn foreign exchange. The capital needed by the township and town enterprises should mainly come from their own accumulations." "Report on the Work of Government," Beijing Domestic Service (March 20, 1989), in *FBIS*-Chi–89–053 (March 21, 1989): 11.

73. Fewsmith, *Dilemmas of Reform in China*, p. 247.

74. In Chinese: *Gongchandang di zhengce xiang yueliang, chuyi shiwu bu yi yang.*

75. Zhongguo Xiangzhen Qiye Nianjian Bianji Weiyuanhui, *1992 Book of Chinese Rural Industrial Enterprises*, p. 196.

76. *New York Times*, December 2, 1993.

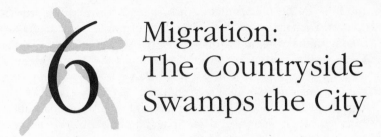

# 6 Migration: The Countryside Swamps the City

Money can make a ghost do the grinding for you.

Chinese proverb

The most important rural influence on the structural changes within the PRC is social and geographic mobility, especially rural–urban migration. Under *baochan daohu*, rural cadres could no longer control the mobility of farmers. As farmers freed themselves from the collectives, they scattered everywhere, seeking opportunities to improve their lives, resulting in perhaps the biggest rural–urban migration in history. According to some estimates, by 1992 over 100 million farmers had migrated from rural to urban environments.[1]

As *baochan daohu* weakened the command system of control in the countryside and rural industrialization ended the state monopoly on industry, so rural migration into cities undermined the core structure of the urban-based state: the *hukou-danwei* system. *Baochan daohu* evoked face-to-face confrontations between urban and rural interests. In some places, the new rural-based drive became more "urban" than its urban counterpart. Rural mobility undermined and bypassed the grain rationing system, the *hukou* system, and the *danwei* system itself, challenging the state even in urban labor allocation. No prereform structure was left untouched.

## State Response to Rural Surplus Labor

The government tried to stop rural-urban migration most of the time. In the 1970s and early 1980s, the state adopted a policy of *jiudi xiaohua* (absorb rural surplus labor locally) in an attempt to prevent rural migrants from entering the cities. When this could not be sustained, it called for *litu bulixiang* (leave land but not the rural areas). The state issued a document in 1984 allowing farmers to settle down in small towns provided that they did not depend on the state grain rationing system and other welfare subsidies that uniquely privileged state workers and urban residents.[2] Although its intention was to deter farmers from going into cities, this document enlarged the hole in the *hukou* dike, a hole already opened by farmers' market activities. The farmer sea surged through that hole. Rural migration soared. To contain the flow, in October 1984, the state published another document specifically indicating that farmers could not go beyond small rural towns, not even to the county seat.[3] After 1986, *nongzhuanfei* (changing of farmers' *hukou* from rural to nonrural) formally ended.

Although there was booming development of small towns in many parts of China, especially Jiangsu and Zhejiang, the state could not prevent the increasingly independent farmers from seeking economic activities in cities. Indeed, as noted above, the very development of small town rural industries increased the access of rural entrepreneurs to urban areas, and the great proliferation of uncontrolled markets overwhelmed the coercive restraints implied in *hukou*. Surging markets guaranteed a source of food and goods for the surge of migrants.

Farmers migrated to cities in large numbers to buy and sell and to take advantage of employment opportunities. This led to the rapid increase of urbanization in direct opposition to the state's attempt to hold it. The farmers migrated on an unorganized basis, planning and acting individually. The sea of unorganized farmers flowed first around the rural cadres and then around the urban cadres. The cadres perceived no local organization and hence no source of danger. Had there been a head to the farmers' movement, it would have been lopped off. The anarchic flow of individuals gave the cadres no organized target to resist.

## Corruption and Migration

Rural people sometimes defied the state's strict control over mobility during the collectivization period. Farmers in Jiangsu, Zhejiang, Gansu, Henan, and Liaoning left collective farms to participate in commerce and in services, but in that period the numbers were comparatively small. Illegal temporary migration (from a few days to several years) has been a feature of Chinese life in varying degrees since decollectivization.[4]

The institutional change of *baochan daohu* in the early 1980s encouraged more efficient use of labor and technology in farming, raised productivity per hectare, created a surplus base for a market economy, and heightened the demand for services in cities. In addition, cadres could no longer arbitrarily determine work assignments. Farmers no longer needed cadre permission to travel or to engage in alternative economic activities. China became more open, more mobile, and more market-oriented. The conventional control methods (grain rationing, *hukou*, and *danwei*) could no longer deter farmers from entering cities to pursue their own economic advancement.

As farming became comparatively less valuable as a source of income, more and more farmers wanted to leave the land to find work elsewhere.

*Liu Weijian, a farmer youth from Zijing County, Guangdong, came to Shenzhen as a taxi driver. In five years, he saved 40,000 yuan and bought a Shenzhen hukou. Now a sophisticated Shenzhenese, Mr. Liu dreams of a career as a banker. Photo by Kate Xiao Zhou*

Some wanted to return the land to the cadres in order to avoid paying the grain quota to the state and cadres. In order to get permission from the village cadres, farmers often gave them gifts (wine, food, consumer goods, or money). For example, Zu Fujiao, a young woman from Tongxin Village, Jingsan County, Hubei, found a job as a maid in Wuhan City in 1986. She bought two bottles of expensive liquor, four packs of cigarettes, and two pieces of clothing for the village head just to ask to return a portion of her contracted land. When the deal was made, the village head asked her family to hold a big banquet for village cadres to "celebrate" her success. The whole deal cost her more than 230 yuan, almost half her wages for the year. When asked why she had to spend so much money, she said, "To be relieved of the burden."[5]

In most cases, farmers had to continue submitting to the state and the local cadres a fixed quota of grain after their departure from their villages. In some cases, family members continue to pay the grain obligation. In other cases, when the whole family migrates, some farmers have to buy grain from the markets to fulfill their obligation. For example, Liu Huafu, a farmer from Sichuan, bought grain and submitted it to cadres on behalf of his family of eight, who all migrated after he made it big as a private construction contractor in Guangdong.[6] With fees and grain quota submitted, there was no reason for cadres to stop villagers from leaving the land. The submitting of grain to the state covered up farmers' migration activities.

Village and township government also collected fees from migrants who wanted to leave villages by giving them a certificate required by the urban governments.

Although the sum involved to buy permission to leave is usually small in the 1990s, farmers spend huge sums of money to get an urban *hukou.* As discussed in Chapter 2, urban *hukou* have become the *minggenzi* (lifeblood) of the Chinese people because they are used to obtain welfare rights (housing, subsidies) and children's education for urban residents. What is more, once one gets an urban *hukou,* one does not have to give grain contributions to the state, that is, one is no longer bound to fulfill the village quota.

Governments at all levels try to make money by selling urban *hukou* to migrants. In September 1994, Beijing announced a policy whereby, beginning November 1, 1994, individuals or their employers could purchase permanent resident status in Beijing city or its suburbs. The price for city residents was 100,000 yuan (about $11,700) for employers and 50,000 yuan ($5,884) for individuals. The price dropped to 30,000 yuan ($3,756) for suburban residence and 10,000 yuan ($1,176) for a "peasant" residential permit in the suburbs.[7]

Li Mingwei, a rural migrant worker from rural Guangdong, spent more than 8,000 yuan (more than one year's pay) to buy an urban *hukou.* Li gave his reasons for such a big investment:

> Can you understand what it means to be a man without [urban] *hukou?* Life is like walking a tightrope. If you have *hukou,* there is a net to catch you when you fall: social welfare, food subsidies, unemployment, social security, and the feeling of being equal in the eyes of others. Without that book, you will fall and you will have nothing. You have to go back to the village to attend water buffalo.[8]

Many farmers were willing to pay a huge sum of money in order to have their status changed from rural *hukou* to urban *hukou.* In the early 1990s, the Shenzhen government charged 40,000–60,000 yuan for a Shenzhen *hukou.* Since cadres were in charge of this *hukou* transfer, corruption involving *hukou* was common. Almost everyone in China had a family member or friend who desperately sought a *hukou* transfer.

Government cadres control this transfer from rural to urban *hukou,* which gives them tremendous power and creates opportunities for corruption. In most cases, farmers approach cadres with offers of bribery. For example, before a young *hukou* police officer in one big town married, strangers showed up with tens of thousands of yuan as wedding gifts.[9] They had heard a rumor that his big town was going to expand to a city.

Since urban *hukou* are also hierarchically ranked, with bigger towns or cities providing higher welfare, transfers to bigger cities require higher

*One of the first toys for rich Guangdong farmer families is a cellular phone—a real one. Photo by Kate Xiao Zhou*

bribes. The bribery also varies from region to region. In general, the richer the place, the higher the amount. For example, Zhang Wenlie, the police chief of Yingde County, Guangdong Province (a rich province), once received 150,000 yuan for a *hukou* transfer.[10] My 1994 interviews with thirty-two rural migrants in Shenzhen indicated that migrants from outside Guangdong paid 50,000 yuan for their Shenzhen *hukou* and rural migrants from Guangdong paid 40,000 yuan for theirs.

One exfarmer became rich after he set up two fashion shops in the busiest street of Yiyang City, Hunan Province. His wife and children, however, were still carrying rural *hukou*. Realizing that his family members would remain "second-class citizens" despite the family's wealth unless he changed their status, the exfarmer entrepreneur sent the police chief 3,000 yuan, a Meihua watch (worth 500 yuan), and a gold ring (worth 1,300 yuan). Mr. Qi signed the transfer for the family.[11]

Apart from personal gains, *hukou* provide a big source of local government revenue. *Hukou* are sold openly to rural migrants in many cities and counties. In some counties, the sale of *hukou* provides 40 percent of government revenue.[12] The *People's Daily* reported that more than thirty county officials were involved in the illegal transfer of 661 *hukou* in Qian County, Shanxi Province.[13] In addition, many city governments in Guangdong set up *hukou* transfer fees, ranging from 3,000 yuan to 10,000 yuan per person.[14] According to one report, in 1993, 3 million farmers bought urban *hukou* by paying 25 billion yuan.[15]

## Grain Coupon Rats

In the very beginning of migration, the most important barrier blocking rural migration was the *hukou* system, which in turn rested on the control of grain rationing. The population in China was defined by the source of their grain: Urban people were provided subsidized grain by the state through the *liangpiao*; rural people received their grain from the production team. If a farmer left his designated work team without permission, his relatives would be punished, often by a reduction or cancelation of grain rations. Rural migrants could not get food in the city because the state prohibited sale of food without *liangpiao*. Since people with a rural *hukou* were not given food coupons, they had to carry their own food to the city. This control of grain made rural–urban migration difficult, if not impossible, for more than twenty years.

After *baochan daohu*, the cadres could no longer use food rationing to control farmers' mobility. Rural migrants dealt with the food problem by buying *liangpiao* on the black market. Also, *baochan daohu* increased the grain under the direct control of the farmers. Grain could be marketed locally, and the funds so gained could be used to fuel the black market system in urban areas.

Although the black market had existed during the collective days, the scale of illegal exchanges of *liangpiao* increased rapidly in the 1980s. After *baochan daohu*, family farming enabled farmers to produce a variety of goods for the market, not the least of which was the grain produced by increased productivity per hectare. In the beginning, rural people swapped their products (both agricultural and nonagricultural) for *liangpiao*. For example, in the Dadongmen vegetable market of Wuhan in 1980, one coupon of *quanguo liangpiao* (national grain coupon) for fifteen jin (approximately sixteen pounds) of grain could be exchanged for twenty eggs.[16] Rural migrants also exchanged services for *liangpiao*. Carpenters, shoe repairers, locksmiths, cotton fluffers, bicycle repairers, and maids would often ask for *liangpiao* as part of their payment. Urban people in need of both goods and services provided by rural people were happy to exchange *liangpiao*.

The continuation of the command economy in the cities in the 1980s provided a prime opportunity for such illegal transactions. Like other countries with a command economy, China experienced endemic shortages in consumption goods and services. Between 1957 and 1979, the population increased more than 50 percent but retail businesses dwindled from 1,950,300 to 1,010,000; the number of restaurants decreased from 470,000 to 103,000. The service sector was reduced from 280,000 to 95,000 businesses; people employed in services decreased from 1.2 percent of the population to 0.8 percent.[17] This severe shortage provided rural migrants with a golden opportunity to get around the grain rationing system by providing services and commercial goods to urban people. It made their presence desirable, even indispensable, in the very core of Chinese urban society. The *liangpiao* black market mushroomed. Such private transactions involved millions of urban and rural people before the state was even aware of it, and when the state did become aware, it was unable to eliminate this illegal activity. The government lacked the will, even though it probably still had the power to do so.

According to one investigation in Shandong (where the consumption of grain was often higher than in the South), the *liangpiao* quota for the average urban person was 15.6 kilograms. In 1988, the actual purchase of grain for the average urban person was only 9.25 kilograms, leaving 40 percent of *liangpiao* for the black market.[18] In fact, *liangpiao* became *dier huobi* (a second currency), despite a 1979 directive that forbade the sale of *liangpiao*.

The state intended *liangpiao* to keep down rural migration, on the one hand, and, on the other hand, to provide cheap agricultural products for urban people. This supported low working wages and acted as a device for extracting the rural surplus. Before 1991, every catty of grain sold to urban people through *liangpiao* included a subsidy of 0.4 yuan. Inadvertently, *liangpiao* trade became a source of nonstate economic power. In fact, more and more people used the price difference to make money through the *liangpiao* trade. According to a 1991 government report, at least 33 percent of urban residents traded *liangpiao* for commercial goods.[19]

Apart from the *liangpiao* black market, the rural migrants also bought grain from *jishi*. The state permitted this as part of the bargain of *baochan daohu*, allowing farmers to sell their leftover products after fulfilling their obligation to the state. Eventually, farmers sold a substantial portion of grain on the open market as the number of migrants increased rapidly.

When *liangpiao* failed to deter rural migration and urban working wages soared during the 1980s, *liangpiao* lost its value to the state.

Providing grain to urban dwellers below the state-imposed purchase price drained the state's budget. Finally, in May 1991, the state reduced urban grain subsidies to allow the grain price to match its purchase price.

When the state grain price for urban dwellers increased, rural grain merchants took over the urban grain market, an event unprecedented in Chinese history. The unorganized farmers not only swamped the structure of the Chinese Communist state, but they stood the urban–rural relationship on its head! By establishing myriad alternative markets, they quietly leached away state control over the markets. Today in China, anyone can buy grain without *liangpiao* in markets dominated by rural merchants, even though in 1994 the government tried its best to restore the use of *liangpiao* in the cities.

## *Jiuji Weicheng* and Street Vending

*Liangpiao* trade suggests that rural migration could never have been maintained without the increase of markets as a source of subsistence. In fact, farmers developed markets to establish and sustain their presence in the city. *Jiuji weicheng* (surround or encircle the city with nine basic commercial goods)[20] proved an effective way for farmers to establish themselves in the city despite both formal and informal discrimination against rural people. The nine goods were vegetables, eggs, fowl, fish, pigs, melons, fruits, flowers, and milk.

Farmers at first peddled small quantities of foodstuffs, vegetables, and handicrafts or, as itinerant repair people, walked around the urban residential streets to sell their goods and services. They had no fixed location and could only operate on a small scale, on an individual basis. Wherever they went, they formed markets.

There was never any rural vender organization as such, and this remains true today. They commanded no great physical capital or access to credit. They operated with cash and *liangpiao*. Rural vendors not only provided urban people with badly needed services, they also provided rural people with market information. When they walked around the urban streets, they became aware of what goods and services were needed. Thus, information found its way to rural people. That is one of the reasons why rural industries were able to produce goods that sell. Rural migrants, especially rural vendors, became cells of the market information network, as indicated by one farmer:

> One day people who went into cities gave me a message that eggs were needed in the cities. They (exfarmers) formed *yitiaolong* (one chain of agricultural specialization). Some collected eggs in villages; others used eggs to buy *liangpiao*; still others used *liang-*

*piao* to buy wheat. Then some made *mantou* (steamed bread) for the city people. They could make a lot of money this way.[21]

## *Jiaoqu Zhazhai* (Settle down in the Fringe Areas)

While the development of *jishi* markets enabled farmers to rid themselves of *liangpiao* restrictions, money-seeking farmers around the city helped migrants overcome the housing problem. Urban people conspired with rural migrants in the *liangpiao* black market, and farmers in fringe areas made themselves the landlords of rural migrants. The *hukou* system, with its control over residence, made it illegal for rural migrants to obtain housing in the city. Early on, rural migrants were not even allowed to stay in hotels; people had to show *jieshaoxin* (a letter of introduction from one's *danwei*) in order to rent a room. Since farmers did not belong to any *danwei*, it was difficult, if not impossible, for them to get *jieshaoxin* from the communal cadres. Although early migrants (in the late 1970s), especially female migrants, shared rooms with their relatives or worked as live-in maids, the crowded housing situation made it difficult even for willing urban people to take in a large number of migrants. Not everyone had a relative or family friend in cities.

The majority of female maids (nearly all from Anhui), especially the early ones (1979–1985), went into the cities as domestic workers on an unorganized basis, pioneering individual job seeking and job creation. (It is important to note that Anhui is one of the first places where farmers began to practice *baochan daohu*.) Those female migrants overcame housing

*Old and new farmer houses in Guangdong.*
*Photo by Kate Xiao Zhou*

problems by living with their relatives or their employers. A 1990 report on rural female migrants in various big cities put the figure at 3 million.[22] These women formed the vanguard of the unregimented army of migrants that invaded the city.

Alternatively, rural migrants overcame housing obstacles by living with suburban farmers. *Baochan daohu* also gave farm families in the suburbs incentives to make money, and one way they accomplished this was by providing housing for migrants. In the early 1980s, Beijing farmers began to rent out their "rooms" to migrants and collected rents. According to *Chinese Business News*, in 1992, the monthly rent for one room in a Beijing suburban farm household ranged from 50 yuan to 700 yuan.[23] This economic benefit encouraged suburban farmers to protect migrants from urban police harassment. There were a thousand leaks in the dike—all etched by the prospect of material betterment.

Few stimuli motivated increases in productivity as did the suburban farmers' desire for income and the cadres' corruptibility. They welcomed migrants and did not ask them for identification papers. Even the local cadres in the suburban areas became the accomplices of the "illegal flow" of rural migrants and protected the illegal transactions of migrants. Neither side wanted to report the migrants because everyone gained by their presence. For example, rural migrants set up a flea market in Wohuqiao Village, a suburb of Beijing, and paid the village 400,000 yuan annually.[24] Everyone benefited. The suburban farmers became the first landlords in Communist China providing housing for rural migrants. Suburbs became the operational base of the rural migrants. The richest group of people in China is the Shenzhen farmers who built rental homes to house migrants.

As in other major cities, the majority of rural migrants in Beijing lived in suburban districts.[25] The majority of rural migrants in Guangdong live in San Yuanli, Liuhua, Kesan, and Guangquan; in Shanghai, they are concentrated in Wujiaochan, Zheru, and Wansan Bang; in Tianjin, they inhabit Hexin Zhuang and Jizhuangzi; in Wuhan, they have taken over Tangjiadun; in Shenyang, they are in Wang Village, Wanghua Village, and Wangjia Hezi.[26] All of these are suburban districts where affordable housing can be found, distant from the most intense police controls.

## Commercial Fever

Once the flow of rural migrants outpaced the capacity of existing suburban houses, satellite villages of migrants grew up around the suburbs. At first, these satellite villages served only as lodging places for rural migrants who worked in the cities as peddlers, merchants, and service people. Gradually, however, these migrant villages became centers of rural enterprises, most of which operated without permission from the state. The state would not allow anyone without a *hukou* to have a business license. This did not stop migrant-dominated Wansan Bang, a suburb of Shanghai, from becoming the center for food processing factories. One government investigation in 1990 discovered thirty underground food processing factories, all of which provided catering and bakery services to urban people in Shanghai.[27] This sort of pattern has become general.

Many of those suburban enterprises are highly specialized. For example, people who specialize in eyeglasses live in the Sanban Zhuang District of Beijing's outskirts. Almost all of those people (4,000 in all) in the eyeglass business are rural migrants from Mayu District, Zhejiang Province, who formed a network of eyeglass enterprises. Buying frames from Guangzhou and low-price glass from Jiangsu, they grind the lenses themselves and sell them in Beijing, dominating the market.[28]

Migrants also used the suburban farmers to evade urban *hukou* restrictions on working licenses. Only those with a *hukou* could get a license to set up restaurants and markets. The suburban farmers acted as fronts for migrants' businesses. As a result, suburbs around cities became an intermediate base from which migrants could maneuver.

Private entrepreneurship in suburban businesses was stronger than in urban private businesses. The flow of rural migrants in the fringe areas around the cities provided rural industries with cheap and efficient labor, while at the same time the closeness to the cities provided technical personnel and information. As a result, rural industries in the suburbs grew much faster than those in the city. Table 6.1 indicates the importance of growth rates for rural industrial development in the suburbs of nine cities and clearly illustrates that rural industries in the suburbs contributed most of urban industrial growth in major cities from 1985 to 1989.

**Table 6.1**
Rural (Suburban) Share of Urban Industrial Growth in Nine Cities (percentages)

|  | *1980–1985* | *1985–1989* |
| --- | --- | --- |
| Shanghai | 17 | 59 |
| Tianjin | 21 | 64 |
| Yantai | 53 | 61 |
| Dalian | 35 | 54 |
| Qingdao | 33 | 65 |
| Langfang | 69 | 88 |
| Wuxi | 59 | 82 |
| Changzhou | 45 | 70 |
| Suzhou | 61 | 72 |

*Source: Bao Yongjiang, Zhongguo chengjiao fazhan yanjiu (A Study of the Developments in China's Suburbs) (Beijing: Zhongguo Jingji Chubanshe, 1991), p.471.*

## Job Creation

Rural migrants were and are able to survive because they created jobs for themselves. They did what was left undone by the state, looking for opportunities in a hostile environment. The shortage of services of many kinds provided the stimuli for migrants to develop private services of all sorts: furniture manufacturing, fluffing quilts, tailoring, restaurants, film developing, barbering, and many others. Rural migrants also took up what urban people did not want to do. The remarks of Huang Aisheng, a rural businessman from Gansu, expressed a common goal of many migrants: "We farmers are able to endure any kind of hardship and suffer any adversity. So long as we can make money to improve our lives, we will do whatever makes the most money. Of course, we cannot violate laws."[29] In fact, to survive and prosper, rural migrants constantly had to violate laws and regulations, creating constant pressures to change discriminatory and irrational laws

Rural migrants took over recycling in all major cities. Because the job is dirty, workers in the state recycling company refused to do it. Rural migrants occupy all Beijing dump sites. At the Xindian dump site alone each month, forty migrants collect 30–40 tons of plastic bags, 20 tons of used papers, 3 tons of plastic bottles, 30–40 tons of glass, 10 tons of used iron and other discarded materials. Some of those used materials ended up in rural factories. In 1993 the forty recycling workers were able to make 8,000–10,000 yuan a month.[30] They are so successful at recycling that they are called *laji dawang* (trash kings). In the late 1980s, rural migrants took charge of trash collection for most cities. The occupation of trash sites and of streets became the spontaneous means used by rural migrants to create informal property rights in spite of the existing *hukou* discrimination against settlement by rural migrants.

Rural migrants created and expanded *jishi* (markets) in the cities, providing jobs for themselves and even some city people. Non-*hukou* holders (most of them rural migrants) dominate Beijing *jishi.* In Xincheng District, 73 percent of *jishi* private business people are rural migrants. The development of *jishi* has enlivened services and commerce, altering their structure. More and more urban people obtain services from *jishi* rather than from state stores. According to a 1991 Beijing government investigation, open markets provided 83 percent of urban residents' vegetables, and 73 percent of the individual businesses on Beijing's open market were operated by suburban or rural merchants.[31] In Wuhan, the rural migrants who dominated vegetable *jishi* quickly developed a major retail and trading center.[32] As early as 1984, before urban reform started, rural merchants and peddlers dominated all *jishi* in Chinese cities. Their share of *jishi* was 80–90 percent in big cities; 70–80 percent in medium-size cities; 50–60 percent in small cities.[33] Most rural merchants were small-scale private traders. Apart from markets, rural migrants were the key service providers. They

*Migrant rural workers are responsible for recycling
in Chinese cities. Photo by Kate Xiao Zhou*

were carpenters, painters, barbers, tailors, quilt makers, restaurant owners, street performers, and repairers.

At first, urban officials reacted to the profit-oriented market with hostility. Some local municipal governments tried to destroy the open markets. When rural entrepreneurs rushed into Beijing to do business in the early 1980s, the Beijing government tried to "seal off all main thoroughfares and districts, and place the others under rigorous restrictions."[34] In 1983, the Wuhan government organized workers and police to rampage through the open markets in Liu Du Qiao and Han Zheng Jie, forcing many migrant businesses to close down for several weeks. In response, those migrants took their businesses to the streets, the apartments, and the *jishi*.

Once urban life came to depend upon migrant services, city governments were forced to tolerate them to some grudging degree. Everywhere they set up rules to restrict the activities of rural migrants. Apart from requiring registration of vendors, many city governments restricted migrants to a few areas. These restrictions did not discourage the commercial activities of rural migrants but instead left a crack in the legal limits for migrants to set up fixed markets. It was against this background that rural *jishi* became established in the cities.

Gradually, the local government, especially the street committees, came to depend on the fees that migrants paid. In 1993, of the total income for Xi Changan Neighborhood Street Government in Beijing, 4,659,000 yuan, 67 percent, came from management fees collected in those migrant-dominated markets.[35] In some cases, funds collected as management fees were even higher than tax revenues. Businesses and peddlers complained: "Small business people have become the 'parents' of management cadres, providing clothes, food, and pocket money."[36] This was a way of accusing the Communist party of parasitism, corruption, and hypocrisy; government officials had always claimed to be the "parents" of the people

Urban government also used the open market as a source of new income. Apart from a growing number of tax collectors, Wuhan's government collected fines. (In the 1980s, the government even set up an urban environmental police, whose sole purpose was to enforce hygiene standards in *jishi*.) Schoolteachers turned their classrooms into night hotels, providing lodging for migrants. As a result, the migrants fell prey to moneymaking urban people while at the same time winning social approval for their stay in the city.

When the urban environment became less hostile to rural migrants, they flooded urban streets, selling ever more goods and services to urban people. Because state-owned services were not able to compete with rural migrants in the markets, there was a rapid decrease in the state sector. Between 1984 and 1985, the state lost 40–50 percent of the agricultural products market to private businesses.[37]

*Facing stiff competition from rural private services in the late 1980s, state services responded by renting their facilities to private businesses to survive.* This was especially true for retail businesses. Many of the tenants were from rural China. These rural merchants or peddlers rented the state counters and promised to pay rent or often to share profits with the state department stores. A 1991 investigation of state and urban collective department stores in Xidan District, Beijing (one of the busiest business sections) suggested that migrant enterprises occupied more than 69 percent of all retail counters. This was especially true for rural businesses in developing coastal areas, such as Zhejiang. Among the rural migrant tenants, *guahu* rural collective enterprises from Zhejiang took the lead. One investigation into the four rental state department stores in Beijing by a Chinese

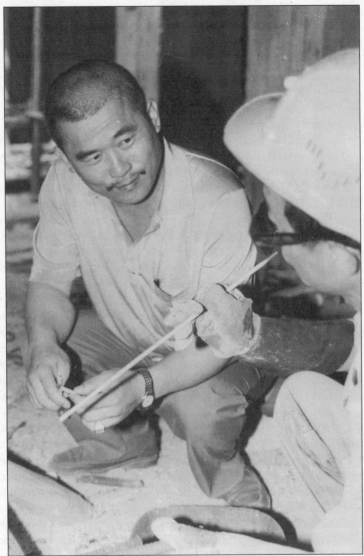

*Farmer Cai Youxin, a multimillionaire, is in charge of real estate development in Shishi District, Fujian. Photo by Xue Qun*

researcher in 1990 found that 77 percent of the tenants in one big state department store came from Zhejiang rural *guahu* collective enterprises; three out of four private renters in a second department store came from rural Zhejiang; the Zhejiang *guahu* enterprises rented all seven rented counters in the third state department store, although one Beijing *getihu* rented a fashion salon in the store; and eleven Zhejiang *guahu* rural businesses took up all the rental space in the fourth department store.[38]

Even in 1989, however, Jiang Zemin, then the mayor of Shanghai, later the party secretary, insisted that the state-owned retail businesses should be the main structure and other forms should only pick up what the state retail outlets had left undone:

> The correct view should be: While carrying out diversity, we adhere to state commerce as the main circulation channel. Without the main channel, there will be no market stability; without diversity, there is no market flexibility. These two features depend upon each other, which is both the feature of the socialist early stage and the character of a planned market economy.[39]

He was whistling in the dark. The development of *jishi* and renting left the state in control of less than 10 percent of all retail business.[40]

Rental activities also influenced workers in the state department stores. Former sales personnel lived on migrant profits in the form of rentals. In some state department stores, more than 50 percent of income came from rents. One former store manager said: "We would not know where [else] to find the money for bonuses for our staff and workers."[41]

Button makers from Qiaotou, Zhejiang Province, rented counters from three thousand state-owned large department stores, monopolizing the button market. Note how this turns socialism on its head. In Zhengzhou, Henan Province, the city's underground mall rented all but 7 of 180 counters to private businesses. The mall's personnel provided security, hygiene, and other management services.[42]

These rentals so alarmed the state that in 1991 its Commerce Bureau issued a document that made large-scale renting illegal. Illegal renting activities continued, though, because there were profits to be made and the state would otherwise have had to bail out all those uncompetitive state companies. Since the state already has to spend huge sums to support its money-losing enterprises (almost one-third of its budget in 1992) and since tax collection is difficult and inflation is feared, the state could not afford to bail them out.

Between 1978 and 1986, the fastest privatization took place in retail businesses, restaurants, and other services. The nonstate sector (both private and collective) rose from 14 percent in 1978 to 83 percent in 1986. Rural-based businesses *first* ended the state monopoly in the service sector, where the state was weak. Second, it was the independent entrepreneurial farmers who subverted the state's socialism.

The development of specialization among rural migrants was accompanied by the revival of *tongxianghui* (an association of people from the same place of birth), which were well known in Chinese history. Rural

*A farmer-built house in Shenzhen. Most of the houses are built by farmers, who then rent them out. As a result, Shenzhen farmers are the richest group in Shenzhen, the capitalist window of China. The door couplet reads, "Longevity and good harvest; strong country and rich family." Photo by Kate Xiao Zhou*

migrants spread information about jobs, housing, and other services among themselves. In every city, especially the big cities, certain parts of the city are so dominated by rural migrants from one province that they are known as a village of that province. They often dominate all services and commerce in one district, usually without formal organization or formal leadership. As their number grows, however, informal organizations also appear. For example, migrant business-people from Zhejiang formed a chain of business stores and service centers, making Zhejiang Cun (Zhejiang Village) a special economic zone in Beijing. The "village" even provided schooling and medical treatment for Zhejiang migrants, who otherwise were denied public services.

Rural migrants were the first group to break the impasse in urban markets and the first group to participate as entrepreneurs in the commodity market. By leaching away many economic functions of the government, they have been transforming China. Because rural migrants entered the private sector before most urban people, they have been able to assert their influence wherever the state's policy is more open to private businesses.

When seven state-owned department stores went on sale in October 1992, Chen Jinyi, a rural entrepreneur from Zhejiang Province, bought six with 145.1 million yuan and set up a corporation to produce food. Chen owned a substantial amount of stock in Guangdong software companies.[43] Chen was not the only exfarmer to purchase state enterprises. In the same year that Chen bought Shanghai state-owned shops, two farmers from rural Zhejiang won the bidding (against rich overseas Chinese investors) for the sale of the Zhejiang provincial government's building in Hangzhou, the capital of Zhejiang. Both leaders and urban people were shocked by this rural takeover and tried to figure out where those farmers could have made so much money. In December 1992, a special meeting was held in Beijing to study the "Chen Jinyi phenomenon."

## A Hostile Urban Environment

Farmers were able to stay more than one step ahead because urban people were still trapped in the *danwei* system. Gradually, rural migrants undermined even this keystone of the social structure of state control of individual lives in the city.

*Danwei* depended on the rigid control of rural–urban migration. The migration itself removed the first buttress of the *danwei* system. After the 1956 collectivization entrenched *hukou* divisions, most jobs in the city included a welfare benefit characterized by lifetime employment known as *tiefanwan* (iron rice bowl). Combined with *santie* (three kinds of iron)— *tiefanwan* (iron rice bowl), *tiegongzi* (fixed wage system), and *tiejiaoyi* (life-tenured cadres)—the *danwei* system meant that there was no labor market, that farmers were kept from urban employment, and that urban folk were kept from alternative employment.

All urban labor recruitment and all wages were distributed by the center and allocated to lower levels of the state bureaucracy. This rigid system discouraged work incentives because seniority, not work effort, determined one's wage increases. The *danwei* system combined welfare (medical care, housing, pension, and child care) with employment, and the state tightly restricted the private sector, so the job turnover rate in China was one of the lowest in the world.[44] Controlled labor limited the flow of information and people to a trickle. Urban workers had no incentive to strive. Aware of the negative impact of *santie*, the State Council issued a document in October 1986 declaring that all newly hired personal in the state sector would be employed on three-to-five-year contracts.[45] Yet there has been little job mobility in urban China because *danwei* still plays a dominant role in the individual lives of its employees.

Actually, after the urban reform that began in 1984, the role of *danwei* as a welfare provider increased because the reform allowed managers to allocate welfare and other benefits for permanent workers. There was also a great increase in temporary and contract workers who lacked full, or any, benefits. This function of *danwei* in urban state enterprises was expressed by a Shougang (Beijing Capital Steel and Iron Complex) slogan: "Improve living standards to speed up production; further improve living standards to further speed up production."[46] This slogan was a revision of a well-known slogan under Mao: "Grasp revolution to speed up production; further grasp revolution to further speed up production."[47] Although the priority has changed from revolution to livelihood, not an insignificant change, efficient production remained a secondary priority in the state sector. Despite rapidly increasing wages, bonuses, and welfare, productivity stayed low.

Because of *danwei*, most urban people still depend on the state for employment in the urban state factories, but urban people were upset that rural people earned more than they did. Snobbery existed even in the PRC. A popular saying went: "The big brother (the worker) is stepping down; the second brother (the farmer) is making money; the ninth brother (the intellectual) is sitting bare-assed in a beautiful sedan chair."[48] Sentiment against the new rural rich and *getihu* who made money put pressure on the state to provide tangible material goods to urban residents. In order to keep urban dwellers satisfied, the state raised their wages in the early 1980s. In addition, fringe benefits were raised more than wages in urban *danwei*. Bonuses, consumption goods, and other benefits increased rapidly. For a while, the state raised pay for everyone legally in the city and increased subsidies for all urban residents as well.

As a result of subsidies from the state and *danwei*, the standard to measure whether a person was employed was to see whether the person was recruited by the state labor department and whether the person was entitled to have medical care, pension, and *danwei* welfare. Other non-state employment was regarded as temporary or unemployed status. The security of state subsidies had great appeal to urban people.

Even young private businesspeople who made money were still considered *daiye qingnian* (youths-waiting-for-government-jobs). In Wuhan, many urban young people used private business jobs as temporary positions in the 1980s. Thus, people who had access to the state bureaucracy would not remain *getihu* (individual private business). When a local cadre offered to help one Beijing pedicab driver with his small business, the young man rejected his offer: "Individual operation? No! If I become a pedicab operator, what girl would accept me? If I'm renting a pedicab now, it's only because I need to do some hard manual work for the sake of self-discipline. I'll sell the cab once I get a regular job."[49] The stigma on *getihu* and preferred dependence on *danwei* left marginal people in the city to become *getihu* as a last resort. For example, *getihu* in Congwei District, Beijing, consisted of former criminals (12 percent), those who have never been employed (11 percent), and fired workers (0.3 percent).[50]

**Table 6.2**

Origins of *Getihu* Employees in Jiaozu City, Henan Province

| Origin | Percent |
| --- | --- |
| Rural migrant | 82 |
| Unemployed | 11 |
| *Daiye* youth | 4 |
| Retiree | 2 |
| *Tingxinliuzhi*[a] and others | 1 |

[a]*Tingxinliuzhi refers to those who stop receiving pay but retain their danwei job title.*

*Source: Li Qiang, "Shixi woguo geti he siying jingji zai chengshi yu nongcun di zhongda chabie" (An Analysis of Great Differences Between Urban and Rural Private Owners), Sociology and Social Research 2 (1992):26.*

The social origins of *getihu* suggest that in the 1980s proper people in the city did not participate in private business. This made them even more dependent on *danwei* and on the state as a source of employment. This urban social structure was in sharp contrast to rural areas, where the able or most educated were engaged in private business ventures. Of the entrepreneurs in rural Zhejiang and Fujian, virtually none came from state sector urban jobs. Furthermore, rural migrants dominated the service industry, where the state was weak. Rural migrants rushed into private business, as shown in Table 6.2. By the end of 1990, 74 percent of all private businesses and 73 percent of all private capital in China belonged to rural people.[51]

To a certain extent, the state exclusion of rural people turned into a blessing for rural migrants. Having no *tiefanwan* and no welfare, farmers became the most daring group, creating markets for themselves. Farmers were the most willing of all social groups to take risks. Self-employment was the standard and *shengchan zijiu* (work to save oneself) was the norm.

In the Chinese socialist economy, stratification of the labor supply was determined by the degree of welfare protection on the one hand and the degree of personal freedom on the other. The higher the welfare protection, the less the freedom to choose and vice versa. Workers in state factories, especially heavy industry, wear *jinshoukao* (golden handcuffs). One expression described workers in the state factories as *buduannai di haizi* (permanently suckling babies).

In state jobs, *dingti* (job inheritance from parents or relatives) had become the norm. Children were employed by a retired parent's *danwei*.[52] As a result, new workers were predominantly the children of employees. Children of employees comprised 90 percent of the new work force in the Wuhan Boiler Works in the 1980s.[53]

## *Mingong Chao* (Tides of Migrant Workers): The Rise of the Chinese Labor Market

Despite the government's reform rhetoric, the urban industrial environment was still rigid in the early and mid-1980s, but the flow of rural migrants loosened up the rigid *danwei* system. This market-driven flow of rural migrants first created a labor market outside *danwei* and then brought changes into *danwei*.

When the state adopted an open door policy, farmers responded to the new opportunity more actively than other groups. A popular saying among rural migrants in the 1980s was: "Wherever you are from, to make money go to Guangdong."[54] In September 1979, the state permitted the assembly and processing of products for foreign companies. Rural entrepreneurs jumped at the opportunity and made good use of cheap labor. Rural people, especially rural entrepreneurs in Guangdong, became the chief beneficiaries of the open door policy. This was especially true in the special economic zones, where hundreds of thousands of rural migrants, including rural young women, assembled imported parts and sent them back to Hongkong. The managers in the newly created factories preferred rural workers because they did not expect to receive welfare from the factories employing them. Also, managers had the right to fire workers. This frightened most urban workers in secure state factories.

The hardworking farmers attracted foreign investment. The first Hongkong businesses that came to China invested in labor-intensive industries, using cheap land and cheap migrant workers from rural backgrounds.

The mobility of rural migrant workers also contributed to the rapid growth and success of rural industries. In fact, the rapid development in many new rural-based industrial cities was linked directly to labor mobility. The industrial takeoff in Guangdong depended upon *mingong chao*, the tides of migrant workers. From 1980 to 1988, a huge free labor market appeared in Guangdong. Millions of farmers from South China flooded into rural industries. In 1988, there were 400,000–500,000 migrant workers in Guangbaoan and Dongwan districts alone, almost all of them working for rural industries or joint foreign companies.[55]

The higher the mobility rate, the higher the growth rate. According to a 1993 five-city survey conducted by the *China Youth News*, rural migrants make up a substantial proportion of newly developed industrial cities. In all these cities, rural industries make up the majority of industrial production, competing successfully with the state factories. A free labor environment is another reason that rural industries are taking over urban state factories.

Migrants and rural industries are creating new cities in China, remaking the Chinese landscape. The new city of Huizhou in Guangdong is a typical example of a migrant city where migrants make up 58 percent of its labor force.[56] Its fast development is catching up with Shenzhen, a special economic zone created by the Guangdong provincial government in the early 1980s. Now there is a saying in Guangdong: "The 1980s looked up to Shenzhen; the 1990s belong to Huizhou."

Of course, Hongkong, Taiwan, and other sources of foreign capital played an important role, especially in coastal areas like Guangdong and Fujian. Many rural people in those areas tried to use their village connections to draw capital from Taiwan Chinese and Hongkong Chinese by using bonds to places of origin. Important as non-PRC capital had been for economic development, it would have gone for naught without a labor market. A migrant-based free labor market guaranteed mobile cheap labor for those rural factories.

Rural migrants dominated five important service sectors in the city: transportation, construction, building materials, repair services, and restaurants. In addition, rural industries, private businesses, and *jishi* markets also provided second-shift jobs for urban people, a topic to be dealt with later in this chapter.

Rural migrants' eagerness to escape the state's trammels and to change their status was the catalyst of mobility. By 1985, more than one-fifth of the farmers had already changed their occupation, residence, and status.[57] Although most rural migrants in the city worked for low wages under poor conditions, they ended the state's position as sole employer in the urban labor market. Many rural people, starved for cash and opportunity, took "dirty" jobs that urban people did not want—as janitors, textile workers, construction workers, and garbage collectors. In the early 1980s, when the state began to build houses in big cities, the old state-run construction outfits were not able to handle the growing demand. They turned to rural migrants as a temporary expedient. Rural migrants became contract workers.

Because the state's *hukou* restrictions forbade rural firms to provide urban construction, a special phenomenon, *zhuanbao* (subcontracting), appeared, assuming three forms: the state or urban collective construction firms contracted out jobs to rural construction businesses, taking a 20 percent construction fee; urban firms contracted the construction to their own employees and those employees hired rural migrants to do the work; and urban firms contracted with private contractors. Huang Wusheng, a thirty-year-old private construction contractor, is a typical example of China's first private construction contractors. Huang left his village to work as a construction worker in 1982, two years after *baochan daohu* brought independent production decisionmaking to his village. At that time he was only eighteen and was quick to learn new concepts and new trades. He endured all sorts of hardship and finally set up his own construction teams in China's West. Huang would not tell others how he managed to get contracts in the hostile urban environments, but Huang was keenly aware of his inferior status because he did not have an urban *hukou*. He struggled hard to overcome adversity and became very successful: "A penniless migrant worker who doesn't want to look up to urban people and who wants to accomplish something must work harder than urban people."[58]

As a result of *zhuanbao* and rural private contracting, rural-based construction firms began to dominate the construction industry, although they were often exploited by urban state construction firms. Rural construction firms have now become the major construction force. In Zhengzhou City, Henan Province, 65 percent of city construction jobs were handled by rural construction firms throughout the 1980s.[59] In Jiangsu alone, 1.7 million rural workers were engaged in construction in 1993.[60] There is no doubt that the mobilization of labor was (and is) one of the most important factors in the Chinese construction industry, as it is in other industries.

The tide of rural migrants contributed not only to the rapid growth of the Chinese economy but also to the equity of distribution between city and countryside. As more and more farmers from poor areas went to work in developed areas, they sent money home. According to Fan Gang, a leading Chinese economist, the rapid flow of rural migrants "has been quite a positive development. It has helped to transfer wealth from rich to poor areas of the country." Rural migrants "from Anhui Province sent home 862 million yuan, which exceeded the provincial government's annual revenue by 230 million."[61]

## The Reform of *Danwei*

There are two ways to change an organization: change its structure substantively, or change its context. The most general form of urban organizational change by rural influence was the latter: changing the context into which the organizations fit. Nowhere was this better illustrated than in the rural impact on *danwei*.

Rural migrants found work even at state enterprises by dealing in "dirty" and strenuous jobs. For example, one Hangzhou silk production factory planned to hire a thousand workers but only recruited twenty urbanites, despite a 5000 yuan advertising campaign.[62] Each workplace had to hire rural migrants in order to get the work done.

Within each *danwei*, workers tried to avoid hard work because wages were fixed and the reward was not related to effort. According to the National Trade Union, one out of every five workers was underemployed on the job.[63] At the same time, workplaces experienced shortages of workers willing to perform dirty jobs. Farmers had a saying about unproductive urban workers: They squat on a toilet without defecating. In order to get those "unpleasant" jobs done, every workplace had to hire contract workers. In 1988, urban on-the-job underemployment reached 15 million people, costing the state 40 billion yuan per year, while at the same time there were 30 million productive job openings, of which rural migrants filled 15 million.[64] Urban workers felt no incentive to shift to less desirable jobs.

In Shanghai, even though there were at least 750,000 overstaffed workers, the number of hired rural migrants was growing at a rate of 9 percent annually.[65] In Guangzhou, rural migrants now occupy half of all jobs in construction, textiles, public hygiene, and chemical manufacturing, and in Wuhan, rural workers number 170,000 in those sectors.[66] Rural migrants with no job guarantees worked harder for lower wages, so managers in state factories hired rural migrants in spite of the state's prohibition. According to Labor Minister Lin Huan, the shortage of personnel in the onerous "productive front" in the state factories is 20–40 percent, whereas superfluous people in the "nonproductive front" (cushy jobs like management and maintenance) are common.

State-sector urban workers enjoy welfare, medical care, housing, and pensions; rural migrants have no fringe benefits. Therefore they are more mobile, moving from job to job looking for the highest pay.

In Wuhan and Shanghai, rural migrants made the textile factories effective, while the old urban workers did not have to do anything. This was true in mining and other sectors as well. There was a working-class aristocracy, despite the official ideology of an egalitarian proletariat. A 1989 survey of eight Shanghai textile factories indicates that contract workers ranged from 18 percent to 39 percent in seven of them. As a popular saying in Shanghai goes, "The party secretary controls the direction; urban workers play around; the work is left to rural hicks."[67] The working-class aristocracy came to fill the roles formerly taken by "capitalist exploiters" of labor.

When the state tried to reform urban enterprises by giving more power to managers, the managers sought more contract workers, making the ban on rural migrants increasingly difficult to enforce. The increased employment of farmers was in direct conflict with state policy, which until 1990 tried to control the social mobility of rural people through *hukou* and other formal restrictions. The state labor organization would often collect a fee from the *danwei* for every rural migrant worker hired, 5–15 percent of the migrants' salary. Many factories underreported their hiring of rural workers in order to avoid paying the fees.

The hiring of migrant workers created problems for the state factories and government cadres. For a long time, the Communist leaders had attacked the notion that labor can be sold as a commodity because, according to Marx, workers inevitably were exploited during the process. By the end of 1988, however, the state factories had hired 10.49 million rural workers, almost all of them based on a free contract system. The party's newspaper, the *People's Daily*, admitted the embarrassment caused by the hiring of rural workers.[68] By selling their labor, rural migrants began to redefine the role of labor relations in China.

The state took notice and tried to control this rapid growth of the mobile labor force. On August 22, 1986, the State Labor Department and the State Planning Commission issued a directive in an attempt to curtail the nonplanned hiring of rural workers. The directive called for an immediate freeze on all nonplanned hiring and to clear out unplanned workers (almost all rural migrants), but this restriction had little effect. In 1989, the State Labor Department had a second clearing out campaign. In Shandong alone, 100,000 rural workers were "cleared out" from the state factories in 1989.[69] In 1990, the labor minister, Yuan Chongwu, stressed the state policy while discussing the increase of rural people in urban factories:

A plan to control rural workers should be reinforced, including the work permit certificate, work registration, and work supervision. We must combine quota control with other policy restrictions. The control of *nongzhuanfei* (changing status from farmer to non-farmer) must be tight. Apart from a few special occupations, all enterprises must clear off all farm workers so that they go back to the countryside to play a role in agricultural production and in rural construction. More room should be left to experiment with remedies for unemployment in the cities.[70]

None of those restrictive policies could stop rural–urban migration, though. Despite the formal restrictions, rural migrants flowed into cities and initiated a free labor market.[71] In 1991, when economist Thomas Rawski asked fellow economists, "Is there a labor market in China?" all said no. His calculation of both the marginal profit of labor and the marginal profit of capital suggests, however, that the market played a significant role throughout the 1980s. Disbelieving his finding, he asked his research associates to recalculate. "But no matter what methods they used, this market effect on labor still exists."[72] Rawski and his research associates did not see that rural migrants had created an underground labor market. Rural migrants went where they found economic opportunities. For example, early in 1989, the daily flow of migrants into Guangdong was 100,000.[73] The Guangdong government had to take measures to restrict the flow.

The presence of rural contract workers influenced workers in the *danwei* system. Rural workers became the envy of urban factory workers. Although the migrant workers did not have work security, they could always leave their jobs for something better, something unthinkable for urban workers in the state factories. Wide choices enabled some rural contract workers to learn new trades and techniques. Some were able to use the experience to release their entrepreneurial spirit.

My 1994 interviews with more than thirty rural migrants in Guangdong suggest that most migrants seized every opportunity to learn new trades. Mr. Liu Wancai, a rural migrant from Hunan, had more than ten kinds of jobs before he began trading computers in 1990:

> I came to Guangdong in 1984 with less than 3 yuan in my pocket. I worked as a janitor, a trash collector, a dishwasher, a taxi-driver, a construction worker, and many other odd jobs. These experiences and hardships have helped me a lot. Now I am much better at personal relationships than city people my age. I know how to strike up a conversation with strangers and what to say. I feel happy that I am always able to do what I want to do and that I can make some money.

Zhu Bosung, a self-made millionaire, was a migrant worker in 1982. He changed his jobs several times to learn survival strategies, eventually becoming the boss of his own small industrial products factory. Zhu attributed his success to having learned while working at all sorts of odd jobs— his capital was his experience as a migrant worker.[74] Success stories like this worked as catalysts for change among urban workers, who came to see a possible alternative to the *danwei*.

## Political Influence

Rural mobility not only increased the opportunity costs of rural labor and expanded the market but also brought their political influence to the fore. At first, the state did not take this unorganized flow of rural people seriously and called rural migrants *mangliu* (wandering migrants). Gradually, however, a large flowing population (100 million) in the cities threatened the state and forced it to deepen reform. The rulers feared the flow of farmers. In the words of He Xin, an influential theorist for the Communist regime: "Once they [rural migrants] get organizations with an educated leadership and a political program, the floating rural population could be molded into a political force, a mobile, armed, and formidable antisocial coalition."[75] *When government leaders noticed this unorganized, apolitical migrant power, they perceived its organizational potential as a political danger.*

The top leaders were on the lookout for the potential leaders of rural migrants and other socially disruptive actions that threatened the regime, but unorganized rural migrants had already breached the *hukou* dam and cut rural labor mobility loose, as Keiko Wakabayashi pointed out:

> The floating population is not only a phenonmenon accompanied by the transformation of cities, but is seen to be a step toward the transformation of China into a freer society characterized by population mobility. One interesting case in this context is a new village that was

established in a very remote area in Fujin County, Heilongjiang Province. The whole village population consists of people who have moved from other areas. In order to obtain the regional government's recognition, the village community elected the leader of the production brigade and secretary of the village party committee.[76]

The influx of rural migrants in the cities threatened the political structure of the PRC which was based on an immobile population: "At all levels and in all localities, administrative management agencies plan their work and projects in accord with the size of the registered permanent population within their respective jurisdictions."[77]

However, the influx of migrants disrupted management. Two systems coexisted side by side: The rural migrants had no administrative control, and urban people were still controlled by administrative bureaucrats. Many rural settlers even named their new settlements *wumingcun* (villages with no names). Ironically, it was precisely the state's antirural exclusion policies that enabled rural migrants to live outside the control of the state in the cities. The government put its policies in place, took conformity for granted, and looked the other way. The migrants continued their anarchic behavior

## *Xiangqiankan* (Money Seeking): The Rise of *Dier Zhiye* (Moonlighting)

One of rural people's most important contributions to the changing face of the PRC has been the emergence of *xiangqiankan* (money seeking). A social survey in Zhejiang suggests that farmers had made moneymaking their first priority in life (see Table 6.3).

Farmers were still looked down upon. Private businesses and peddlers were derisively called *erdao fanzi* (secondhand peddlers), with pronunciation of *fan* (peddler) the same as *fan* (criminal). The state treated peddlers and itinerant traders like criminals. Because the state tried to make it impossible for rural migrants to own businesses in the city, they became peddlers, or worked at the bottom of the service sector. Despite rural migrants' economic improvement, their social status was slow to improve.

Gradually, rural entrepreneurs have begun to represent a new way of thinking, a transformation of values. At first, the growth of rural industry provided a *new nonstate job market*. In Wuhan and Beijing, scientists and professors were hired to help suburban rural people with their new factories and business firms. This new source of income created a stir in the city. Many intellectuals and technicians went to those places on Sundays or holidays. Rural people called them "Sunday engineers." Since the pay those "Sunday engineers" received from the rural enterprises was much higher than their state salaries, their marriage to the *danwei* was shaken. Some even dared to leave their state jobs to work for rural enterprises full time.

*"Money comes in through the door with the rising sun; good luck comes into the household with the spring wind," a typical door couplet in rural China. Modern moneymaking leaves room for ancient geomancy—the couplet refers quite literally to luck brought by the morning sun through the (properly oriented) door. The children are wearing clothes like those worn in the city. Photo by Kate Xiao Zhou*

Rural industry also contributed to the weakening of *danwei*'s control of job transfers in urban China. For a long time, *danwei* cadres and police made it difficult for people to change their jobs. Changing jobs required permission from the *danwei*; changing residence, permission from the local police. In addition, the *danwei* had to release the secret personnel file that recorded the political behavior and attitude of each worker in *danwei*. A party member also had to transfer his or her party affiliation. Throughout

**Table 6.3**
Do You Agree That the Goal of Life Is to Make Money?
(percentages)

| Occupation | Agree | Don't Care | Disagree |
|---|---|---|---|
| Cadre | 40 | 19 | 41 |
| Worker | 66 | 5 | 31 |
| Farmer | 81 | 6 | 13 |
| Private business person | 59 | 15 | 26 |

Source: Li Qian, Yu Xianyan, and Shi Xilai, "Studies on Elements That Influence Social Values and Social Behavior," Sociology and Social Investigation, no. 5 (1992): 11–20.

the reform period, *hukou*, secret personnel files, and party connections were barriers to mobility for urban people, but 80 percent of farmers did not have any of these, so they were not important for rural industries. Farmer-run industries were far more flexible.

Rural industries hired urban people to work for them on the side. Rural industries paid a bounty to urban people if they could help them set up joint ventures with Taiwanese and Hongkong businesses. Rural industries needed government workers who had contacts with foreign businessmen. They bought research and development results on the black market from state-employed scientists. These government employees are called ghost workers because although their bodies sit at a government desk their spirits work for the rural enterprises. Urbanites got welfare from *danwei* and income from the rural industries; the rural firms gained connections and experience.

The money that migrant entrepreneurs made began to win the envy of urban people. Sayings caught the discrepancy between what one made at his or her *danwei* and what the "uneducated farmers" made at the market or in the service sector. Government cadres would say, "One can make more money traveling with a carrying pole over one's shoulders than (Party Secretary) Hu Yaobang makes." Intellectuals liked to complain: "A missile researcher makes less than an egg seller."[78]

More and more people became attracted to service and open market activities, trying to get rich. Because money assumed more importance, "this would give them [private business people] a certain status in society as well as threaten a key source of cadre power: the ability to allocate scarce goods."[79] The state was not able to provide more money to satisfy urban residents, so a restriction on the second shift was weakened, and moonlighting spread quickly. In Shanghai by 1990, at least two hundred thousand people had a second job; 8 percent of the people in Tianjin, 9 percent in Beijing, 12 percent in Hangzhou, and 20 percent in Guangzhou were engaged in second shifts in 1987.[80] The numbers grew rapidly. By

1992, in Shanghai, 30 percent of professionals, 40 percent of scientists, and 40 percent of high school and elementary school teachers had taken up a second shift.[81] By 1994, many more urban people were on the lookout for a second shift.

Moreover, the success stories of self-made millionaires stirred the hearts of many urban people. One migrant-turned-multibillionaire, Liu Yanlin, attracted national attention. In 1981, Liu left his village in Sichuan and went to Guangdong with only 9 yuan (less than U.S. $2). At first he worked as a construction worker, then he became a contractor. Using his savings and a loan, he managed to buy a small brick factory. In 1988, Liu became a millionaire and began to spread his efforts into real estate. Now Liu is a billionaire, a new Chinese dream for rural migrants and the envy of urban people as well. Like many other rural migrants, the desire to rid himself of his inferior status pushed him forward: "When I came to Guangdong with only nine yuan and twenty cents, I did not know that I would make it big like today. At that time what I thought of most was to prove myself, which helped me endure hardship. Of course, to prove oneself requires economic success."[82]

Rural entrepreneurs are participating in new ways of life. Many of them have become regular clients of karaoke nightclubs and expensive restaurants, many of which were opened by rural people. This is particularly true for Guangdong rural entrepreneurs, who have used the money they made to buy Hongkong fashions and are referred to as *tuhuaqiao* (native overseas Chinese). Given the important role of overseas Chinese in China's economic development, especially in the southeast coastal regions, this new identification links the oceans and the countryside and sends a new perception of farmers as bold, open, and dynamic

Money-oriented rural people have led Chinese people in *xiangqiankan* (money seeking). A new saying is now popular in China: "If one wants to look forward, one must first of all look for money; only looking for money can one look forward."[83] By 1990, urban people no longer looked down upon free-marketers. Even the cadres and professors began to "moonlight" in the labor market. When prize-winning mathematician Chen Jinrun went to sell meat cakes on the side, it caused a stir in China. Rural people took the initiative; urban folk followed.

*Xiangqiankan* is weakening dependence on the *danwei*. Commerce is breaking "feudal" fetters. Dynamic job choice is replacing static status identity. Urban Chinese are increasingly more likely to ask, "What do you do?" than "To what *danwei* do you belong?" Values and behavior are being transformed. People are willing to leave *danwei* to look for opportunities elsewhere. A deputy editor left a state-owned newspaper to work as a secretary for a rural enterprise in Guangdong. When people asked him whether money was the motivation for him to leave his *danwei*, he replied, "It is a joy to work here because work is work and play is play. I feel

*A color TV and a modern set of furniture are*
*required items for newlyweds in rural Hubei.*
*Photo by Kate Xiao Zhou*

depressed thinking of my past big iron rice bowl because it was a life of half death and half living."[84]

Moonlighting threatens the *danwei*. When people make more money on their second shift, their already low motivation at the *danwei* declines even further. According to a popular saying, "The worm at work becomes a dragon after hours."[85] The worry is no longer that a missile designer makes less than an egg seller but that the missile designer is focusing his energy on selling eggs. Now taking a second job has become such an ideal pattern that married women in the city proclaim, "Men without a second job are not able men."

The second job has become a liberating force for urban workers, much as *baochan daohu* was for farmers. Urban workers saw little or no possibility of bettering themselves in their state jobs, but the second job opened new horizons.

## Conclusion

The impact of rural migrants on urban life has been tremendous. Today, traveling to any city in China, one walks on roads and bridges built and cleaned by rural migrants and stays in hotels or houses built by rural migrants. One wears clothes made by rural factories or rural migrant workers. Urban people have to depend on services (restaurants and repairs) provided by migrants. Urban people buy fresh vegetables and meat from migrant-dominated markets. In short, rural migrants touch every aspect of urban life.

Rural migrants have altered the social structures of the urban-centered state. Rural migrants' market-driven mobility undermined the planned economy. The rural-dominated service sector is overtaking the state sector. By 1986, private businesses and cooperatives, which were increasingly dominated by rural people, controlled 83 percent of retail business, such as restaurants, and other service industries in China as a whole.[86] They provided a second occupation for urban workers. Social differentiation has been undergoing rapid changes. *Hukou* is losing its importance for status differentiation, especially in the rapidly developing coastal areas. Private entrepreneurs are becoming a new and increasingly respected group. A new reference group is emerging.

Meanwhile, state subsidies to less efficient, legally protected urban residents are breaking the state budget. Urban workers are putting pressure on the state for more subsidies to keep up with rural entrepreneurs despite the budget crisis. The state is on the verge of bankruptcy and may have to surrender its controls fully. It will not be long before urban workers will have *nifanwan* ("clay rice bowls," i.e., no job security), as do rural migrants. The farmers are moving toward victory.

Rural migrants have exacerbated the problem of public goods in the city. They enjoy hidden urban subsidies from the state in the form of public transit, water, electricity, and other daily necessities, thereby adding to the state budget crisis. Most public services in the cities are subsidized at great cost to the state. The migrants' presence is making the provision of public goods too costly for the state to bear. Unless the state takes strong measures to change its policy on urban subsidies, the state public service will go bankrupt.

In 1992, in response to this budget crisis, the state raised prices on many goods in the cities, including housing, grain, and meat. According to Dorothy Solinger, the price increase may target rural migrants who could benefit from urban subsidies, because urban people can still get compensation through their workplace.[87] This suggests rural migrants' impact on state policy formation.

The elimination of formal subsidies in the cities eventually will benefit rural people, however. The end of formal subsidies means more market allocation of goods and services. Farmers were the victims of the state allocation of goods and services, so more market-based allocation may bring more opportunities to farmers. Moreover, as farmers gained no help from the state, their ability to survive in the market was strengthened. The new policies forced on the state may end with the farmers rather than the state becoming the chief supplier of public goods—a libertarian outcome indeed!

Rural entrepreneurs represent a new life style in direct opposition to Communist ideology. Its bold consumer culture is drowning out the message of state ideology. *Xiangqiankan*, or always looking for money, is leading to fundamental changes in the Chinese social structure, breeding a new materialistic civil society. The impetus for basic structural change in both urban and rural areas is coming largely from the farmers, who since 1978 have increasingly moved outside the state. The huge population of rural migrants, without intending reforms, is reshaping Chinese politics.

Nonetheless, both the state and urban people continue to discriminate against rural migrants. In some cities, migrants are treated as disposable, second-class people. Without paying high fees, children of migrants could not go to school. The Shenzhen government used *hukou* to differentiate between two groups of migrants: temporary and permanent. Almost all rural migrants belong to the temporary class, although they outnumbered the permanent residents (usually children of urban elites) two to one in the late 1980s and five to one in the early 1990s.[88]

Many rural migrants are worried that they will be forced to go home because they lack urban *hukou*. But the experience of migrant life has transformed many migrants. The very migration of migrant workers has contributed to the growth of the Chinese economy. Professor Richard Baum calls the migrants "a shock absorber." They "cushion the transformation of the Chinese economy," by flowing from regions with surplus labor to those with a shortage.[89] They also help equalize income distribution because many migrants send money to their home village. In fact, many migrants are bringing information and technology to their home areas. Today's migrant workers may become the future entrepreneurs of less developed areas.

Many migrants try to avoid being sent home by purchasing an urban *hukou*. Urban cadres still use *hukou* privileges to benefit themselves. In order to get more revenue, many local, provincial, and city governments have developed *lanka zhidu*, a system of legal urban residence (literally, the blue card system). Unlike urban *hukou*, *lanka zhidu* does not provide the resident any state subsidies. Like the green card in the United States, the Chinese blue card gives rural migrants permission to stay once they pay certain fees. The cost of the blue card varies from a couple of thousand to tens of thousands of yuan. One of the goals of the high fees is to limit the flow of rural migrants. In 1994, the Beijing government tried to impose huge fees ($11,600 per head) to limit rural migrants.[90] In Guangdong alone, more than a million farmers have purchased the blue cards. Governments at all levels began to sell *hukou* to rural migrants as a source of revenue. As with the demise of feudalism in France, poverty-stricken members of the old aristocracy are selling their status categories, thereby further undermining the system. Moreover, the sale of blue cards and *hukou* provides more revenue for local governments, further weakening the financial power of the central government.

The People's Republic of China, originally based on the farmers, is sinking in a sea of restless farmers, who increasingly acquire the means to move even if they lack permission to move or certainty as to where to move. This became the dramatic and ironic new form of Mao's *nongcun baowei chengshi* (the countryside encircles the city). Unlike the period 1927–1949, there is no Mao in this farmers' movement. Mao organized the farmers by playing shrewdly on their frustrations and deprivations. This new movement of the farmers is endogenous. With no Mao mobilizing this movement, it has proved invulnerable to all the government's mechanisms for keeping the people in their place.

Rural migrants succeeded in leaching away the state's mobility control without making a direct assault on the government's discriminatory *hukou* policies. The mobility of rural people took shape outside official channels. Personal networks (kinship, friendship, and village fellowship) and productivity provided migrants with the tools for social change. At one level, the purchase of *hukou* and blue cards constituted an act of accommodation to the system, but when millions of farmers could buy food without *hukou* and began to gain access to *hukou*, the function of *hukou* lost its value. Many migrants who are not wealthy enough to buy *hukou* or the blue card try not to be noticed. Many go to the cities without the registration that the state requires. Chinese social scientists point out that 60 percent of rural migrants in Chengdu City, Sichuan, do not register, while in Guangzhou, the capital of Guangdong, fewer than one-third of migrants register at all.[91]

The mobility of the unorganized farmers contrasts sharply with organized students' protests. Students' protests seek the attention of the state, the public, and the international community, whereas rural migrants go to great lengths to avoid attracting attention. While China's political leaders were transfixed by Tiananmen and other organized protests, the unorganized farmers surged everywhere, through country and city. While attention was focused elsewhere, and with no self-conscious organization or intent, the Chinese farmers transformed the system, politically, economically, and socially.

## Notes

1. Jiang Liu, et al., eds, *Shehui lanpishu 1992–1993 nian Zhongguo: Shehui xingshi fenxi yu yuce* (China in 1992–1993: Analysis and Forecast of Social Situations 1992–1993 China) (Beijing: Zhongguo Shehui Kexue Chubanshe, 1993).

2.   For the 1984 no. 1 document from the central government, see Zhonggong Zhongyang Wenjian Yanjiushi, ed., *Shi er da yilai zhongyao wenxian xuanbian* (Selections of Important Documents Since the Twelfth Party Congress), vols. 1 and 2 (Beijing: Renmin Chubanshe, 1986), p. 424–438.

3.   State Council, "The State Council: Information on Peasant's Settling into Towns October 13, 1984," in *Zhongguo nongcun fagui 1984* (Chinese Agriculture Regulations 1984) (Beijing: Nongye Chubanshe, 1986).

4.   Akira Koshizawa, "China's Urban Planning Treats Development Without Urbanization," *Developing Economies* 16 (March, 1978):9–13.

5.   Personal interviews with Zu in 1986.

6.   *Zhongguo qingnian bao* (China Youth News), February 17, 1994.

7.   *China News Digest,* September 12, 1994; *World Journal,* September 17, 1994.

8.   *Zhongguo qingnian bao* (China Youth News), February 26, 1994.

9.   He Xiaoping, "Nongjia you" (Farmers' Worry), *Shehui* (Sociology Journal) (March 1991):13–17.

10.   Ai Xue, "Suohui jiuzhang luowangji" (The Capture of Bribe Seeking Director), *Falüyushenghuo* (Law and Life) 7 (1991).

11.   Ma Fei, "Beigao xi shang de gongan jiuzhang" (Police Chief on Trial), *Falüyushenghuo* (Law and Life) 8 (1991).

12.   Personal interviews with Zheng Yongnian, August 1993.

13.   *People's Daily*, September 24, 1992.

14.   Yang Hui, "Zhongguo shuizhi de 'heihezi'" (The "Black Box" of the Chinese Tax System), *Minzhu Zhongguo* (Democracy and China) 11 (1993):35–39.

15.   *Central Daily News*, February 9, 1994.

16.   There were three kinds of coupons for grain: one issued by the city government; one issued by the provincial government; and one issued by the state. The state grain coupon could be used nationally; the provincial one was used within the province; the city one was only used by the city. All the coupons were distributed by the state urban organizations.

17.   Min Yaolian and Li Binkun, eds., *Zhongguo nongcun jingji gaige yanjiu* (Study on Chinese Rural Economic Reform) (Beijing: Zhongguo Zhanwang Chubanshe, 1988), p. 156.

18.   Guo Shutian and Liu Chulin, eds., *Shehen de Zhongguo* (Unbalanced China) (Shijiachuang: Hebei Renmin Chubanshe, 1991), p. 78; and Chu Songlin, "On the Function of Liangpiao," *Beijing Daily*, January 26, 1991.

19.   Nongyebu Jingji Zhengce Yanjiu Zhongxin (Economic Policy Research Center of the Agricultural Ministry), *Zhongguo nongcun: zhengce yanjiu beiwanglu* (Rural China: Memorandum of Policy Research), vol. 2 (Beijing: Nongye Chubanshe, 1991), p. 197.

20.   This is a play on Mao's slogan, "The countryside surrounds the city."

21. Li Xianfu, "Tudi de shengyin" (The Complaint of the Earth), in Shanghai Wenyi Chubanshe, ed., *Minyishi weitian* (People Depend on Food) (Shanghai: Shanghai Wenyi Chubanshe, 1991), p. 142.

22. Lu Xueyi and Li Peilin, *Zhongguo shehui fazhan baogao* (A Developmental Report on Chinese Society) (Shengyang: Liaoning Renmin Chubanshe, 1991), p. 138.

23. *Zhongguo gongshang bao* (Chinese Business News), October 29, 1992.

24. Li Mengbai and Hu Xin, *Liudong renkou dui dachengshi fazhan di yingxiang ji duice* (Impact of Migrants on Big City Development and Policy Implications) (Beijing: Jingji Ribao Chubanshe, 1991), p. 57.

25. Li Mengbai and Hu Xin suggest that of rural migrants in Beijing, 18 percent live in the city, 57 percent in near suburbs, and 26 percent in far suburbs. See ibid., p. 18.

26. Ibid., p. 56.

27. Huang Weiding, *Zhongguo de yinxing jingji* (China's Hidden Economy) (Beijing : Zhongguo Shangye Chubanshe, 1993), p. 69.

28. Li and Hu, *Impact of Migrants*.

29. *Zhongguo qingnian bao* (China Youth News), February 16, 1994, p. 1.

30. Huang, *China's Hidden Economy*, p. 42.

31. Shi Xianmin, "Beijing getihu difazhan licheng ji neibie fenghua" (The Development Process of Small Businesses with a Detailed Breakdown: A Case Study of the Western District in Beijing), *Zhongguo shehui kexue* (Social Sciences in China) 5 (September 1992):25.

32. Personal investigation in 1984, 1985, 1986.

33. Gao Xiaomeng and Xiang Ning, *Zhongguo nongye jiage zhengce fenxi* (Policy Analysis of Chinese Agricultural Price) (Hangzhou: Zhejiang Renmin Chubanshe, 1992), p. 32. In small towns and cities, farmers themselves sold the goods. Thus, the share of rural merchants is smaller.

34. Shi Xianmin, "Beijing's Privately-Owned Small Businesses: A Decade's Development," *Zhongguo shehui kexue* (Social Sciences in China) 14, no. 1 (1993):156.

35. Ibid., p. 161.

36. Personal interviews with rural entrepreneurs in Wuhan, in 1985.

37. Gao and Xiang, *Policy Analysis*.

38. Shi, "Development," p. 34.

39. Jiang Zemin, "Speech on the Commerce Work in Shanghai, February 23, 1989," *Zhongguo shang bao* (Chinese Business News) (April 12, 1990):1.

40. Jiang, et al., *China in 1992–1993*, pp. 3–10.

41. Shi Ai, "Beijing saimachang zhengzhi fengyun" (Political Clouds over the Beijing Horse Racing Course), *Zhongguo shibao* (China Times) (September 5–11, 1993):68.

42. Huang, *China's Hidden Economy*, pp. 183–202.

43. Tian Zhiwei and Wu Xiaopo, "Chen Jinyi tingjin shanghaitan" (Chen Jinyi Marches into Shanghai), *Banyuetan* (1993):18–20.

44. Andrew Walder, *Communist Neo-traditionalism: Work and Authority in Chinese Society* (Berkeley: University of California Press, 1986).

45. "Temporary Regulations on Implementing Labor Contracts in State Industry," *Bulletin of the State Council* (October 10, 1986): 739–750.

46. *People's Daily*, August 20, 1988. In Chinese: *Zhuashenghuo cushengchan; zaizhuashenghuo zaicushengchan.*

47. In Chinese: *Zhuageming cushengchan; zaizhuageming zaicushengchan.*

48. "Bare-assed intellectuals in a beautiful sedan chair" means that although the social prestige of intellectuals rose, their economic position was low. Intellectuals under Mao were called *chou laojiu* (the stinking ninth).

49. Shi, "Beijing's Privately-Owned Small Businesses," p. 155.

50. Li Qiang, "Shixi woguo geti he siying jingji zai chengshi yu nong-cun di zhongda chabie" (An Analysis of Great Differences Between Urban and Rural Private Owners), *Sociology and Social Research* 2 (1992):21–28.

51. Ibid.

52. See Deborah Davis, "Job Mobility in Post-Mao Cities: Increases on the Margins," *China Quarterly* 132 (December 1992):1062–1085; and Susan L. Shirk, "Recent Chinese Labor Policies and the Transformation of Industrial Organization in China," *China Quarterly* (December 1981):575–593.

53. Personal interviews with managers at the Wuhan Boiler Works in 1985 and 1986.

54. In Chinese: *Dong xi nan bai zhong, zhuanqian dao Guangdong.*

55. *People's Daily*, February 25, 1988.

56. *Zhongguo qingnian bao* (China Youth News), March 1, 1994.

57. Fazhan Yanjiusuo (Development Research Institute), *Gaige mian-lin zhidu chuangxin* (Reform and System Innovation) (Shanghai: Sanlian Chubanshe, 1988).

58. *Zhongguo qingnian bao* (China Youth News), March 10, 1994.

59. Huang, *China's Hidden Economy*, p.63.

60. *Zhongguo qingnian bao* (China Youth News), March 3, 1994.

61. Patrick E. Tyler, "China's Migrants: Economic Engine, Social Burden," *New York Times*, June 29, 1994, A3.

62. Li and Hu, *Impact of Migrants* , p. 33.

63. Guo Shutian and Liu Chulin, eds., *Shehen de Zhongguo* (Unbalanced China) (Shijiachuang: Hebei Renmin Chubanshe, 1991), p. 55.

64. Nongyebu Jingji Zhengce Yanjiu Zhongxin, *Rural China: Policy Research Memorandum*, vol. 1. (Beijing: Nongye Chubanshe, 1988), p. 97.

65. Guo and Liu , *Unbalanced China*, p. 56.

66. Huang, *China's Hidden Economy*, p. 61.

67. In Chinese: *Shuji guan fangxiang; gongren da baixiang; gongzhou kao laoxiang.* (*Da baixiang* means "play around" in the Shanghai dialect.)

68. *People's Daily,* January 3, 1989.

69. Feng Lanrui, *Lun Zhongguo Laodongli Shichang* (On Chinese Labor Markets) (Beijing: Zhongguo Chengshi Chubanshe, 1991), p. 38.

70. *Qiu Shi* (Seeking Truth), no. 4 (1990):38.

71. In addition to farmers, *getihu* "private retail traders" in the city were also successful. Most *getihu* were exconvicts who were unable to find jobs because of their past behavior. The state allowed them to open some retail stores to keep them out of trouble, but their numbers were small.

72. Thomas Rawski, ed., *How to Study China's Economy Today* (Hongkong: Chinese University Press, 1991), p. 8.

73. *Zhongguo baikei quanshu, 1990* (Chinese Encyclopedia 1990 Year Book) (Beijing: Baike Daquan Chubanshe), p. 59.

74. *Zhongguo qingnian bao* (China Youth News), March 10, 1994.

75. He Xin, "Analysis of the Current Student Protests and Forecasts Concerning the Situation," *Australian Journal of Chinese Affairs* 23 (1990):64–76.

76. Keiko Wakabayashi, "Migration from Rural to Urban Areas in China," *Developing Economies* 28, no. 4 (1990):520–521.

77. Wu Ruijun, "Defining the Floating Population," *Renkou yu jingji* (Population and Economy) 3 (1990):53–55. Translated in Joint Publications Research Services CAR–90–073 (September 28, 1990).

78. In Chinese: *Gao daodande buru mai jidande.* There is a pun here in that both "missile" and "egg" are pronounced *dan.*

79. Thomas B. Gold, "Urban Private Business and Social Change," in Deborah Davis and Ezra F. Vogel, eds., *Chinese Society on the Eve of Tiananmen: The Impact of Reform* (Cambridge: Harvard University Press, 1990), p. 175.

80. Yan Gaihua and Lu Sishan, *Zapo 'santie' houde Zhongguo ren?* (Chinese People After Breaking *Santie?*) (Beijing: Ligong Daxue Chubanshe, 1992). *Santie* refers to the iron rice bowl, iron salary, and tenured positions.

81. *Liaowang* (Outlook), May 31, 1993.

82. *Zhongguo qingnian bao* (China Youth News), February 25, 1994.

83. The farmer saying in Chinese is: *Renyao xiangqian kan, xianyao xiangqiankan, zhiyou xiangqian kan, caineng xiangqiankan.* The pronunciation of *qian* can mean "money" or "forward." In Mao's time, *xiangqiankan* carried the sole meaning of looking forward.

84. Yan Zi, "Fengyu piaoyao po santie; shitan Zhongguo jingji gaige di genben wenti" (Breaking *Santie* in Hard Times: On the Basic Problem of Chinese Economic System Reform) *Jingji gaige* (Economic Reform) 2 (1993): 16–20.

85. In Chinese: *Shangban yitiao chong; xiaban yitiao long.*

86. Xiao Qingfu, *Wuci langchao* (Five Waves) (Beijing: Zhongguo Renmin Daxue Chubanshe, 1989), p. 201.

87. Dorothy Solinger, "China's Urban Transients in the Transition from Socialism and the Collapse of the Communist 'Urban Public Regime,'" *Comparative Politics* 27, no. 2 (1995):127.

88. Hou Dongmi, "Shenzhen fangshi" (The Shenzhen Way), *Renko yanjiu* (Population Studies) 2 (1991):25; and personal interviews with Shenzhen officials in 1994.

89. Tyler, "China's Migrants," A3.

90. Patrick E. Tyler, "Beijing to Impose Huge Fees to Limit Migrants in City," *New York Times*, September 15, 1994, A10.

91. Li and Hu, *Impact of Migrants*, pp. 228–29

# Farmers Engulf the One-Child Family Policy

A tree of a thousand feet must have roots;
water of a thousand miles must have a
source;
a man lives but once, so he must have
sons.

Farmer proverb

After *baochan daohu*, farmers brought about changes not only in economic arenas but in other social structures as well, including altering the government's one-child policy. The coercive one-child policy of the People's Republic of China illustrates that despite the Deng regime's loud claims to undo Maoist political campaign methods, the important political continuities remain.[1] Under Deng, in addition to economic reform, the one-child law became basic state policy, as expressed in 1979 by Vice-Premier Chen Yun: "The immediate primary task is to advocate that each couple have just one child; the resultant problems are secondary."[2]

China's top leaders agreed on the one-child policy, as Chen Muhua, the head of the Family Planning Commission, pointed out:

> The Central Committee of the Party attaches great importance to the development of programs in fertility planning and the control of population growth. These programs are launched under the direct leadership of the Central Committee. Comrade Deng Xiaoping, Li Xiannian, Chen Yun, Hu Yaobang, Zhao Ziyang have all personally directed the development of these programs.[3]

In 1982, the constitution was revised to state that "both husband and wife have the duty to implement fertility planning."[4] China is probably the only country in the world whose constitution contains such a provision. In 1988, Premier Li Peng stressed the one-child policy at the National People's Congress: "To keep the country's population at about 1.2 billion by the end of the century, China must strictly carry out the policies of promoting later marriages and restricting each couple to only one child."[5] Each provincial government drafted rules to carry out the one-child policy.

For more than two thousand years, Chinese have placed a high value on the birth of sons, as represented by Mencius's well-known words: There are three unofficial sins; of these, to lack posterity is the greatest.[6] For the Chinese, posterity has meant sons because the family line and ancestor worship were carried on exclusively through male descendants. For them, a sense of immortality exists in the line of descent, which gives meaning to their lives and prescribes their duties in life:

> Reproduction of the line was a man's most fundamental obligation, a repayment to the ancestors who had given him life and the means of subsistence. In prerevolutionary China failure to reproduce the line was considered an offense to the ancestors, the ultimate unfilial act that brought disgrace in the eyes of the ancestors and opprobrium in the eyes of the community.[7]

The revolution failed to change these attitudes significantly. The one-child family policy in fact forces millions of Chinese to accept the extinction of the family line when the only child is a girl, for rural parents rely on sons for support in their old age. The Chinese one-child family policy is one of the most far-reaching social engineering policies in human history.

It is important to recognize the urgency of family planning for China. For two decades, the government did not develop a sound birth control program. Starting in the 1970s, the government used coercion to impose its one-child policy in order to sharply reduce the national birthrate. Although the state succeeded in sharply and rapidly reducing the birthrate, especially in the cities, it failed to force many desperate rural people to have only one child. This chapter illustrates how *baochan daohu* empowered the farmers to resist the one-child policy, how farmers evaded the one-child family law, and how, eventually, what they brought about even helped urban people to resist the one-child family law.

## The One-Child Family and State Coercion

Beginning in the 1960s, the state launched many campaigns to reduce the birthrate in the cities because of the urban unemployment problem. In the mid-1970s, the state included rural people in its family planning. The pressure reached its peak after the government formally issued a one-child per family regulation in 1979. In order to reach its goal to sharply reduce births, the government established comprehensive measures ranging from free contraceptives and abortions to mass propaganda, heavy fines, and other forms of direct intervention, including the most draconian policy of forced abortions, even into the third trimester, and sterilization of women.

The state welfare structure plus urban crowding made it relatively easy for most city people to accept (if not like) the one-child policy. Also, higher educational levels in the city contributed to the demographic transition. But even in the city, the state had to use coercion as well as incentives to carry out its one-child family program. In the city, the state used the confiscation of *hukou* and the loss of jobs to enforce its birth control policy. Urban people who violated the policy faced both economic and political punishment. Party members could be kicked out of the party, and workers could lose their jobs altogether. Urban working women with more than one child faced heavy fines during the second pregnancy and for seven years after the child was born, at a rate equivalent to 10–20 percent of the couple's income.

In some cities, urban residents lost their urban *hukou* if they violated the one-child plan. Children born *jihuawai* (out of plan) would not be provided with *liangpiao* (cheap food rationing coupons) and would be deprived of free health care and education. Apart from negative incentives beginning in the 1970s, the state also provided money to urban couples who promised to have only one child, with regional variation ranging from 5 yuan to 30 yuan per month. At a state factory, mothers of one child are provided with extensive paid maternal leave. The child receives health care and education benefits unavailable to second children.

The state developed a systematic program to control women's fertility. Women fell victim to the state one-child family regulation. Cadres watched women closely—even checking on their menstrual flows. The cadres literally decided when a woman could give birth and dictated how many children a woman could have.

The state's one-child planning sought complete control over women's fertility. Given the population problem, it is important to develop a sound family planning program, but Chinese state family planning sought to control women and ignored both women's and men's wishes. In early 1983, the state launched a family planning month campaign, forcing pregnant women even in the third trimester to undergo abortions and sterilization.[8] Every workplace had someone investigating family planning. Even one's fellow workers became a part of the team watching menstrual cycles, the symptoms of pregnancy, and the means of contraception.[9] Reproduction merged with simple production statistics, but the goal was to reduce rather than increase production. The state regarded women's bodies as a means of production owned and administered by the state.

Leaders at all levels boasted about increasing abortions and used abortion statistics as the measure of their success. A document from a county office reports: "This year there were 8,830 abortions, which means 8,830 fewer babies. At the rate of 400 yuan per baby, the county has saved 3,532,000 yuan. This has played a positive role in promoting the four modernizations."[10]

Every work unit (*danwei*) and village was assigned a fixed reproduction quota in addition to its production quota. After a reproduction quota was filled, no one in that organization was allowed to give birth. Without a birth allowance certificate from the workplace, no hospital would deliver a baby. A woman had to apply for a quota slot before she conceived, or else she had to undergo abortion. For example, one woman over thirty five got pregnant and asked for an exception, promising her party secretary that the baby would be the only one, but her request was turned down because her workplace's quota had been filled. Despite the pleading of her doctor, her workplace forced her to have an abortion. When she finally was given a quota, she was not able to conceive due to complications from the previous abortion. Tragic stories like this are commonplace in the city.

The strategy worked best in the city because urban working couples were tightly controlled and easily observed in their workplace. What is more, tight urban housing made it more difficult for urban couples to raise more than one child. When the state was the only employer, urban people depended entirely on the state. Urban women complied with the one child policy against their own wishes because they feared discrimination at work, lack of promotion, or more stringent reprisals. As a result, most couples in the city had only one child regardless of their preferences. In 1988, in Shanghai, for example, only 0.6 percent of Shanghai residents with an urban *hukou* violated the one-child regulation. Combined with the above-mentioned measures, the control over women's bodies succeeded in preventing urban people from having a second baby. *Throughout the 1980s, more than 95 percent of urban couples who gave birth obtained the one-child certificate.*

One of the important reasons that urban people accepted the coercive one-child policy is that urban *danwei* provided welfare and pensions for old people. They no longer depended on their sons to provide for their old age. The effectiveness of the one-child policy in the city does not mean that urban people were happy and willing to have only one child, however. Several social surveys in China indicate that the majority of women both in the city and in the countryside wanted to have more than one child. Only 13 percent of all women in Hebei, 8 percent of all women in Shanxi, and 20 percent of all women in Beijing wanted to have only one child.[11] According to a survey reported by the state's Xinhua News Agency in 1995, more than 40 percent of young mothers under twenty-five would like to have a second child if the one-child policy were not enforced.[12]

Moreover, women have to endure both psychological and social pressure during and after pregnancy. The desire to have a son to carry on the family name still survives under communism in the countryside and in the city. The one-child policy may be an actual pattern in urban areas, but it is most definitely not the ideal pattern in rural or urban areas. The birth of one daughter will end the male line for the family, threatening the basic Chinese patrilineal ideal. Although urban people were not as strong believers in the male line for the family as rural people, many people still preferred sons. Even in cities, life choices for a man were much brighter than a woman's. Mothers who gave birth to female babies were often beaten and sometimes driven to suicide in urban and particularly in rural areas. The pressure to have a son haunted most pregnant woman both in the city and the countryside. Women were blamed for producing a girl whose existence meant the end of the family line. The joy of being pregnant turned into the fear of having a girl.

Although Chinese women before communism also wanted to produce male children, the birth of a girl baby was a small happiness because it at least showed that the woman was fertile. She could hope for a boy later. The one-child law, if enforced, means that the first child must also be the last child, placing women under further emotional stress. Many family disputes have occurred as the result of the one-child law. Some men have sought a divorce after their wife gave birth to a girl. Incidents of abusing mothers after the birth of a girl are rising, particularly in the city, where the one-child family law has been most successful. Still, the woman bears the blame for infertility, birth defects, and the sex of the child. Those matters are never blamed on men. One female worker wrote to the *Workers' Daily* to complain about the ill treatment from her husband after she gave birth to a girl:

> However, after I gave birth to a baby girl in March 1981, I was subjected to beating, scolding, and maltreatment by Xu Baocheng's entire family. My mother-in-law despised me, and screamed at me, "There is land, yet the grass does not grow; you have given birth to a girl and snuffed out the Xu family's incense burner. . . ." He tried to force me and our daughter out of the hut, telling me to go live in the chicken coop. He refused to give me any daily necessities except for bedding. I lived through the next four months in an inhuman state.[13]

Birth-of-a-girl-related divorce increased in many cities. One 1991 survey in Hexi District, Tianjin City, suggests that 55 percent of divorces in that district resulted from the birth of girls.[14]

The state-sponsored one-child policy also created conflicts between generations. Combined with an increase in life expectancy, the rapid decline of birth means that China will face a crisis in caring for the aged. Ansley Coale projects that if China can achieve the zero population growth planned by the state, by 2035 over 25 percent of the population will be over sixty-five years of age.[15] The low percentage of working people will threaten China's economy. Who will provide for these elders?

## Farmers' Wishes vs. State Planning

The one-child policy enjoyed notably less success in the countryside than in the urban setting. In the long run, the main reason for this discrepancy was, again, *baochan daohu*. The one-child law was issued after the farmers had begun to dismantle the commune system. In other words, the state attempted its most intimidating policy just as it was losing direct control over rural people. Increasing independence after *baochan daohu* gave farmers more control over their lives, including reproduction. First of all, the distribution of labor and goods came to be in the hands of the family, not the cadres. Second, with family farming, the cadres could not effectively "cut off" their grain rations. Third, villagers could come and go, disguising pregnancy and giving birth beyond the reach of village cadres.

The state's one-child family policy directly conflicted with farmers' wishes. All farmers wanted to have at least one boy. A son will care for his parents. Most daughters marry out of the village; even if girls marry within the village, their responsibilities are to their new families. A son will carry on the family line. Sons represent power and even protection in the village. A family with no sons may be bullied by the neighbors. Finally, sons are stronger laborers to work in the fields. A son adds labor power to the farm or, increasingly, rural industry or marketing. Daughters "marry out."

The farmers' reproductive wish was in conflict with the state quota of one child per family. In the countryside, the incentives to have a son were stronger than those in the city as a result of *baochan daohu* and the exclusion of farmers from the welfare system. First of all, farmers did not fear cancelation of their *hukou*. Under collective farming, rural *hukou* gave residents a share of subsistence. After *baochan daohu*, the family provided subsistence. In most cases, newborn babies did not gain allocation of land after 1982. The threat of forcing farmers off the land had little effect because farmers could farm for others. More importantly, they could do non-farm-related work. Secondly, the state could not fire farmers or throw them out of their own houses without great effort.

Other forms of negative incentives, including fines and failure to allocate land and housing space for the "excess" babies, were minor compared with the benefits of having a son. The positive incentives to restrict births were limited and dwindled before the alternative possibility of having a (or another) strong boy. Strong measures from the state, both economic and political, could not force farmers to obey state family planning directives. In fact, *baochan daohu* wiped out much of the cadres' basis for sanctions.

When all else failed, naked force was used to make farmers toe the official line. In the early 1980s, the state forced millions of women to wear IUDs. Any woman who gave birth to a second child was pressured to undergo sterilization. In some cases, women in third trimesters were forced to have abortions. Due to lack of medical care, many rural women had to bear the burden of the state's coercive birth plan. All these measures could not make farmers comply with the one-child regulation, however, because the law violated not only the social value of having sons but also economic rationality and long-term security. Most important of all, farm families with increasing economic and political independence were able to resist the sanctions that reinforced the one-child policy in urban settings.

*Baochan daohu*, the structural change in the countryside, provided farmers the means to resist the one-child regulation. *Baochan daohu* placed family heads in charge of economic resources. The cadres lost control over farmer families. When cadres in charge of family planning went to farmhouses, they were often driven out by farmers. A common complaint of farmers was, "Our children do not eat nor drink anything from the cadres. What business have they got to tell us how many children we should have."[16] Across rural China, farm families have created myriad means to evade the enforcement of the one-child policy.[17]

## Marriage Boom in the Early 1980s

Linked with the one-child family policy in the late 1970s and early 1980s was the policy of a late marriage age, set at twenty-three for women and twenty-five for men, although the state's 1950 marriage law set the legal marriage age at eighteen and twenty for women and men, respectively. This late marriage age was the state family planning policy of the 1970s. Under the collective arrangement, cadres were able to carry out the official late marriage policy quite successfully in many rural areas. They could give high work points to couples who complied with the late marriage requirement and reduce work points for those who failed to comply. The most effective means of cadre control was the cancelation or reduction of grain rationing, the essential means of survival for most villagers under the collective system. The control of marriage registration was another way to enforce compliance. In order to get a marriage license, the couple had to get an official age certificate from their brigade cadres, who kept the *hukou* records. Couples who married without a marriage license were subject to punishment. Although there were many cases of bribing cadres or distorting records, the apparatus for late marriage generally succeeded. The percentage of young women marrying before age eighteen fell to only 3.5 percent in 1978.[18] Marriage age for women in general rose from less than nineteen before 1950 to more than twenty-three in 1979.

In the late 1970s and early 1980s, *baochan daohu* in rural China affected social structures in general, including the marital age structure. For quite a few years, late marriage stopped and many young rural couples married. First of all, cadres' control in the countryside weakened when farmer families regained their decisionmaking power. Farmers did not have to obey the official late marriage policy because the cadres could not use cancelation of food rationing to enforce the late marriage requirement. For most farmers, seeing to the marriage of their children was one of their most important duties in life. Second, the increase in productivity and reduction in state controls after *baochan daohu* gave most farmers more income. With money in their hands, many farmers bribed village cadres to falsify the ages of their children. In addition, farmers' increased wealth after *baochan daohu* offered many of them the material means to have a wedding for their sons, a most important event in life. Many farmers did not bother to register the marriage of their children. In some areas, the old practice of customary marriage (without legal license) resumed. For example, in Feidong County, Shanxi, 81 percent of newlyweds between 1986 and 1987 married without marriage licenses.[19]

These factors gave rise to a marriage boom in China after *baochan daohu* that affected the overall demographic trend. In 1980, to offset the rural marriage boom, the state raised the marriage age from eighteen for women to twenty, hoping to ban early marriage, but farmers did not pay attention to the new law. As a result, the minimum age for marriage fell in the early 1980s.[20] In Xizhou District, Shanxi Province, 22 percent of all married women in 1987 had not reached the age specified in the 1980 law.[21]

The violation of the marriage law in the countryside has demographic consequences. The *baochan daohu* marriage boom led to a rapid increase in births in the early 1980s, and this rapid increase attracted the attention of the state. The leaders attributed this rapid increase in fertility to a breakdown of family planning in the countryside. Thus, a comprehensive antinatal program was developed in the early 1980s to force farmers to reduce births.

The state was effective in reducing births, especially in reducing urban birthrates—the percentage of women having a second child in the city declined rapidly from 60 percent in 1980 to 11 percent in 1983. But the government was never able to achieve the one-child-per-family goal in the countryside. Even in 1984, when the rural birthrate declined rapidly, more than 75 percent of rural women had a second child. In 1987, the percentage of rural women having a second child rose rapidly, reaching 89 percent.[22] This is one indication that the one-child policy has had its greatest effect in the cities, not the countryside. What follows are varied patterns of unorganized farmers' resistance to the one-child policy.

## Rural Violence

One way to resist state intrusion was open defiance. The tension between farmers and cadres over the issue of family planning became so explosive that many rural cadres did not dare to push too far. Revenge against the cadres in charge of family planning and their children occurred in many rural areas. For example, in Yangtian Village, Huangzhuzhong District, Hunan Province, one female cadre forced a farmer's wife to have an abortion in her third trimester and to be sterilized because the farmer had two girls already. When the farmer learned that the aborted child was a boy, he became enraged and went to the cadre's home and drowned her two sons. His reason was simple: the cadre had cut off his family line so he wanted to end her family line, too.[23] Between 1986 and 1990, there were 935 reported incidents of physical abuse against cadres in charge of family planning in Hunan alone.[24]

Violence also took place when cadres forced the sterilization of rural women. One farmer in Shuangliu County, Sichuan Province, killed every member of the village party secretary's family after his two children were drowned in a swimming accident. The secretary had sterilized the farmer's wife after she gave birth to two children.[25]

This kind of eye-for-an-eye revenge occurred in the countryside because some farmers regarded the life of a son as more important than their own. This sentiment made state control of family planning costly, sometimes to rural cadres. Even the official *Farmers' Daily* reported that rural violence against cadres over birth planning took away their security.[26] Many cadres had to accommodate farmers' wishes for a son. A popular saying among cadres on how to deal with the family planning went this way: "Shout loud; control less; report fewer; allow more; live an easy life."[27]

According to one social survey, 32 percent of the violent crime in one rural district of Jiangsu Province was related to family planning.[28] In her 1987 book, *China's Changing Population,* Judith Banister also reports incidents of violent attacks against cadres in family planning.[29] It is important to note that rural violence took the form of individual reprisals. Organized resistance against the one-child policy was rare. Here, too, the farmers' movement was spontaneous, unorganized, leaderless, nonideological, and apolitical. Sheryl WuDunn of the *New York Times* reported from Guangdong: "The peasants seem little interested in challenging the Government on freedom of expression, for instance, preferring to put their energies into defying Government limits on having children."[30]

## *Maiyijiaerzi* (Buying Sons at Negotiated Prices)

*Baochan daohu* enabled farmers to evade the one-child law because the increase in productivity increased the wealth of farmers, many of whom have been willing to pay high fines to secure the birth of their sons. They call this practice *maiyijiaerzi*.[31] They reason that it is worthwhile to buy a son to take care of the parents until their death. One case of *maiyijiaerzi* involved two rural entrepreneurs from Sanzai Village, Hua County, Henan Province. One was fined 10,000 yuan for having six boys and four girls; the other was fined 100,000 yuan for having four boys and four girls.[32] Paying for birth rights became so common in rural China that even the minister of the Chinese Communist Organization Department discussed *maiyijiaerzi*:

> The *xiang* government permits one child per couple. The violators will be fined 5,000 yuan per birth. People call it *maiyijiaerzi*. Some specialized households do not mind the fine and continue to violate the regulation. In 1985, one *xiang* government reported four cases of violators and was criticized by the county government. But this figure was fake. In fact, there were 104 excess births that year.[33]

Monetary fines turned the one-child policy into a new rule: *The bottom line on compliance was money.* As farmers put it, "As long as we are able to pay the fine, we will decide how many kids we should have." One rich farmer who had two daughters came to the *xiang* government and cried: "I beg you: please let me have a son. Here is 30,000 yuan. One half is the fine; the other half serves as propaganda fees to teach others not to learn from me."[34]

When fines became common, the meaning of the economic sanction disappeared. This can be observed in a village meeting in Shanxi Province:

> The announcement of names for fines and the process of collecting fines should scare farmers who violated the plan but in reality embarrasses cadres. When Wang Gengguan's name was called, he walked to the platform with pride. Wang handed in a big red bag [money] for two over-quota babies, one yet to be born. Afterward, he walked back to his seat with pride as if he had won a good prize.[35]

The pattern of shaming someone at a public meeting became an opportunity for someone to show off his wealth and his guts; it became a form of conspicuous corruption.

Although the rich could buy their way out of the one-child regulation, the very poor were not afraid of being fined, as one rural saying goes: "If you have too many fleas, you no longer itch; if you have too much debt, you no longer worry."

## *Quxian Shengyu* (Circuitous Childbirth, Evading Childbirth Regulations)

Rural people were able to defy the one-child policy because they could "get around" the medical control of the state. First of all, almost all rural babies are delivered at home. Home delivery gives farm families discretion in going beyond the rules of the one-child policy. Although in some cases female infanticides do occur, the majority of farm families have been able to use other means to secure the birth of sons without resorting to female infanticide. Some families declare their new baby stillborn while arranging adoption or hiding the new baby. Hence, they are able to have a second baby, especially if the first baby was a girl. One study discovered that as many as one-half of the "missing" girls" in demographic surveys of the 1980s may have been adopted by other families.[36] In fact, adoption arrangements became so common that the state policy "denounced this practice, explicitly excluding such couples from eligibility for further childbearing."[37]

In the area of contraceptives, rural women have more discretion than urban women. Few rural brides in Hubei and Hunan villages employed contraception during the one-child law period despite the state call for delay of childbirth after marriage. Pregnancy immediately after marriage was common in the countryside. Whereas contraceptives were delivered to the workplace in the city, in the countryside contraceptives were delivered to the village. The village cadres then had to deliver them to each household. It was considered unacceptable in the village for cadres to deliver contraceptives to newlyweds because it was considered unlucky for newlyweds to accept a device to stop the birth of a child. The Chinese wedding is full of rituals that symbolize the conception and birth of a son. Consequently, the quota baby phenomenon that has frustrated many urban newlyweds did not actually disturb rural reality prior to the first birth. Despite the pressure, most rural women would not use any form of contraceptive before they had at least one boy.

One of the most important means for rural women to carry an unauthorized pregnancy was to hide with relatives in other rural places. Such activities were more difficult under collective farming because everyone had to ask permission to leave the village. After *baochan daohu,* farmers did not have to ask for permission to go anywhere. Incidents of pregnant women hiding with relatives were so common that village women began to congratulate the family when a wife or daughter-in-law of child-bearing age took a long "visit." "Congratulations, Mother Wang, your daughter-in-law is taking another visit to her relatives. When are you going to give us red eggs to eat?" Finally, it was easier for rural women to disguise a pregnancy because they were simply less subject to direct cadre observation.

## Corruption

Farmers used bribery to go around the state birth regulation, just as they got around other restrictions by bribery. *Once the farmers had money, the corruptibility of cadres became a major means for whatever ends.* Additional children were certainly one such end. It was common for farmers to get away with violating the one-child directive by having a second or a third child if they were on goods terms with the local cadres. One of the most common ways was to obtain an official certificate stating that the first baby was handicapped. Farmers with resources and connections would "pay off" doctors and the local cadres in order to get a handicap certificate. Since the strategy of "fake handicap firstborn" saved money, farmers tried hard to bribe local cadres and doctors to get a handicap certificate for the firstborn regardless of the sex of the baby. In fact, rural cadres themselves used these excuses to go beyond the one-child regulation. For example, Wang Wenhua, a village cadre in Tongxin Village, was able to help his son arrange a handicap certificate for his first grandson. With the certificate, his son was officially allowed to have a second child. The fake certificate saved 2,000 yuan, a substantial sum of money that Wang would have been fined when a second baby was born in 1985.[38]

Farmers also tried to obtain fake certificates in order to avoid sterilization. For example, one investigation in Shuangqiao Village, Sichuan Province, discovered that of fifty-seven sterilization certificate holders, thirty-seven were not sterilized at all.[39] In another example, a doctor in Wutong Xiang, Anhui Province, often sold sterilization certificates to farmers, at 50 yuan or 100 yuan apiece. With the sterilization certificate, farmers' wives could get pregnant without fear of forced abortion because the pregnancy would be considered a "medical mistake." In other cases, farmers would pay the doctor so that he or she would not sterilize their wives during the sterilization operation. The operation scar became the best proof of their having been sterilized. Doctors in many rural areas accepted *gan-xieqian* (gratitude money) from farmers for performing fake sterilizations on their wives.

Farmers also used fake twins to get around the one-child regulation. To do so, they had to establish good relations with village cadres. Usually, a farmer would not report the birth of the first baby and report a twin baby when the second baby was born. In fact, local cadres in charge of birth control welcomed such innovations because they were pressured by the higher authorities to reduce births. Fake twins gave them excuses for the excess births in the village.

Other forms of corruption developed when farmers tried to bribe local cadres by giving gifts and feasts, as one survey in Shanxi reports: "Whenever the family planning campaigns starts, these farmers would invite local cadres to a feast and give them gifts. Cadres would give them 'privileges' to have excess births."[40]

One rural saying has this to say about rural cadres: "One will say okay holding a pair of chopsticks; the policy will become loose holding a wine cup." On October 22, 1988, the *People's Daily* exposed a birth control–related corruption case in Tongliang County, Sichuan. Between late 1984 and mid-1988, the county government collected more than

8.2 million yuan in fines from violators, but cadres at all levels misused 20 percent (at least) for their personal use (drinking, eating, and pocket money). As a result of cadre corruption in this county, 20,000–30,000 children were born outside of the plan.[41]

Corruption became so widespread that some provinces even issued regulations to punish corrupt family planning cadres. For example, Sichuan Law 26 specified punishment for the corruption in family planning:

> Regarding doctors, nurses, and working personnel in charge of birth planning work and marriage registration and state functionaries who violate these regulations, practice fraud, and accept bribes, the units where they work or the higher level competent departments should educate them through criticisms and disciplinary sanctions. If their practices constitute an offense, the judicial organs will investigate and affix the responsibility for the offense according to law.[42]

Corruption involved village cadres embezzling fines from "over-quota" births. In one case, three village cadres embezzled 60,000 yuan:

> In order to have more fine money to satisfy their own greed, they even helped and encouraged villagers to give "excessive births." As a result of their greed and seeking bribes, 70 more babies were born within two years in Yingmin Village, where the whole population was only 740, with only 140 fertile women.[43]

As a result, nonquota births became normal in the countryside, as one popular saying goes: "Those with money buy birth rights; those with power have birth rights; those with guts seize birth rights; those with nothing steal birth rights."[44] The resistance of farmers and the corruption of cadres made the accepted official statistics on family planning irrelevant to actuality. Table 7.1 suggests the discrepancy between the accepted family

**Table 7.1**

A Comparison of Statistics Between Family Planning Records and the 1982 Third Nationwide Census in One Rural District (thousands)

|  | Family Planning Records | Third Census |
|---|---|---|
| All births | 1,664 | 2,069 |
| Births of a third child | 278 | 553 |

*Source: Zhou Xiaozheng, Renkou weiji: laizi shehui gongzuozhe de jinggao (The Population Crisis: Warnings from Social Scientists) (Tianjin: Zhongguo Funü Chubanshe, 1989), p.58.*

*No one in this picture is from a one-child family.*
*Photo by Kate Xiao Zhou*

planning figure and the Third Nationwide Census of 1982. It indicates a 24 percent birth discrepancy and almost 100 percent difference between the reported family planning statistics for a third child and the Third Nationwide Census.

## The Rise of *Chaosheng Youjidui* (Over-Quota Birth Guerrillas)

The most effective way to evade state family planning was migration. Since so many rural women used migration to have unauthorized births, they were referred to in China as *chaosheng youjidui* (over-quota birth guerrillas), because the strategies they used in their hiding out resembled Mao's guerrilla strategies. One well-known Maoist guerrilla strategy, *dayiqiang huan yige difang* (after the shot, change site), was used in the 1980s by rural women who had more than one birth by constantly changing their residence.

The chief aim of these guerrilla mothers was to protect their newborn babies. Many underground railways (mainly consisting of relatives and friends) came into being to help those mothers. Members not only help pregnant women but also deliver babies because hospitals refuse to take women with over-quota births. Nothing is more ancient in China than the practice of midwifery, however.

Like any other guerrilla movement, the guerrillas for more births were flexible, constantly changing their residence, successfully escaping state control. For example, in my 1985 interview with Zhou Xiaoping of Hunan Province, Zhou recalled having to hide in five different places before she was able to give birth to her daughter. This strategy helped rural women evade the attention of local family planning cadres.

Much of rural women's resistance to the one-child policy resembles Mao's sixteen-character jingle:

When the enemy advances, we retreat;
When the enemy halts, we harass;
When the enemy is exhausted, we attack;
When the enemy retreats, we pursue.

But the "we" of guerrilla mothers were individuals not organized groups.

### When the Enemy Advances, We Retreat

Throughout the 1980s, several campaigns were launched to control rural births. Sometimes the state launched a "birth control month" and forced village women to have IUDs inserted or be sterilized. When the state used radical means to force rural women to use contraceptives, the most common form was the IUD. In order to make sure that IUDs stayed in women's bodies, the state used a special IUD with no strings attached. The removal of an IUD had to be surgical. A woman had to ask for permission to have her IUD removed. Unauthorized removal was illegal. Anyone caught assisting a woman to take out her IUD was subject to criminal charges, but these measures did not prevent some women from removing their IUDs.[45] In one rural district of Guizhou Province, more than 30 percent of those with IUDs had them illegally removed.[46] Bribery worked here, too. Rural women paid for their reproductive freedom with money, pain, and even physical danger.

Local officials even used militia to round up unauthorizedly pregnant women, surely one of the strangest military missions in all human history! Very often local government used heavy fines to enforce abortion and sterilization. The following story was told by a local party secretary:

They [farmers] hated three things: (1) tax collection; (2) yaoming [literally, "want life," i.e., family planning]; (3) cremation of their parents. Yaoming refers to family planning. Fuck their mothers, we do not care. At first, we tried to persuade [women] by going to their homes once or twice, but to no avail. Want to hide? But when they came home, I used militia men to send them to the clinic to have "operations." When someone escapes successfully by having unauthorized babies, when we wanted to fine him, he had no money saying, "Take whatever you can including the human being. I have no money." We would destroy his house. But the house was not worth much. When we had no way out, we took their cooking pots.[47]

When the situation got tough, rural women migrated in order to avoid the abuse. Migration, in fact, became the most effective way for farmers to escape state coercion in family planning.

### Rural–Rural Migration for Illegal Births

Many farm women tried to escape the coercion of local authorities by fleeing to other rural areas. Of course, women helped one another on this underground railway birth movement. Female relatives and friends used their personal networks to help pregnant women deliver babies. Some hid the women in their attics, vegetables, and watermelon huts; some sent them food; others helped deliver babies and took care of the new mother and her baby. Since cadres had formal control over the population within a district and could hardly keep up their surveillance against the people of their own district, they did not and could not control migrants. Some women became migrants just to have over-quota babies, and others settled with their families in a different rural area to start a new life. Since most of those migrants transferred their residence without permission from cadres, they did not have *hukou* in the new place. All the birth quotas were calculated according to the *hukou* statistics. As soon as a rural baby is born, the baby is recorded by the village cadre. Thus, migrants became free people in terms of having babies. My 1986 investigation in both Wuhan and Guangdong suggests that almost all migrant families violated the family planning policy. Some even managed to have four children.

To some extent, cadres paid no attention to the over-quota babies of rural migrants in their areas. At the place of origin, the cadres were happy to leave those violators out in order to reduce the number of over-quota babies. At the new place, the cadres did not want to count the new migrants as over-quota statistics. Everyone collaborated in this evasion of policy. Moreover, after *baochan daohu*, all farm families tried every means available to make money. Some farm families tried to make money by charging high fees for pregnant women and their families. For example, Changzheng *xiang*, a rural town near Shanghai, became a birth hiding place. Local people had only one article of creed: "Whoever pays more money gets his or her rent-room, it does not matter what you are doing or how many children you will have here."[48] As a result, the migrant population often surpassed that of locals.

### *Wandering Migrants: A Big Crack in the Birth Planning Dike*

Birth guerrilla bases were often situated in remote areas, minority regions, and border areas where official controls were lax. State family planning allowed "minority people" in the sparsely populated regions to have more than one child. Rural Han Chinese people went to those places to give birth to their babies. Many farmers tried hard to claim minority status. Xinjiang, a sparsely populated region, became a safe haven for rural pregnant women trying to escape family planning. For example, in the Manansi Valley of Xinjiang, rural migrants set up a village for over-quota births.[49] Most birth-oriented migrants came from rural Sichuan, Gansu, and Anhui. (Anhui is far away from Xinjiang, an illustration of farmers' desperation). They lived a primitive existence. Their goal was to produce a baby boy. They endured hardship in order to secure the birth of their sons, and many of them were successful. Since the valley was not populated, it took the state quite a while to discover its existence. When the state discovered that valley, rural migrants moved somewhere else.

Rural people also tended to hide between border regions, where control was loose. Some adjacent areas between provinces became *shiwai taoyuan* (an ideal place) for excess births. Quanxi Village, Hunan Province, was such an area and became well known as a base for over-quota birth migrants. Farmers who hid out in these places were so happy to be able to have sons safely delivered that some even had a saying for the experience: "Carry two girls wandering about, hold a boy coming home."[50]

In other places, women hid or were hidden with fishing families, who were happy to provide the service for a fee. In Zhejiang and Fujian, such a substantial number of babies were delivered illegally that a mother who gave birth on a boat was known as *shuishang chaoshengdui* (waterborne over-quota birth guerrillas). In Hubei and Hunan, two provinces well known for their numerous lakes, *shuishang chaoshengdui* was popular. On one riverside of Shanghai, farmers set up many duck-raising huts, and many babies were illegally born in those huts. On Xishui Lake in West Hunan, some rural migrants hid by staying afloat on the boats. They took advantage of the mobility of the boats to give birth outside of the plan. Some even gave birth to six children.

## Underground Excess-Birth Guerrillas in the City

More and more farmers used the market to kill several birds with one stone. Many farm families opened small restaurants, shops, and service-related businesses to escape the countryside. Moreover, once they were on the road, only they could control their fertility. In 1988, when the illegal birthrate rose sharply as a result of farmers' migration, the state issued a new directive demanding local government not issue documents to rural merchants who violated the family planning policy.[51] But rich merchants are able to bribe local leaders to get permission to have babies and to continue their business, and increasingly, anyone could buy food and other necessities, without coupons, at the rapidly spreading markets and send children elsewhere if needed.

Rural migrants were able to go beyond the one-child family policy even in the city, where strict birth control was practiced, because they were beyond two major controls that faced every urban resident. First of these was the control of the workplace. Many women who had unauthorized pregnancies did not work in the state-controlled *danwei*. Many worked for themselves in the markets or some rural-based service business. Second was the control of *hukou*. Almost none of those rural birth guerrillas had urban *hukou*. Thus, they were beyond the control of urban cadres. As a result, rural migrants in general and rural birth guerrillas in particular existed in a special state, free of the state's three instruments of control: the cadres, *hukou*, and *danwei*.[52]

A good illustration of this situation involved migrant construction workers and their families or relatives. Once a rural construction team signed a contract, workers were under the direct control of rural entrepreneurs, whose only concern was to finish the project. Many small shanties were built near dirty and dangerous construction sites, which most people avoided as much as possible. Those sites became major bases for the over-quota birth guerrillas. Some of them were the families of the rural migrants; some of them were relatives or fellow villagers. For rural people, those construction sites were a safe haven where they could have babies without fear of being fined or punished. As a result, more and more unplanned babies were born in those shanties on the construction sites at the very heart of the city. At five major airport construction sites in Hainan Province, 95 percent of construction workers came from the countryside. *The average family on the site had three children. Some even had four.* Word spread to other parts of China: Want a boy, go to Hainan. Because so many migrant women were able to give unauthorized birth, they referred to their retreats as *fangkongdong* (bomb shelters).[53]

Of course, some rural women wanted to have a son and joined the guerrilla army to secure the birth of a son. As one rural saying goes: "Push the little cart wandering around; don't return home until a baby son is born."[54] It is important to realize that the pressure to have a son combined with the state birth control policy threatens the lives of baby girls (especially if the girl is a second or third try). The underground birth railway can save the little girl who may otherwise be killed by her grandmother or her father upon birth.

The use of the term "guerrilla" does not capture the essence of the rural women's resistance to state family planning because these facilities were unorganized, leaderless, and nonideological. (The underground rail-way involved informal cooperation.) Even the most violent attacks against local family planning cadres were individual acts. The effect of the daring acts of those rural people, however, broke one of the most important projects of the Chinese state. Here again, as so often in Chinese history, the state was neither as strong nor as creative as the farmers.

As a result of rural resistance, between 1980 and 1987, 9 million newborns exceeded the plan, more than one-third of the planned births.[55] Whatever the success of the one-child per family law in the urban setting, the childbearing rate of rural women could not be pushed below 2.8. Although the Chinese state was able to reduce the birthrate greatly by coercion and through other means, it could not realize the goal of the one-child law.

## When the Enemy Is Exhausted, We Attack

As a result of farmers' resistance, compliance with the one-child law in some rural areas was as low as 10–20 percent.[56] The fear that widespread defiance of the one-child law might lead to the breakdown of family planning altogether forced the state to modify its one-child policy, and in 1984 a new family policy came out with specific terms to address the rural population. The modified family plan may be summarized as follows: (1) one couple, one child, for all urban residents, with exceptions for a seriously handicapped first child; (2) some rural residents with difficulties or farmers living in mountainous areas are allowed to have a second child only after several years' interval and by permission if the first is a girl; (3) no third child is ever allowed; (4) late marriage and late birth.[57]

By allowing farmers to have a second try if the first child was a girl, the government gave in to the farmers' desire for a son.[58] Many farmers continued to try to have a third child if the first two were girls. In fact, the 1984 compromise by the state did little to prevent farmers from having more children:

> This relaxation has partially accommodated the demand for male offspring that frustrated earlier enforcement efforts, but it has not put an end to peasant resistance. Couples with one son or two daughters often bear additional children; the required four-year interval between the first and second birth is routinely ignored; and village leaders conspire with relatives and friends to conceal "excess" births from higher authorities.[59]

When the state opened a small hole in the dike of family planning, farmers widened it, and every family in the countryside tried to have a second child, regardless of their situation. The goal of the modified policy in

1984 was to prevent the total breakdown of family planning by loosening up control, as represented by the guideline "open a small hole to close a large one."[60] But farmers surged through that hole. Most farmers had two children regardless of whether their first-born children was male and regardless of their economic situation.

## "Missing Baby Girls"

All the above-mentioned rural resistance has created a problem for accurate statistics on birthrates. This situation is made worse when cadres at local levels simply cast out the migrant women and their children and "cheat" on the real birthrate.

One of the problems is the "missing baby girls." Since the one-child law was put in effect in 1979, there has been a rapid increase in an already high male-to-female ratio. According to the 1990 census, the primary reason for the sex imbalance came from underreporting of baby girls, although other factors, like female infanticide and ultrasound-determined abortion also existed. Between 1983 to 1990, according to one informal estimate, the underreporting of girls accounted for half to two-thirds of the high ratio of boys to girls.[61]

This problem worsened when many farmers refused to register the birth of their babies, especially the birth of girl babies. In 1987, the government journal *Liaowang* (Outlook) reported that in Zhangyu County, Liaoning Province, one-third of baby girls were not registered at birth, leading to a reported "sex ratio" of 158:100 in 1984. The same journal also reported that in 1986 the family planning birth report in Anhui was 670,000, but the survey from the Anhui Statistics Bureau reported the births at 970,000.[62] There must exist a huge number of "unregistered" children.

In some cases, refusing to register one's children is a form of rural defiance against the *hukou* system and a way to evade the one-child policy. For example, in Qingtian County, Zhejiang, there has been a rapid increase in girls with no *hukou*. Some farmers sent their girls for adoption; others hired people to take care of daughters. Many rural couples refused to register the birth of their daughters until they had a son. As a result, the sex ratio from the birth record in 1986 showed a constant biased ratio for high male births (133:100). In fact, investigation showed that the actual sex ratio in that county was 105:100 in that year.[63] One investigation into two Shanxi *xiang* discovered that more than 88 percent of babies born in the 1980s were not registered under rural *hukou*.[64] In some rural areas, not registering does not deprive them of benefits because the family will not have new allocation of land use with a new additional baby. For example, rural women who worked in the factories had to register their children as "rural households." Fearing that their children would be discriminated against by *hukou*, many women from the countryside refused to register the birth. The reporting of births is so distorted that a 1988 national survey on birth and sterilization reveals that there is a 33 percent discrepancy between the reported birthrate and survey estimates.[65] In one investigation, the State Public Security Ministry in charge of *hukou* found 1 million children without *hukou*.[66] Children without *hukou* have no official access to education, land, or labor allocation. They become, in effect, a group outside the system altogether.

## The Decline of Hukou as a Form of Control

To a great extent, *hukou*, a product of a planned state, actually became irrelevant to the increasingly independent farmers. Under the collective economy, farmers had to report their births because the collective production team was the only place where their children could get grain. But *baochan daohu* placed grain distribution in the hands of the family. More and more farmers ignored *hukou* altogether. Rural people could get away with underreporting babies because rural people no longer took *hukou* seriously. Nevertheless, *hukou* is still the most important record used by the state to trace population statistics.

In fact, one of the best ways to illustrate the decline of *hukou* control in the countryside is to look at the acceptance of one-child certificates by *hukou* type in Hebei between 1979 to 1988. Table 7.2 presents family planning by *hukou* types. From it, we can see that the majority of women with rural *hukou* (88 percent) refused to comply with the one-child policy, whereas 89 percent of urban mothers accepted the one-child policy. Since women with rural *hukou* were the majority, approximately 80 percent, overall compliance with the one-child policy was as low as 22 percent. Table 7.2 also suggests that rural women who became pregnant with a second child had fewer abortions than did urban women, although they still

**Table 7.2**

Fertility Event After the First Live Birth, by Type of *Hukou*, Hebei, 1979–1988 (percentages)

| Fertility Event | Total | Rural Hukou | Urban Hukou |
|---|---|---|---|
| One-child certificate acceptance | 22 | 12 | 89 |
| Contraceptive use | 48 | 45 | 67 |
| Subsequent pregnancy | 66 | 68 | 48 |
| Abortion | 26 | 20 | 89 |

*Source: Jiali Li and Rosemary Cooney, "Son Preference, Government Control, and the One-Child Policy in China, 1979–1988," Paper presented to the 1993 Annual Meeting of the Population Association of America, Cincinnati, Ohio, April 1–4, p. 18.*

use contraceptives. This suggests that rural women are able to use the contraceptive services provided by the state while at the same time resisting the state's coercion. Rural women have more freedom in terms of reproductive rights.

## Cadre Cheating

Almost all rural cadres lied about the real number of births, for several reasons. First, the real statistics would force them to pay heavy fines to the higher authority. Second, it is difficult to force sterilization on farm women with no sons. Cadres fear offending too many people and being the target of revenge. In addition, they are sympathetic to the girl-only families. Third, cadres fear criticism if they admit they failed to carry out family planning. Fourth and last, cadres are themselves influenced by the social environment and do not want to stir up trouble.

The discrepancy between actual births and reported births has grown so large that it threatens not only the one-child law but also the state's control over the population as a whole. Unreported children and over-quota babies become nonpersons in the eye of the state. Some even called them the phantoms (*youling*) of China. In general, the children born out of plan are referred as *heihaizi* ("black children," i.e., illegal children).

Throughout the 1980s, nearly half of all women (almost all from the countryside) who had two children went on to have a third child.[67] In a joint letter to the State Family Planning Commission in 1990, China's top leaders, Jiang Zemin and Li Peng, expressed their concern:

> Family planning touches the whole project of the economy and other social development. Party committees and governments at all levels must regard this task as a major routine work and organize all related departments and mass organizations to do a good job on this matter. Quota management for births must be carried out in order to guarantee the family planning policy to be carried out at the basic level. We must do everything to correct the slack family planning work in some parts of rural China.[68]

## Developmental Impact

There is no doubt that China has experienced a rapid decline in its fertility rate. No one can doubt that the state's coercive family planning policy has played an important role in reducing the birthrate. One must not, however, attribute the decline of the birthrate and the rural resistance solely to the one-child policy. The decline of the birthrate in rural areas in recent years seems to correlate with the expansion of markets, the development of rural industry, and the increase in rural migration. Thus, this decline was also linked to an increase in farmers' decisions to have smaller families, a familiar accompaniment of modernization.

As more and more rural women participate in market activities, the perceived cost of having an additional child increases. From Table 7.2 we can see that about half of rural women used contraceptives. Female rural merchants have a saying: "First make money, then have babies." Thus, markets provided a safe harbor for rural women to give birth out of the plan, on the one hand; on the other hand, rural merchants in the markets tended to have smaller families than those who remained in villages as farmers. As more and more rural women become active in market activities, they are likely to have fewer children than women who stay on the farm.

The rapid increase in rural industry also may cause a decline of rural births. As more and more rural women worked in rural enterprises, it became burdensome to have more children. As young rural women joined the factories, the marriage age in the countryside began to rise, bringing down the rural birthrate. There seems to be a striking correlation between the decline of the birthrate and the increase in rural industries. After 1987, when nonagricultural production in China surpassed agricultural production in the countryside, the rural birthrate also declined.

For example, Jiangsu Province took the lead in rural industrial development throughout the 1980s, and the birthrate for Jiangsu was the lowest in the nation. Within Jiangsu, the higher the level of rural industrial development in one region, the lower the birthrate, suggesting that rural industrialization reduces family size.[69] There seems to be a consistent relation between high economic development (markets and rural industry) and lower rural birthrates. It could also be that it is easier for factory managers to control the fertility of factory workers.

The developmental impact on demography is more important in those fast-growing regions. Rural factories tend to employ unmarried young rural women, so those women tend to remain unmarried in order to keep their jobs. This means that a large number of rural women have to delay marriage or remain single in order to keep their factory jobs. A 1989 survey of rural industries in Guangdong indicates that almost all the women in those factories were single.[70] My own interviews in 1994 with young female workers in rural Guangdong indicate a structural difficulty for those female workers to get married at a younger age. Many rural factories provided no maternity leave or child care for young mothers. Many have to delay their childrearing. Many factories fire female workers if they become pregnant. Because women comprise the majority of workers in rural factories in those areas, their impact on demographic change is important.

The increase in rural migration also may contribute to the decline of the rural birthrate because it is easier for rural migrants if they have smaller families. Frequent contact with modern cultural life, either through television or through other cultural effects, has influenced the way of life. *For rural women, there is increasingly a life apart from being a wife and a mother.*

There is little doubt that China will experience a further decline of the rural birthrate. Moreover, as more and more urban people now have started to work for private businesses, to become self-employed, and to have nonstate housing, even some urban people will have the means to have a second child, away from the stifling supervision of the *danwei* (workplace). *The urban birthrate will rise.* In fact, in 1986, studies within China already indicated the trend. A 1986 social survey in Tianjin suggested that 80 percent of people working in private businesses or self-employed were considering trying for a second child.[71] Some even remarked, "With money in hand, one should not worry about having a son." In any case, the control of fertility is being leached from the government.

China seems to confirm the findings of other studies that more development will lead to a decline in the birthrate even if state intervention is more limited. Other countries and areas, especially Chinese neighbors (Taiwan, Hongkong, South Korea, and Kerala), were able to achieve similar declines without coercion.[72] The rising cost of raising a child, wider opportunities for women, and the influence of modern culture all contribute to the decline of births in fast developing East Asian neighbors. China is following the trend.

While resisting blatant state interference, especially the one-child policy, to a large extent, farmers reduced their family size at their own decision, apart from their compliance with the state antinatal policy. In addition, the corruptibility of local cadres and the cost of carrying out the state's one-child policy suggest that compliance on birth planning was traded for farmers' other interests.

## Conclusion

The discussion of rural resistance to the one-child family reveals that the farmers undermined the one-child policy by enlarging the gap between policy goals and practice. This is another indication of the power of the unorganized farmers to alter or annul state policies. This unorganized power greatly affects Chinese demography. One by one, farm families created a striking demographic difference: Whereas almost all urban residents obeyed the one-child family requirement, large numbers of villagers used every resource at their command to foil the government's wish. Demographers Rosemary Cooney and Jiali Li have shown that there is a significant *hukou* difference, that the state has less control over farmers' fertility independent of cultural and socioeconomic factors.[73]

This unorganized resistance alarmed the top leaders. On March 20, 1995, General Party Secretary Jiang Zemin pointed out that farmers and

rural migrants have taken the lead in violating state family planning strategy and called for strong measures to deal with them.[74] Once again, the
unorganized farmers' power altered the state's intended policy outcome.

Farmers' resistance and the existence of the urban one-child reality
have far-reaching social consequences. First of all, rural resistance to the
one-child policy posed a dilemma for women. On the one hand, rural
women gained a certain degree of freedom of reproductive rights by hiding
out to give birth. By so doing they saved the lives of many baby girls who
might have been killed if the one-child regulation had been carried out in
the countryside. On the other hand, both farmers' resistance and state policies catered to farmers' demand for sons, increasing the male–female ratio.

Given the available technology, despite state efforts to exercise control,
it is more likely that sex-selective induced abortion will increase in both
the city and the countryside. As a result, the struggle for reproductive freedom and the state's family planning have combined to reinforce patriarchal
values. Making the birth of a girl as worthy as that of a boy will continue to
be a great challenge in China, especially rural China. There will be a shortage of brides, especially in poor rural areas. Unless the government also
provides welfare and pensions to rural people, rural people will continue
to depend on their children, especially sons, for support in old age.

Second, the planned decline in fertility will rapidly change the population age structure,[75] particularly in the cities. The new generation of urban
people (from one-child families) will have no relatives. This means that
core elements of the Chinese family structure will disappear or have to be
reinvented in urban settings. In addition, the social security system in
which relatives take care of each other will disappear. The new generation
of urban people coming of age will have to take responsibility for the care
of their elders. It is a 4–2–1 phenomenon, an inverted pyramid, in which *a
single child will have to take care of four grandparents, two parents, and
one child*. Urban people will have to turn to the state for help. For more
than two thousand years, family structure was the linchpin holding the
Chinese together, as John Bongaarts and Susan Greenhalgh pointed out:

> By fundamentally altering the basic social and economic unit, the
> one-child policy may tear the fabric of Chinese society in a way
> that uproots people's sense of their place in the world; undermines
> the family's ability to take care of the old; and precludes the kind
> of economic development that has spurred the post–World War II
> industrial miracle in other parts of East Asia.[76]

The overwhelming success of the one-child policy in the city means the
disappearance of this social structure and a threat to social stability.

Rural resistance to the one-child family has, in fact, helped preserve
the Chinese family system. From an economic point of view, rural resistance to the one-child policy may also benefit Chinese people in the long

run. If the one-child family had succeeded everywhere as it did in the cities, the demographic consequence would have been devastating.[77] The rapid decline in population, especially in the cities, and the rise of life expectancy mean that the state will have to take from younger rural producers to finance welfare for the urban aged. To do so, the state will have to give rural people more space to develop economically.

Third, the clash between urban children from one-child families and rural children from nonconforming families will create social problems in China. The urban "little emperors" *(xiaohuangdi)* will not be available for military service because the state's own law stipulates that an only child need not join the army. Moreover, the army has long been rural. Unless the state changes its law (which will not make the state popular), the state will have to depend on rural children whose births may even be unrecorded and who resulted from conflict with the state. It will be difficult for China to have loyal soldiers if the state continues its policy against the children from multiple-child families. If they do not accept these "illegal children," they will not have enough candidates to fill the armies that they want to raise. Urban children from one-child families will use their political influence to increase their power and prevent competition from the countryside. How can the Chinese state continue its urban-centric policy without losing the support of rural people? Can the state afford this policy?

In short, the state's overall control over fertility succeeded more in the cities than in the countryside. In rural China, state coercion and the usual pressures of modernization (high productivity, markets, industrialization, and migration) may also have forced farmers to increase their tolerance of small families, an important attitude change that may translate economic gains into gains in per capita output and income. Moreover, new markets, new private housing, and second-shift job opportunities will bring urban fertility rates closer to rural fertility rates. Urban couples, too, will have sons if they can. No matter what happens, though, future success in China depends on the very rural children whom the state has tried so hard to eliminate. There will be so many of them!

## Notes

1.   Tyrene White, "Postrevolutionary Mobilization in China: The One-Child Policy Reconsidered," *World Politics* 43, no. 1 (1990):53–76.

2.   Wong Siu-lun, "Consequences of China's New Population Policy," *China Quarterly* 98 (1984):220.

3.   Chen Muhua, "Developing Population Science and Making It Serve the Goal of Controlling Population Growth," *Renkou yanjiu* (Population Studies) 3 (1981):8–11, esp. 10.

4.   Craig Dietrich, *People's China: A Brief History* (New York: Oxford University Press, 1986), p. 290.

5.　Karen Hardee-Cleaveland and Judith Banister, "Fertility Policy and Implementation in China, 1985–1988," *Population and Development Review* 14, no. 2 (1988):134.

6.　Marion J. Levy, Jr., *The Family Revolution in Modern China* (New York: Atheneum, 1948), p. 94.

7.　John Bongaarts and Susan Greenhalgh, "An Alternative to the One-Child Policy in China," *Population and Development Review* 11, no. 4 (1985): 595.

8.　Qiao Xiaochung, et. al, *Chaozai de tudi* (Overpopulated Land) (Shenyang: Shenyang Chubanshe, 1989), p. 132.

9.　For a discussion of the abuse of women's bodies in China's family planning, see Steven W. Mosher, *Broken Earth: The Rural Chinese* (New York: Free Press, 1983); and Steven W. Mosher, *A Mother's Ordeal: One Woman's Fight Against China's One-Child Policy* (New York: Harcourt Brace, 1993).

10.　Zhou Xiaozheng, *Renkou weiji: laizi shehui gongzuozhe de jinggao* (The Population Crisis: Warnings from Social Scientists) (Tianjin: Zhongguo Nüren Chubanshe, 1989), p. 12.

11.　Ibid., p. 57.

12.　*China News Digest* , January 27, 1995.

13.　*Gongren ribao*, (Workers' Daily), December 20, 1983, quoted in Emily Honig and Gail Hershatter, *Personal Voices: Chinese Women in the 1980s* (Stanford: Stanford University Press, 1988).

14.　Wu Baosheng, "Shangdi de youyu" (The Worry of God), in Lü Ye, ed., *Zhongguo: xiong yong de renchao* (China: The Rushing Tides of People) (Beijing: Sheyue Wenyi Chubanshe, 1989), pp. 74–105.

15.　Ansley J. Coale, *Rapid Population Change in China, 1952–1982* (Washington, D.C.: National Academy Press, 1982).

16.　In Chinese: *Women de ya yibuchi ganbude erbuhe ganbude. Women shengduoshao ya guanta pishi! Ya* means "children" in many rural areas of Hunan and Hubei provinces. The common complaint was frequently expressed by farmers in different regions. During my visits to several villages in Human and Hunan, many farmers used the same expression.

17.　Jeffrey Wasserstrom, "Resistance to the One-Child Family," *Modern China* 3 (1984):345–374.

18.　Ansley J. Coale, et al., "Recent Trends in Fertility and Nuptiality in China," *Science* 251 (1991):390.

19.　Chen Shi and Mi Youlu, eds., *Zhongguo nongcun jiating di bianqian* (The Transformation of Rural Families in China) (Beijing: Nongcun Duwu Chubanshe, 1989), p. 326.

20.　Coale, et al., "Recent Trends," p. 390.

21.　Meng Chanshou and Bei Shuangxiu, "Nongcun zaohun he feifa tongju qing kuang diao cha fenxi ji jian yi" (A Survey on Early Marriage and Illegal Cohabitation in Some Rural Areas in China), *Renkou xuekan* (Population Journal) 4 (1989):53–55.

22.   Griffith Feeney and Wang Feng, "Parity Progression and Birth Intervals in China," *Population and Development Review* 19, no. 1 (1993): 61–101.

23.   Personal interview with Zhou Xuanhua of Hunan Province, October 1985.

24.   Zhu Xiaoyang, "Zhongguoren-Benxiang tiantang" (Chinese Rush into Paradise), *Jiushi niandai* (The Nineties) (1991):86.

25.   Yang Zuquan, *Xianda jiating de yuang yu liu* (The Origins of Modern Family) (Henan: Renmin Chubanshe, 1988).

26.   *Nongmin ribao* (Farmers' Daily), August 7, 1989.

27.   In Chinese: *Han xiong xie; fang cong xie; shao bao xie; duo rang xie; shufu xie.*

28.   Su Suining, "There Are Many Causes of Strained Relations Between Cadres and Masses in the Rural Areas," *Nongmin ribao*, September 26, 1988, p. 1, in *FBIS* (October 7, 1988): 13.

29.   Judith Banister, *China's Changing Population* (Stanford: Stanford University Press, 1987), p. 365.

30.   Sheryl WuDunn, "China's Peasantry Takes Measure of Its Prosperity," *New York Times*, July 4, 1993.

31.   The literal translation of *maiyijiaerzi* is to buy a son at a negotiated price, that is, the highest price the state pays farmers when they fulfill their basic quota for grain. Here it means paying heavy fines for violating the one-child policy.

32.   Sheng Maochang, et al., *Rang renkou jinzhong changmin*, (Let the Population Alarm Ring Forever) (Nangjing: Nangjing Chubanshe, 1991), p. 101.

33.   *Qiushi* (Seeking Truth), no. 8 (1988).

34.   Li Qiouhong, *Zhongguo nongmin de xinli shijie* (Psychology of Chinese Farmers) (Beijing: Zhongyuan Nongmin Chubanshe, 1992), p. 204.

35.   Li Zhenglun, "Jihe jishu de jingbao" (Alarm of the Geometric Population Growth), *Falü yu shenghe* (Law and Life) (1989):19.

36.   Sten Johanson and Ola Nygren, "The Missing Girls of China: A New Demographic Account," *Population and Development Review* 17, no. 1 (1991):35–51.

37.   Susan Greenhalgh, "Controlling Births and Bodies in Village China," *American Ethnologist* 22, no. 1 (1994): 3–20.

38.   Personal interviews with Wang Wenhua in February 1986.

39.   Sheng, et al., *Let the Population Alarm Ring Forever*, p. 102.

40.   Zhou, *The Population Crisis*, p. 88.

41.   *People's Daily,* October 22, 1988.

42.   Sichuan Provincial Government, "Sichuan Birth Planning Provincial Regulations," *Population and Development Review* 14, no. 2 (1988):373.

43.   Xie Yaoping and Luo Bing, "Zhaosheng zhimi" (The Secret of Over-quota Birth), *Faluyüshenghuo* (Law and Life) (1990):28.

44. In Chinese: *Youqian maizhesheng; youquan mingzhesheng; youdan qiangzhesheng; yiwu suoyou touzhesheng.*

45. For a good discussion on the illegal removal of IUDs, see John S. Arid, "Coercion in Family Planning: Causes, Methods, and Consequences," in *China's Economy Looks Toward the Year 2000* (Washington, D.C.: Government Printing Office, 1986).

46. Johns Hopkins Population Information Program, "Population Reports, Population and Birth Planning in the People's Republic of China," Working paper, Johns Hopkins Population Information Program, 1992.

47. Zhu, "Chinese Rush into Paradise," p. 84.

48. Ying Shen and Quan You, "Chaocheng youjidui zai xingdong," (The Actions of Over-Quota Birth Guerrillas), in Lü, *China: The Rushing Tides of People*, p. 206.

49. Sheng, et al., *Let the Population Alarm Ring Forever*, pp. 99–100.

50. In Chinese: *Baozhe erjiao zoutaxiang, baozhe erzi huijiaxiang.*

51. De Ming, "China's Population Situation Remains Grim," *Liaowang* (Outlook) 17 (April 15, 1988): 10–11, in *FBIS* (May 11, 1988): 28.

52. Personal interviews with Liu Liu, a family planning cadre in Wuchang District, Wuhan City, in August 1985.

53. Interviews with rural migrants in Wuhan, May 1986.

54. In Chinese: *Tuizhe xiaoche zousifang, busheng naner bu huixiang.*

55. *Far East Economic Review* (July 19, 1990): 19.

56. Elizabeth Croll, *Chinese Women Since Mao* (London: Second Books, 1983), p. 54.

57. Sheng, et al., *Let the Population Alarm Ring Forever.*

58. This policy has important gender implications. For a good description on this topic, see Delia Davin, "Never Mind if It's a Girl, You Can Have Another Try," in Jørgen Delman, et al., eds., *Remaking Peasant China: Problems of Rural Development and Institutions at the Start of the 1990s* (Aarhus, Denmark: Aarhus University Press, 1990), pp. 81–91.

59. White, "Postrevolutionary Mobilization in China," p. 63.

60. In Chinese: *Kaixiaokou, du badong.* Susan Greenhalgh, "Shifts in China's Population Policy, 1984–1986: Views from the Central, Provincial, and Local Levels," *Population and Development Review* (1986): 492.

61. Zeng Yi, et al., "A Cause-analysis for the Rising Sex Ratio at Birth in Recent Years in China and Its Consequence," *Population and Economics* 1 (1993):3–15.

62. *Liaowang* (Outlook), no. 20 (1987).

63. Wu Baosheng, "Shangdi de youyu" (The Worry of God), in Lü, *China: The Rushing Tides of People*, pp. 91–92.

64. Li, "Alarm of the Geometric Population Growth," p. 20.

65. Zhe Guiqiong, "An Analysis of Unreported Birth Rate," *Population Studies* (1991): 43–44.

66. *People's Daily,* June 30, 1988.

67. Feeney and Wang, "Parity Progression and Birth Intervals," p. 78.

68. Jiang Zemin and Li Peng, "Gei guojia jihua shengyu weiyuanhui de yifeng gongkaixin" (An Open Letter to the State Family Planning Commission), *Zhongguo renkou bao* (Chinese Population Journal) (1990): 1.

69. George P. Brown, "The Changing Status of Chinese Women in Rural Jiangsu Province," Paper presented to the AAS meetings, Washington, D.C., April 6–9, 1995.

70. Denise Hare, "Rural Nonagricultural Activities and Their Impact on the Distribution of Income: Evidence from Farm Households in Southern China," *China Economic Review* 4, no. 1 (1994): 65.

71. Wu, "The Worry of God," pp. 91–92.

72. Richard Leete and Iqbal Alam, *The Revolution in Asian Fertility: Dimensions, Causes and Implications* (Oxford: Clarendon Press, 1991).

73. Rosemary Cooney and Li Jiali, "Household-Registration Type and Compliance with the One-Child Policy in China, 1979–1988," *Demography* 31, no.1 (February 1994): 21–32.

74. *China News Digest*, March 31, 1995.

75. Banister, *China's Changing Population.*

76. John Bongaarts and Susan Greenhalgh, "An Alternative to the One-Child Policy," *Population and Development Review* 11, no. 4 (1985): 595.

77. Personal communications with Ansley Coale, January 1994.

# 8 Rural Women: Floating to Power

Women can hold up half the sky.

Mao Zedong

Most analyses of rural China ignore women. Nevertheless, rural women constitute about 50 percent of the rural population. Any social change of the magnitude of the Chinese economic reforms will profoundly affect the lives of women. Chapter 7 discussed rural women's role in family planning and its impact on rural women. This chapter examines how *baochan daohu*, markets, rural industrialization, migration, and corruption affect the lives of rural women and the roles rural women have played in this historical transformation.

## Baochan Daohu

There is little doubt that *baochan daohu* strengthened the power of family heads, most of whom were men. As households gained autonomy and strength, the family head assumed a great degree of control over production decisions, labor and capital allocation, consumption, and even reproduction within the family. How did rural women fare under this new arrangement? Was men's gain necessarily women's loss?[1] Was the movement toward family farming a male conspiracy against women? Were women worse off within the family economy than under collective farming?

Women actively participated in dismantling the collective-commune system in the late 1970s and the early 1980s. They voted their preference by "exiting" from the commune system. Women's active role in the restoration of the family economy suggests that they were fed up with the collective system.

Women helped to bring about *baochan daohu* in two important ways. First, in the 1970s, rural women turned to household sidelines to avoid the low pay and long hours of collective work.[2] Some were able to do so by asking for sick leave; others pretended to work and saved their energy for family chores. They were behind their husbands or fathers in pushing for family farming, as part of the movement toward *baochan daohu.* Ellen Judd discovered this pattern in North China: "The strategy of evading restrictions in more public and male-defined economic spheres in favor of more autonomous activity carried on in the household, usually by individual women, could be seen *as a practical strategy spontaneously devised by rural women and later advocated by the Women's Federations as legitimate.*"[3]

Second, they helped to spread the practice of *baochan daohu.* In Chapter 3, I discussed how women used marriage to show their preferences by marrying farmers who adopted *baochan daohu.* Women also helped the spread of *baochan daohu* by visiting relatives, carrying information between their village of origin (their parents) and their village of procreation (their husbands). The knowledge of *baochan daohu* occurring elsewhere was crucial for farmers to have the guts to seek *baochan daohu* for their own families.

Women's role as information bearer was not restricted to intervillage networks within a region. It was also cross-regional. In Hubei and Hebei, *Sichuan po* (wives from Sichuan) played a significant role in spreading *baochan daohu.* In the 1960s and 1970s, many rural women from poverty-stricken Sichuan fled from their collective farms.[4] They were said to be strong workers—thus desirable brides. They may also have been good at *baochan daohu.* Many women established families outside Sichuan in order to avoid being sent back to their famine-stricken villages because of the strict controls of the household registration system. Some of those women already had families of their own before they came to Hubei. When *baochan daohu* and other changes in Sichuan improved farmers' lives, some of these *Sichuan po* wanted to return to their homes in Sichuan. Their departure created family disputes in some Hubei villages, while at the same time providing *baochan daohu* information to Hubei farmers.

Why did women push so actively for *baochan daohu?* For most rural women, it is far easier to deal with their husbands or fathers than to deal with local cadres, who are nearly all male and are not family. The family economy is patriarchal, but it was double patriarchy under the collectives. Most rural women supported the *baochan daohu* movement. They were not under the spell of false consciousness. Under collectivization, institutionalized discrimination assured that women's pay was inferior to that of men, varying from approximately 50 percent in the North to 70 percent in the South. The lower pay encouraged women to seek to escape collective work. Women had more excuses not to go to work under the collective system and stayed home to attend their small vegetable plots.

After *baochan daohu,* women gained a certain degree of control, and they began to share in making many family decisions although they still have not achieved total equality, as indicated by the Table 8.1.

The survey suggests that rural women share in making most family decisions with their husbands. In children's education, mothers and fathers

**Table 8.1**

Major Decisionmaking Within Rural Families (percentages)

| Item | Husband | Wife | Both |
|---|---|---|---|
| Buying animals | 29 | 4 | 57 |
| Buying tools | 27 | 4 | 60 |
| Housebuilding | 17 | 2 | 76 |
| Buying durable goods | 18 | 13 | 67 |
| Money gift sending | 14 | 10 | 73 |
| When to send children to school | 10 | 6 | 82 |
| Whether to continue children's education | 9 | 6 | 82 |
| Children's mate selection | 4 | 9 | 67 |
| Prepare for sons' wedding | 5 | 7 | 74 |
| Prepare for daughters' wedding | 5 | 8 | 73 |
| Accounting and management | 10 | 7 | 81 |
| Birth decision | 2 | 7 | 83 |

Source: Zhongguo Shehui Kexue Yuan Renko Yanjiu Suo, Dangdai Zhongguo funü diwei chouyang diaocha ziliao (Sampling Survey Data of Women's Status in Contemporary China) (Beijing: Wanguo Xueshu Chubanshe, 1994).

shared almost equal decision making power. In children's mate selection, wedding preparations, birth, accounting, and management, women have more power than men.[5] This has never happened before in Chinese history.

The sexual division of labor in production was less rigid under the family economy, although a sharply differentiated division of labor remained in terms of housekeeping and childbearing. After baochan daohu, women still were responsible for most child care, cooking, and washing. However, with most work carried out within the household context, women's traditional role as mothers in addition to other productive roles became easier and often was better appreciated. Women have more flexibility working both in the fields and at home. It is common knowledge that women worked harder than men in the countryside. More importantly, women together with men have the decision power of labor allocation for family members.

Of all the villages in the rice production area I visited in the early 1980s, women and men shared more productive work under family autonomy than under collective farming. This was especially true for farmers in rice-growing areas. (Of course, this situation changed after the rise of rural industry and migration in the mid-1980s.) Both husbands and wives began to have control over allocation of labor at home.

Edward Friedman and Mark Selden, studying the collectives in North China, found an almost complete separation of women from men in daily labor, even during the harvest, when both men and women harvested. Under the collective, women's teams (sometimes one for older women and one for younger) almost always worked separately. Men and women share more work under family autonomy than they did under collective farming. This gender pattern is broadly representative of those across rural China.

Men and women both contributed to sideline production after *baochan daohu*, but women were more important in sideline production because women historically dominated agricultural sideline production. Most sideline production took place at home—raising pigs, chickens, geese, ducks, and goats, growing vegetables, gathering eggs. Women were regarded as specially fit for these kinds of work because they were thought to be nurturing. This important productive element was strictly controlled under the commune system, when each family was assigned a quota for pigs and chickens. Under family autonomy, quick money often came from the sale of those sideline products, and women's contribution became clearer in the family, even though other productive roles in the family were often diffused. The money brought in from the sale of the sideline products further benefited women in the sense that women gained with the prosperity of the family.

Women also contribute to the spread of technology and new knowledge. In rural China, the phrase *zou qinqi* means going to visit relatives. Since women marry out of the family and village, *zou qinqi* refers to visiting relatives from the female side of the family. After *baochan daohu*, farmers, especially farm women, increased *zou qinqi* rapidly. Married women increased their visits to their parents' villages. Since married women more than men have close extravillage ties, they became an important source of information on new seeds and new products. As a result, innovation and new technology spread very quickly. This is another "chicken pest" in rural China, and women have a major role in the diffusion of new productive means.

Women preferred *baochan daohu* because they had more control over their time. After *baochan daohu*, both women and men had more leisure hours than under the commune system, although they had to work very hard during the busy seasons. After *baochan daohu*, women did not have to work on the big collective land reclamation and water conservancy projects in winter. For most women, that was a big relief.

In short, *baochan daohu* increased women's economic status in terms of control over time, income, and knowledge, but more importantly, the *baochan daohu* movement gave rise to markets, rural industrial enterprises, and migration, all of which had a great impact on the position of women.

## Markets and Women

*Baochan daohu* was directly responsible for women's participation in market activities. After two or three months of intensive agricultural work, depending on the region, almost all adults in rural families participate in some sort of market activities, either sideline production, transportation, or selling of goods. In the 1980s, the family economy allowed women to get

*Rural peddlers, all farm women, crowd the street
in Shenzhen. Photo by Kate Xiao Zhou*

involved with the outside world through market exchanges. The markets
themselves became less localized. Under the commune, even localized
marketing had been very much controlled by the commune staff.

Women played an important role in creating and expanding markets in
China. Throughout the 1980s, rural women occupied a conspicuous place
in *jishi* of all sorts. In many local and intermediate *jishi*, there were often
more women than men. My investigation in Hubei and Hebei indicates that
rural women occupied markets because of a new form of sexual division
of labor within the family economy. Rural men tended to be responsible
for transporting goods to the markets. Selling did not require a lot of
strength and thus was regarded as more suitable for women. More importantly, women were thought to be good at human relationships such as
selling and dealing. A rural couplet in Hubei expressed this new division of
labor: "Men transport goods and women count money; donkeys grind and
oxen cultivate—each according to his ability."[6]

This new form of sexual division of labor may come from gender
stereotyping. In an era of trucks, carting goods to market may not be a
matter of brute strength beyond the strength of women. The greater obstacles may have been the fear of women being out on roads alone.
Nonetheless, the presence of rural women in markets did provide many
rural women new ways of life that were not possible under the collectives.

*A Shenzhen farmer woman who also runs a grocery shop downstairs in her new house. Photo by Kate Xiao Zhou*

Widespread female participation in nonlocalized market exchange has never occurred before in Chinese history. In Imperial China, Chinese women were confined to their own homes and more specifically to the kitchens. The most visible curtailment of women's physical mobility in human history was the practice of foot binding in China, which started in the Song dynasty. Although the government leaders of the People's Republic of China tried to indoctrinate the ideology of independent women, for a long time the closed nature of its social structure provided little potential for women to achieve independence. There was no vehicle for women to go beyond the confinement of the patriarchal village.

*Baochan daohu* gave rise to farmer-based markets across China, which provided the means to go beyond the confines of the family and village. More and more rural women are becoming merchants. Some even conduct long-distance trade. In recent years, tens of thousands of Chinese rural women have been either directly or indirectly engaged in international trade.

Markets add more responsibilities and opportunities for rural women, leading them into a more complex and modern world. Female rural migrants play a conspicuous role as street vendors. In Mao's hometown, Xiangtan, there are about two thousand female vendors selling tofu. They are from rural areas of Hubei, Anhui, Jiangxi, Guizhou, and Hunan.[7] They are all making good money.

Even in Shanxi, where economic development lagged behind many regions in China, by the early 1990s, three hundred thousand rural women had become professional merchants selling agricultural by-products. The annual sale of eggs and chickens by those rural women reached 630 million yuan.[8] In Lingtong County, Shaanxi, hundreds of rural women sell horse-soldier replicas beside the Horse-Soldier Museum. Those local women even learned English and Japanese in order to sell the replicas to foreign visitors. Xiao Lan, one of the vendors, proudly said: "In this market those who have good language skill and know several foreign languages have more opportunity to make money."[9] Most female vendors are independent owners of their small businesses. Many rural women liberated themselves by becoming entrepreneurs, vendors, merchants, and salespeople.

Another common way for rural women to gain independence is to open small restaurants along the road. Many rural women become owners of those small businesses. One Henan woman, Wu Meishu, is a well-known restaurant owner along the Yellow River Road: "The old saying goes, 'Poor at home and rich on the road.' Those travelers and drivers have a lot of money. But they need a place to rest and food to eat. I will provide them with those services."[10]

Interviewing several female restaurant owners and dozens of female vendors in late 1994, I discovered that their success lies in their hard work, shrewdness, and good business sense. One vendor from rural Sichuan told me that her secret in the busy street in Shenzhen is *boli duoxiao* (small profit but large quantity). Urban people often call those rural female restaurant bosses Aqingsao, after the female boss of a teahouse and a heroine in one of Madame Mao's modern operas during the Cultural Revolution. Aqingsao used her teahouse as a cover to work for the party. Her shrewdness enabled her to deal with Japanese and Guomindang officers. The contemporary Aqingsao is also shrewd in dealing with customers and government inspectors.

Many rural female migrants try to create jobs and opportunities for themselves. In many rural areas and in the cities, rural migrants become the owners of barbershops and beauty shops. In Imperial China and under collective farming, only men were barbers. In fact, it was considered an offense for a woman to touch a man's head because it would bring bad luck to the man. Barbers would often go door to door to provide their service, and no women were allowed or willing to become barbers because women's proper place was at home. Now it is fashionable for a man to have a haircut by a female barber. Rural women constitute the main body of barbers and beauticians. In Guangzhou, in 1994, one beauty shop owner from rural Hunan told me: "When I first set up this beauty shop, some people looked down upon me. But I believed a wise saying, 'Of seventy-two occupations, every occupation will have one moneymaking champion.' Now I am a champion of beauty shops."

Another example of the changing gender division of labor is butchery. In traditional China and under the collectives, women were banned from butchery. In fact, slaughtering pigs was an important male ritual in many villages in China. The cooperation of several men during the process showed strong male bonding. Women were not even allowed to observe the slaughter or cut meat for sale at the market. Now, it is very common to see female butchers at markets both in the city and in the countryside.

Truck drivers will be the next frontier for rural women to cross.

Many Chinese rural women are filled with entrepreneurial spirit. Stevan Harrell's study of Southwestern villages suggests that rural women are running vegetable businesses: "But it is not merely the potential for entrepreneurial activity that is shared by men and women in Renhe; many of the actual prime movers in Renhe's entrepreneurial families are women."[11]

Market activities in China evaded not only state oppression but also the traditional patriarchy. Before 1949 and under the collectives, no rural women could earn more than men within the same village, but the scale of income earning for rural women is no longer constrained by the institutional gender inequality.[12] Some women make more than men within the same village, although on the whole rural women still make less than men.[13] It is even possible for some wives to make more than their husbands. The market provided many rural women with alternatives in life that were not possible under Mao or the emperors. Furthermore, just as the central figures of the People's Republic of China have so far been unwilling to crack down on the rural sources of China's rapid economic growth, the males of the patriarchal family and village are not willing to forgo the increased family and village productivity of women in their new roles. There is even a popular tune in rural China to express the approval of women's moneymaking role:

In the ancient time, Hua Mulan joined the army for her father;
Now the new army of women are busy making money.[14]

## Rural Industry

Rural women also actively participated in the process of rural industrialization. After *baochan daohu*, both men and women were able to leave the

*Twenty-six-year-old Tan Liu-qiong (middle, with long hair) learned carpet weaving while working in Xingjiang and set up a carpet factory in her village in Sichuan. She has sold carpets to more than ten countries. Photo by Liu Qiangang*

land due to increasingly high agricultural productivity and to their relative political independence. Once the family submitted the quota grain and paid the cadres their due, they could do pretty much what they wanted. A substantial proportion of rural women, literally tens of millions, especially the young and the unmarried, became workers in local rural industries or migrated to find employment elsewhere.

Women's contribution to rural industrial development was great. According to the official statistics, by 1989, 40 million rural women, one-fifth of the female labor force in the countryside, were employed by rural factories. By 1993, there were 50 million female workers in rural industry, 42 percent of the entire rural industrial labor force.[15] From 1980 to 1994, the growth rate for female nonagricultural employment was 52 percent; the corresponding growth rate for males was 42 percent.

From a purely economic viewpoint, the massive flow of female workers to rural industry increased the pool of labor. Women's desire to become industrial workers combined with the low level of development to keep wages low. This cheap source of labor made rural industries more competitive both in relation to the city and internationally. There is no doubt that women's participation has stabilized low wage rates for China.

Exploited though those women may have been in rural industries, most of them improved their livelihood, both in economic terms and in other social respects. Even given the labor surplus, most of those women could earn much more in rural factories than on the farm. In addition, farm work, especially in the busy season, can be much more laborious than work in the factories.

Rural factories of different types (collective, semi-collective, and private) exploded in the 1980s and provided rural women with alternative sources of employment. The most important impact of rural industrial development on women was the separation between work and home. Although Chinese women, especially women in the South and the Eastern coastal areas, traditionally participated in handicraft production, only on rare occasions (the silk factories in imperial times and in the Republic period) was work separated from the home. Most new industrial workers in the 1980s worked outside their homes. The separation between work and home produced a fundamental change in all aspects of these working

*Zhang Qi set up a glove factory at her village in Yishang County, Anhui, and helped to employ many unemployed rural workers in her village. Photo by Yu Jie*

women's lives. The new female factory workers had a degree of personal autonomy their former sisters in Chinese society lacked.

In Imperial China and under collective farms, rural income and material distribution (often in the form of grain) were under the name of the family head (often male). Now many rural women bring their income-home, and their contribution is clear. When a female worker's income is separated from that of the rest of the family and to a high degree under her control, every member of her family knows very clearly how much she earns. "How much money do you make a month?" has become a standard greeting in the countryside nowadays. There is little doubt that the clear knowledge of a woman's economic contribution enhances her social status at home. Women have become increasingly autonomous in the factory as well as at home, more so than ever before.

Within the factory setting, women's roles as mothers, wives, and daughters lost importance, although these roles may continue to affect their daily life. Female factory workers had to articulate their working roles by learning how to negotiate with their boss and how to interact with other workers on a more or less equal footing. For example, Chang Xiaofu, a rural woman from Pingjiang County, Hunan, went to work in one of Shenzhen's Hongkong factories. She learned how to deal with her bosses very soon, as she recalled: "When the young girls first came to work for the Hongkong boss, we were very afraid of the boss, enduring hardship and mistreatment. As soon as we become skilled workers, however, we could be picky. If he treats us badly, we can fire him before he fires us."[16] More importantly, they had to do this on their own, which increased the complexity of their social relations.

The new social role of rural women as co-workers also altered the general hierarchical structure in Chinese society. These young workers were increasingly more autonomous and played an important role in assimilation of ever changing technology. This shift of power from older women to younger women also affected social roles in the family. The economic power of younger women balanced the customary power of their older mothers-in-law.

As a result of these changes, more and more rural women from rural factories began to have more input into their marriage and reproductive decisions. For thousands of years, it was her parents who decided whom a rural girl should marry. Under the usual family arrangement, most marriage decisions were based upon the families' social and financial considerations; little thought was given to the two young people involved. Although it is true that young people began to acquire a greater role in these decisions even under the Republic of China and that this increased in the People's Republic, now the day of the purely arranged marriage is past for most Chinese (see more on this point later in the chapter). The new factory women are much more involved in their marriage decisions.

It seems that women's new power and independence, including their marriage decision power, is also linked to their improved living standard and to alternative outside opportunities.

Rural industrial development provided rural women more responsibilities and, above all, more opportunities. The increased possibilities for individual autonomy allowed women to reduce the importance of their domestic roles. More flexible career opportunities allowed women to combine the responsibilities of job and family.

Since the state did not offer jobs to rural people, rural women who wanted to change their occupational status had to seek nonstate employment. Although family connections and friends played an important role in getting a factory job (especially at local factories), women themselves were also involved in bribing officials and offering gifts to factory managers. More and more rural young women have had to depend on themselves if they wanted a job in profitable coastal factories.

Today, rural women, especially the young, have made the best use of rural industrial development to express their independence. This time, however, the women in their factory and other employment are not necessarily "sending their wages home," although they may buy gifts for their relatives when they visit their relatives in the village. This is especially true for migrant workers in South China. For most of those working women, the most important thing is to secure their urban employment. They need savings to find other alternatives because they do not have secure work. In addition, their reference group now is co-workers in the factory. Most of them are young. Fashion is more important in these new groups than filial piety. They want money to buy fashionable clothes, to go to movies and other entertainments, to go to restaurants, and to wear makeup. More importantly, the money comes from their own efforts rather than from a bride price or their parents.

In rural China, rapid industrialization has also weakened institutionalized sexual discrimination. In the agricultural setting, women's physical weakness often gave rise to sexual discrimination in both sexual division of labor and material distribution within the family. In factories, physical strength is a less important focus among co-workers. This work environment encourages many rural women to develop greater self-confidence. Many women work in light industries and assembly lines making toys, shoes, and clothes. Many rural factories pay piece-rate wages, so *women in light industries often do as well as or even better than men*. This increases their self-confidence and gives them a sense of pride in their labor.

There are also problems for rural women. A sharp gender division of labor exists because almost all managerial personnel, headmen, skilled workers, and *caigouyuan* (purchasing agents) are male. Moreover, the *hukou* constraint makes it difficult for those migrant workers to have the institutional protection women workers in state factories enjoy. After they work for several years, the possibility of being fired is high. Chinese employers like employers elsewhere have a tendency to hire young women. In order to keep their job, many young factory workers go to night school to learn new skills for more job opportunities. Some have to return to their villages. Although they may bring back new ideas and new information for economic development in their villages, the forced return also creates problems. Some find they no longer fit into village life. For some of those *dagong mei* (working sisters), marriage to an urban citizen has become a goal in itself. For those who refuse to accept or fail in the marriage settlement strategy, spinsterhood is possible. We may see a high rate of female spinsters in those industrial centers. Many working women experience job discrimination and lower pay. Many face job loss if they marry. Employers prefer married men over married women.

Despite those problems, rural women in general have benefited from rapid rural industrial development. In fact, rural women have played an important role in the rapid economic development in China. Rural female workers are the vanguard of Chinese industrialization. Most working women have benefited from the separation of the workplace from the home. The process of rural industrialization provided many women more life chances and, above all, a greater degree of independence. Some may send the money home to contribute to their family incomes; others may save for marriage (dowry). No matter what they do with the hard-earned money, the new wage work has fundamentally changed the way of life for those rural women and enhanced their status at home, as Graham Johnson has discovered in South China: "It is tempting to conclude that increased economic participation of Wantong women in wage labor has enhanced their importance as family managers."[17] In short, women's participation in industry has influenced gender relations both in the family and in society.

## Migration: Looking for New Ways of Life

Just as rural industry affected women, so did the rapid increase in rural–urban migration. Rural women also contributed to the rise of free labor markets in China. As more and more women migrated, leaving the land for alternative employment, the occupational choices became more complex and ever changing. Migration also has had important implications for women's autonomy.

Some became peddlers, saleswomen, merchants, restaurateurs, and small shop owners. Others became waitresses and housemaids. By 1989, there were 3 million rural women in the city working as nannies. Some rural female migrants have taken up dirty and heavy work that urban people scorn. As discussed in Chapter 6, rural young women have become the main labor force in many textile mills. Female migrants also sweep roads. The migration of rural women provided cheap labor and threatened gov-

ernment control over labor allocation. Those rural workers received no welfare benefits from the state. They had nothing to lose in a free labor market
but the chains by which the state had bound them to their villages, especially the chains of patriarchy. The flow of rural migrants, both men and
women, broke the Communist feudal arrangement that tied 80 percent of
rural people to the land. *The migrant flow of free labor is one of the most
important reasons that China has been able to sustain double-digit growth
for almost fifteen years, and women constitute an important part of the flow.*

After the beginning of the migration, both male and female farmers
were able to sell their labor. This was an improvement over their former
serfdom, when rural labor was locked up and worth nothing. Under the collective arrangement, almost all rural women were completely denied any
opportunity for nonagricultural work. The few chances of upward mobility
(joining the army and party promotion) were almost completely reserved for
men, although a few exceptional rural women were regularly showcased.

Rural female migrants now flow where the opportunities are. They are
very competitive. In fact, light industries, especially export-oriented factories,
prefer women to men because many people believe the stereotype that
women are more disciplined and thus better workers. Many rural factories,
especially export-oriented ones, practice task rates under which both men
and women may receive the same pay. In some cases, women who are willing to endure hardship receive higher wages for their overtime workload.
According to one estimate, the wage differential was often 120 for men to
140 for women per month.[18] This higher income differential gave those
female workers a strong sense of self-worth. That is one of the important reasons that female migrants want to go to those rural factories. There is even a
popular song among female migrants: "I would like to have a home; it does
not matter the location of the home, so long as it is on the banks of Pearl
River."[19] The Pearl River is the most important industrial center in China.

In some cities, the massive influx of rural young women into those
light factories has upset the sexual ratio in favor of women. In the Special
Economic Zones, the sex ratio is 7 (women) to 3 (men).[20]

Migration provided women with opportunities never before possible
in Chinese history. In Imperial China, the major employment for women
outside the village was prostitution and concubinage. Although prostitution also exists in today's China and is increasing, it is far from the main
employment opportunity. For most rural women, their life cycle had for a
long time focused on two villages, the village of their parents and the village of their husband. In each village, the social circle was perhaps
200–500 people. A woman spent most of her life working and socializing
in contact with those people. Although this closeness did provide some
solidarity and networks of social relations, village communities also stulti-
fied individual empowerment and controlled women. In many villages,
the punishment for adulterous women was stoning or drowning. Village

gossip was sharp as a knife, able to kill any individual initiative (especially among women).

For almost two thousand years, almost every member of any Chinese village spent most of his or her time working and living within eyesight or earshot of other members of his or her family or other villagers. For women this was particularly true. Never before the past decade and a half have so many women worked outside the family and village context.

Now, outside their village, women can do things that would be impossible in their villages. There is no one gossiping about them. For women who do not have sons, migration has provided a way out of discrimination. As one migrant told me in a 1986 interview in Guangzhou: "I was a damned woman in the village because I failed to have a son. Villagers with several sons would always make fun of me. Now I am a migrant. No one knows that I do not have sons. I no longer feel sad." Although rural migrants still prefer to have sons, when they interact with new people their social status is no longer determined by their ability to carry sons.

Migration offers women a potential to gain the degree of personal freedom. A young woman from rural Hunan told me in a 1985 interview why she ran away from her home: "I felt so choked at home. I had to act according to the expectations of my parents and of my neighbors. I could not fart without them knowing it. When they forced me to marry a man in another village in 1984, I ran away from home. Life outside the village is not easy, but it is free."

Migration produced a paradox for rural migrants. On the one hand, migrants were alienated from the familiar social setting in which they had formed their identity. Lonely on the road, they had to endure social and political discrimination of all sorts. On the other hand, they encountered new sources of social relations, which often were more pluralistic and more complex. The experience and interaction with people from different regions and with different dialects enriched their personal experiences. Several female migrants used the phrase *ren huo le* (more flexible and more complex) to describe their situation.[21]

Living as migrants also changed women's life style and values. More and more migrants take a broader view of the world. In order to overcome language barriers, they have to learn *putonghua* (the standard Chinese language) or local dialects (Cantonese or Shanghainese). More frequent interactions with people of different backgrounds and their experiences in different places provide them rich experiences in life and enable them to form a multiplicity of relationships. Of course, they still experience discrimination and cadre intimidation. Many women who run small shops and restaurants in towns and cities have to learn to deal with bureaucrats and fend off local hooligans. They have to learn to be shrewd; as a saying goes, "Female bosses are like an oily watermelon, round and slippery."[22] "Round and slippery" carries the connotation of shrewdness in Chinese.

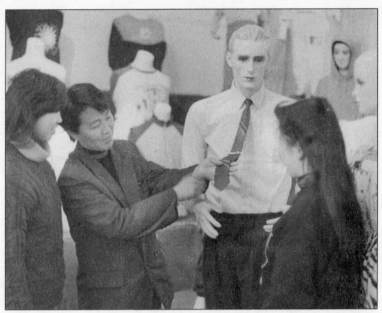

*Ji Zhihang, executive manager of Jiangsu Gold
Key Corporation, is from the rural town of
Changan, Wuxi, Jiangsu. In 1992, her corporation set up more than fifty branches across China,
including clothing, chemicals, and metal processing. Photo by Xu Peng*

Migration experiences also enriched their own individual growth. One
Chinese social scientist investigated 172 housemaids and asked them to
indicate the changes they experienced after their migration to the city.
Fifty-one percent of them placed "acquiring new knowledge" as the most
important reason for them to change jobs.[23]

Migration also provides women with more opportunities to make
money. In many cases, the income from migrants is an important source of
cash for farmer families.

Opportunities for industrial employment and migration have made
women more valuable as "commodities," as goods to be traded with other
families who want their labor power and potential for family prosperity. The
rise in bride prices and increased kidnapping of women are cases in point.
Some poor men have to depend on human traffickers to buy cheaper
brides. The outcry against trafficking in women in recent years points to the
problem, but it is important to note that what was regarded as normal (the
use of women as goods) has become illegitimate and problematic.

The massive flow of rural women, especially young women, is changing China and bringing about new social problems. In most booming cities

in South China, the sex ratio is so much influenced by those female migrants that many call those cities *huacheng* (cities of flowers).

Of course, female migrants also encounter numerous difficulties and discriminations. Without urban *hukou*, it is difficult for them to establish a family or find a secure job in the cities, but they always work hard to improve their status. One song, "I Bet Tomorrow with My Youth," expresses the feelings of young migrants:

> Fate is my challenger;
> I will not bow to it;
> Never complain and never ask why;
> I bet my youth against tomorrow—
> Walking ahead.[24]

Migration also occurs between rural areas. Female migrants, especially those from poor rural areas, take the opportunity to find a better life. Many try to establish a home in a rich rural area, resulting in the prevalent female marriage migration from poor to rich farm areas. According to one survey in the rich area of Zhejiang, more than one hundred thousand women from other provinces had married Zhejiang farmers. The main motivation for the migration of those rural women was to "find a rich husband" and "live a better life."[25] This pattern of marriage was suppressed under the collectives. The growth of markets, rural industrialization, and rural–rural migration have diversified marriage alliances and the marriage scope of farmers has broadened as well.

## Corruption

Just as rural women participate in all sorts of economic activities, they are also involved in corruption. In the context of the People's Republic of China, corruption means the violation of official rules for personal gain. Apart from money and gift bribery, women have an additional source— sex—to entice officials to get what they want. A new term describing this practice, *sexiang huiluo* (proffering sexual favors or seduction), has appeared in Chinese since the rise of the market economy. Some women became *gongguan xiaojie* (public relations misses) working for rural industries and rural construction terms. Other female entrepreneurs themselves would use *sexiang huiluo* to get what they want. Those women would target officials in charge of banking, taxes, public security, business, transportation, and customs.

Bribery and beauty work so well to get around government regulations that there is a saying in China: "With money, an official will slowly do what you want, with beauty, he will do it immediately, without money and beauty, nothing can be done."[26] Providing sexual favors plays such an important role in rural female migrants' search for a secure environment that there is a saying to describe the decline of sexual morality: "Women cannot make a lot money unless they are bad."[27] One female entrepreneur from rural Sichuan told me in a 1994 interview: "As a rural migrant without urban *hukou*, I had to use all I had to make a living in Shenzhen. Women are like water, flowing over all walls. A woman's youth is short. She should make the best use of it. Now I have important 'male friends' to support me." What surprised me during my interview is that she had no sense of shame or embarrassment when she said this.

Sex-related corruption is increasing. According to one government report, proffering sexual favors constituted 20 percent of all bribery charges against the government officials in one district.[28] The emergence of proffering sexual favors is new and different from the old social patterns of prostitution. Although prostitution in China still involves the old practices of violence and gangsters, the new prostitution may also be characterized by less patriarchy than was commonly the case for China (and most other societies as well) because many new prostitutes are independent contractors.

## New Farm Women

Markets, rural industry, and migration provided more opportunities for both men and women. Of course, not every woman has been able to use the opportunity to leave farming. The majority of farm women still live in villages and still spend much of their time in agriculture-related work. But farm women have also experienced changes both within their own home and in the village community. Indirectly, farm women themselves gain from the nonagricultural opportunities available to others.

This comparison is most salient in those farm families whose husbands work outside doing nonagricultural work. Despite the fact that many rural women work in rural industries, the sex ratio of industrial workers still favors men. Because each farm family had to produce a grain quota for the state, more men quit agricultural work, leaving the farming to women because women have to take care of young children at home. A recent social survey from China suggests that farm women make up 60–70 percent of the agricultural labor force.[29] In Imperial China and under the collectives, the gender pattern in Chinese villages had been either *nan geng nü zhi* (men farm and women weave) or *nannü gong geng* (men and women farm together). Now two new patterns—*nan gong nü geng* (men work outside and women farm) and *nannü gong gong* (both men and women work outside)—have begun to take root in rural China.

The feminization of agricultural work has far-reaching significance. In those families where the husbands have left for nonagricultural work, wives are responsible for almost all production and marketing decisions. In fact, women become the heads of the households. This is especially true for those women whose husbands work in other regions. In many Hunan villages, local women call those men "holiday" husbands (many of them construction workers and rural merchants) because they come home only once or twice a year. The new female heads not only have to work hard physically as laborers but also have to plan for their family's affairs on their own. They hire farmhands to help out during the busy seasons. Since crop surplus and sideline products are sold at the market, women's agricultural activities are directly linked to market activities. The long absence of the male family head leaves him ill-equipped for major family decisions, even though he may continue to enjoy patriarchal social status. Sometimes, farm women have to support their husbands when those men fail in their businesses or are not able to find jobs in the cities. The new female family heads have decision power to buy whatever they deem important for the family.

Although a Chinese woman in Imperial China could also become a family head by default, she could never become one ideally even after the death of the family patriarch, not even Mother Jia in *The Dream of the Red Chamber*, who had age and generation to support her role, did that. The new female heads assume family responsibility when they are in their twenties, thirties, and forties.

Women are more prominent in less developed regions with fewer rural factories, but in other places women also gain more control in family decisionmaking, as Ellen Judd's study of North China suggests: "Women—not simply as laborers, but as especially skilled or able persons—are often decisive in enabling a household project to flourish, either by virtue of their own particular abilities or by virtue of their capacity to act as effective partners."[30]

Graham Johnson's research in the Pearl River delta, a region with strong rural industrialization, also indicates that rural women dominate in the agricultural economy.[31] Moreover, most farm women are not subsistence farmers. They are small-scale commercial farmers. In Shandong alone, out of 14 million working rural women, 12 million participated in commercial endeavors of all sorts (grain production, handicrafts, animal husbandry, garden economy).[32]

## New Village Life

Rapid economic change affects every aspect of village life. Moneymaking has become the most important part of village life in today's China. The price of goods and knowledge of new ways to make money dominate village women's gossip. Visitors to Chinese villages may be surprised at the market knowledge of Chinese farm women, which ranges from the price of

Chinese cabbage at local markets to currency exchange rates between Chinese yuan and U.S. dollars.

Farm women have also played an important role in the high savings rate and the new patterns of consumption. In rural China, high levels of consumption are paired with high rural savings rates. Women's interest in consumer goods and the changing life style in the village have intensified the silent competition among village households for the possession of durable goods. In the early and mid-1980s (varying according to the region), farmers saved to build houses. After houses, the most desirable goods were *sanzhuan yixiang* (three wheels and one sound)—sewing machines, watches, bikes, and radios. From the mid-1980s to the early 1990s, this changed to include washing machines, tractors, trucks or motorcycles, tape recorders, and color televisions. In most rural families, women are in charge of finances because they are believed to be better in careful calculation and strict budgeting. Although both men and women are responsible for saving for big projects, women are most responsible for saving for durable consumer goods. The competition for better goods also creates village tensions. The widespread *hongyanbing* is obvious in the village.

Moreover, the traditional norms that bind the community have weakened. One important Chinese village norm dictates, "Even a rabbit knows not to eat grass beside his nest," suggesting that there should be no stealing in one's neighborhood or within the village. But nowadays many property-related crimes take place within the village and among neighbors. Sex outside marriage and before marriage has become more common. The weakening of traditional authority also brought about some increased autonomy for young people and for women.

Arranged marriages are decreasing. This is especially true for rural female migrants and female migrant workers. According to a 1990 survey by the *Journal of China's Women,* 74 percent of new marriages in China are not arranged marriages.[33] Young boys and girls now have much greater power over their marital decisions. I saw engaged couples riding their bicycles to go to the county seat to see the local opera. Some young women have even talked about sex in front of their parents. Those rural women will have to travel a long way to achieve sexual equality, but they have achieved a certain degree of freedom and independence surpassing anything they ever knew before. Personal freedom is crucial to women's independence.

The rapid movement of rural people and the rapid development of rural industrialization also means that more and more couples live their lives apart from their in-laws. The nuclear family was the dominant pattern of rural migrants throughout the 1980s. For most Chinese women, that in itself is a liberation. The period of subordination as a daughter-in-law has been regarded as the most stressful stage of a woman's life. The rapid development in the countryside achieved without effort a feat that neither the PRC nor the Republic was able to achieve in eighty-three years, and with little investment from the state.

Kindergarten became more popular after the economic change in the countryside. For the first time in the history of China, rural parents and grandparents are no longer the sole caretakers and educators of the children. This has significant gender implications. Women have more time to engage in outside activities. Nonetheless, rural women are still the main transmitters of social values, and the changing role of women is associated with the disruptions or weakening of the patriarchal order.

The new basic structures reshape urban and even village life, and most Chinese still live in villages.

## Conflict Among Women

Of course, women encounter numerous problems as they enter the market. Urban state female workers confront a host of new challenges. The standard procedure of the socialist state in China required that factories provide welfare for workers, medical care, child care, and maternity leave. Competition from rural factories has forced urban state factories to pay attention to efficiency and to attempt to cut costs. Women workers in those urban factories are under pressure. In a worker exchange meeting held in Beijing in April 1987, 80–90 percent of enterprises expressed their intention to hire only male employees.[34] Because the costs of maternity leave are now borne by the enterprise, women are considered a burden.

Rural women did not get any welfare from either the state or the employers, so they are less troubled by market forces. Market reform in fact divided Chinese women into two segments: Rural women have been able to take advantage of the opportunity to expand their life opportunities; and urban women, especially urban workers in state factories, have been left out by the market forces. Many urban factory workers, male and female alike, became conservative forces during this transition. They wanted to maintain the status quo. Many urban women believed that socialism benefited them, as indeed it did. Thus, while rural women are busy (in many cases together with their men) creating space free from government control, many urban working women are trying to use their political power to keep the government in.

The conflict between rural and urban interests divided rural and urban women. *Whereas rural women prefer more liberty and less state control, urban working women want the state to act on their behalf to secure benefits won long ago by state workers.* In most cases, the state has been on the side of urban women and against the interests of rural women. The *hukou* restriction is one example. Rural people without an urban *hukou* could not find permanent employment in the state factories. Recently rural people have had to pay city governments a fee to be able to stay. All these factors create problems for rural migrants. In addition, some urban women have sought employment in rural-initiated industries and enterprises in the urban setting.

## Conclusion

Markets, rural industrial development, and migration provided new opportunities for rural women. For the first time in Chinese history, alternative employment outside the home became an ideal pattern for many and even most women. The numbers of rural women in nonagricultural occupations have increased. Women are not only workers but also managers of firms, although their percentage is still low in comparison to men. Moreover, women use markets to acquire independent sources of income and new networks of social relations away from the family.

Rural women did not seek to make a revolution in women's position, but they have achieved one nevertheless. Most changes in women's social status and empowerment in the past fifteen years have come as a result of the wide range of social and economic changes within the countryside. Women are also agents for those changes, but they achieved this without organization: "Women are active agents in the processes that are reconstructing class in the Chinese countryside, but they are not acting in an organized or conscious sense as women. They may be a collectivity in itself, but they are not a collectivity for itself."[35]

Nevertheless, more Chinese women changed their social and economic positions and gained some degree of individual freedom than during any previous period. This grass-roots women's movement was able to bring about more radical changes than either the official attempt to impose an authoritarian patriarchy in the post-Mao era,[36] or Mao's mobilization of women.[37]

China has a long way to go to achieve sexual equality. Rural women, despite their gains, are still defined mainly by their role as daughters and mothers. It would be misleading to claim that economic development is a guarantee for the improvement of women's life. After all, not every woman is able to grasp the opportunities provided by markets, rural industrial development, and migration. Nonetheless, most women gain from *baochan daohu*, markets, rural industrial development, and migration, which provide a necessary although insufficient condition for women's future liberation. These changes have not only changed the substantive patterns of women's lives, they have also changed the context into which women's lives fit.

In short, the changed pattern of Chinese women has been a SULNAM within a SULNAM. It too has been a spontaneous, unorganized, leaderless, nonideological, and apolitical movement (SULNAM), and it has been the more effective for each of those characteristics.

## Notes

1. For a negative evaluation of *baochan daohu*'s impact on women, see Delia Davin, "The Implications of Contract Agriculture for the Employment and Status of Chinese Peasant Women," pp. 137–146, in S. Feuchtang, ed., *Transforming China's Economy in the Eighties: The Rural Sector, Welfare and Employment* (Boulder: Westview Press, 1988) and Laurel Bossen, "Chinese Rural Women: What Keeps; Them down on the Farm?" Paper presented at the conference, "Engendering China," Wellesley College and Harvard University, Boston, February 7, 1992.

2. Margery Wolf, *Revolution Postponed: Women in Contemporary China* (Stanford: Stanford University Press, 1985.)

3. Ellen R. Judd, *Gender and Power in Rural North China* (Stanford: Stanford University Press, 1994), p.237. Emphasis added.

4. Many Sichuan brides were perhaps sold by marriage brokers. My own investigation in Hubei and Mark Selden's research in Hebei suggest that these Sichuan brides were valued as good workers in their new homes. Personal communication with Mark Selden in November 1994.

5. Zhongguo Shehui Kexue Yuan Renko Yanjiu Suo (Institute of Population Studies, Chinese Academy of Social Sciences), *Dangdai Zhongguo funü dewei chouyang diaocha ziliao* (Sampling Survey Data of Women's Status in Contemporary China) (Beijing: Wangguo Xueshu Chubanshe, 1994).

6. In Chinese: *Maolü lamo niu geng tian, nanren lahuo nü shuqian ge you benshi.*

7. Yuan Zhixin, *Guo zhong zhi guo* (A Country Within a Country) (Guangzhou: Jinan Daxue Chubanshe, 1992), p. 112.

8. Quanguo Funian Nongcun Chu (Rural Work Division, Chinese Women's Federation), "Zhongguo nongcun de 1.8 yi" (Chinese Rural 180 Million), *Zhongguo funü* (Chinese Women)11 (1993): 23.

9. Yuan, *A Country Within a Country*, p. 111.

10. Ibid., p. 94.

11. Stevan Harrell, "Geography, Demography, and Family Composition in Three Southwestern Villages," in Deborah Davis and Stevan Harrell, eds., *Chinese Families in the Post-Mao Era* (Berkeley: University of California Press, 1994), p.97.

12. Lu Aiguo, "Farming System and Woman Labor Participation: The Case of Rural China in Economic Transition," Paper presented at the international symposium, "Social and Cultural Development in the Context of Economic Growth in Asia," Hanoi, November 24–26, 1994.

13. On gender inequality in post-Mao rural China, see Barbara Entwisle, et al., "Gender and Family Businesses in Rural China," *American Sociological Review* 60, no. 1 (1995): 36–57.

14. Hua Mulan is a legendary heroine in China. She dressed up as a man to join the army so that her father would not have to be drafted. She returned as a general. The music of the song is from a revolutionary song in the modern ballet, *The Red Female Regiment.* In Chinese: *Gu you Hua Mulan ti fu qu cong jun, jin you nianzijun zhuanqian mang buying.*

15. *Zhongguo funü* (Chinese Women) 11 (1993): 23.

16. Personal communication with Chang, December 26, 1994, Shenzhen.

17. Graham E. Johnson, "Family Strategies and Economic Transformation in Rural China: Some Evidence from the Pearl River Delta," in Davis and Harrell, *Chinese Families,* p.124.

18. Meng Xiaofan, "Chinese Rural Women in the Transfer of the Rural Labor Force," *Social Sciences in China,* no. 1 (Spring 1994): 109–118.

19. In Chinese: *Wo xiang yao ge jia, yinge buguan zenyang de difang, zhiyao tazai zhujiang liangan.*

20. Wu Ping, *Baiwan funü xia tequ* (Millions of Women Go to the Special Economic Zone) (Guangdong: Renmin Chubanshe, 1993), p. i. My personal communications in 1994 with two cadres from the Shenzhen government suggest the ratio is 5 to 1. Those figures refer only to Special Economic Zones in Guangdong.

21. Based on my personal interviews in Wuhan, Shijiazhuang, Beijing, and Guangdong, between 1982 and 1986.

22. In Chinese: *Laobanniang xiang yousigua: you yuan you hua.*

23. Meng, "Chinese Rural Women," pp. 109–118.

24. In Chinese: *Mingyun shi duishou; yongbu ditou; congbu baoyuan banju, buqu wen liyou; wo na qingchun du mingtian—douzai wangqian zuo.*

25. Wang Jinling, "New Characteristics of Marriages Between Zhejiang Farmers and Women from Outside the Province," *Social Sciences in China* (Summer 1994):59–64.

26. In Chinese: *Songshang jinqian tui zhe gan, songshang meinü mashang gan, wuqian wunü kao bian zhan.*

27. In Chinese: *Nüren buhuai mei yong qian.*

28. Yu Yongjun, "Sexiang huiluo mianmian guan" (All Sorts of Proffering Sexual Favors), in Li Xiao and Zhou Yan, *Gongheguo shutan neimu jishi* (Records of Clearing up Bribery in the People's Republic) (Beijing: Tuanjie Chubanshe, 1993), p.351.

29. *Zhongguo funü* (Chinese Women), no. 390 (1991): 8; no. 392 (1991): 13; and no. 402 (1992): 2.

30. Judd, *Gender and Power,* p.159.

31. Johnson, "Family Strategies," pp. 103–136

32.   Quanguo Funian Nongcun Chu, "Chinese Rural 180 Million," p. 23.

33.   Wang Jian, "Shuju xianshi Zhongguo funü shehui diwei" (Data Reveals Social Status of Chinese Women), *Zhongguo funü* (Chinese Women) 1 (1992): 24–25.

34.   Ran Maoying, "Women's Employment Challenge," *Beijing Review* 5 (July 11–17, 1988): 25.

35.   Judd, *Gender and Power*, p.162.

36.   Edward Friedman, *National Identity and Democratic Prospects in Socialist China* (Armonk, N.Y.: M.E. Sharpe, 1995), chap. 9.

37.   Kay Ann Johnson, *Women, the Family and Peasant Revolution in China* (Chicago: University of Chicago Press, 1983). Johnson argues that "politics in command" and the ideological attack on gender inequality left structural gender issues untouched.

# Conclusion: Farmers Changed China

Revolutions, genuine revolutions, not
those which simply change the political
forms and members of the government but
those which transform institutions and
alter property relations, advance unseen
for a long time before bursting into the
sunlight impelled by some circumstance.

Albert Matheiz, *The
French Revolution*

China is being transformed, in both the countryside and the cities. Despite the formal claim of socialism, markets and the private sector now play an increasingly important role in peoples' lives. Central planning, the symbol of the socialist state, controlled only a little over 10 percent of all industrial production by 1992. It has been the rapid economic growth from the nonstate sector that has enabled China to maintain double-digit growth for more than fifteen years. Other formal Communist structures are losing their relevance to Chinese people's lives. The *hukou* system, which once controlled mobility, especially rural mobility, has lost much of its power. Rural–urban migration has increased rapidly, reaching 100 million in 1992.[1] The system of rationing food and other consumer goods came to an end in 1992. The People's Republic of China is changing from a closed class society to an open class society—not a democratic society, but a far more open class society nonetheless.

The transformation of communism in China involves two unique aspects. First, the farmers, including many who no longer earn their living tilling soil, stand at center stage in the great transformation. The economic development that counted did not begin as urban development with growth trickling down to the rural sector but rather flowed from rural to urban sectors. The impact of that development on Chinese modernization exceeded all previous urban-centered development in the People's Republic of China. Second, the Chinese farmers' movement that started and

energized the transformation of the People's Republic of China was a spon-
taneous, unorganized, leaderless, nonideological, apolitical movement
(SULNAM) that spread like a flood, affecting the macro structures of the
People's Republic of China.

In Chapter 2, I discussed the status quo ante, the People's Republic
from 1949 to 1978, the setting of the action. Two major changes took place
under the People's Republic of China that established the foundations of
what occurred later. One had to do with the place of families in the general
social structure. Early on, the People's Republic took economic decisions
out of the hands of family heads. The family unit, which had been the ultimate decentralized focus of Chinese society, was set aside as the major
focus of social life. Loyalty to family members took second place to everyone's supposed loyalty to the Communist regime. The other change was
the "feudalization" of China. Cadres controlled the communes as "feudal"
lords in everything but inheritance (and they even achieved a bit of that by
way of nepotism and *hukou* control). The countryside was cut off from the
city, even villages from market towns. The state bound 80 percent of
China's population in a newly created closed class system by tying them to
the collective-owned land.

The particular elements of this "feudalism" that set the scene for the
breakout were two: (1) for the first time in two thousand years, political
leaders who often lacked agricultural experience directed Chinese farming,
instead of rural family heads buttressed by generations of agricultural experience; and (2) *hukou* restrictions and the grain rationing system prevented
farmers from leaving their designated collective teams without the permission of cadres.

I examined the farmers' reaction to these two main changes in six
chapters, looking at *baochan daohu* (turning production over to the
household), markets, rural industrialization, rural migration, rural reproduction, and Chinese rural women. My examination revealed the farmers'
spontaneous and simultaneous transformation of their social system in general and their economic systems in particular. I focused on both the economic structural changes (the spread of *baochan daohu*, rural markets,
and rural industries) and other key social structures (mobility, especially
migration, reproduction, *danwei*, and *hukou*).

## Transformation of the Economic System

Before the spread of *baochan daohu*, Chinese economic ownership took
two distinct forms: state-owned enterprises (mainly urban-based), and collectives (mainly rural-based). With the exception of urban fringe areas and a
few coastal regions, the rural economy was mainly a subsistence economy
with little market activity. Indeed, revolutionary processes cut many of the
economic, political, and cultural ties that had previously linked villages to

market towns. The ways in which *hukou*, together with antimarket collectivism, isolated villages affected not only the economy but also other elements of society and culture. After *baochan daohu*, farmers began to produce under their own independent management as they had done before 1949, fundamentally changing the economic and political structure of the Chinese Communist regime. This structural change gave farmers incentives to increase productivity both per hectare and per worker. These incentives brought into play advances previously made by the People's Republic in fertilizers, seeds, and machines. Within a few years, Chinese agricultural production doubled. Subsistence farmers practically disappeared overnight. Now, almost all farm households produce for markets, although the percentage of commercial agriculture varies from region to region.

Chinese farmers are no longer "collective peasants." They are no longer the farmers of pre-Maoist China because of the rapid increase in market activities, rural industries, and migration. They are now, increasingly, independent producers and managers—with a difference. Now they have wrested initiative for themselves. Their horizons for material betterment have expanded explosively. The sky's the limit for their economic productivity and diversification, *if only the cadres leave them alone*. The farmers quickly see and accept new methods that increase their productivity. By 1990, farmers used 150 fewer "person-days" per hectare as they had in producing the same amount of output under collective agriculture.[2] Under Mao, the government had provided the *means* for increasing productivity but gave farmers' no incentives to exploit those newly available means. Farmers are now so quick to learn that they may "mine" the land they use to increase its productivity in the short run, even at the risk of environmental degradation.

After this rural institutional transformation, China's state has been swamped and outmaneuvered by millions upon millions of farmers. First of all, the farmers increased and diversified farm production as they perceived market opportunities. They sought markets. Producing for markets and even producing markets became the most important way for farmers to enrich themselves. The planned state could hardly keep its head above water in terms of strict party doctrine with 80 percent of its population flooding the markets. By 1992, the state controlled only 20 percent of grain purchases and 25 percent of agricultural sideline products.[3] Rural merchants became the backbone of Chinese markets as well as models for other farmers. From 1978 to 1989, rural *jishi* increased from 33,302 to 59,019, while "the volume of business rose from 12.5 to 125 billion yuan."[4]

Farmers' ideas are changing, and many are on the move. One social survey of farm households in Lin County, Shandong Province, reports that 90 percent of farmers wanted to be merchants or workers in factories.[5] A popular rural saying goes: "One year's hard work in the field is not worth one day in the market." By 1992, there were 62,000 rural *jishi* and 9,500 specialized and wholesale markets in the countryside, 160 of which reached 100 million yuan in annual trade turnover. Also there were 6.5 million farm merchant networks, involving 15 million farmers.[6] The cadres went with the flow. After all, increased productivity had long been a main goal, and even Deng himself bestowed his blessing on the private wealth that he had in no way planned! Of course, Deng's support was not constant. He wavered in his support and sometimes called for socialist egalitarianism.[7]

One important indicator of the farmer-based increase of markets was the rapid growth in retail sales. Between 1978 and 1989, when few urban people were involved in commercial activities, the total volume of retail sales rose from 155.86 billion to 810.14 billion yuan (a 4.2-fold increase).[8] In the countryside, the root of Chinese commercial vitality, retail sales experienced a 4.6-fold increase. Farmer-based market achievements have led to the privatization of the service industry in China. In 1979, there were only 103,000 restaurants and 1 million retail businesses in China, all controlled by state or local government; by 1993 there were 6.5 million rural-based service firms, most of which (4.5 million) were controlled by private farmer households.[9]

Second, the released surplus rural labor and the shortage of consumer goods in the planned economy provided farmers with opportunities to develop rural industries further:

In 1989, the total output value of village and town enterprises reached 842.28 billion yuan, which accounted for one-fourth of the gross national product and 58 percent of the total rural output value, and the number of employees in village and town enterprises reached 94 million, which accounted for 23 percent of the total rural labor force.[10]

According to a 1993 New York Times report, rural industries (township, village, and private enterprises) "now contribute more than half of China's overall industrial output."[11] Rural industries developed so fast that even the government itself used the term yijun tujin (a strange army suddenly appears) to describe the sudden rise of rural industry. The growth of rural industry continues. They provide most of China's double-digit growth, offsetting the inefficient majority of state-owned enterprises, of which more than one-third run in the red. A Chinese economist has this to say about the rural industries and state industries: "There are two almost independent economies here. The non-state economy is incredible. It is. . . doing it profitably and competitively. There is no comparison in modern times with what is happening here. At the same time, you have a basically bankrupt state sector supported by various methods of subsidy."[12]

According to a 1993 report from the *Asian Wall Street Journal Weekly*, "Production by state factories grew only 4 percent in October, and many are predicting negative growth by January due to a shortage of capital."[13] Yet rural industrial growth overcame the slow growth of the urban state sector and maintained China's double-digit growth for 1993.

The increase of rural industry is endogenous and the ownership structure is nongovernmental. Originally, the government hoped rural industry would be a sop to ward off rural–urban migration. As such it failed, but it did afford the farmers a vital vehicle for capital growth. The government itself acknowledged in 1991 that it invested almost nothing in the development of rural industry.[14] State-led rural industrialization occurred in 1958, involving 18 million farmers, but that development failed, leading the state later to try to ban rural industries.[15]

The recent rapid growth in rural industries has led to a rapid increase of nonfarmers in the countryside, as illustrated by Table 9.1. Nonfarmers are former farmers who have taken up other occupations. The rate of increase in nonfarm labor over the decade was ten times that of farm labor.[16]

The rapid development of rural industry has altered the Chinese social structure: "The proportion working in agriculture decreased from more than 70 percent in 1978 to 60.2 percent in 1989." By 1989, one decade after *baochan daohu*, 23 percent of the rural labor force worked in rural industries and 58 percent of total rural productivity value came from rural industries.[17] By 1992, nonagricultural employment in the countryside reached 98 million.[18] The trend continues.

Third, rural-based private businesses are spreading all over China in both manufacturing and services, challenging the state-owned sectors. Private and semi-private *(guahu)* enterprises and existing family farms altered the effective ownership structure of the planned state. In rural China, private enterprises flourished, reaching 54 percent of Chinese firms in 1993.[19]

**Table 9.1**

A Comparison of Rural Labor Distribution, 1978–1988 (percentages)

| Year | 1978 | 1988 | Increase | Annual Increase |
|------|------|------|----------|-----------------|
| Farmers[a] | 90.5 | 78.5 | 14.6 | 1.4 |
| Nonfarmers | 9.5 | 21.5 | 197.3 | 11.5 |

[a]*Farmers include grain producers, fishermen, herdsmen, and lumberjacks.*

*Source: Zhu Qingfang, "Shinian lai woguo gejieji, jieceng jiegou yanbian de fenxi" (An Analysis of Structural Evolution of Various Classes and Strata in China During the Last Decade), Shehuixue yanjiu (Sociological Studies), no. 3 (1990): 6.*

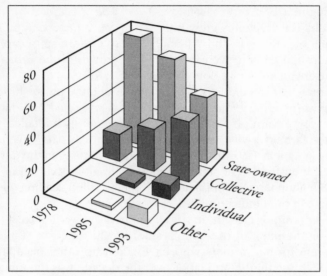

**Figure 9.1** Transformation of Industry Ownership
in China
*Source: Zhongguo Xiangzhen Qiye Nianjian Bianji
Weiyuanhui (Editorial Commision of Chinese Rural
Industrial Enterprise), Zhongguo xiangzheng qiye
nianjian 1992 (1992 Book of Chinese Rural Industrial Enterprises) (Beijing: Nongye Chubanshe, 1992).*

In 1978, 78 percent of industry consisted of state-owned enterprises, with 15 percent urban collectives, and 7 percent rural collectives. By 1993, only 43 percent of industrial firms were state-owned enterprises (see Figure 9.1). The spread of rural industry caused a rapid drop in the state's share.

The rapid development of rural industries has changed the context into which the government fits. In 1992, even the state had to accept the fact that China was becoming a market economy. China's leaders did not plan to replace state enterprises with nonstate rural industries, but the competition from rural industries and the bankruptcy of the government budget may force the government to close down some state factories. State leaders may in the end take credit for the success of this economic structural transformation.

In short, the rural economy leads China's growth. As a 1993 government report states:

Amid the fast economic growth in 1992, the growth in the rural sector was much faster than the urban sector. Of the national income growth rate of 12.5 percent, about 8 percent, or a proportional 64 percent, came from the rural sector, whereas about 4.5

percent, or a proportional 36 percent, came from the urban sector. Of the acceleration of national income growth rate of 5 percentage points in 1992 (comparing the growth rate in 1992 with that in 1991), about *96 percent was realized in the rural sector.*[20]

The picture was quite different before 1978. Although China achieved a 6 percent growth rate during those years (1949–1978), the urban share of growth was 63 percent. In 1952, the rural share of the national growth rate was 47 percent, but the figure dropped to 28 percent in 1978.[21] These figures suggest that the rural growth rate during the collective days was decreasing, leaving a major part of the growth rate to the urban sector. After *baochan daohu*, the tables turned. Chinese people's living standard improved rapidly when the rural sector began pushing and pulling the economy.

## Transformation from a Closed to an Open Class Society

Late Imperial China and the Republic of China maintained the ideal and legal structure of an open class pattern of social mobility, although in reality mobility was highly constrained.

For decades, the People's Republic used *hukou, danwei, liangpiao,* and other forms of political control (class labeling and secret personnel files) to freeze and control social mobility in China. As a result, China became, in effect, a closed class society with little social mobility. Birthplace (rural or urban) and family origin (as a result of class assignment) often determined one's lifelong occupational status. After *baochan daohu,* economic independence in the countryside increasingly forced open the pattern of social stratification. When given a chance, the farmers reopened the class structure, except in regard to the state, which remained closed.

First of all, the "feudalization" of Chinese farmers was swept away. Farmers became not only producers but also managers of their family farms, reclaiming responsibility for myriad decisions from choice of crop and technology to financing and marketing, yet without technically "owning" their land. Cadres could no longer order them about in terms of production and other important economic decisions, although they still possessed power over farmers in terms of tax collection and could at least raise barriers to free choice in reproduction. The farmers began moving ahead at an ever accelerating rate.

Second, residential and occupational mobility increased rapidly in rural China. Farmers could leave their villages on the family's decision. They were no longer tied to the land. As early as 1985, one-fifth of all farmers changed either their occupation or place of residence.[22] *If one compares social mobility in terms of wealth, status, and migration, rural people have been the most mobile of all.* Between 1981 and 1987, close to 10 million farmers moved annually.[23] By 1988, more than 86 million farmers had changed their occupation from farmer to nonfarmer. In the 1980s, despite the formal system of constraints and informal urban discrimination, rural migrants invented ways of surviving in the hostile urban environment. Rural migrants encircled the cities, filling urban streets with peddlers, rural merchants, service people, performers, and even beggars. Some found success on their own. As the number of rural migrants grew, self-employment and various kinds of private businesses flourished in the cities. There is no doubt that the farm-led mobilization of labor played a crucial role in Chinese economic growth. Before 1980, no one could have imagined that farmers would dominate urban free markets or that most exchange in urban areas would take place in urban free markets.

Spatial mobility was not only rural–urban but also regional. Farmers in less developed regions migrated to work in those regions with booming rural industries and services. Some found work in newly built rural-based factories; others began to work on contract land for rich exfarmers, particularly in Zhejiang, Jiangsu, and Guangdong. For example, the annual flow of migrants from the Mount Dabie area bordering Hubei, Henan, and Anhui provinces reached 1 million.[24] At the same time, rural factories in those developed regions moved into less developed regions in order to take advantage of cheap labor. *The market, not the cadres, determined plant locations.* At the same time, rural migrants from poor areas find work in developed areas and mail money home, redistributing income from rich to poor areas.

According to a government report, rural migrants have overloaded the whole Chinese transportation system.[25]

Such rapid rural mobility contrasts sharply to the relative lack of mobility for longtime urban dwellers, but rural mobility and rural industry changed labor mobility in the cities as well. *Rural industries, especially those close to the cities, provided a "second shift" job market for urban people.* More and more urban people moonlight to make money. Some even dare to leave secure jobs for private employment, although most urban people still stay in their designated workplace (*danwei*) for employment and welfare. After all, the government still has a welfare contract with urban dwellers, which it never had with rural people. By 1992, 10 percent of urban working people participated in a "second shift."[26] The number is increasing rapidly.

Successful rural service businesses, self-made millionaires, and rich rural merchants are transforming social values. Everyone is trying to make money. Careers in state organizations are not the prize they once were. Farmers emerged from the Maoist "feudal" period as libertarians and opportunists. In the 1980s, it was farmers who turned Chinese values upside down. Farmers substituted *xiangqiankan* for *xiangqiankan* (look forward) collectivism. Individualism by default replaced communal spirit.

They became inadvertent champions of capitalism. They have discovered and practice a new materialism that powers economic development in China as never before. They seem never to care for, mention, or even think of the term "capitalism."

Third, the opening of social mobility increased varieties of social strati-fication. Gone are the days when rural dwellers were homogenous "blue ants," sharing their leveling poverty. Some rural people may even feel nos-talgia for the old days of shared poverty, but few would give up their improved material life and family economy. The increasing variations in the countryside illustrate the rapid social mobility in China. Regional differ-ences in fact facilitate population mobility from the less developed to more developed areas. The majority of migrants are from Hunan, Sichuan, Hubei, and other hinterland areas. Compared with a few rich farmers and rural entrepreneurs, many rural people may feel bypassed and frustrated, but the frustration comes more from the comparison with the rural rich. Few would simply give up and not do anything. Rural apathy is no longer a problem. Almost all farmers are engaged in market activities of various kinds, and new social strata are forming among farmers. They are rural fac-tory workers, private workers, merchants, peddlers, private entrepreneurs, rural collective factory managers, migrant workers, temporary and contract workers. There are even some rural intellectuals, but no one seems to be paying much attention to them. They do not even get arrested.

Like state enterprises, the bureaucracy also declined as farmers tried to bribe their way out of restrictions. Corruption eroded the party apparatus. It may also be argued that the farmers saw an opportunity, a hole in the Communist dike against rural change, and they flowed through it. They recognized the corruptibility of cadres, of officials of all sorts, and they exploited it, all the way to comparative economic independence. Corruption played an important role in the farmers' defeat of the system. Through corruption, they changed the rules of the game. This was crucial for the transformation of the Chinese Communist system, whether intended or not. If the cadres had been incorruptible, *baochan daohu* would have been stopped in its tracks. There is a saying in China, "No winds of corrup-tion, no rural enterprises." Corruption weakened party discipline and the party apparatus, greatly reducing the power of the central government despite its continued control of the military and the armed police.

Corruption has run like a unifying thread throughout this book. The farmers' movement could never have worked if the cadres had been incor-ruptible. In the long run, corruption is a sure sign of trouble. In this period of farmer-based revolutionary change, corruption has been a major means for shifting resources from relatively unproductive uses to spectacularly more productive employments.

The comparative failure of the state one-child family policy in rural China (in contrast to urban areas) reveals the strength of farmers. Despite the reduction of the birthrate (even in rural China), the government never carried out the one-child policy as successfully in rural areas as in the cities. It didn't even try. Rural fertility rates are beginning to decline as a function of modernization, but urban birthrates are beginning to rise as second shift jobs, the end of rationing, and the possibility of private housing give urban people greater freedom to resist cadre control.

Like the economic means of markets and rural industries, migration, corruption, and defiance of the one-child policy are also changing the People's Republic of China. As Havel points out: "Anything which leads people to overstep their predetermined rules is regarded by the system as an attack upon itself. And in this respect it is correct; every instance of such transgression is a genuine denial of the system."[27]

Finally, the position of women in China, both substantively and in context, has changed. Patriarchy has not been overthrown, but the forces that created economic growth have carried with them new economic and political roles for women. It is doubtful whether even the still intact military power of the government can reverse these changes. Women will be one-half of the world in China in a way never contemplated before.

## Implications

Development in China in the past fifteen years has undermined or superseded many existing theories of social change, especially many of those applied to China.

First, this analysis departs from the state-centered and elite-focused approaches that dominate the study of politics in general and Chinese politics in particular. It pays particular attention to the words and deeds of ordinary Chinese farmers (*laobaixing*, 80 percent of all Chinese). When such a radical social transformation is taking place, it is quite understandable that scholars trace the remarks of powerful leaders and the acts of members of existing organizations. Yet, throughout this analysis I have shown that the development of markets and services, rural industry, and migration did not originate in, although they were often conditioned by, government action. They originated in and were propelled primarily by farmers' actions. Farmers have demonstrated their initiative through *baochan daohu*, market activities, rural industries, and migration. Their confidence in their own abilities has been stronger than that of urban people. Many urban people, in contrast, fear competition from rural people. Farmers formed a broad entrepreneurial base and accumulated the capital for economic takeoff in China. Yet, in all this time (1978–1993), the farmers never tried to overthrow the government; they sought merely to get out from under it, to get the government off their backs. They sought always to make the government irrelevant, and so, to a perfectly astonishing degree, they did. The motto of farmers has not been, "We appeal to the state for help," but rather, "Let the state get out of the way. Damn the cadres, full speed ahead," or *shengchan zijiu* (work to save oneself). More recent studies of China suggest that the state reform policies after 1978 always followed several steps behind farmers' actions.[28] The government did achieve some agricultural improvements, mostly of a technological nature, before *baochan daohu*. Deng Xiaoping should be credited for not suppressing *baochan daohu* as Mao did in the early 1960s. We should probably give Mao credit for developing some new material means to increase agricultural productivity, although his policies killed incentives for growth. But when the family farmers took charge of their own work, productivity gains exploded.

To write history from the point of view of the farmers is difficult. This treatment is frequently "anecdotal," even "anthropological." But writing from the point of view of farmers also has several virtues. It provides readers a sense of what the vast majority of actual Chinese are doing. Beneath the anecdotes and the farmers' pithy sayings, the reader will grasp a few hints that go further—to the great drama of social transformation in China. Chinese farmers remind us that ordinary individuals also make history; maybe they always make history. When there is actual change, they change, too. When things are quiet, as they are much of the time, the general people must be quiet, too. By concentrating too heavily on leaders, we may overlook the farmers' force; we may in fact have sold the role of the people, the sun of political analysis, for the sovereign of formal political leadership.

Second, this analysis shows that most Chinese farmers' actions were spontaneous, unorganized, leaderless, nonideological, and apolitical, yet cumulatively they are revolutionizing Chinese society. Study of social movements tends to emphasize organization, leadership, and ideology. The familiar theme underlying farmers' movements is that of the Maoist peasant revolution. In almost all cases in Asia, Africa, and Latin America, leadership came from outside. Often nonfarmers were "a factor of supreme importance" in peasant movements.[29] *Baochan daohu* and other farmers' actions suggest that revolutionary movements may not require organization, leadership, and ideology. Indeed, those may make the movements more vulnerable. The experiences of organized Chinese farmers' movements before 1978 furnish some evidence for this (see Chapter 3).

This type of farmers' movement is a world away from the predominant type of farmers' movement that has been endemic in Chinese society for over two thousand years.[30] When taxes, rents, usury, or cost of essential goods took, say, 30 percent of their crops (varying by regions), farmers saw this as normal, even natural. When the percentage rose to, say, 60 percent, there were "peasant revolts." These revolts were conservative. They sought not to overthrow the system but only to clear out and restore the old system. Those movements differ from the subject of this book in important ways. They were organized, planned, and led, and in many cases they articulated a social vision. Such movements were repeatedly crushed by the state. Occasionally their victories brought new dynasties to power.

Analysis of organized rural movements and the state's response to them has centered on leadership. The Chinese farmers' movement discussed here suggests a micro history moving from "the bottom up." Compared with overt student protest in China, the farmers' unorganized and leaderless movement has accomplished far more. Had farmers organized their movement and demanded the end of the *hukou* system and collective agriculture, had they carried banners and marched on Tiananmen, state leaders would surely have smashed them just as they smashed the students at Tiananmen in 1989.

Third, the analysis here is suggestive about development in general. It shows what can happen if farmers have both means and incentives. Most previous studies emphasize urban- and elite-powered change. Chinese farmer-led growth provides an alternative model to the general pattern. Given the fact that rural people constitute the majority of all developing nations, this alternative might have far-reaching effects on the analysis of development elsewhere, but its grass-roots and anarchic quality does not lend itself to the formulations of development planners. Nor is it evident how to unleash the power of SULNAM elsewhere.

Fourth, there can be no denying that corruption in the PRC has been directly and vitally relevant to what may well be the most dramatic sustained rates of economic development of any latecomer to modernization. Farmers have been successful in disentangling the inefficient state apparatus by getting around the formal restrictions through bribery and building up personal connections: "Bribes are given even for a small matter. Bribes must be given before anything happens. Bribes must be given for an important deal. It seems that everyone is giving and taking bribes while absolving himself or herself from blame."[31]

Although corruption has weakened Communist control and the planned economy, its deepening will create problems in the long run for China in its ambition to become a powerful modern state. Further development of markets requires laws that stress universalism rather than particularism. As the industries mature, the networks and corruption may hinder their further development, but given the importance of family particularism, it is doubtful that a highly impersonal bureaucracy will take root again in a short time. Will farmers' successes in the end prove their undoing?

Finally and more importantly, the book goes further than James C. Scott's proposition about the weapons of the weak and the state-centered approach that typifies the China field. Here I explore an historical instance where weakness becomes strength. By using ingenious and surprising methods and taking advantage of historical circumstances, farmers contested successfully with the Chinese party-state and decisively contributed to the transformation of the social system (and not only that of rural China). As raindrops begin a torrent, the unorganized farmers quietly initiated a storm of social change. Their method: SULNAM.

## SULNAM and the Collapse of the Urban Public Good Regime

The relevance of SULNAM is well nigh incontestable. How could such a large movement escape the notice of the government? Some scholars suggest that the lack of state intervention into the farmers' pursuit for economic gain came out of a benign neglect. Deng and his followers chose to look the other way. That view is contradicted by their unremitting though increasingly ineffective resistance to rural-urban migration. I argue that the nature of SULNAM itself and the urban focus of the government are the main reasons for the success of SULNAM in China.

First, the movement was spontaneous. The participants themselves cannot say or know where a spontaneous movement will lead. They can only hope. How can cadres know or see it very quickly?

Second, the movement was unorganized and thereby exhibited no focus for governmental attack.

Third, the movement was leaderless. It highlighted no individuals for disciplinary action.

Fourth, the movement was nonideological. No authors of pronouncements presented themselves. No one was caught preparing posters. No walls bore their proclamations.

Fifth, the movement was apolitical. The farmers did not seek to defy authority. They went where authority was weak or absent.

In the last analysis, China's recent spectacular growth rests on three pillars: the initiative, ingenuity, and greed of the farmers; the corruptibility of the cadres; and the fact that the central leadership was preoccupied with other matters. The farmers carried it off because the urban-centric national government was exclusively focused on the cities. Political leaders were virtually unaware of what the farmers, 80 percent of the Chinese population, were accomplishing until they had succeeded in providing double-digit growth rates, something that all developing country political leaders have eagerly sought. The farmers had proved to be alchemists. They had turned their mundane agrarian dross into agricultural, industrial, and commercial gold.

The nature of the urban preoccupation of the Chinese leadership was essential to the success of the farmers' SULNAM. The attention and structure of the People's Republic were so urban-centric that some scholars call it the "urban public good regime."[32] From an economic point of view, urban state industries provided most of the state revenue apart from their "confiscation of grain." Almost all bureaucracies (with the exception of the Agricultural Ministry) are concerned with urban state factories. The urban-centered bureaucracy remain largely unaware of the power and potential of the countryside and the farmers.

The political leadership remained preoccupied with urban stability. To buy stability in the city, the politicians increased subsidies for urban people and urban factories through the reform period (1978–1994). From 1978 to 1988, social security and welfare for urban people increased from 7.81 billion to 65.3 billion yuan, a sevenfold increase, reaching 24 percent per year. Meanwhile, the state also bailed out money-losing factories. From 1978 to 1988, the state spent 44.583 billion yuan to feed money-losing factories, a 22 percent increase.[33] In 1990, state subsidies for urban food and money-losing state factories reached 40.8 billion yuan.[34] At the same time, the state decreased capital investment in the countryside, from 10 percent in 1978 to a little over 2 percent in 1991.

Consequently, urban cadres have paid little attention to the rural sector, providing leeway for farmers' unorganized movements to grow. *Even now, when rural industries contribute more than 50 percent of China's overall industrial output, there is no Ministry of Rural Industry in Beijing.*

In short, the spontaneous, unorganized, leaderless, nonideological, apolitical movement of the Chinese farmers avoided all direct challenge. When bribery was ineffective, they avoided contact with authority as much as possible. The farmers did not confront. They sought only to achieve their ends as best as they might with as little fuss, feathers, and vainglory as possible. They seize no power; they leach it away from the government and are assisted in this by an increasing interdependency that they neither sought nor realized. The farmers had already done much to enrich themselves before Deng Xiaoping told the Chinese that to be rich was glorious. Basically, the farmers changed Communist China not because the government was prescient, flexible, and benign but because the powers-that-be were looking the other way and were ideologically hidebound—and the farmers caught them at it.

## And in the Future. . .

The farmers of China have leached away most of the economic dominance of an authoritarian, urban-oriented government that maintained its focus of political control. The farmers replaced state economic dominance with a phenomenal economic growth rate sustained for some fifteen years. This economic power has recently influenced both the social structures in general and economic structures in particular in the city. An urban-centric government that ignored or was in some cases unaware of this movement powered by farmers' initiative and ingenuity is now clearly aware of it—even proud of it. The political leadership actually attributes much of it to their own "reform program," and many scholars have followed this lead eagerly. Nothing is more likely than that this still prominent, well-organized, political regime will attempt to take over and give active direction to the farmers' movement. If it does and is "successful," it will almost certainly slay the goose that lays the golden eggs. The leaders in charge have not in the past been able by constructive action to stimulate the initiative and ingenuity of the Chinese farmers. Since 1978, the farmers have done that for themselves.

The SULNAM is largely responsible for the dramatic increases in China's economic development. Moreover, there is no doubt that the SUL-NAM has leached away many of the central functions and practices of the government of Communist China. Both of these accomplishments continue apace. There is, however, a downside to this. Sooner or later, what the farmers have made irrelevant will have to be replaced, but the farmers have no plans, no tactics or strategies even, to replace what they have leached away. The spontaneity, the lack of organization, the absence of leadership, the lack of an ideology, the apolitical nature of their move-ment—all those qualities that made their movement possible can change into anomie. Political functions may be badly performed, but they cannot be ignored or neglected. That is the weakness of libertarianism. The farm-ers show no sign of developing either an alternative to or a talent for gov-ernment. Their talents have been for material productivity (economic development) and family living, not for governance. They could care less about the creation of public goods. They are diminishing the powers of the state, but they may in their turn be drowned in what they have created. Anomie is the ultimate nemesis of libertarianism.

What does all this mean for China's political future? The farmers are radical individualists by default. They believe, "'It's every man for himself and God for us all,' said the elephant as he danced among the chickens." But as development continues, to the very degree that it is successful, there will have to be more and more concern for the chickens. As the elephants grow and multiply, more chickens will take notice. Rapid economic devel-opment will likely create more self-assertive social groups. Many will want to have more of a voice than the government is willing to allow. Students and intellectuals may even turn from their preoccupation with state political leaders and turn on the farmers. Can spontaneous, unorganized, leaderless, nonideological, apolitical movements continue indefinitely? The farmers of China believe and hope they can and will. If the farmers have their way, China will become the leading libertarian state by default. In China, farmers' energies have been unleashed by the farmers themselves and are still unharnessed. The world of development has never seen anything like it.

The sun rising in the villages is the future of China.

# Notes

1. Jiang Liu, et al., eds., *Shehui lanpishu 1992–1993 nian zhongguo: shehui xingshi fenxi yu yuce* (China in 1992–1993: Analysis and Forecast of Social Situations 1992–1993 China) (Beijing: Zhongguo Shehui Kexue Chubanshe, 1993), pp. 4–14. Even in state enterprises, a substantial amount of production is beyond the reach of the state.

2. Vaclav Smil, *China's Environmental Crisis: An Inquiry into the Limits of National Development* (Armonk, N.Y.: M. E. Sharpe/East Gate Books, 1993).

3. Zhongguo Shehui Kexueyuan Nongcun Fazhan Yanjiusuo (Rural Development Institute, Chinese Academy of the Social Sciences), *1992 nian Zhongguo nongcun jingji fazhan niandu baogao* (A 1992 Report on Chinese Rural Economic Development) (Beijing: Zhongguo Kexue Chubanshe, 1993), p. 47.

4. Group for Research on Social Development, Sociology Institute of CASS, "Changes Marking the Beginning of a Period of Transition in Chinese Society," *Social Sciences in China* (Spring 1994): 67.

5. Lu Xueyi and Li Peilin, *Zhongguo shehui fazhan baogao* (A Developmental Report on Chinese Society) (Shengyang: Liaoning Renmin Chubanshe, 1991), p. 47.

6. Zhongguo Shehui Kexueyuan Nongcun Fazhan Yanjiusuo, *A 1992 Report*, p. 46.

7. Joseph Fewsmith, *Dilemmas of Reform in China: Political Conflict and Economic Debate* (Armonk, N.Y.: M. E. Sharpe, 1994).

8. Group for Research on Social Development, "Marking Changes," p. 72.

9. Zhongguo Xiangzhen Qiye Nianjian Bianji Weiyuanhui, *Zhongguo xiangzheng qiye nianjian—1994* (1994 Book of Chinese Rural Industrial Enterprises) (Beijing: Nongye Chubanshe, 1994), p. 39.

10. Lu and Li, *A Developmental Report*, p. 593.

11. Patrick E. Tyler, "Communist Makes Good, as a Ruthless Capitalist," *New York Times*, December 2, 1993.

12. Ibid. Emphasis added.

13. Kathy Chen and Julia Leung, "Economists Fear Surging Inflation as China Rolls Back Austerity Plan," *Asian Wall Street Journal Weekly* (December 6, 1993):3.

14. *People's Daily*, December 24, 1991.

15. Dong Fureng, *Industrialization and China's Rural Modernization* (London: Macmillan Press, 1992).

16. Zhu Qingfang, "Shinian lai woguo gejieji, jieceng jiegou yanbian de fenxi" (An Analysis of Structural Evolution of Various Classes and Strata in China during the Last Decade), *Shehuixue yanjiu* (Sociological Studies) 3 (1990):6. "Farmers" include grain producers, fishermen, herdsmen, and lumberjacks.

17. Lu and Li, *A Developmental Report*, pp. 592–593.

18. Zhongguo Shehui Kexueyuan Nongcun Fazhan Yanjiusuo, *A 1992 Report*, p. 4.

19. Zhongguo Xiangzhen Qiye Nianjian Bianji Weiyuanhui, *Zhongguo xiangzheng qiye nianjian—1994* (1994 Book of Chinese Rural Industrial Enterprises) (Beijing: Nongye Chubanshe, 1994), p.4.

20. Zhongguo Shehui Kexueyuan Nongcun Fazhan Yanjiusuo, *A 1992 Report*, p. 177. Emphasis added.

21. Ibid., p. 167.

22. Fazhan Yanjiusuo (Development Research Institute), *Gaige mianlin zhidu chuangxin* (Reform and System Innovation) (Shanghai: Sanlian Chubanshe, 1988).

23. Group for Research on Social Development , "Marking Changes," p. 70.

24. Ting Jianzhong, "Nongye laodong cong 'kuanxiang' xiang 'xiaxiang' zisheng qianyi xianxiang fengxi" (Analysis of the Spontaneous Rural Labor Migration Phenomenon from Less Populated Areas to Densely Populated Areas), *Shehui kexue* 1 (1993):47–50.

25. Lu and Li, *A Developmental Report*.

26. Jiang, et al., *China in 1992–1993*.

27. Vaclav Havel, *The Power of the Powerless: Citizens Against the State in Central-Eastern Europe* (Armonk, N.Y.: M. E. Sharpe, 1985), p. 30.

28. Daniel Kelliher, *Peasant Power in China: The Era of Rural Reform 1979–88* (New Haven: Yale University Press, 1992), p. 33; and Chen Yizi, *Zhongguo: shinian gaige yu bajiu minyun* (China: Ten-Year Reform and 1989 Democracy Movement) (Taiwan: Lianjing Chuban Shiye Gongsi, 1991).

29. Charles D. Brockett, "The Structure of Political Opportunities and Peasant Mobilization in Central America," *Comparative Politics* 23 (1991):268.

30. Elizabeth Perry, *Rebels and Revolutionarism, North China, 1845–1945* (Stanford: Stanford University Press, 1980); and Susan Naquin, *Millenarian Rebellion in China* (New Haven: Yale University Press, 1976).

31. *Gongren ribao,* (Workers' Daily), May 12, 1989, translation from Gong Xiaoxia, "Corruption and Abuses of Power During the Reform Era," *Chinese Sociology and Anthropology* 26, no. 2 (Winter 1993–94):4.

32. Dorothy Solinger, "China's Urban Transients in the Transition from Socialism and the Collapse of the Communist 'Urban Public Regime,'" *Comparative Politics* 27, no. 2 (1995):127.

33. Guo Shuqing and Han Wenxiu, *Zhongguo GNP di fenpei he shiyong* (The Distribution and Management of China's GNP) (Beijing: Zhongguo Renmin Daxue Chubanshe, 1991), pp. 125–127.

34. Nongyebu Jingji Zhengce Yanjiu Zhongxin (Economic Policy Research Center of the Agricultural Ministry), *Zhongguo nongcun: zhengce yanjiu beiwanglu* (Rural China: Policy Research Memorandum), vol. 2 (Beijing: Nongye Chubanshe, 1991), p. 23.

# Selected
# Bibliography

Banister, Judith. *China's Changing Population*. Stanford: Stanford University Press, 1987.

Bates, Robert H. *Markets and States in Tropical Africa: The Political Basis of Agricultural Policies*. Berkeley: University of California Press, 1981.

Chan, Anita, Richard Madsen, and Jonathan Unger. *Chen Village: The Recent History of a Peasant Community in Mao's China*. Berkeley: University of California Press, 1984.

Chen Jianyuan. *Zhongguo shehui: yuanxing yu yanhua* (Chinese Society: Original Pattern and Transformation). Shengyang: Liaoning Renmin Chubanshe, 1988.

Chen Shi and Mi Youlu, eds. *Zhongguo nongcun jiating di bianqian* (The Transformation of Rural Families in China). Beijing: Nongcun Duwu Chubanshe, 1989.

Chen Yizi. *Zhongguo: shinian gaige yu bajiu minyun* (China: Ten-year Reform and 1989 Democracy Movement). Taipei: Lianjing Chuban Shiye Gongsi, 1991.

Chen Yun. *Selected Works of Chen Yun: 1956–1985*. Beijing: Renmin Chubanshe, 1986.

Cheng Tiejun. "Zhongguo hukou di xianzhuang yu weilai" (Household Registration System in China: Retrospect and Prospect) *China Report* 13, no. 2 (1991):1–25.

Coale, Ansley J., Wang Feng, Nancy Riley, and Lin Fu De. "Recent Trends in Fertility and Nuptiality in China." *Science* 251 (1991):389–393.

Cong Jin. *Ouzhe fazhan de suiyue* (Years of Torturous Development). Zhengzhou: Henan Renmin Chubanshe, 1989.

Cooney, Rosemary, and Li Jiali. "Household-Registration Type and Compliance with the One–Child Policy in China, 1979–1988." *Demography* 31, no. 1 (1994):21–32.

Croll, Elizabeth. *Chinese Women Since Mao*. London: Second Books, 1983.

Davis, Deborah. "Job Mobility in Post-Mao Cities: Increases on the Margins." *China Quarterly* 132 (December 1992):1062–1085.

Davis, Deborah, and Stevan Harrell, eds. *Chinese Families in the Post-Mao Era*. Berkeley: University of California Press, 1994.

Davis, Deborah, and Ezra F. Vogel, eds. *Chinese Society on the Eve of Tiananmen: The Impact of Reform*. Cambridge: Harvard University Press, 1990.

Delman, Jørgen, et al., eds. *Remaking Peasant China: Problems of Rural Development and Institutions at the Start of the 1990s*. Aarhus, Denmark: Aarhus University Press, 1990.

Deng Xiaoping. "On Problems Concerning Our Rural Policy," pp. 275–277. In *Selected Articles of Deng Xiaoping*. Beijing: Renmin Chubanshe, 1983.

————. "Gaige de buzi yaojiakuai" (To Speed up Reforms), pp. 1441–1449. In *Shierda yilai zhongyao wenjian xuanbian* (Selections of Important Documents Since the Twelfth Party Congress). Beijing: Renmin Chubanshe, 1988.

Dittmer, Lowell. "Tiananmen Reconsidered: Review Article." *Pacific Affairs* 64, no. 4 (1991):529–535.

Dong Fureng. *Industrialization and China's Rural Modernization.* London: Macmillan Press, 1992.

Du Runsheng. *Zhongguo nongcun jingji gaige* (The Reform of China's Rural Economy). Beijing: Zhongguo Shehui Kexue Chubanshe, 1985.

Entwisle, Barbara, et al. "Gender and Family Businesses in Rural China." *American Sociological Review* 60, no. 1 (1995):36–57.

Fazhan Yanjiusuo (Development Research Institute). *Gaige mianlin zhidu chuangxin* (Reform and System Innovation). Shanghai: Sanlian Chubanshe, 1988.

Feeney, Griffith, and Wang Feng. "Parity Progression and Birth Intervals in China." *Population and Development Review* 19, no. 1 (1993):61–102.

Fei Xiaotong. *Chinese Village Close-up.* Beijing: Xin Shijie Chubanshe, 1983.

————. *Fei Xiaotong xuanji* (Selected Works of Fei Xiaotong). Tianjin: Renmin Chubanshe, 1988.

Feng Lanrui. *Lun Zhongguo laodongli shichang* (On Chinese Labor Markets). Beijing: Zhongguo Chengshi Chubanshe, 1991.

Fewsmith, Joseph. *Dilemmas of Reform in China: Political Conflict and Economic Debate.* Armonk, N.Y.: M.E. Sharpe, 1994.

Friedman, Edward. "Maoism and the Liberation of the Poor." *World Politics* 39, no. 3 (1987):408–428.

————. "Deng Versus the Peasantry: Recollectivization in the Countryside." *Problems of Communism* 39 (September 1990):30–49.

————. *National Identity and Democratic Prospects in Socialist China.* Armonk, N.Y.: M.E. Sharpe, 1995.

Friedman, Edward, Paul Pickowicz, and Mark Selden. *Chinese Village, Socialist State.* New Haven: Yale University Press, 1991.

Gao Xiaomeng and Xiang Ning. *Zhongguo nongye jiage zhengce fenxi* (Policy Analysis of Chinese Agricultural Price). Hangzhou: Zhejiang Renmin Chubanshe, 1992.

Greenhalgh, Susan. "Controlling Births and Bodies in Village China." *American Ethnologist* 21, no. 1 (1994):3–30.

Guo Shutian and Liu Chulin, eds. *Shehen de Zhongguo* (Unbalanced China). Shijiachuang: Hebei Renmin Chubanshe, 1991.

Guojia Nongye Weiyuanhui Bangongting (General Office of the State Agriculture Commission). *Nongye jitihua zhongyao wenjian huibian* (Compendium of Important Documents on Agricultural Collectivization). Beijing: Zhongyang Dangxiao Chubanshe, 1981.

Guojia Tongji Ju Nongcun Shehui Jingji Tongji Shi (Rural Social Economic Statistics Group of the State Statistical Bureau). *Zhongguo nongcun tongji nian jian, 1992* (Chinese Rural Statistics, 1992). Beijing: Zhongguo Tongji Chubanshe, 1992.

Guowuyuan He Guojia Tongji Ju (State Council and State Statistical Bureau). *Zhongguo gongye jingji tongji ziliao 1986* (Statistical Materials on China's Industrial Economy 1986). Beijing: Zhongguo Tongji Chubanshe, 1987.

Guowuyuan Yanjiu Shi Geti Siying Jingji Tiaochazu (State Council Investigation Team). *Zhongguo de geti he siying jingji* (Chinese Private Enterprises). Beijing: Gaige Chubanshe, 1990.

Harding, Harry. *China's Second Revolution: Reform After Mao.* Washington, D.C.: Brookings Institute, 1987.

Havel, Vaclav. *The Power of the Powerless: Citizens Against the State in Central-Eastern Europe.* Armonk, N.Y.: M.E. Sharpe, 1985.

He Xin. "Analysis of the Current Student Protests and Forecasts Concerning the Situation." *Australian Journal of Chinese Affairs* 23 (1990):64–76.

Heilongjiang Sheng Nongye Hezuo Shi Bianweihui (Editors of History of Agricultural Cooperatives in Heilongjiang Province), ed. *Heilongjiang nongye hezuoshi* (History of Agricultural Cooperatives in Heilongjiang Province). Beijing: Zhonggong Tangshi Ziliao Chubanshe, 1990.

Hinton, William. *Fanshen: A Document of Revolution in a Chinese Village.* New York: Vintage Books, 1972.

Honig, Emily, and Gail Hershatter. *Personal Voices: Chinese Women in the 1980s.* Stanford: Stanford University Press, 1988.

Hu Heli. "1988 nian woguo zhujin jiazhi de gusuan" (Estimation of Rent-Seeking in 1988). *Jingji shehui tizhi bijiao* (Journal of Comparative Economic Social Systems) 5 (1989):10–15.

Huang Shu-min. *The Spiral Road: Change in a Chinese Village Through the Eyes of a Communist Party Leader.* Boulder: Westview Press, 1989.

Huang Weiding. *Zhongguo de yinxing jingji* (China's Hidden Economy). Beijing: Zhongguo Shangye Chubanshe, 1993.

Huo Da. "Minyishi weitian" (People Depend on Food), pp. 217–280. In Shanghai Wenyi Chubanshe, ed., *Minyishi weitian* (People Depend on Food). Shanghai: Shanghai Wenyi Chubanshe, 1991.

Investigation Group, Institute of Economics, CASS. "Survey of the Rural Commodity Economy in Wenzhou." Working paper, Institute of Economics, CASS, 1988.

Jiang Liu et al., eds. *Shehui lanpishu 1992–1993 nian Zhongguo: shehui xingshi fenxi yu yuce* (China in 1992–1993: Analysis and Forecast of Social Situations 1992–1993 China). Beijing: Zhongguo Shehui Kexue Chubanshe, 1993.

Jiang Zemin. "Speech on the Commerce Work in Shanghai, Feb. 23, 1989." *Zhongguo shang bao* (Chinese Business News) (April 12, 1990):1.

Jiang Zemin and Li Peng. "Gei guojia jihua shengyu weiyuanhui de yifeng gongkaixin" (An Open Letter to the State Family Planning Commission). *Zhongguo renkou bao* (Chinese Population Journal) (1990): 1.

Judd, Ellen R. *Gender and Power in Rural North China.* Stanford: Stanford University Press, 1994.

Kelliher, Daniel. *Peasant Power in China: The Era of Rural Reform 1979–88.* New Haven: Yale University Press, 1992.

Kornai, Janos. *The Socialist System: The Political Economy of Communism.* Princeton: Princeton University Press, 1992.

Levy, Marion J., Jr. *The Family Revolution in Modern China.* New York: Atheneum, 1948.

———. "The Problem of Our Policy in China," *Virginia Quarterly Review* 25, no. 3 (Summer 1949):360–362.

————. "Contrasting Factors in the Modernization of China and Japan." *Economic Development and Cultural Change* 2, no. 3 (1953):161–178.

————. *Modernization and the Structure of Society.* Princeton: Princeton University Press, 1966.

Li Mengbai and Hu Xin. *Liudong renkou dui dachengshi fazhan di yingxiang ji duice* (Impact of Migrants on Big City Development and Policy Implications). Beijing: Jingji Ribao Chubanshe, 1991.

Lin Qingsong and William A. Byrd, eds. *China's Rural Industry: Structure, Development, and Reform.* New York: Oxford University Press for the World Bank, 1990.

Liu Xuemin. "Speech on National *Jishi* Conference." *Zhongguo gongshang pao* (Chinese Commerce News), October 11, 15, 18, 1990.

Lou Xiaopeng. "Ownership and Status Stratification," pp. 134–171. In William A. Byrd and Lin Qingsong, eds., *China's Rural Industry: Structure, Development, and Reform.* New York: Oxford University Press for the World Bank, 1990.

Lu Xueyi and Li Peilin. *Zhongguo shehui fazhan baogao* (A Developmental Report on Chinese Society). Shengyang: Liaoning Renmin Chubanshe, 1991.

Ma Qibin, et al. *Zhongguo gongchandang zhizheng sishi nian 1949–1989* (Chinese Communist Party's Forty Years in Power, 1949–1989). Beijing: Zhonggong Dangshi Chubanshe, 1991.

Mao Zedong. "Report of an Investigation into the Peasant Movement in Hunan," pp. 21–59. In *Selected Works of Mao Tse-tung.* New York: International, 1954.

Meng Xianfan. "Chinese Rural Women in the Transfer of the Rural Labor Force" *Social Sciences in China* (Spring 1994):109–118.

Min Yaolian and Li Binkun, eds. *Zhongguo nongcun jingji gaige yanjiu* (Study on Chinese Rural Economic Reform). Beijing: Zhongguo Zhanwang Chubanshe, 1988.

Moore, Barrington, Jr. *Social Origins of Dictatorship and Democracy.* Boston: Beacon Press, 1966.

Mosher, Steven W. *Broken Earth: The Rural Chinese.* New York: Free Press, 1983.

Myrdal, Jan. *Return to a Chinese Village.* New York: Pantheon Books, 1984.

Nathan, Andrew, and Shi Tianjian. "Cultural Requisites for Democracy in China: Findings from a Survey." *Daedalus* 122, no. 2 (1993):95–123.

Naughton, Barry. "Implications of the State Monopoly over Industry and Its Relaxation." *Modern China* 18, no. 1 (January 1992):14–41.

Nongchanpin Pifa Shichang Ketizu (Wholesale Market Research Group). "Woguo nongchanpin pifa shichang gean tiancha yu fengxi" (Agricultural Wholesale Markets in China: Analysis on Selected Case Studies). *Nongye jingji wenti* (Problems of Agricultural Economics) 4 (1992):2–9.

Nongyebu (Agriculture Department). *Woguo nongmin shenghuo de juda bianhua* (The Tremendous Change in the Peasant's Life in Our Country). Beijing: Zhongguo Tongji Chubanshe, 1984.

Nongyebu Jingji Zhengce Yanjiu Zhongxin (Economic Policy Research Center of the Agricultural Ministry). *Zhongguo nongcun: zhengce yanjiu beiwanglu* (Rural China: Policy Research Memorandum). Beijing: Nongye Chubanshe, 1988.

Oi, Jean. "Fiscal Reform and the Economic Foundations of Local State Corporatism in China." *World Politics* 45, no. 1 (1992):99–126.

Parish, William L., and Martin King Whyte. *Village and Family in Contemporary China.* Chicago: University of Chicago Press, 1978.

Peng Peiyun. "China's Population Policy." *Beijing Review* (April 13–19, 1992):

Perry, Elizabeth, and Christine Wong, eds. *The Political Economy of Reform in Post-Mao China.* Cambridge: Harvard University Press, 1985.

Platte, Erika. "Private Sector in China's Agriculture: An Appraisal of Recent Changes." *Australian Journal of Chinese Affairs* 10 (1983):81–96.

Polanyi, Karl. *The Great Transformation.* Boston: Beacon Press, 1957.

Popkin, Samuel. *The Rational Peasant.* Berkeley: University of California Press, 1979.

Potter, Sulamith Heins, and Jack M. Potter. *China's Peasants: The Anthropology of a Revolution.* New York: Cambridge University Press, 1990.

Pryor, Frederic L. *The Red and the Green: The Rise and the Fall of Collectivized Agriculture in Marxist Regimes.* Princeton: Princeton University Press, 1992.

Putterman, Louis. "Institutional Boundaries, Structural Change, and Economic Reform in China." *Modern China* 18, no. 1 (January 1992).

Pye, Lucian W. "An Introductory Profile: Deng Xiaoping and China's Political Culture." *China Quarterly* 135 (September 1993):412–443.

Qiao Xiachung, et al. *Chaozai de tudi* (Overpopulated Land). Shenyang: Shenyang Chubanshe, 1989.

Rawski, Thomas, ed. *How to Study China's Economy Today.* Hongkong: Chinese University Press, 1991.

Riskin, Carl. *China's Political Economy: The Quest for Development Since 1949.* New York: Oxford University Press, 1987.

Scott, James C. *Weapons of the Weak: Everyday Forms of Peasant Resistance.* New Haven: Yale University Press, 1985.

Selden, Mark. *The People's Republic of China: A Documentary History of Revolutionary Change.* New York: Monthly Review Press, 1979.

———. "Family Strategies and Structures in Rural North China," pp. 139–164. In Deborah Davis and Stevan Harrell, eds., *Chinese Families in the Post-Mao Era.* Berkeley: University of California Press, 1993.

———. *Political Economy of Chinese Development.* Armonk, N.Y.: M.E. Sharpe, 1993.

Shambaugh, David. "Introduction: Assessing Deng Xiaoping's Legacy." *China Quarterly* 135 (September 1993):409–411.

Shandong Sheng Nongye Hezuohua Shi Bianji Weiyuanhui (Editorial Commision of History of Agricultural Cooperatives in Shandong Province). *Shandong sheng nongye hezuohua shiliao ji* (Collective Agriculture in Shandong Province). Jinan: Shandong Renmin Chubanshe, 1989.

Shang Xiaoyuan. *Zhongguo guoming de ziwo yizhixing renge* (Self-inflicted Depressed Personality in China). Kunmin: Yunnan Renmin Chubanshe, 1989.

Sheng Hua, et al. *China: From Revolution to Reform.* London: Macmillan Press, 1993.

Sheng Maochang, et al. *Rang renkou jinzhong changmin* (Let the Population Alarm Ring Forever). Nanjing: Nanjing Chubanshe, 1991.

Shi Xianmin. "Beijing getihu difazhan licheng ji neibie fenghua" (The Development Process of Small Businesses with a Detailed Breakdown: A Case Study of the Western District in Beijing). *Zhongguo shehui kexue* (Social Science in China) 5 (September 1992):19–41.

————. "Beijing's Privately Owned Small Businesses: A Decade's Development." *Zhongguo shehui kexue* (Social Sciences in China) 14, no. 1 (1993):153–164.

Shirk, Susan L. *The Political Logic of Economic Reform in China.* Berkeley: University of California Press, 1993.

Shue, Vivienne. *The Reach of the State: Sketches of the Chinese Body Politic.* Stanford: Stanford University Press, 1988.

Sichuan Provincial Government. "Sichuan Birth Planning Provincial Regulations." *Population and Development Review* 14, no. 2 (1988):369–375.

Sicular, Terry. "China's Agricultural Policy During the Reform Period," pp. 340–364. In Joint Economic Committee, Congress of the United States, ed., *China's Economic Dilemmas in the 1990's: The Problems of Reforms, Modernization, and Interdependence.* Washington, D.C.: Government Printing Office, 1991.

Siu, Helen F. *Agents and Victims in South China: Accomplices and Victims in Rural Revolution.* New Haven: Yale University Press, 1989.

Skinner, G. William, ed. *The City in Late Imperial China.* Stanford: Stanford University Press, 1977.

Smil, Vaclav. *China's Environmental Crisis: An Inquiry into the Limits of National Development.* Armonk, N.Y.: M.E. Sharpe/East Gate Books, 1993.

Solinger, Dorothy. "China's Urban Transients in the Transition from Socialism and the Collapse of the Communist 'Urban Public Regime.'" *Comparative Politics* 27, no. 2 (1995):127.

Stark, David, and Victor Nee. "Toward an Institutional Analysis of State Socialism," pp. 1–31. In Victor Nee, and David Stark, eds., *Remaking the Economic Institutions of Socialism: China and Eastern Europe.* Stanford: Stanford University Press, 1989.

Statistical Bureau of China. *Statistical Year Book of China 1986.* Hongkong: Longman, 1986.

————. *Statistical Year Book of China, 1987.* Hongkong: Longman, 1987.

Sun Fangmin, et al. "Nongcun shangpin liudong zhong de 'zinan' wenti" (Four Difficulties in Rural Commodity Circulation), pp. 246–254. In Zhongguo Nongcun Fazhan Wenti Yanjiu, ed., *Nongcun jingji, shehui* (Rural Areas Society and Economy). Beijing: Zhishi Chubanshe, 1985.

Tyler, Patrick E. "Communist Makes Good, as a Ruthless Capitalist." *New York Times,* December 2, 1993.

————. "Between Marxism and the Market, a Chinese Manager Finds Corruption." *New York Times,* May 25, 1994, D3.

————. "China's Migrants: Economic Engine, Social Burden." *New York Times,* June 29 1994, A3.

————. "Beijing to Impose Huge Fees to Limit Migrants in City." *New York Times,* September 15, 1994, A10.

Vogel, Ezra F. *One Step Ahead in China: Guangdong Under Reform.* Cambridge: Harvard University Press, 1989.

Wadekin, Karl-Eugen, ed. *Communist Agriculture: Farming in the Soviet Union and Eastern Europe.* London: Routledge, 1989.

Wakabayashi, Keiko. "Migration from Rural to Urban Areas in China." *Developing Economies* 28, no. 4 (1990):503–523.

Walder, Andrew. *Communist Neo-traditionalism: Work and Authority in Chinese Society.* Berkeley: University of California Press, 1986.

Wang Genjin and Zhang Xuansan. *Woguo nongye xiandaihua yu jilei wenti yanjiu* (A Study on Agricultural Modernization and Capital Accumulation in China). Tanyuan: Shanxi Jingji Chubanshe, 1993.

Wang Jian. "Shuju xianshi Zhongguo funü shehui diwei" (Data Reveals Social Status of Chinese Women). *Zhongguo funü* (Chinese Women) 1 (1992):24– 25.

Wang Lixin. "The Years after Mao Zedong." *Kunlun* 6 (December 1988):4–53, trans. in JPRS-CAR–89–079 (July 1989):1–65.

Wang Ruipu. *Zhongguo nongcun 1978–1988* (Rural China 1978–1988). Beijing: Jiefangjun Chubanshe, 1989.

Wang Shiyuan, et al. *Zhongguo ganke daquan* (Chinese Reform Encyclopedia). Dalian: Dalian Chubanshe, 1992.

Wang Xiaoqiang, et al. "Nongcun shangpin shengchan fazhan de xindongxiang" (New Trends of Rural Commodity Production Development). *Nongcun, jingji, shehui* (Rural China, Economy and Society) 3 (1985):69–93.

Wang Xueqi, et al. *Zhongguo shehui zhuyi shigao* (A Manual of Chinese Socialist History). Hangzhou: Zhejiang Renmin Chubanshe, 1988.

Wang Yu, ed. *Da zhuanbian shiqi* (Great Transformation). Shijiazhuang: Hebei Renmin Chubanshe, 1987.

Wasserstrom, Jeffrey. "Resistance to the One-Child Family." *Modern China* 3 (1984):345–374.

Watson, Andrew, et al. "Who Won the 'Wool War'?" *China Quarterly* 118 (June 1989): 213–241.

"When China Wakes: A Survey of China." *Economist* (November 28–December 4, 1992):4.

White, Lynn T. *Careers in Shanghai: The Social Guidance of Personal Energies in a Developing Chinese City 1949–1966.* Berkeley: University of California Press, 1978.
———. *Policies of Chaos.* Princeton: Princeton University Press, 1990.

White, Tyrene. "Postrevolutionary Mobilization in China: The One-Child Policy Reconsidered." *World Politics* 43, no. 1 (1990):53–76.

Whyte, Martin K. "Chengdu diaocha: nongcun jiating xingshi shiying chengshi shenghuo wenti" (Chengdu Survey: Rural Family Pattern in Urban Life). *Shehui xue yanjiu* (Sociological Studies) 3 (1990):66–73.

Wolf, Margery. *Revolution Postponed: Women in Contemporary China.* Stanford: Stanford University Press, 1985.

Wong, Christine P. W. "Fiscal Reform and Local Industrialization: The Problematic Sequencing of Reform in Post-Mao China." *Modern China* 18, no. 2 (April 1992):197–227.

Wong Siu-lun. "Consequences of China's New Population Policy." *China Quarterly* 98 (1984):220–240.

Wu Baosheng. "Shangdi de youyu" (The Worry of God), pp. 74–105. In Lü Ye, ed., *Zhongguo: xiong yong de renchao* (China: The Rushing Tides of People). Beijing: Sheyue Wenyi Chubanshe, 1989.

Wu Ping. *Baiwan funü xia tequ* (Millions of Women Go to the Special Economic Zone). Guangdong: Renmin Chubanshe, 1993.

Wu Ruijun. "Defining the Floating Population." *Renkou yu jingji* (Population and Economy) 3 (1990):53–55.

WuDunn, Sheryl. "China's Peasantry Takes Measure of Its Prosperity." *New York Times,* July 4, 1993, p. 2.

Xiao Qingfu. *Wuci langchao* (Five Waves). Beijing: Zhongguo Renmin Daxue Chubanshe, 1989.

Xie Yaoping and Luo Bing. "Zhaosheng zhimi" (The Secret of Over-Quota Birth). *Faluyüshenghuo* (Law and Life) (1990):28.

Yan Gaihua and Lu Sishan. *Zapo "santie" houde zhongguo ren?* (Chinese People After Breaking *Santie*). Beijing: Ligong Daxue Chubanshe, 1992.

Yang, Dali. "Making Reform: Great Leap Famine and Rural Change in China." Ph.D. dissertation, Princeton University, 1993.

Yuan Zhixin. *Guozhong zhi guo* (A Country Within a Country). Guangzhou: Jinan Daxue Chubanshe, 1992.

Zeng Yi, et al. "A Cause-Analysis for the Rising Sex Ratio at Birth in Recent Years in China and Its Consequence." *Population and Economics* 1 (February 1993):3–15.

Zhang Zhiwen. *Zhongguo nongcun jiating jingying* (Family Management in Rural China). Beijing: Jingji Guanli Chubanshe, 1989.

Zhao Ziyang. "Zai zhongguo gongchandang dishisanjie zhongyang weiyuanhui disanci quanti huiyi shang de baogao" (Report at the Third Plenary Session of the Thirteenth Central Committee of the Chinese Communist Party). *Xinhu yuebao* (Xinhu Monthly) 10 (1988):6–11.

Zhonggong Zhongyang Wenjian Yanjiushi. "Zhonggong zhongyang guanyu 1984 nongcun gongzuo de tongzhi" (1984 No. 1 Document from the Central Government)," pp. 424–438. In Zhonggong Zhongyang Wenjian Yanjiushi, ed., *Shi er da yilai zhongyao wenxian xuanbian* (Selections of Important Documents Since the Twelfth Party Congress). Beijing: Renmin Chubanshe, 1986.

*Zhongguo baikei quanshu 1990* (Chinese Encyclopedia 1990 Year Book). Beijing: Baike Daquan Chubanshe, 1990.

*Zhongguo funü* (Chinese Women) 11 (1993).

*Zhongguo gongye jingji tongji zilian 1986* (Statistical Materials on China's Industrial Economy 1986). Beijing: Zhongguo Tongji Chubanshe, 1987.

Zhongguo Jingji Tizhi Yanjiu Suo (Chinese Economic System Reform Research Institute). *Gaige de sheshui xinli: bainqian yu xuanze* (Reform and Social Psychology: Changes and Choices). Chendu: Sichuan Renmin Chubanshe, 1988.

Zhongguo Nongcun Fazhan Yanjiu Zu (Chinese Rural Development Research Group). *Baochan daohu ziliao xuan* (Selected Material on Contracting to the Household). Beijing: Internal Government Document, 1981.

Zhongguo Nongcun Fazhan Yanjiu Zhongxin (Chinese Rural Development Research Center). *Nongcun, jingji, shehui* (Rural China, Economy and Society). Vol. 1 Beijing: Zhishi Chubanshe, 1985, 1986, 1987.

Zhongguo Shehui Kexue Yuan Renko Yanjiu Suo. *Dangdai Zhongguo funü diwei chouyang diaocha ziliao* (Sampling Survey Data of Women's Status in Contemporary China). Beijing: Wanguo Xueshu Chubanshe, 1994.

Zhongguo Shehui Kexueyuan Nongcun Fazhan Yanjiusuo (Rural Development Center of the Chinese Social Science Academy). *1992 nian Zhongguo nongcun jingji fazhan niandu baogao* (A 1992 Report on Chinese Rural Economic Development). Beijing: Zhongguo Kexue Chubanshe, 1993.

Zhongguo Xiangzhen Qiye Nianjian Bianji Weiyuanhui (Editorial Commision of Chinese Rural Industrial Enterprise). *Zhongguo xiangzheng qiye nianjian 1992* (1992 Book of Chinese Rural Industrial Enterprises). Beijing: Nongye Chubanshe, 1992.

Zhongguo Xianzhen Qiye Nianjian Bianwei Hui (Editorial Board of Chinese Rural Industrial Enterprises Yearbook). *Zhongguo xianzhen qiye nianjian: 1978–1987*, (Yearbook of Chinese Rural Industrial Enterprises: 1978–1987). Beijing: Nongye Chubanshe, 1989.

Zhou Jianming. *Geren zai jingji zhong de quanli (Individual Rights in the Economy)* Beijing: Renmin Chubanshe, 1989.

Zhou Xiaozheng. *Renkou weiji: laizi shehui gongzuozhe de jinggao* (The Population Crisis: Warnings from Social Scientists). Tianjin: Zhongguo Funü Chubanshe, 1989.

Zhou Xueguang. "Unorganized Interests and Collective Action in Communist China." *American Sociological Review* 58, no. 1 (1993):54–73.

Zhu Xiaoyang. "Zhongguoren-benxiang tiantang" (Chinese Rush into Paradise). *Jiushi niandai* (The Nineties) (1991):81–89.

Zweig, David. *Agrarian Radicalism in China 1968–1981*. Cambridge: Harvard University Press, 1989.

———. "Struggle over Land in China: Peasant Resistance After Collectivization, 1966–1986," pp. 151–174. In Forrest D. Colburn, ed., *Everyday Forms of Peasants' Resistance*. Armonk, N.Y.: M.E. Sharpe, 1989.

———. "Internationalizing China's Countryside: The Political Economy of Exports from Rural Industry." *China Quarterly* 128 (December 1991):716–741.

———. "Rural Industry: Constraining the Leading Growth Sector in China's Economy," pp. 418–436. In Joint Economic Committee, ed., *China's Economic Dilemmas in the 1990s: The Problems of Reforms, Modernization and Interdependence*. Washington, D.C.: Government Printing Office, 1991.

# Chinese Glossary

| | | |
|---|---|---|
| baochan daodui | 包產到戶 | output quotas contracted to the production team |
| baochan daohu | 包產到隊 | contract production to the household |
| baochan daolao | 包產到勞 | contract production to labor or task rates |
| baochan daozu | 包產到組 | contract production to work group |
| biandan | 扁擔 | carrying pole |
| boli duoxiao | 薄利多銷 | small profit, but large quantity |
| buduannai de haizi | 不斷奶的孩子 | unweaned babies |
| caigouyuan | 採購員 | purchasing agents who specialize in buying and selling goods |
| caishichang | 菜市場 | free vegetable market |
| chaosheng youjidui | 超生游擊隊 | over-quota birth guerrillas |
| cu | 粗 | coarse |
| dabaogan | 大包干 | comprehensive household contracting, returning everything—distribution, production, labor—to the household |
| dagong mei | 打工妹 | working sisters |
| daiye qingnian | 待業青年 | youths-waiting-for-government-jobs |
| dang'an | 檔案 | files; refers to the secret personal dossier |
| dangjiaren | 當家人 | master of one's own house |
| danhu guahu | 單戶掛戶 | single household or individual who practices *guahu* |

| danwei | 單位 | urban work unit |
| daodan jidi | 倒蛋基地 | a pun, that sounds like both "egg trading base" and "causing trouble" |
| dier huobi | 第二貨幣 | second currency |
| dier zhiye | 第二職業 | moonlighting |
| dinge daoqiu | 定額到丘 | the output of land was fixed and anyone responsible for the land could decide how many work points a worker could receive |
| dingti | 頂替 | job inheritance from parents or relatives |
| erdao fanzi | 二道販子 | secondhand peddlers |
| erduo yiziyou | 二多一自由 | two "mores" and one "autonomy," i.e., *more* private family plots, *more* allocation of grain, and the *freedom* to go to work |
| fangkongdong | 防空洞 | bomb shelter |
| fanxiaoliang | 返銷糧 | grain supplied by other rural places |
| fengding | 封頂 | capping, or setting a ceiling, i.e., to limit the amount that farmers can sell |
| ganji | 趕集 | going to the local market |
| ganxieqian | 感謝錢 | gratitude money |
| getihu | 個體戶 | individual private business |
| gongguan xiaojie | 公關小姐 | public relations misses |
| guahu | 掛戶 | attach oneself to somebody's household; in common usage, to act using the name of a legal organization |
| guandao | 官倒 | official profiteers |
| guanxi | 關係 | use of personal connections |
| gufen guahu | 股份掛戶 | joint-stock holders |

| | | |
|---|---|---|
| guojia de ren | 國家 的人 | people of the state |
| guojia liang | 國家糧 | government grain |
| guojia zhidao jia | 國家指導价 | the state guided price |
| heihaizi | 黑孩子 | black children, meaning illegal children |
| hongyanbing | 紅眼病 | red-eye disease, or envy |
| huacheng | 花城 | cities of flowers |
| huanglian | 黃蓮 | a bitter Chinese herbal medicine |
| hui | 會 | association |
| huikou | 回扣 | kickback money |
| huitou | 會頭 | the head of an organization |
| hukou | 戶口 | household registration system or internal passport |
| jiajiti | 假集體 | fake collective enterprise |
| jiandao ganbu | 剪刀幹部 | cadres with scissors |
| jiandaocha | 剪刀差 | "scissors price"—high prices for industrial goods and low prices for agricultural goods |
| jiang | 醬 | a Chinese soy bean pastelike dip |
| jianzu jianxi | 減租減息 | reduce taxes and rents |
| jiaoqu zhazhai | 郊區扎寨 | settle down in the fringe areas |
| jiben guoce | 基本國策 | basic state policy |
| jie | 借 | borrow or lend |
| jiedi | 借地 | lending land |
| jieshaoxin | 介紹信 | letter of introduction from one's danwei |
| jihuawai | 計劃外 | out of plan, not included in the plan |
| jinshoukao | 金手銬 | golden handcuffs |
| jishi | 集市 | farmers' markets |
| jiudi xiaohua | 就地消化 | to absorb rural surplus labor locally |

| | | |
|---|---|---|
| jiuji weicheng | 九基圍城 | surround or encircle the city with nine basic commercial goods |
| jiumingtian | 救命田 | lifesaving grain field |
| kandejian | 看得見 | visible |
| kaoshan | 靠山 | a reliable mountain, i.e., a big shot, a backer |
| laguanxi | 拉關係 | cultivating relationships |
| laji dawang | 拉圾大王 | kings of trash |
| lanka zhidu | 藍卡制度 | a system of legal urban residence, literally, the "blue card" system |
| laobaixing | 老百姓 | "old one hundred surnames," or ordinary people |
| laodage | 老大哥 | big brothers |
| li | 禮 | showing proper respect to one's relations |
| lianchan daolao | 聯產到勞 | contract production to labor |
| lianghu guahu | 聯戶掛戶 | more than two households' joint-*guahu* |
| liangpiao | 糧票 | food rationing coupons |
| litu bulixiang | 離土不離鄉 | Leave the land but not the rural areas. |
| maiyijiaerzi | 買議價兒子 | buying sons at negotiated prices |
| manchan | 瞞產 | hidden production quota |
| mandi | 瞞地 | hidden land |
| mangliu | 饅頭 | wandering migrants |
| mantou | 盲流 | steamed bread |
| minggenzi | 命根子 | lifeblood |
| mingong chao | 民工潮 | tides of migrant workers |
| modezhao | 摸得著 | tangible |
| nifanwan | 泥飯碗 | "clay rice bowls," i.e., no job security |

| | | |
|---|---|---|
| nongzhuanfei | 農轉非 | changing farmers' *hukou* from rural to nonrural |
| paigou | 派購 | government cadres sent to purchase the grain quota |
| putonghua | 普通話 | the standard Chinese language |
| quanguo liangpiao | 全國糧票 | national grain coupon |
| qiong | 窮 | impoverished |
| quxian shengyu | 曲線生育 | circuitous childbirth, evading childbirth regulations |
| ren huo le | 人活了 | a resourceful, flexible, and clever person |
| renqing | 人情 | good human feeling |
| sanbao yijiang | 三包一獎 | three contracts, one reward |
| sandai sanjie | 三代三借 | three substitutes, three borrowings |
| sanguagou | 三掛鉤 | three links |
| sanjiudi | 三就地 | the three locals: get material locally, process locally, and sell locally |
| santie | 三鐵 | three kinds of iron |
| sanzhuan yixiang | 三轉一響 | three wheels and one sound |
| sexiang huiluo | 色相賄賂 | proffering sexual favors or seduction |
| shengchan zijiu | 生產自救 | work to save oneself |
| shiwai taoyuan | 世外桃源 | an ideal place |
| shourongsuo | 收容所 | temporary jail for rural people |
| shuishang chaoshengdui | 水上超生隊 guerrillas | waterborne over-quota birth |
| siqian jingshen | 四千精神 | four thousand spirits |
| siying | 私營 | private enterprises |
| suo | 所 | taxation office, police office, and commercial office |
| tiefanwan | 鐵飯碗 | iron rice bowl |

| tiegongzi | 鐵工資 | fixed wage system |
| tiejiaoyi | 鐵交椅 | life-tenured cadres |
| tingyuan jingji | 庭院經濟 | garden economy |
| tonggou tongxiao | 統購統銷 | compulsory procurement system |
| tongxianghui | 同鄉會 | an association of people from the same place of birth |
| tongyi jingji | 統一經營 | unified management, e.g. by team leaders |
| tuhuangdi | 土皇帝 | local emperors |
| tuhuaqiao | 土華僑 | native overseas Chinese |
| wenbao buzu | 溫飽不足 | not enough to eat or to wear |
| wumingcun | 無名村 | villages with no names |
| wutong shizi | 五統十自 | five coordinations and ten independences |
| xian | 縣 | county |
| xiang | 鄉 | township |
| xiangqiankan | 向錢看 | money-seeking |
| xiangxia ren | 鄉下人 | rural people |
| xiaohongbao | 小紅包 | a small red bag containing money |
| xiaohuangdi | 小皇帝 | little emperors |
| xiaojingui | 小金櫃 | small gold treasure boxes |
| xiaozu | 小組 | the work group |
| xiehui | 協會 | mutual assistance association |
| yangguangdao | 陽光道 | shining road |
| yaoming | 要命 | literally, "want life" i.e., family planning |
| yidaoqie | 一刀切 | one knife that cuts everything, i.e., a Procrustean bed |
| yijun tujin | 異軍突進 | a strange army suddenly appears |

| | | |
|---|---|---|
| yinyangtou | 陰陽頭 | half-man and half-woman haircut |
| yitiaolong | 一條龍 | one chain of agricultural specialization |
| youjie | 游街 | parading someone through the streets |
| youling | 幽靈 | phantoms |
| yu | 愚 | ignorant |
| zang | 髒 | dirty |
| zeren daohu | 責任到戶 | each household responsible for part of the production quota |
| zerentian | 責任田 | responsibility land system |
| zerenzhi | 責任制 | the responsibility system |
| zhaokaoshan | 找靠山 | looking for a reliable mountain |
| zhenzheng de jiefang | 真正的解放 | authentic liberation |
| zhuanbao | 轉包 | subcontracting |
| zhuanye chengbao | 專業承包 | the production team contracted with individual households to produce specific sideline items |
| zijiu zizhu | 自救自助 | self-reliance and self-help |
| ziliuren | 自流人 | free people, i.e., free of collective controls |
| zongshejishi | 總設計師 | the great architect |
| zuoyezu | 作業組 | small work group |
| zou qinqi | 走親戚 | visit relatives |

# About the Book and Author

In this original and provocative book, Kate Zhou argues that Chinese farmers—who comprise one-fifth of the world's population—have been the driving force behind their country's phenomenal economic growth and social change over the past fifteen years. Guided by their own interests rather than by directives from Beijing, farmers have restored family autonomy in farming, created new markets, established rural industries that now generate over half of China's industrial production, migrated to cities despite rigid government controls, shaped their own family-size policy, and redefined the role of women.

Drawing on rich primary source material and her own years of experience in the countryside, the author focuses on the farmers' initiatives and the stories of ordinary people who collectively have played a central role in the economic upsurge. She takes issue with most current interpretations, which credit China's economic success almost entirely to reforms put in place by the Chinese leadership. Indeed, Zhou argues that the farmers were effective precisely because their movement was spontaneous, unorganized, leaderless, non-ideological, and apolitical.

In stark contrast to the turmoil surrounding the Tiananmen Square protests, farmers have been gradually yet remorselessly leaching power away from the central government without overt confrontation or violence. Their "reform from below" may well have generated the most long-lasting and fundamental changes contemporary China has witnessed.

Kate Xiao Zhou is assistant professor of Chinese politics and comparative politics at the University of Hawaii at Manoa.

# Index